D1458119

Maoist Economics and the Revolutionary Road to Communism

The Shanghai Textbook

Maoist Economics and the Revolutionary Road to Communism

The Shanghai Textbook

**Edited with an Introduction and Afterword
by Raymond Lotta**

BANNER PRESS • NEW YORK

Banner Press, P.O. Box 21195, New York, NY 10129

Library of Congress Catalog Card Number: 94-94131

ISBN 0-916650-41-3

Raymond Lotta is a Maoist political economist who has written and lectured extensively on issues of world economics and politics and also on the experience of socialist revolution. His books include *America in Decline*, *The Soviet Union: Socialist or Social-Imperialist?* and *And Mao Makes Five*.

Cover art: "New Upsurge in Revolution and Production," a 1973 painting by Sun Shuang-cheng, an assembly worker in Shanghai's Hutung Shipyard. This work was part of a 1974 Beijing graphic art exhibition by workers from Shanghai and several other cities in the People's Republic of China.

Contents

CONTENTS

PUBLISHER'S NOTE

Maoist Economics and the Revolutionary Road to Communism: The Shanghai Textbook on Socialist Political Economy was originally published in China in December 1975 under the title *Fundamentals of Political Economy*. The first part of the Chinese edition was an exposition of the political economy of capitalism and imperialism. That portion is not included here, as what is most pathbreaking and enduring about this work is its discussion of socialism—hence, the title change. However, the opening chapter to the work as a whole, which deals with the content and method of Marxian political economy, has been retained.

For this new English-language edition, an Introduction and an Afterword by Raymond Lotta, a list of suggested readings on socialist political economy, and an index have been furnished. Major Study References and Notes at the end of each chapter are from the original Chinese edition; explanatory bottom-of-page footnotes have been added by the editor. An article that appeared originally in *Red Flag* and subsequently in the *Peking Review* in 1976 has been excerpted and added as an appendix to Chapter 4. Study questions that appeared at the end of each chapter of the Chinese edition have been dropped. A chapter on socialist China's external economic relations has been deleted. The chapter was less a continuation of the work's theorization of socialist society than it was an accounting of certain diplomatic, aid, and trade policies during the early and mid-1970s, and the presentation of the class nature and possibilities for economic development of independent Third World

i

states departed in significant ways from the theoretical framework of the rest of the book. An English translation of an earlier (1974) edition of the entire work, including the section on capitalism, is available as *Fundamentals of Political Economy*, translated and edited by George Wang (Armonk, New York: M.E. Sharpe, 1977).

This translation was done by a team working from the 1975 Chinese text and making use of the Wang translation of the 1974 edition. English translations published by the People's Republic of China at the time the work was brought out have been used as a standard for phrasing and style. Quotations are taken from and references and citations are, wherever possible, given to official Chinese translations and authoritative English-language sources. Most of the Chinese names, terms, and places in the text have been romanized according to the Wade-Giles system, which was the system of transliteration most widely in use at the time this work first appeared. Even though the phonetic (pinyin) system has since come to replace it, this translation preserves the Wade-Giles system of spelling to aid readers in searching out bibliographic citations and references.

INTRODUCTION: MAOIST ECONOMICS AND THE FUTURE OF SOCIALISM

by Raymond Lotta

Maoist Economics and the Revolutionary Road to Communism: The Shanghai Textbook on Socialist Political Economy should be of interest to anyone who sees the present social order as cruel and unjust and has dreamed of the possibility of something fundamentally and radically different. For this book tells of a liberating socialism. It tells of a liberating economics. It tells of Maoism.

Can society be organized on a foundation other than that of exploitation, competition, and private gain? Are alienation, social fragmentation, and bureaucratic domination the unavoidable consequences of economic and technological development? What was probed and achieved in revolutionary China between 1949 and 1976 challenge deeply-held assumptions about what humanity is capable of. This book was written in 1975 and reflects the most advanced experience of socialist economics that the world has seen.

China's socialist revolution began in 1949 with the countrywide seizure of power by the workers and peasants led by the Chinese Communist Party. The revolution passed through several important stages marked by changes in the ownership system, the creation of new socialist economic and institutional forms, and mass political campaigns and upheavals. China's socialist revolution met defeat and came to an end in 1976 when a military coup overthrew working class power. In historical time, 27 years are scarcely a blip on the radar screen. But in terms of what was accomplished between 1949 and 1976, we're dealing with something quite epochal. One-quarter of humanity had struggled heroically to forge a path to the future and had embarked on a journey of unparalleled political, economic, and social transformation. This book is part of that endeavor's enduring legacy. This book is suppressed in China today!

A liberating economics? You will search in vain in bourgeois economics for concern with, much less solutions to, great social problems such as poverty, inequality, or environmental degradation. Its compass is rather more narrow and self-justifying. There are the discourses on how the price mechanism leads to efficient allocation of resources— efficiency to what end and for whom never questioned; the idealized models of decisionmaking and "perfect competition" in a market economy that assume away the real (unequal) structure of economic and political power and paper over the real world of conflict (capitalist against worker, capitalist against capitalist, imperialist rival against imperialist rival); the mythology of "general equilibrium," when in fact capitalism is a crisis-prone system that cannot secure full employment of resources and labor; and the arcane mathematical treatments of issues such as international trade that somehow can't fit world hunger into the equations.

Confronted with the stark gap between the world depicted in their abstract theory and life-crushing reality, the bourgeois economists explain that such things as racial discrimination or industrial pollution are "imperfections" or "negative externalities" of a market economy— that is, unfortunate but peripheral aberrations of the workings of a self-correcting system. And worry not, because the market will eventually perform its magic. It is the core idea of capitalism, going back to Adam Smith's famous metaphor of the "invisible hand," that individuals pursuing their own selfish ends, and acting as autonomous agents, will contribute their share to what is rationally best for everybody.

That economics might have anything to do with overcoming the division of society into haves and have-nots and with creating the conditions for the all-round development of freely-associating human beings would be dismissed by its bourgeois practitioners as an absurdity. And they are right . . . from the standpoint of capitalist economic laws. Bourgeois economics, like bourgeois society, is sensitive only to what can be bought and sold, to profit and loss. Indeed, capitalism is a system in which human needs are addressed and met only as byproducts of the pursuit of profit. It is a logic of profit maximization based on exploitation and oppression. And it shapes and subordinates everything in its domain—from the physical landscape, to the labor process, to relations between men and women.

The vision, the economic theory, and the experience of building a new society summed up in *Maoist Economics and the Revolutionary Road to Communism* (hereafter referred to as *The Shanghai Textbook*) point in a radically different direction. A socialist revolution creates a new kind of economy. The means of production are no longer the private property of a minority of society but are placed under society's collective control. Economic resources are no longer employed to maximize profit but are utilized to meet the fundamental needs and interests of the masses of people. Social production is no longer carried out without prior plan or social purpose but is now shaped according to consciously adopted aims and coordinated as a whole. The mechanisms and motivations of capitalism give way to something new: social planning, social cooperation, and conscious mass participation in all aspects of economic and social development. The potential for varied and all-sided human activity that the powers of social production have put within reach can begin to be realized.

All of which is to say that the misery, the dehumanization, and the inequality that are daily life under capitalism need not be. The great gap between rich and poor, the scourge of unemployment, the oppression and degradation of women, the subjugation of and discrimination against whole nations and nationalities, the problems of health care, housing, and urban decay . . . these and other sores of class society can be taken on and overcome. The desperate, competitive struggle of all against all to survive and claw their way ahead need not be. The creativity, energy, and fierceness of purpose of the "nobodies" on the bottom of society can be unleashed on a vast and transformative scale. Problems can be taken up for collective solution; the needs and direction of society can be wrangled over by people in their millions. And through this process of struggle and debate, people can change in ways unimaginable under the present order. Socialism makes this possible.

We live in a world in which the life activities of the laboring majority are subject to the controlling power of a minority whose interests are opposed to theirs. We live in a world in which people's lives are ruled by blind economic forces: the spontaneous movement of a stock or commodity price can, literally overnight, alter the lives of millions throughout the world. But with the creation of a system of socially organized and socially directed production, humanity crosses an historic threshold. The structure and functioning of society will no longer be wrapped in mystery but can become known to the community of individuals who make it up. The economic system and society as a whole will no longer confront the masses of people as something external, alien, and dominating but rather will be something they are more and more consciously taking hold of, transforming, and mastering in their own interests. At bottom, that is what this book is all about.

Maoism emphasizes that economic development by itself is not enough, nor is it the essence of socialism. Growth must serve and be guided by larger political and social goals—fundamentally, the quest of the proletariat and laboring people to master all of society and ultimately to eliminate classes on a world scale. Economic change and the creation of social wealth must be accompanied by change in every sphere of society, including very importantly change in people's outlook and thinking. Maoism emphasizes that people not "things" are decisive. The conscious activism of the laboring people, not the capital stock or level of technology as such, are the crucial variables of economic and social development. The laboring people must master technology, not the other way around. And Maoism emphasizes that the socialist project hinges on its constant reinvigoration: the revolution must continue and the class struggle must be continually waged in order to transform society and the world. Yes, this is a radically different approach to economics and to the development of society overall.

When *The Shanghai Textbook* was published in 1975, China was still undergoing the extraordinary struggle and ferment of the Great Proletarian Cultural Revolution. Factories in Shanghai and in many other cities were experimenting with new forms of worker participation in management. Peasants were discussing the ways that Confucian patriarchal and authoritarian values still influenced their lives. Scientists were conducting research among and sharing understanding with workers rich in practical experience. Administrators were routinely called on the carpet for losing touch with the people. Engineers became workers, teachers became students, political officials became garbage collectors, and vice versa! This was a society, and friend and foe alike would scarcely disagree, that was consciously ranging itself against capitalism.

No aspect of economic development and organization was taken for granted—whether it be the supposedly inescapable trajectory of "modernization" and urbanization (revolutionary China took bold steps to break with the traditional Western and the more recent Third World patterns of chaotic and lopsided city and industrial growth, and to integrate industry with agriculture and town with countryside); or technology (the Maoists emphasized that the design, applications, and relationship of people to technology are shaped not only by the development of the productive forces but also by the social relations of an economic system); or the very notion of what constitutes economic efficiency and optimality (which were seen in broader economic and social terms rather than in a narrow cost-effectiveness frame). This was a socialism that dared challenge not only the brutal profit-above-all calculus and stultifying methods of organization of capitalism but its whole "me first" mind-set as well. "Serve the people" was not just a slogan emblazoned on the walls of factories, schools, hospitals, and retail stores; it was an ideological benchmark against which tens of millions judged themselves and others. This was a revolution that promoted initiative, creativity, and daring . . . but for the sake of the collectivity not for oneself.

China, it need hardly be said, is a very different society today. After Mao Tsetung died in 1976, rightist forces led by Deng Xiaoping staged a military coup.[*] The systematic dismantling of socialism, the restoration of capitalism, and the resubordination of China to imperialism were to begin.

This sea-change is perhaps best captured in the slogan promoted in the early 1980s by the new leadership: "to get rich is glorious." And so it has been . . . for a few. Shanghai has opened a stock market; speculation in urban real estate is now legitimate economic activity; special economic zones have been carved out to serve multinational corporations. China's leaders have turned the country into a low-wage assembly complex and production base for domestic and foreign capi-

---

[*] Deng's role in the coup was played out from behind the scenes. Hua Guofeng was the nomimal leader, but all along, Deng represented the leading force behind the coup and the consequent restoration of capitalism. Hua, having served Deng's reactionary purpose, was nudged aside and retired into obscurity.

tal—in early 1992, an average of 45 new foreign-financed ventures were being contracted each day. Workers are told to keep their noses to the grindstone and out of politics. In the countryside, under the banner of reform, the communes were broken up and rural collective assets grabbed up by the well-positioned. The resulting social polarization has forced millions of disadvantaged peasants to migrate to urban areas. Economic and social inequalities are widening rapidly between the favored coastal rim (where most of China's growth is taking place) and the vast inland regions of the country (where stagnation and poverty are the norm).

The economy now shows all the earmarks of boom-bust cyclical development. It is also on an ecological disaster course. Short-term interests of growth and profit have resulted in the neglect and abuse of irrigation and flood works, the chopping down of much of the country's mature forests, and massive industrial dumping that is polluting clean water sources. China's external debt and dependency are mounting. Old social ills have reemerged: in the countryside, the killing of girl babies (since male labor power is now viewed as a vital asset in the every-family-for-itself economy that is being foisted on the rural majority) and clan violence; in the cities, unemployment, beggary, and prostitution. Culturally, revolutionary images of women "holding up half the sky" have given way to icons of women as dutiful housewives, "dressed-for-success" consumers, and sex objects. Corruption is so widespread in Chinese society that it no longer arouses shock.

These are the economic and social realities behind China's vaunted growth rates. And the 1989 Tiananmen Square massacre of workers and students served to bring political reality into sharp focus. Such is the new (old) China. China today is socialist only in name. But the story run in the West is that the "pragmatic" leaders grouped around Deng Xiaoping have brought sanity to a society that had been held in the grip of totalitarian Maoist madness. Yes, the apologetics continue, there are distasteful political practices, but when the octogenarians in charge die off, democratization (Western-style institutionalized control and deception) will then flower completely. The truth is that the rule of workers and peasants has been crushed; property and hierarchy reenshrined; and profit put in command of economic development. A new exploiting class has restored not sanity but capitalism—exactly what Mao had warned would happen if the rightists within the

Communist Party seized power. What these "capitalist roaders" have overthrown and undone is precisely what this book details and upholds.

The Shanghai Textbook is one of the most complete presentations by the Maoist revolutionaries of their views on the nature and functioning of the socialist alternative to capitalism. It makes a major contribution to socialist economic theory. That would be valuable under any circumstances. But in the current world climate, the book takes on heightened importance—because the claim is made that there is in fact no alternative to capitalism. Socialism, we are to believe, has failed . . . and can only fail.

As anyone who has lived through the last few years knows, the ruling classes of the West have staged an ideological victory parade. It started with the collapse in 1989 of the Soviet-dominated regimes in Eastern Europe. And it became an epic celebration with the disintegration of the Soviet Union itself. But what collapsed in the former Soviet Union was not socialism. It was a particular form of capitalism, a highly centralized state-monopoly capitalism in which state ownership and state planning were invested with capitalist content. There was nothing revolutionary about this class-divided, exploitative, and oppressive society. In fact, socialism in the Soviet Union was overthrown in the 1950s—and the lessons of the Soviet experience are major themes of this book.[*]

What the ruling classes are celebrating is Western-style capitalism. No other set of economic arrangements, they tell us, can perform as efficiently or rationally; no other political system can provide scope for individual development. Never mind that the gap between rich and poor nations in the wondrous world market economy has doubled over the last 30 years, or that each day 40,000 children die of malnutrition and preventable disease in a Third World dominated by international capitalist economic and political institutions. Never mind that the West is experiencing the most painful and protracted global economic slowdown of the postwar period. Never mind the obscenity of the claim that a Western-style market that ravages the U.S.'s inner

---

[*] For an analysis of the basic features of the state-monopoly capitalism that had existed in the former Soviet Union, *see* Raymond Lotta, *The Soviet Union: Socialist or Social-Imperialist?* (Chicago: RCP Publications, 1983).

cities is somehow going to solve Russia's housing crisis. Never mind three centuries of industrial development that has been as blind as it has been rapacious toward the ecobalance of the planet. Never mind a system that requires people to perfect themselves as salable products in the marketplaces of work and human relationships. Ignore all that . . . the market ensures the best of all possible worlds.

If Western capitalism has declared triumph over exploitation and corruption that masqueraded as socialism in the Soviet bloc, it is also using the occasion to declare null and void the possibility that humanity can move beyond exploitation, inequality, fragmentation and a social environment of greed and selfishness to create a very different kind of society. The ruling classes are proclaiming not just the "verdict of history," but "the end of history;" society and history can advance no further—the West, as if by divine providence, has realized the ideal of all civilized peoples. Anything that challenges capitalism is at best a pipedream, and at worst an unworkable utopia imposed from above that can only lead to nightmare. The victory parade is, as the historian Arno Mayer described it, a "thunderous celebration of dystopia." Which is to say, since you can't have a perfect world, long live greed and oppression and meanness. And all this has not been without political effect. Among many who at one time or another embraced alternatives to capitalism, the collapse of the Soviet economic and political system, erroneously identified as socialist, and the ideological assault against socialism have led to deep questioning and doubt about the nature and future of socialism.

What is at issue here is the feasibility of revolutionary communism: whether or not it is possible to end all oppression and class distinctions on the basis of the voluntary and collective efforts of millions; whether or not political leadership and economic institutions can serve such ends; whether in fact a socialist economy can work. In raising such questions, Mao and the experience of revolutionary China until his death in 1976 are a fundamental point of departure. The state-bourgeois ideologues of the former Soviet Union peddled a vulgar pseudo-Marxism that equated socialism with formal and legal state ownership, benevolent welfarism, technocratic efficiency, and political passivity. In contrast to this, Mao Tsetung reclaimed Marx and Engels's vision of communist society and Lenin's brief but historic experience in leading practical efforts toward creating a new socialist society as a transition to full communist society, in which men and women would consciously and voluntarily, and through great struggles, change the world and themselves. At the same time, while learning from the positive experiences of the first efforts to build a socialist economy in the Soviet Union, Mao profoundly rethought and recast the prevailing model of a planned socialist economy that became institutionalized under Stalin.

Mao was conceptualizing and implementing a set of solutions to the real problems of developing a planned socialist economy that does not rest on bureaucratized regulation or reproduce oppressive capitalist relations. His approach meant subjecting growth and development to social and political criteria, linking the question of economic coordination to the question of mass initiative and participation, putting emphasis on issues of motivation and collective benefit, and on the ideological and political environment in which decisions are taken at all levels, and combining a system of coordinated planning with decentralized management.

The Maoist model also represents a complete rejection of the orthodox Western approach to "underdevelopment," which sees underdevelopment as nothing more than delayed development that can only be sped up and put on track through absorption of foreign capital and participation in the international division of labor. Revolutionary China, by contrast, delinked itself from the world imperialist system. It formulated and implemented a developmental strategy based on giving priority to agriculture, utilizing simple and intermediate technologies that could be spread and adopted throughout the economy while seeking to develop and apply advanced technology in a way that would not distort and disarticulate the economy, promoting self-reliance, and, above all, unleashing people. On such a basis, a poor country, whose development had been twisted and scarred by semicolonial domination, was able to achieve sustainable and balanced growth and to meet the basic needs of its population.

To be sure, there were problems and mistakes. The economy had certain weak points; the new social institutions certainly had some flaws; and in the sweep and swirl of mass struggle, errors were unavoidable—sometimes due to people getting carried away in their zeal to change things, other times due to rigidity. But all this was in the context of a revolution uprooting exploitation and class oppression and drawing the broad masses into political life. The CIA couldn't deny the favorable growth rates. Observer after observer couldn't help but be struck by the forging of new values and attitudes. Yet as impressive as all that was, these mechanisms and principles were part of a larger solution to a deeper set of problems: how to revolutionize society and people in order to make the stormy passage to classless society, to communism. In short, Mao's political economy is what might be called *the political economy of a visionary and viable socialism.*

The guardians of the present order vilify the Maoist experience for rather obvious reasons—it stands so totally opposed to their whole system and outlook of exploitation. But it has also become a fashion in some more "enlightened" intellectual circles to dismiss Maoism as an artifact of an era bypassed by history. Whether intended as such or not, it is an argument for the status quo. Still, the question remains: Is this experience and understanding relevant to achieving genuine liberation? For those seeking to really understand and change the world, and radically so, it is nothing less than essential.

Marxism and the Nature and Building of Socialism

A political economy of socialism refers to two things: the theorization and continuing investigation of the economic substructure (the relations of production) of socialist society; and a model of and operational approach to economic development and planning. The doctrine of socialist reorganization of the economy and society has long been part of the arsenal of the workers' movement. But a comprehensive and revolutionary political economy of socialism is actually a relatively recent development.

Until the Bolshevik Revolution, Marxian economics had focused its analytic attention almost exclusively on the capitalist mode of production. There was historical reason and necessity for this. By the mid-19th century, industrial capitalism had matured. It had revolutionized productive technique, spawning modern industry and a vast, new class of industrial wage-laborers. It had widened the scope and accelerated the pace of technological change as had no economic system before it. Industrial capitalism was literally—and quite brutally—remaking the world. It had created a capitalist world market and forged an international division of labor suited to its requirements. Developmentally, this system was given to a characteristic pattern of rapid growth punctuated by severe economic disturbance; it was unstable and crisis-prone. And, of great historical moment, its class relations and contradictions had led to the emergence of a new political force—the proletariat, or working class—that was waging a struggle for emancipation. This capitalist mode of production had to be understood; a revolutionary strategy and tactics to serve the rising struggle of the working class had to be formulated.

Karl Marx theorized the capitalist mode of production. He placed it in historical perspective—showing it to be but a specific and transitory stage of social development founded on a particular organization of social labor and a particular mechanism by which the propertied ruling class extracts surplus labor from the subordinated producing class.* He identified the key relationship in capitalist society as between wage-labor and capital. He disclosed the fundamental contradiction of this system as between socialized production and private appropriation—large-scale and highly developed productive forces usable only if they are used in common by thousands and millions of workers, yet productive forces utilized for the competitive enhancement of particular (private) interests. And he unearthed capitalism's inner economic contradictions and laws of motion (development trends).

These discoveries enabled Marx to show that capitalism creates both the material basis (the enormous growth and socialization of the productive forces) and the agency (the proletariat) for a higher, cooperative mode of production (socialism), leading finally to communism, with the abolition of class distinctions and all social divisions containing the seeds of class division. But Marx never sought to lay down a detailed blueprint for this future society. Socialism, in Marx's view, would be fought for and forged in the concrete; the exact forms taken by socialism and ultimately communism would be conditioned by prior historical development and the specific circumstances of revolution.

Reviewing the course of Marxian economics after Marx's great discoveries, it really should come as no surprise that Marxism's theorization of socialism and communism would lag behind its analysis of capi-

---

* Surplus labor is the labor time over and above that required to provide for the needs of the laboring classes themselves.

talism. The socialist movement of the late 19th and early 20th centuries had to solve certain pressing (and more immediate) political questions thrown up by the particularities of capitalist development and the demands of the class struggle. This was especially so in Germany and Russia, where the workers' movement was growing apace, and both the German and Russian Marxists had made important analyses of the structural changes that had brought capitalism to a new stage of development. (Lenin's work *Imperialism* was the culminating and most outstanding of these analyses.) Not that the socialist movement prior to 1917 showed no interest in the political-economic organization of the future society. It did, and thorny issues of the time, like the agrarian question, were considered with an eye towards socialist reorganization. Still, this was of secondary theoretical concern, and in the case of the most influential wing of that movement, German Social-Democracy, socialism was more often than not conceived of in erroneous and nonrevolutionary terms: as the evolutionary extension and rationalization of capitalism's tendencies towards socialization, centralization, and organization.

Yet something more fundamental explains the lag in conceptualizing socialism: in a very real sense, socialism had to reveal itself before it could be grasped in theoretical depth. Socialist revolution had to be made and the practical challenges of socialist transformation taken on as a condition for comprehensive knowledge. But that was neither the beginning nor end of the problem, because socialism's inner nature was by no means obvious or transparent—it had to be penetrated.[*]

"To know the objective laws," Mao wrote in his *Critique of Soviet Economics,* "you must go through a process." The process of knowing the laws of socialist society—and by this is meant the structure and dynamics of socialist society—has been one of theoretical deepening and reconceptualizing based on and carried out in connection with the social practice of building socialism. It is a process that has involved the investigation of concrete social(ist) reality, the addition to and correction of previous knowledge, and the class and ideological struggle

---

[*] In the early part of the 20th century, many Marxist theorists, such as Rosa Luxemburg and some prominent Bolshevik economists, erroneously assumed that the workings of a socialist economy would be so readily knowable and its management so eminently practicable that political economy as a distinct science would wither away.

xiv

in socialist society over the road forward. There are markers in this process—pivotal historical episodes that have not only required but also enabled Marxism to elaborate and extend a political economy of socialism. Here we are referring to the first attempt to construct a socialist society and economy that took place in the Soviet Union between 1917 and 1953, the subsequent restoration of capitalism there after the death of Stalin, and China's Cultural Revolution of 1966-76 led by Mao. There is also a milestone in this process: Mao Tsetung's theoretical synthesis of the underlying contradictions of socialist society and the historical tasks facing the proletariat in power.

Marx and Engels laid the foundations of socialist political economy. As indicated, they identified the tendencies in capitalist production that were not only hurling capitalist society into greater crisis but also opening up the material possibilities for a higher form of economic and social organization. Only a system based on social ownership and social planning could overcome the anarchy (the spontaneous and destructive "regulation" of the economy by the market) of capitalist production and resolve the contradictions that capitalism continually generates. And only a violent political revolution could clear the way to create such a system. The task before the proletariat was to seize power and set up its dictatorship: the rule of the majority of producers over the minority of former exploiters. The proletariat would transform the private basis of control over technically advanced social productive forces, put an end to exploitation, and begin to collectively master society. No longer would the products of human activity govern their creators; no longer would mental and manual work be opposed and class-specific realms of human activity. The proletarian revolution would initiate a world-historic process through which the working class would emancipate itself and all of humanity from exploitative economic relations and oppressive social relations as a whole.

For Marx, the new society was not the realization of an ethical idea or a utopia created outside of capitalist society. Socialism would be born out of the conditions and contradictions of the old society. Thus Marx saw the communist revolution as passing from a lower to a higher stage: from socialism, which replaces capitalism yet still bears its material and ideological birthmarks, to communism, which is marked by the absence of classes, the abolition of the state, and the creation of common material abundance. For Marx, the socialist revolution entailed two "radical ruptures": with traditional property relations and with traditional ideas.

This was scientific socialism (and Lenin would restate and deepen these theses in his *State and Revolution*). But Marx and Engels did not live to see the working class conquer power and launch the historically unprecedented task of transforming class society.[*] They could only theorize the nature of socialist society and the character and duration of the transition to communism in broad, yet powerful and telegraphic strokes. Moreover, they made certain assumptions about the economic underpinnings of socialism that turned out not to be in correspondence with the actual material conditions in which socialist society has developed. They expected that all means of production would, more or less immediately, become common social property; that the production of society's needed goods would no longer have a commodity character (involving production for exchange against money) once unplanned production-for-profit was replaced by planned production-for-use; that money-wages would cease to exist in the socialist stage.

No socialist society has achieved this. It has not been possible, especially given the persistence and economic weight of peasant-based agriculture in the countries where socialist revolutions have so far taken place, to effect a rapid socialization of all means of production to the level of public-state ownership; it has been necessary to introduce collective ownership as an intermediate stage between private and public-state ownership. It has not been possible to do away with commodity-exchange relations among production units. And although the socialist principle of "from each according to their ability, to each according to their work" was implemented in socialist societies, the distribution of consumer goods still took place through the medium of money and involved payment of money-wages.

Marx and Engels also expected socialism to make its initial breakthrough in the advanced capitalist countries, where the productive

---

[*] The Paris Commune of 1871 did occur during their lifetimes, and Marx was quick to sum up profound lessons from this brief but rich experience. But the Commune lasted only two months and, on an economic level, was unable to establish a new mode of production.

forces were highly developed. Obviously, this is not how things worked out. Capitalism evolved to a higher stage, imperialism, marked by the dominant economic role of huge monopolies and finance capital, the internationalization of capitalist production, the acute rivalry between imperialist nation-states, and the dominance of a few rich capitalist countries over the oppressed nations of the Third World, where the majority of humanity lives. The development and contradictions of the imperialist system have profoundly affected the course of socialist revolution. The proletarian movement spread to the colonized and oppressed countries while its progress has been impeded in the advanced capitalist countries (where the ruling classes have utilized the vast wealth accumulated through international exploitation and plunder to secure relative stability for extended periods).

Some bourgeois critics of Marxism suggest that its explanatory value is called into question since socialism unfolded somewhat differently than Marx had anticipated. It is a rather superficial argument. Marx's suppositions were entirely plausible (and they were not cast as hard and fast predictions—Marxism makes no claim to forecasting all the particular features of future social development). More to the point, and what the experience of the 20th century has powerfully validated, is Marx's view of revolution and of socialism as historical phenomena flowing from the contradictions of capitalist production and development, which must now be understood even more fully as a global process.

But the fact that not all of Marx's specific expectations did materialize does have important practical and theoretical significance. Bob Avakian, Chairman of the Revolutionary Communist Party, USA, has summed up the problem this way. Socialism as it actually emerged in the 20th century has proven to be a more complex and unstable social formation, and socialist transformation a more difficult and protracted process, than either Marx or Lenin had foreseen. This "complicatedness" is very much bound up with the historic problem that confronted the international workers' movement during its "first wave" of socialist revolutions: the problem of making, sustaining, and advancing revolution in a world still dominated by capitalism-imperialism. This is not only a question of the political-military strength of imperialism, important as that is, but also of the continuing dominance on a global scale of capitalism as a mode of production—which has exerted pervasive material and ideological effects on newly-emergent socialist societies and limited and distorted what they have been able to accomplish. That socialist states have existed in a sea of capitalism-imperialism underscores that a socialist state is not an end in itself. The highest task of the revolution in power is not to develop and defend socialism within its existing confines, although this is a crucial task. A socialist state must function first and foremost as a "base area" to support and spread the world proletarian revolution.* There is an important point of orientation here that is stressed in *The Shanghai Textbook*: final victory in the proletarian revolution can only be won on an international level, and the working class cannot be free until all of humanity is free.

Secondly, the complexity of socialist revolution is bound up with the nature of socialism itself. Historical experience has revealed socialism to be a unique, transitional form of society. This applies on all levels: economic, political, social, and ideological. Take the question of commodity production under socialism, which is a major topic of the *Textbook*.

In commodity-producing systems, of which capitalism is the most developed type, goods are produced for exchange (sale to others). This process of exchange is based on multiple divisions of labor (people specializing in this or that activity), and these divisions of labor are deepened and extended by the exchange process. The producers of commodities are objectively interconnected with one another—they depend on each other as suppliers and customers. But they are also socially isolated from one another—because the individual units of production are privately controlled, making separate production decisions. That is, products are created as the property of particular agents of production. The social process of determining what gets produced and in what quantity, and how labor should be allocated, is not the result of conscious society-wide coordination but occurs through the exchange of commodities. Individual commodity-producing units

---

* Avakian has written extensively on the experience and lessons of proletarian revolution. A good point of entry is "Conquer the World—The International Proletariat Must and Will," *Revolution*, No. 50 (1981). For those for whom these questions are largely new, Avakian's book *Phony Communism is Dead . . . Long Live Real Communism!* (Chicago: RCP Publications, 1992) provides a good introduction as well as exposition on these questions.

respond to market and price signals, which ultimately reflect underlying conditions of social production.

The commodity form of production obscures and distorts the real social relations that bind individuals to one another. It makes it seem as though things (commodities and money) have a life of their own rather than expressing social relationships. A Nike sneaker, for example, is produced by superexploited workers in South Korea, a neocolony of the United States. But this rather crucial social information is not conveyed by price. People define themselves in relation to things, and the acquisition of things becomes the be-all and end-all, while people themselves are treated and used as things. Commodity production creates the illusion that we are all private actors taking unlinked actions to pursue our own purposes; and the competitive struggle of the independent commodity producers/sellers—including the proletarians, whose essential salable commodity is their ability to work (labor power)—underlies the "me-first" mentality of a market-based society. Under capitalist commodity production, everything becomes subject to "coldhearted calculation" (Lenin's phrase); what does not register as price is not worthy of attention.

Socialist society must restrict and eventually overcome commodity production; if this is not happening, the new society cannot be built. Why? Because commodity production and the law of value[*] that regulates it cannot be allowed to determine what gets produced and how; if profit-efficiency considerations dominate, then social need—the fundamental needs and interests of the masses of people—will not be met. Because in commodity production, and exchange through money, lies the germ of capitalist oppression: the separation of workers from the means of production and the exploitation of wage-labor. Because in commodity production, and the divisons and separations it engenders, lies a barrier to people grasping their social connectedness and mastering their own social organization and activity as a "community of free individuals carrying on their work with the means of production in common" (Marx's phrase).

---

[*] The law of value is an objective law of commodity-producing society. It regulates the exchange of commodities according to the quantities of socially necessary labor expended in their production. In regulating capitalist commodity exchange, this law also regulates the distribution of labor and means of production between different branches of production. Labor power ceases to be a commodity under socialism.

The Shanghai Textbook explains how socialist society concretely subordinates the commodity form of production (and money relations) as the primary vehicle for organizing social production. It explains how the proletariat sets out to initiate a form of "direct social production" involving a different way of organizing an economy (socially planned production for social need); to transform the labor process (the producers dominating the conditions of production rather than vice versa); and to develop a different social psychology (people working for the common good). But this new type of production has not and can not break free totally of commodity elements, and various types of commodity-money relations persist under socialism and continue to influence people's thinking. The principle of exchange based on equivalent amounts of labor still plays a role. Socialist enterprises must pay attention to efficiency and must still utilize monetary calculation to compare between the planned cost and the actual cost of producing something. The *Textbook* explores the reasons for this and the complications and dangers posed. By the same token, while the working class rules in socialist society and aims to abolish classes and class distinctions, socialist society continues to reproduce classes and social differences and inequalities that find expression as class antagonisms. Socialism is a society in which the danger of reversion to capitalism is omnipresent.

One could of course dispense with the complexity of socialism definitionally: since workers' rule in the Soviet Union during the 1917-53 period and in China under Mao did not correspond in important ways to what Marx prefigured, then what existed there was not really socialism. It is a tack taken by some. Others, recognizing real difficulty, have concluded that socialism has simply failed and must be reinvented.* These approaches would substitute abstract and ideal categories for the complexity of real life. Worse, they negate the rich and liberatory experience that socialist revolution, for all its difficulties and setbacks, has in fact yielded up.

---

* This notion that socialism has failed and must be recast is addressed in the Afterword to this work.

The Soviet Union: Breakthrough and Limitations

This brings us to the Bolshevik Revolution and the Soviet Union. The October Revolution is the first case of a working-class state carrying out the expropriation of the former propertied classes and establishing a socialist form of economy. Privately-controlled means of production were converted into public property and economic development was subjected to conscious planning. Through the instrumentalities of their party and state, workers and peasants set out to collectively control and rationally utilize society's economic resources. This planned form of economy required not only coordination and social mobilization but also a guiding theory of economic development and transformation. And so it was in the first workers' state that research into the political economy of socialism was inaugurated and that a systematic socialist political economy was first propounded. It was a theoretical enterprise infused with the spirit of discovery, debate, and ferment that character-ized the early years of the revolution. But it was not, nor could it be, a self-contained intellectual exercise. The course of understanding and policy formulation was shaped by the sharp struggle within the Communist Party over the direction and viability of the revolution and by the life-and-death struggle to defeat counterrevolution from within and from without.

What emerged from this first attempt was a certain conception of the nature of socialist society and of the tasks and methods of socialist construction. There were elements of theoretical advance here, reflect-ing the sweeping changes taking place in Soviet society. On the other hand, the understanding of socialist economy and society was partial, owing mainly to the limitations of historical experience. It was also flawed in key respects, owing to problems in approach and methodol-ogy. Here only a few summary points can be offered.

The Soviet revolution triumphed in a backward capitalist country with a huge peasantry (the working class represented only five percent of the population). That reality alone posed an awesome challenge. Could the revolution consolidate its support and survive? Could social-ism be built if the material prerequisites, like a highly-developed indus-trial base and large-scale agriculture, were not yet present? The Bolsheviks were acutely aware of the difficulties. In the immediate flush of victory, they anticipated and counted on support in the form of revolution and the spread of socialism to the more developed countries of Europe. But the revolutionary movement in Europe, in particular Germany, ran aground. It soon became clear to the Bolsheviks that the newly-formed Soviet republic would have to go it alone, and perhaps for some time. Lenin was determined that the revolution make its way: after all, the Bolsheviks had taken the risk of leading the masses to make revolution, and now they would take the risk of leading them to carry it forward. The revolution would and did fight for its life. It had to crush the counterrevolutionary efforts of the old possessing classes aided by foreign imperialist intervention. Economic policy swung from the radical market-restricting measures of "war communism" to the temporary market-widening provisions of the New Economic Policy.

But it was a *revolution* fighting for its life, and it continued to unfold economic and deep-going social transformation. New political and social organs of popular rule were established, and battle-steeled workers staffed important governmental and managerial positions. The former Tsarist "prisonhouse of nations" ceased to be: the revolution recognized the right of self-determination, and a multinational state based on equality of nations and nationalities was established. Great strides were made towards emancipating women—by 1921, divorce was easily obtainable, the formal stigma attached to illegitimacy was removed, abortion legalized, and equal rights and equal pay became policy and law. Mass campaigns were launched to eradicate illiteracy (written languages were created for national languages that had previously had none).

In the years following Lenin's death in 1924, the question of whether socialism was possible under conditions of internal economic and cultural backwardness and imperialist encirclement was posed anew and even more sharply. Stalin fought for the view that socialism could and must be built in one country absent the near-term spread of revolution—for the survival and continued development of the revolution in the Soviet Union and for the cause of world revolution. Relative to the alternative positions advanced at the time, Stalin's was the most correct. But as Bob Avakian points out in "Conquer the World," the "socialism in one country" debate and struggle to a certain degree begged the most important question . . . just what *is* socialism?

For the Soviet leadership, socialism came to be identified with two things: the elimination of antagonistic classes, and the establishment of modern, large-scale industry under state ownership. These were problematical notions that Mao would critique and that Maoism has continued to probe. With respect to the question of classes, the dominant view among the Bolsheviks was that the economic and social basis of exploiter/exploited relations and of a bourgeois class ceased to exist once private ownership of the means of production was abolished. In other words, after the resistance of the overthrown classes was broken, classes and class struggle would no longer play a significant or determining role in economic and political life.

The Bolsheviks were aware that the issue of classes and social polarization was not so simple a matter as decreeing an end to exploitation. Lenin in *State and Revolution* had dwelled on the persistence of inequality under socialism and saw in the continuing division between mental and manual labor a chief source of this inequality. In the 1920s he had also begun to grapple with the phenomenon of bureaucratic degeneration among some government officials and with the problem of the regeneration of commodity relations under socialism—and the dangers this posed for the revolution. But these were exploratory investigations, and informed by a conception that tended to connect commodity production under socialism only with private small-scale production, and classes only with private property forms. The complexity and contradictory nature of "public-state" property, a point that will be returned to, was not understood at the time.

In the mid-1930s, Stalin tended to formulate the issue of class in the following way: with the overthrow of the old propertied classes and with the nationalization of industry and the collectivization of agriculture, the economic basis of exploitation was eliminated. Society consisted of two nonantagonistic classes, the working class and the collectivized peasants, along with a stratum made up of the intelligentsia and white-collar groupings. The old ruling classes were liquidated as classes. What remained were remnants of these overthrown classes, that is, individuals associated in some way with the prerevolutionary class formation. But these remnants of the old order could only be propped up externally; thus the threat to society came from agents of the deposed classes cultivated and supported by foreign capital.

Again, antagonistic classes and class struggle were not seen as playing a crucial role in socialist society, since a bourgeois class was seen to exist only in relation to readily detectable forms of private ownership. It was a line that did not correspond with reality and social practice, since society was in fact teeming with class differences and contradictions.

This notion of class was linked to a conception of the developmental foundations of socialism. There was a tendency to view socialism in material-technical terms. That is, socialism was equated with the attainment of a certain level of development of the productive forces under public ownership. From this flowed a particular programmatic and historical approach to the achievement of communism. State ownership of the means of production combined with industrialization would lead to higher levels of socialism and, ultimately, to the relatively harmonious passage to communism. Socialist industrialization would lay the basis for and be the stimulus to the transformation of social relations, division of labor, and ideologies inherited from class society. These changes were expected to follow almost as automatic adjustments to socialist industrialization. Thus, once social ownership of the means of production was achieved, the key task was to develop the material productive forces. In its specific conditions of backwardness, the Soviet Union needed more factories, machinery, modern technology, transport, and infrastructure; it needed more trained technical personnel, engineers, etc., and an educational system geared toward turning out such people; it needed a shift of population from countryside to the towns.

Socialist construction came to be identified with the mobilization of resources for the rapid development of capital-intensive heavy industry.* And the destruction of the legal basis of private property in the major means of production and the establishment of state ownership were seen as the guarantee that the process of industrialization would serve working class rule. The complexity and contradictoriness of state property forms and the fact that juridical (formal/legal) worker-state ownership can mask bourgeois relations was not understood.

---

* "Capital-intensive" here does not mean "capitalist," but industry with a large technical component, as opposed to "labor-intensive" industry, which has a relatively low technological level and relies considerably on human labor.

(*The Shanghai Textbook* sheds important light on this point, emphasizing the need to go beyond form to the actual *content* of state ownership: Who is really running state enterprises? Is a political-ideological orientation of restricting or expanding inequalities and differences in command?)

These were not particularly or peculiarly Bolshevik or "Stalinist" notions; they were the prevailing understanding within the international communist movement. But Mao broke with this conceptual framework. He developed a theory of classes and class struggle under socialism, grounding it in the material, social, and ideological contradictions of socialist society. And he approached the problem of the foundations of socialism rather differently. Technological advance and economic growth are not the fundamental guarantor of socialism and communism. The mere increase in productive forces (economic development) will not in and of itself eliminate exploitative relations and other oppressive social and ideological relations (like patriarchy). There is, Mao emphasized, a dialectical relationship between economic development and ongoing and deep-going social and ideological transformation: "if a socialist society does not promote socially collectivistic aims, then what of socialism remains."*

The key issue confronting socialist society, and what determines its overall character, is the *road* on which it is traveling. Is society overcoming the relations of class society to the greatest degree possible? Is the labor of the working class serving this end? And does the working class through its state and political leadership have the overall initiative in carrying forward and persisting on this road? In short, what is key is whether the revolution is continuing and deepening on all fronts. If this is not happening, then the ground is being laid for the working class to lose state power, and capitalism will be restored. If the revolution is continuing, then working class state power will be strengthened, and the struggle for communism will be propelled forward. There will be times when great leaps can, and must, be made in pushing the revolution forward; at other times, consolidation becomes the necessary emphasis; and there will be twists and turns. Through this wave-like process, revolution advances.

---

* *Mao Zedong sixiang wan sui* (Taipei: n.p., 1969), p. 197.

But this occurs within and is conditioned by the international framework—by the development and contradictions of the world imperialist system, including its rivalries, military interventions, and the direct and indirect effects of the structure and turns of the imperialist world economy on the socialist economy; and by the relative strength, forward thrusts, and requirements made of the socialist state by the world revolution. The proletarian revolution and its conditions of development must in fact be grasped fundamentally as an international process. At those historic turning points when the world revolution can make major breakthroughs, and these are invariably moments of great danger and crisis as well, any already existing socialist state must be prepared to put its material and ideological strength on the line to advance the world revolution. This is a critical summation of the experience of socialist revolution.

With this understanding in mind, let us return to Soviet theory and practice. The view of socialism described earlier was deeply embedded in Soviet political economy. It was clearly in evidence in the debate over industrialization strategy that occurred in the 1920s and in the economic theory that guided the implementation of the First Five-Year Plan and collectivization of agriculture in the years 1929-32. Valuable work was undertaken; this was the real and creative beginning of practical socialist political economy, and a vast new literature was produced. Theoretical discussion ranged over such issues as the nature of socialist construction; the relationship between the structure of the economy which the proletariat inherits and must transform and the economic structure which the revolution aims to bring into being; methods and forms of industrialization; investment priorities and the means to generate investment resources; the desirable tempo of socialist growth; intersectoral relationships (such as between agriculture and industry) and the establishment of material balances within and between sectors (the Soviet economists pioneered what has since come to be called input-output analysis); the role of money and prices in economic calculation, in the mobilization of society's surplus, and in balancing the distribution of income between the urban and rural populations. Advances were also made in the development of mathematical techniques to serve planning.[*]

---

[*] On the development of socialist economic theory in the Soviet Union and associated debates over economic strategy during the 1920s, *see* N. Spulber (ed.), *Foundations of*

And this was *political* economy. Social and political issues figured in the discourse—for instance, the effects of various policies on the worker-peasant alliance and other social relations. Economic problems and policies were seen, to varying degrees, in the context of the old social order being transformed into a new one. But by and large the political economy practiced had a decidedly productivist and technicist edge to it. On the one hand, what largely drove and delimited inquiry and debate was the imperative of finding the way to the most rapid expansion of state industry resting on modern technique, which was seen as the underlying foundation of socialism. On the other hand, planning tended to be approached as technical activity in pursuit of this goal, mainly as a means of rationally organizing the productive forces and coordinating growth.

The experience of developing and planning a socialist economy in the Soviet Union in the years 1917-56, when the Soviet Union was a socialist society, could not but be highly contradictory. Not only was something new being tried; it was happening under very difficult and hostile circumstances. Imperialist military threats and encirclement forced the new Soviet power to divert resources to build up military-industrial capacity to defend itself and conditioned the whole strategy of rapid industrialization that was embarked upon and the forms of industrial organization that were adopted. Indeed, for the better part of its existence, the first workers' state had to wage war, prepare for war, and dress the wounds of war.

But if the challenges of constructing a socialist society and economy were formidable, the achievements were truly remarkable. A new mode of production which neither rested on exploitation nor experienced the destructive economic crises of capitalist market forces was established. A modern socialist industrial base and a system of collectivized agriculture were created. A central planning mechanism was able to give overall direction to economic development. It was a system of planning that made it possible to rapidly expand aggregate industrial capacity, to promote the development of the more backward republics and regions, and to marshal resources and capabilities on a monumental scale as part of the heroic effort to defeat German imperi-

---

Soviet Strategy for Economic Growth: Selected Soviet Essays, 1924-30 (Bloomington: Indiana University Press, 1964); and Maurice Dobb, *Soviet Economic Development Since 1917* (London: Routledge & Kegan Paul, 1948).

alism (1500 major factories were relocated eastward in the span of a few weeks). The slogan of the First Five Year Plan was "we are building a new world," and millions of workers and peasants, especially during the late 1920s and early 1930s, were fired with a spirit of "storming the heavens" and doing this for the cause of world revolution.

The collectivization drive ignited a genuine upheaval against centuries-old authority, tradition, and oppression in the countryside. The old educational system was overhauled and opened up to the masses, and young workers were mobilized as a social force to confront the old and hidebound. Artists, writers, and other cultural workers chronicled the great changes taking place in society, and an art to serve the revolution was struggled for and debated over. And the new workers' state gave support to and helped to formulate the line for revolutionary struggles throughout the world. In all, these were real and historic accomplishments. But, and here the focus is on the economic planning front, there were serious problems as well.

The Soviet planning system was able to steer a major portion of society's investment resources to key industrial sectors, and this promoted rapid growth. But the system overemphasized heavy industry. This created serious imbalances as heavy industry absorbed a tremendous share of economic resources at the social and economic expense of peasant agriculture (and, secondarily, at the expense of adequate development of transport and distribution). At the same time, the goal of high-speed industrial development and the preference for large-scale investment projects, with many being located in already industrialized areas, contributed to a huge increase in the urban population and an unnecessary concentration of industrial activities. This had the effect of reinforcing some of the inequalities between town and country and of intensifying to an excessive degree aspects of occupational specialization.

Stalin recognized the need to overcome such differences as between town and country and mental and manual labor. But he approached the problem mainly from the standpoint of developing production. The task of restricting these differences and relations to the greatest degree possible within the existing material conditions; of waging, and drawing the masses into, political struggle against bourgeois forces and lines and policies that would widen the gap between city and countryside and break the worker-peasant alliance; and challenging elitism, the worship of expertise, disdain for manual labor, and old habits and ideas—this was not sufficiently grasped. The political and ideological struggle was not recognized as the essential aspect. There were also problems with the institutions and methods of planning. Socialist construction and management in the Soviet Union rested on an overcentralized planning apparatus. The Soviet planning system, as it had evolved by the early 1950s but especially as it was formalized into a model to be adopted by other socialist countries, put a premium on tight control by the top industrial ministries and planning agencies, extending down to details at the enterprise level. Built into this model was a reliance on specialists and hierarchy that cut against the conscious activism of the producers. Its strict lines of authority and forms of one-man management tended to reproduce certain aspects of the traditional social division of labor. Motivationally, the system relied too much on material incentives, on stimulating hard work and sacrifice by offering people higher pay and bonuses—and with this came a certain ideological endorsement of wage and income differentiation.

The Soviet planning system proved administratively bulky and bureaucratic, overloading itself with tasks beyond its capabilities. When it came to figuring out material balances (for example, how much steel would be needed by local enterprises) and allocating materials, the system operated in such a way that everything had to be calculated and balanced at the highest levels. The rigidity of planning and its lack of flexibility at lower levels held back local dynamism and made it harder to adjust to unforeseen circumstances. This led to waste and actually made it more difficult to insure that plans would be suitably modified in order to be carried through.

Mao's Conceptual Leap

Mao rethought and recast this model of a planned socialist economy. While learning from the positive aspects of this first attempt to build socialism, he criticized the top-down methods and the strong tendency toward technological determinism that characterized Soviet planning. Yes, socialist construction requires a state economic plan to represent the fundamental interests of the working class. But Mao approached the question of centralized planning in a more dialectical way than had Stalin. That is, he understood the unity and struggle of opposites— between agriculture and industry, heavy and light industry, between the center and the localities, and between balance and imbalance. He understood that a plan could not be approached either in its formulation or implementation as an exact blueprint, and that production targets could not be treated as though they were simply laws subject to administrative enforcement. The socialist transition period is one of great struggle, transformation, and experimentation. The dynamism and change that is socialism is one of its great strengths, the more so as the masses are unleashed. And economic development will of necessity reflect this; it cannot be smooth and even. This understanding must inform planning methodology.

At a deeper level, Mao was critical of the view of a plan as a technical instrument of control over the economy. On the contrary, a plan is an expression of ideology, of the goals and outlook of a class. A plan is a class-based reflection of social reality that in turn acts on reality, and which, from the standpoint of the working class and its emancipation, seeks to bring about the conscious, social control of production.* The formulation of a plan is never merely a question of gathering technical information and anticipating economic developments. It involves class struggle in the ideological realm over the goals and direction of society. In reaching these conclusions, Mao was summing up both the Soviet and China's own revolutionary experience.

Let us draw together Mao's key insights into the nature of socialist society. Socialism, Mao emphasized, is not some sort of economic machine and set of political institutions that just tick along. It is a momentous struggle to replace production for profit by production for social use, a struggle to revolutionize all institutions and social relations in society, to forge new values and attitudes, to establish all-round control of society by the working people so they can master and transform all aspects of society, and to narrow and ultimately abolish all class distinctions. In short, it is a struggle to uproot the old and build a new world. Capitalist ideologues delight in sarcastically describing socialism

---

* In contrast with Mao, Stalin, in his 1952 essay *Economic Problems of Socialism*, had defined planning as a practical, policy-oriented enterprise as opposed to political economy, a theoretical pursuit.

as a "supposed workers' paradise." But socialism is not some kind of utopian endpoint. It is a period of revolutionary transformation between capitalism and communism. It is a form of class rule—proletarian dictatorship—that itself constitutes a transition and a means to carry out the struggle to transform the material and ideological foundations of class society and to continue the revolution to achieve classless society.

For Mao, socialism is a highly contradictory phenomenon. On the one hand, it is a great leap. Production is carried out to meet the needs of society according to a plan and is organized on the basis of conscious social initiative and coordination. Labor power is no longer bought and sold as a commodity; it is no longer controlled by a force alien to it; it is no longer reproducing economic relations that perpetuate domination and servitude. Yet, as much as a leap as socialism is, it remains a transitional society, containing both the scars of capitalism and the seeds of communism.

Socialist society will either move forward to communism or backward to capitalism. Two roads open up: the socialist road and the capitalist road. And what direction society goes in will be determined in the furnace of intense class struggle and upheaval. This is a struggle between the formerly oppressed who aspire to run and transform society and reactionary forces, *especially new bourgeois* forces, who seek to reimpose the old order and restructure society according to capitalist principles.

These new bourgeois forces are generated out of the contradictions of socialist society—out of differences in income, the specialized positions different individuals occupy in production, the particular roles that people play in administration and leadership, the gaps between town and country, and other major social contradictions that still exist under socialism—as well as the general environment of commodity-money relations.* In particular units and spheres of socialist economy it becomes possible for capitalist relations of control and exploitation to gain ground and even ascendancy. And various elements of the

---

* With respect to socialist state enterprises, *The Shanghai Textbook* points out that even though ownership is socialized and relations between these enterprises are built on a foundation of social cooperation, there persists an important degree of enterprise separateness (a relative independence of operation and management) that can lead to competition and fragmentation.

superstructure, such as education and culture, can also become bourgeois strongholds when a bourgeois-elitist line is dominant.

As a class, the new bourgeoisie represents the bourgeois aspects— the inequalities, social differences, etc.—*within* socialist relations of production and actual relations of exploitation that can develop within a collective property form. This class develops inside the framework of socialist ownership. As a political force, its strength is concentrated in, and organized through, power centers at the highest echelons of the governing party-state apparatus in socialist society, including the armed forces.[*] In other words, with the overthrow of the old exploiting classes, the defeat of their subsequent attempts at comeback, and the consolidation of a new mode of production, class relations change and the ground and terms of the class struggle shift. As Mao pointed out in 1976, "You are making the socialist revolution and yet don't know where the bourgeoisie is. It is right in the Communist Party— those in power taking the capitalist road."[**]

Mao's focus on the party is crucial to a correct understanding of the class struggle under socialism. The masses still need a leading core in order to wage the complicated and protracted battle to rule and remake society and achieve communism worldwide. The proletarian party becomes the leading political force in the exercise of mass political power. It becomes the main directing force of an economy based on state-public ownership. This vanguard position and role are essential to proletarian rule. But this vanguard position has a dual character—because it is precisely within this leading institution, especially at its highest reaches, where a new bourgeoisie will be centered. The party thus emerges as a decisive arena of the class struggle under socialism and must itself be revolutionized.

Socialist society is characterized by the extremely close, and direct, links between the exercise of political and economic power. Not only

---

[*] For Mao, bureaucracy in economic planning and in other aspects of party and state functioning was not simply a problem of administrative overgrowth and elitism that had to be curbed. Bureaucracy is also a form of organization through which a new bourgeoisie reproduces itself and a method of control by which it seeks to consolidate power in particular spheres.

[**] Mao Tsetung, quoted in "Reversing Correct Verdicts Goes Against the Will of the People," *Peking Review* (11), 12 March 1976, in Lotta, *And Mao Makes Five*, p. 261.

is the power to allocate and manage means of production expressed in a concentrated way as political leadership (over ministries, finance, trade, and individual production units, etc.), but also the overall direction society moves in hinges on what line (aims and outlook) and policies are leading at the top levels. Those in the highest positions of power and influence who depart from the socialist road and divorce themselves from the masses, and who champion and seek to implement a neocapitalist line, will ultimately organize into a bourgeois headquarters. These "capitalist roaders" are the main force of the bourgeoisie (understood as an actual class) and the main target of the continuing revolution. The political program of the capitalist roaders is to seize on and expand the capitalist factors within socialist society in order to transform socialist ownership into a mere shell. And when the conditions are ripe the capitalist roaders will, as they must, make a bid for power.

The Cultural Revolution led by Mao was a means and method to defeat the forces that wanted to restore capitalism. Through the mobilization of and the heroic determination of the masses, the bourgeois centers of power within the party and state institutions were politically bombarded, leading bourgeois elements were struck down, and many of the portions of power they had usurped were seized back from below through revolution. Most importantly, society was sprung into the air, and on the basis of mass upheaval, economic, political, and social relations, as well as people's thinking, were revolutionized. In this way, by continuing the revolution, the proletariat attacks the material and ideological foundations of privilege, a bourgeoisie, and a social base in support of it; the proletariat digs up the soil out of which classes arise.

The class struggle in socialist society is a struggle over whether a plan will serve socialist development—or serve capitalist development; whether the results of the proletariat's labor will be used to build up the basis to eliminate classes—or be used against the producers; whether the capitalist aspects in society and their manifestations in the realms of ideas and culture will be restricted and overcome—or expanded; whether the scope of participation and initiative of the masses in running society will be widened—or hemmed in; whether the socialist state will act as a base area for world revolution—or turn its back on the international proletariat. In short, will the revolution continue, or will it be reversed?

Of course, the economy must be developed and the productivity of social labor must be raised. But, the productive forces must be developed not as an end in itself, nor even with the guiding principle of maximizing material welfare, but rather to provide the necessary material basis for carrying forward the social, political, and ideological transformations that are at the heart of the transition and revolutionary struggle to a higher form of society no longer divided by classes. Politics must command production. And Mao emphasized that the productive forces have to be developed *on the basis of* continually revolutionizing production relations and people's outlook. As Mao said, class struggle is the key link; grasp revolution, promote production.

Once political leadership departs from this standpoint, once production is taken as the key link in moving society forward and the "most efficient" methods of production become the all-important yardstick, then what sets in is production for its own sake, the domination of dead labor (means of production produced by previous labor) over living labor . . . and that puts you on the capitalist road. Once planning is construed as a technical activity of administering and controlling, then the plan begins to dominate the proletariat rather than the other way around . . . and that puts you on the capitalist road.*

The struggle to create a world without classes and class distinctions, to make and deepen socialist revolution, has required the application of Marxism to a new set of problems and the formulation of new concepts adequate to the complexity of socialist society. Mao Tsetung decisively extended the range of Marxism. He did so on the theoretical level of conceptualizing what is being acted on—socialism as a transitional form of class society. And he did so on the political level of developing an orientation for how that society must be acted upon—persisting in class struggle and continuing the revolu-

---

* Stalin veered very much in the direction of these erroneous approaches, and many of the economic policies he promoted gave oxygen to the forces of capitalist restoration. But this must be put in context. To begin with, there was no prior socialist experience, positive or negative, to serve as a measuring rod. Secondly, for all his mistakes, Stalin was attempting to build socialism *not* capitalism and, in fact, ranged himself against those who wanted to put profit mechanisms in command of planning and economic construction.

tion. Mao systematized the fullest understanding yet achieved by Marxism of the economics and politics of the transition from socialism to communism. As to the subject at hand, the point can be put this way: With Mao a scientific and comprehensive political economy of socialism can now, for the first time in the history of the workers' movement, be said to have been established. *The Shanghai Textbook* is persuasive testimony.

The Shanghai Textbook: Its History and Legacy

The Shanghai Textbook was conceived of as a rigorous exposition of socialist political economy, yet one accessible to broad numbers. The text and the larger work from which it is derived are the product of a process of struggle and learning.

Socialist political economy became a matter of intense theoretical concern to the Chinese revolutionaries after the countrywide seizure of power in 1949. How would China make the transition from the national-democratic to the socialist revolution? What path would socialist development take given China's concrete conditions? How would a socialist China link up with the Soviet-led socialist camp, confront the forces of imperialism, and aid revolutionary struggles internationally? These were among the critical issues facing the revolution in power. And these issues framed more particular problems of socialist development and planning—the relationship between industrialization and agricultural collectivization, investment priorities, the law of value and planning, the role of different incentive systems in spurring the growth of the productive forces, the place of advanced technology, etc.

The Chinese communists were hardly coming from nowhere in leading the masses in transforming and running society. They had accumulated valuable experience and understanding from waging more than 20 years of people's war. In the revolution's base areas from the late 1920s, up through the anti-Japanese war over more or less a decade ending in 1945, and then until nationwide victory in 1949, the party had mobilized the populace to carry out economic construction and transformation as well as to wage military combat. And Maoist war-fighting involved principles, such as combining centralized military line and command with decentralized operations, that had wider applicability. There was also the Maoist party tradition of conducting deep social investigation among the masses to understand their needs and experiences and politically winning over the masses to take up lines and policies that concentrate their higher interests. But in terms of unfolding socialist construction, what was most relevant was the Soviet Union. It had pioneered the way to developing and managing a full-fledged socialist economy, and China's initial approach to planning and development was heavily influenced by Soviet experience and thinking.

The Chinese had translated and closely studied Stalin's essay *Economic Problems of Socialism* (1952) as well as a comprehensive Soviet textbook, *Political Economy: A Textbook*. This Soviet textbook, the drafting of which was guided by Stalin's essay, though it did not appear until the mid-1950s, after his death, looms large in the narrative of Maoist political economy. It was the most advanced and systematic presentation of socialist political economy available to revolutionaries. In 1959, Mao instructed party members to study the third edition of the Soviet political economy text with certain problems in mind. But the book soon became an object of critique by Mao—with regard to its methodology as well as specific theoretical formulations.

China had adopted much of the Soviet planning and developmental-industrialization model when it embarked on socialist construction—"let's be modern and Soviet" was a slogan of the First Five-Year Plan. But as the Plan drew to a close in 1956-57, with very mixed results, Mao began to rethink the Soviet paradigm. Huge heavy investment projects threatened to absorb too high a level of resources; agriculture required more attention and stimulation so as to raise growth rates; planning mechanisms and management methods were not fostering mass participation. In this period the revolution was also moving to socialize ownership to higher levels (completing the nationalization of industry in the cities, and pushing forward collectivization in the countryside) and was experiencing new social struggles.* In his 1956 speech "On the Ten Major Relationships," Mao set forth a different

---

* In the countryside, poor peasants began redistributing and pooling land and productive assets. (Mao hailed this high tide.) In the cities, there were some outbursts of dissatisfaction and anti-socialist unrest among sections of intellectuals and students.

approach to developmental priorities—including placing more emphasis on agriculture and light industry relative to heavy industry (without sacrificing heavy industry's core role) and putting more responsibility in local hands—and development itself was seen as a series of economic–social relationships and contradictions rather than simply a matter of technical–production variables. In 1958, at the time of China's Great Leap Forward, Mao criticized Stalin's *Economic Problems of Socialism* for, among other things, its one-sided emphasis on the productive forces and its downplaying of questions of politics, ideology, and culture: "From the beginning to the end of this book, Stalin says nothing about the superstructure; he does not take man into consideration; he sees things but not people."* He also took issue with the elevation of technology over politics, and of cadre over the masses.

In 1961-62, Mao wrote his *Reading Notes on the Soviet Text Political Economy*. Wide-ranging in its observations and thematic considerations, and written with characteristic pungency, the essay stands as an essential work of Marxian political economy. In it, Mao attaches great importance to the need to revolutionize the relations of production after socialist ownership has been achieved. He views the movement from lower to higher social property forms as a process of political-revolutionary struggle and conceptualizes the passage from socialism to communism as nothing less than a social revolution.

So during the 1956-64 period, Mao was articulating an alternative approach to socialist development. It was an approach rooted in revolutionary struggle and mass participation. During this period, there had been direct experience from which to learn: the negative impacts of the Soviet-influenced growth strategy and industrial organization model that had been adopted in the early 1950s, and the positive experience of the Great Leap Forward in China. The Great Leap was the crucible through which the new approach was initially forged. It had led to the formation of peasant communes in the countryside, experiments in new forms of worker management, broad efforts to restrict the differences between town and country and mental and manual

---

* A slightly different translation can be found in Mao Tsetung, "Critique of Stalin's *Economic Problems of Socialism*," in *A Critique of Soviet Economics* (New York: Monthly Review Press, 1977), p. 135.

labor, and the introduction of new planning priorities and mechanisms to serve these goals.

During this same period, Mao was further developing and synthesizing the understanding of the question of classes and class conflict under socialism. In a 1962 party congress speech, Mao put forward an important thesis on class contradictions and class struggle under socialism (which he now begins to see as being of relatively long duration). And the Chinese party's polemics with the Soviet Union of 1963-64, written under Mao's overall guidance, pointed to the existence of a privileged ruling stratum that had reversed the revolution in the Soviet Union. This was very much related to the issues of economic development and transformation: the struggle raging on the economic front and over economic policy in China was definitely revealing that such a stratum (later to be understood as a bourgeois class) existed in China too.

Indeed, Mao was leading the class struggle against the conservative-revisionist[*] forces in the Chinese party who had attacked and tried to sabotage the Great Leap Forward. These forces were pushing a capitalist program under a banner of modernization and efficiency. Not surprisingly, they too were systematizing a political economy of socialism (in name!). From the 1950s until the overthrow of the revolutionary forces in 1976, the conservative-revisionist forces, sometimes split among themselves and sometimes shifting their positions, basically advanced two economic models: a decentralized economy in which individual production units enjoyed considerable autonomy in production and marketing decisions; and a more centralized economy in which ministries, planning agencies, and the upper reaches of the party concentrated decision-making and economic power (over the allocation of investment and financial resources, etc.). Despite the surface differences, what they shared in common was a vision of industrialization and modernization as ends in themselves, and reliance on effi-

---

[*] "Revisionism" is false communism. It is a bourgeois current within the workers' movement that "revises" and distorts fundamental principles of Marxism—as regards the nature of capitalism, political revolution, and socialism-communism. Revisionism guts Marxism of its emancipatory heart. It appeals to workers on a basis of reformism and narrow material interest. And its aim and effect is to perpetuate or to restore capitalism in the name of Marxism and in pursuit or defense of bourgeois class position and interest. Revisionism is capitalism disguised as socialism. *See* Chapter 2 of the *Textbook*.

ciency norms and rate of return indicators, as well as capitalist mechanisms of control, management, and motivation, to get there.*

The Cultural Revolution of 1966-76 was the quantum leap in Maoist theory and practice. In the wake of the Cultural Revolution's first and tumultuous phase of power seizures and radical institutional transformations, the Maoist forces decided to consolidate a political economy of socialism. To sum up and draw on, they had the experience of this "second revolution," as *The Shanghai Textbook* describes the Cultural Revolution, and what had been learned about the nature of socialist society and its class relations. And to build on, they had Mao's summations of the paths and strategies of socialist construction in the Soviet Union and China, his analysis of the revisionist takeover in the Soviet Union, and his theory of continuing revolution.

A comprehensive analysis of the economic structure and social contradictions of socialism, and of the causes of capitalist restoration, was now possible. It was also vitally needed—as a theoretical compass for understanding and navigating what was now understood to be a protracted socialist transition period, and, more immediately, as theoretical support for policies being implemented and promoted by the revolutionary forces in the face of fierce opposition from the conservative-revisionist forces. Some background is necessary to more fully appreciate this.

In the early and mid-1970s, the political situation in China had grown more complicated and dangerous. This was very much bound up with shifts and developments in the overall world situation. Starting in the late 1960s, the Soviet Union was threatening and making serious moves towards attacking China; by 1969, they had massed an enormous military force on their border with China, and were openly talking about a nuclear option. How China would face this mounting Soviet danger became a focus of policy debate and the class struggle in the ensuing years. Lin Piao, the head of China's armed forces, had argued for a policy of accommodation with the Soviet Union. Rebuked by Mao, Lin attempted an unsuccessful coup against Mao in 1971.

---

* On the debates over issues of economic theory in the 1950s and 1960s, *see* E.L. Wheelwright and Bruce McFarlane, *The Chinese Road to Socialism* (New York: Monthly Review Press, 1970); "Socialist Construction and Class Struggle in the Field of Economics," *Peking Review* (16), 17 April 1970; Stephen Andors, *China's Industrial Revolution* (New York: Pantheon, 1977); and Christopher Howe and Kenneth R. Walker, eds., *The Foundations of the Chinese Planned Economy* (London: Macmillan, 1989).

The largely pro-Western conservative elements within the party leadership saw an opening and sought to take advantage. They exploited the fact that Lin was identified with the Cultural Revolution to discredit its achievements. They used the threat of Soviet attack as an argument that China must strengthen itself through full-scale military alliance and economic integration with the West and the adoption of capitalist modernization and management. And they argued that China could no longer tolerate the upheaval and experimentation of the Cultural Revolution. The gains of the Cultural Revolution and the policies and programs of the Maoists were coming under increasing attack. A major struggle was shaping up. This was to be Mao Tsetung's last great battle to prevent capitalist restoration, and that battle, as it unfolded and deepened between 1973 and 1976, very much influenced theoretical work.

In June 1971, research and writing of a political economy of socialism text commenced.[*] It was to be an authoritative study of the foundations and dynamics of a socialist economy—identifying the key properties of a socialist economy and the key tasks and struggles posing themselves in the transition to classless society. Its method was to take Marxist categories of political economy and of class struggle and to apply them to the complex historical reality of socialism.

Political Economy of Socialism was seen as an ongoing work. The process of writing and circulating and improving drafts was a fertile one. Between 1972 and 1976, four drafts of the book were published, each a significant marker of a deeper theoretical grasp and each implicitly setting an agenda for further research. In tracking the changes in the successive drafts of the text, it becomes apparent that the Maoists were creatively tackling many of the most vexing issues of socialist political economy—from the character of the socialist labor process, to the status of economic laws under socialism, to the relationship between economics and politics, to the nature of the contradictions between the forces of production and the relations of production under socialism. The fifth manuscript of the *Political Economy of*

---

[*] The account that follows draws on Peer Moller Christensen and Jorgen Delman, "A Theory of Transitional Society and Mao Zedong and the Shanghai School," *Bulletin of Concerned Asian Scholars*, April-June, 1981, pp. 2-15. This essay has been of great assistance in reconstructing the history of the text.

Socialism never saw the light of day. It was seized off the printing presses immediately after the October 1976 rightist coup.

The Shanghai Textbook is a popularization of *Political Economy of Socialism*. The overall organization and argumentation of the two books are basically the same; textual comparison shows very little difference in matters of theoretical substance, and the revisions that *The Shanghai Textbook* underwent roughly correspond to successive editions of the larger work. The version of the textbook translated here is based on the fourth manuscript of *Political Economy of Socialism* dating from late 1975. The economists who had worked on the project were connected with the Institute of Political Economy at Fudan University in Shanghai, and Shanghai in general was a center of radical Maoist activity—hence the title change for this English edition of the *Fundamentals of Political Economy* textbook.

The key figure giving direction to the political economy of socialism project was Chang Chun-chiao [Zhang Chunqiao]. Chang was part of the national leadership core on whom Mao had relied to guide and sum up the complicated struggles of the Cultural Revolution. He first came to prominence during the Great Leap Forward, having written several important articles on wages policies and issues of socialist ownership. But it was in 1967, as the Cultural Revolution gathered hurricane force, that Chang emerged as a major figure. He had played a pivotal role in the 1967 worker uprising in Shanghai that came to be known as the January Shanghai Storm. He eventually became a vice-premier and member of the Standing Committee of the Politburo of the Communist Party Central Committee, the party's highest leadership body, and he helped steer the political campaigns launched by the Maoist forces to prevent capitalist takeover. He was also a major revolutionary theoretician. In October 1976, Chang and Chiang Ching, Mao's wife, were arrested along with Yao Wen-yuan and Wang Hung-wen. They were the "gang of four." Tried before a kangaroo court in 1980, Chang and Chiang Ching stuck by revolutionary principle, defending Mao and the Cultural Revolution (while Yao and Wang caved in). They received life sentences. Chiang Ching died in jail in 1990. At this writing, it is still not clear whether Chang is alive or dead.

It was Chang who had approved the initial plans for the *Political Economy of Socialism*. He had issued directives about its contents, had led several important discussion meetings concerned with the text, and had, according to accounts by the current Chinese leadership, reviewed final drafts. After the first manuscript appeared in September 1972, Chang evidently identified three key themes to be elaborated on in the text: why there are capitalist factors inside socialist relations of production; why the question of ownership is a question of power; and why relations between people in the production process are class relations. His essay "On Exercising All-Round Dictatorship Over the Bourgeoisie," published in 1975, advanced important theoretical issues expanded upon in the last two editions of *Political Economy of Socialism.*

The Shanghai Textbook is a work of considerable synthesis and originality, and given the scope and complexity of the subject, its clear-eyed and sharp-edged presentation of ideas is no small accomplishment. The *Textbook*, following Mao, conceptualizes socialism as three interrelated things. First, it is a *form of class rule* through which the proletariat (in alliance with other popular strata, most especially the poor peasantry in the oppressed Third World nations) rules over old and newly-engendered bourgeois and exploiting forces. Second, it is a *mode of production* in which social ownership replaces private ownership of the means of production and social need replaces private profit as the purpose and measure of social production. Third, it is a *period of transition* marked by intense class struggle and deep-going transformation, the aim of which is to eliminate classes and class distinctions on a world scale and as part of a worldwide process of revolution.

The opening chapter explains that the object of inquiry of Marxist political economy is the relations of production of society, and the book goes on to examine these relations in China. The role of politics, ideology, and culture in economic development is examined. The path and tempo of the socialization of the means of production in China's industrial and agricultural sectors, and the relations between these sectors, are surveyed. There are chapters dealing with the transformation of the social division of labor within the workplace (and social production is treated richly, as involving social relations, not just technical functions); planning methodology; forms of wage payment, distribution of society's output of goods, and the goal of simultaneously raising the living standards of people and creating greater equality between people; the role and dangers of money and monetary calculation. The task of narrowing and eventually overcoming what Maoists call the "three great differences"—between industry and agriculture, town and country, and mental and manual labor—runs as a theoretical thread through the work. The text is anything but formulaic and dogmatic in approach. It poses provocative questions: how can the proletariat delegate certain powers to representatives yet guard against the abuse and monopolization of these powers and loss of control over the means of production? how does one determine the real nature of state ownership?

Of particular importance in this 1975 edition is the issue of "bourgeois right." Bourgeois right is a "birthmark" of capitalism within socialist society. Bourgeois right refers to economic and social relations, as concentrated in law and policy, that uphold formal equality but which actually contain elements of inequality. The socialist principle of distribution—"from each according to one's ability, to each according to one's work"—is one example: on the one hand, an equal standard is applied to all—payment according to the amount of work performed; on the other hand, not everyone has the same needs and not everyone can work as productively as the other—and so this equal standard actually serves to reinforce inequality. The text draws attention to the forms of existence of bourgeois right and the ideological influence of bourgeois right (using the term more broadly to signify all the relations of socialist society that contain the seeds of capitalist commodity and social relations). China at the time was conducting a nationwide campaign to educate people about why bourgeois right is a breeding ground for capitalism (capitalist roaders try to widen social and economic differences by expanding bourgeois right) and why it must be restricted and ultimately transcended—which, in the case of distribution, requires the application of the communist principle of "from each according to one's ability, to each according to one's need."*

This 1975 edition of *The Shanghai Textbook* builds on the advanced understanding that Maoism had developed of the material

---

* Restricting bourgeois right in the realm of distribution under socialism involves such measures as developing more social forms of consumption; providing vital services, like health care, regardless of individual income; taking social initiatives to overcome inequalities between men and women; and narrowing wage differentials.

and ideological conditions in socialist society giving rise to new privileged forces and emergent capitalist relations. But it does not incorporate Mao's later analysis of the nature and location of the new bourgeoisie under socialism. Up until then, rightists and revisionists had generally been viewed as *agents* or *representatives* of bourgeois and feudal classes. Several months after this text was originally published, Mao issued a series of statements explaining that the core of the bourgeoisie in society was to be found at the highest levels of the party and state organs. Guided by these insights, Mao's followers carried their research further, and there is strong evidence that this theoretical development was substantively addressed in the 1976 edition of *Political Economy of Socialism*.

This work was not intended as an analysis of the performance of the Chinese economy or of policy disputes at the time.* It does, however, speak to broad growth and developmental trends as well as basic lines of demarcation between revolutionary and revisionist approaches to China's socialist developmental needs. One of the strengths of the work is precisely that it breathes the rich lessons of China's socialist revolution. These are its experiential reference points. But all this serves the larger purpose of the work: to provide a comprehensive theoretical accounting of socialist political economy.

Beyond that theoretical contribution, *The Shanghai Textbook* can also be read on several other levels. Written in direct and nonacademic language, it was designed to reach an audience that was not necessarily professionally trained. The text was one of several titles published between 1972 and 1976 comprising a Youth Self-Education Series. Books like this played a vital role in Maoist China. A key aim of the Cultural Revolution was to create an educational system that attacked rather than reinforced elitism. As part of this effort, a "down to the countryside, up to the mountains" movement was launched. Some 12 million young people, most of them of college age from the urban areas, took up assignments in China's rural areas, where the majority of the population lived. This book was written for these young people. They studied it, alongside companion volumes dealing with philosophy, literature, the social and natural sciences, and agricultural technol-

---

* The Afterword examines the performance of China's economy during the Maoist years.

ogy, to help prepare them for work and learning and political struggle in the countryside. Thus we learn something about how a new generation was being trained to look at socialist society. And we also get a sense of how Marxist theory was being made available to a broad audience—because this information was to be shared with peasants at the same time that students learned from the peasants. Broad public study and discussion of theory, including political economy, were a vital feature of political life in Maoist China.

The text is polemically charged in sections. The grounds for this should, in retrospect, be obvious: a momentous struggle was shaping up in China . . . and those who wanted to restore capitalism eventually won out. Thus the book can be read on yet another level. It reveals how the Chinese revolutionaries were preparing for battle, how they were training people to identify the structures and mechanisms within socialist society that had to be transformed and to understand what was ultimately at stake—to continue the revolution or see it defeated and reversed.

The Shanghai Textbook is a valuable source book for students and scholars of comparative economics, China studies, and Third World development. It should be of special interest to all who thirst for fundamental change. One thing that cannot be forgotten: the Chinese revolutionaries intended their theoretical work as a contribution to and aid for the international struggle of the working class and oppressed people. For those engaged in revolutionary struggle in various corners of the world, the book should help to clarify the scope and tasks of socialist political economy and indeed the socialist transformation of society overall. And the dialectics of struggle and knowledge will continue to assert itself. Out of one or several of these triumphant revolutions will no doubt come the next manuscript of the *Political Economy of Socialism*.

June 1994

ABBREVIATIONS OF
FREQUENTLY CITED WORKS

Engels, *Anti-Duhring*	Frederick Engels, *Anti-Duhring* (Peking: Foreign Languages Press, 1976).
Engels or Marx, *MESW*, followed by volume number	Karl Marx and Frederick Engels, *Selected Works* (Moscow: Progress Publishers), volumes 1 and 2 (1969), volume 3 (1970).
Lenin, *CW*, followed by volume number	V. I. Lenin, *Collected Works* (Moscow: Progress Publishers, various dates).
Lenin, *The State and Revolution*	V. I. Lenin, *The State and Revolution* (Peking: Foreign Languages Press, 1973).
Lotta, *And Mao Makes Five*	Raymond Lotta, ed., *And Mao Makes Five* (Chicago: Banner Press, 1978).
Mao, *SW*, followed by volume number	Mao Tsetung, *Selected Works* (Peking: Foreign Languages Press), volumes 1, 2, and 3 (1967), volume 4 (1969).
Mao, *SR*	Mao Tsetung, *Selected Readings* (Peking: Foreign Languages Press, 1971).
Mao, *The Red Book*	*Quotations from Mao Tsetung* (Peking: Foreign Languages Press, 1966).
Marx, *Capital*, followed by volume number	Karl Marx, *Capital* (Moscow: Progress Publishers, 1971).
Marx, *Critique of the Gotha Programme*	Karl Marx, *Critique of the Gotha Programme* (Peking: Foreign Languages Press, 1972).
Stalin, *Economic Problems of Socialism*	Joseph Stalin, *Economic Problems of Socialism in the U.S.S.R.* (Peking: Foreign Languages Press, 1972).

1

Study Some Political Economy

The Object of Political Economy

The great Chairman Mao teaches us: "Why did Lenin speak of exercising dictatorship over the bourgeoisie? It is essential to get this question clear. Lack of clarity on this question will lead to revisionism. This should be made known to the whole nation."[1] Studying some political economy is very important if we are to master Marxism, if we are to persevere in exercising all-round dictatorship over the bourgeoisie, and if we are to consciously implement the Party's basic line and policies for the entire historical period of socialism.

The youth fighting on the front lines in the countryside and factories are our country's hope and the successors to the proletarian revolutionary cause. To better engage in combat, to become politically fit more quickly, the youth must study some political economy.

The object of political economy is the relations of production

What kind of science is political economy? We must start from its object of study. The object of study of Marxist political economy is the relations of production. Engels clearly pointed out that "economics deals not with things but with relations between persons, and, in the last resort, between classes."[2] How do the relations of production among people arise? We must start from man's productive activities.

Chairman Mao said, "Marxists regard man's activity in production as the most fundamental practical activity, the determinant of all his

1

other activities."[3] But prior to the development of Marxism, a little over a hundred years ago, people did not have this scientific understanding. Thinkers of the exploiting classes all denied this viewpoint. They either championed the fallacy that human society developed according to god's will or peddled the nonsense that heroes make history. These supposedly great thinkers glossed over the simplest fact, namely, that people must first be able to feed, clothe, and shelter themselves before they can engage in politics, science, fine arts, and religious activities. And if people are to have food, clothing, and shelter, they must engage in productive activities. Therefore, the direct production of material goods is the basis of development of human society. Without the productive activities of the laboring people, humanity cannot survive and society cannot develop. It was Marx who discovered this law of development of human history.

To produce, people must enter into certain mutual relations. Isolated individuals cannot engage in production. Just as Marx pointed out: "In order to produce, they enter into definite connections and relations with one another and only within these social connections and relations does their action on nature, does production, take place."[4] These relations formed by people in the production process are called the relations of production. In class society, these relations are ultimately manifested as class relations.

The relations of production consist of three aspects:

(1) the form of ownership of the means of production;

(2) the position and mutual relations of people in production;

(3) the form of distribution of products.

The form of ownership refers to who owns the means of production (including means of labor such as machines, factories, and land, and objects of labor such as raw materials). The form of ownership of the means of production is the most important aspect of the relations of production and the basis of production relations. The form of ownership of the means of production determines the nature of the relations of production. Primitive society, slave society, feudal society, capitalist society, and socialist society are classified according to the differences in the forms and patterns of ownership of the means of production. The form of ownership determines people's roles in production and their mutual relations, and thus the form of distribution of products. To produce, it is necessary not only to have relations among people but also relations between people and nature. Human beings must conquer and transform nature. The power which humans develop and utilize to conquer and transform nature is called the productive forces. Productive forces are composed of people and materials (the latter called means of production). Among the productive forces, tools of production are the most important. The types of tools used for production reflect the magnitude of humanity's power to conquer nature. But we cannot regard tools of production as the determining factor in productive forces. "It is people, not things, that are decisive."[5] "Of all things in the world, people are the most precious."[6] Tools have to be used by people, created by people, and renovated by people—thus, without people, there would be no tools and no know-how. Without people, the best "automatic" tools are never really "automatic."

The relations of production and the productive forces constitute the two aspects of social production. In overall historical development, the productive forces generally play the principal and decisive role. Any transformation of the relations of production is necessarily a result of a certain development of the productive forces. The relations of production must correspond to [the demands of development of] the productive forces. When certain relations of production fetter the development of the productive forces, these relations of production must be replaced by some other, new relations of production which correspond to the development of the productive forces. This is to say, the form of production relations is not determined by man's subjective will but by the level of development of the productive forces. The relations of production must conform to the development of the productive forces. This is an objective law independent of human will. The emergence, development, and disintegration of certain relations of production unfold with a corresponding evolution of the contradictions of certain productive forces. Therefore, in the study of production relations, Marxist political economy also studies productive forces.

If in the overall development of history the productive forces are revealed to be the principal determining factor, does this mean that the relations of production are entirely passive in relation to the productive forces? Definitely not. When the relations of production correspond to the productive forces, they are an active spur to the development of the productive forces. When the relations of production no longer correspond to the productive forces, they will fetter the development of the productive forces. When the productive forces cannot be developed without changing the relations of production, the transformation of the relations of production plays the principal determining role. When old China was under the rule of imperialism, feudalism, and bureaucrat capitalism, the landlord and the comprador classes represented the most reactionary and backward relations of production in China. The development of the productive forces was severely restricted and undermined. Before liberation in 1949, China did not have any machine-building industry or any automobile or airplane manufacturing. Outside of Northeast China, the annual output of steel was only several hundred thousand tons. Even daily necessities were imported. Cloth was called foreign cloth, umbrellas were called foreign umbrellas. Even a tiny nail was called a foreign nail. Under those circumstances, the overthrow of the reactionary rule of imperialism, feudalism, and bureaucrat capitalism, the transformation of comprador-feudal relations of production, and the establishment of socialist relations of production played the principal determining role in promoting the development of the productive forces.

The major development of the productive forces generally occurs after changes in the relations of production. This is a universal law. The major development of the productive forces in capitalist society took place after the disintegration of feudal relations of production brought about by the bourgeois revolution and the rapid development of capitalist relations of production. In England, for example, the Industrial Revolution of the late eighteenth and early nineteenth centuries was carried through only after and on the basis of the bourgeois revolution of the seventeenth century. All this gave great impetus to the development of the productive forces. Similarly, large-scale modern industry in France, Germany, the United States, and Japan developed rapidly only after the old superstructure and relations of production had been transformed in various ways.

On the question of the relations of production and the productive forces, one of the principal issues in the long struggle between

Marxism and revisionism has always been whether one insists on upholding the theory of the dialectical unity between the productive forces and the relations of production, or promotes the reactionary "theory of the productive forces." Lin Piao, in league with Chen Po-ta, advocated that the principal task after the Ninth Party Congress of 1969 was to develop production. This is the same revisionist fallacy inserted into the Resolution of the Eighth Party Congress by Liu Shao-chi and Chen Po-ta, which held that "the contradiction between the advanced socialist system and the backward social productive forces" was the principal contradiction in Chinese society. In China, the socialist relations of production are basically in harmony with the growth of the productive forces. This opens up whole new horizons for the development of the productive forces. But these relations of production are still far from perfect, and this imperfection stands in contradiction to the growth of the productive forces. The practice of socialist revolution teaches us that it is always the superior socialist system that promotes the development of the productive forces. It is always after the transformation of those parts of the relations of production that do not correspond to the development of the productive forces that the development of the productive forces is promoted. Where is "the contradiction between the advanced socialist system and the backward social productive forces"? The criminal intention of Liu Shao-chi, Lin Piao, and other such swindlers who peddled this nonsense was to futilely attempt to use the "theory of productive forces" as a weapon to oppose continuing the revolution under the dictatorship of the proletariat and exercising all-round dictatorship over the bourgeoisie and to oppose the Party's basic line. This is their impossible dream.

The relations of production must correspond to the development of the forces of production. The development of the productive forces necessitates the destruction of old relations of production that are not compatible with their development and their replacement by new relations of production that are compatible with the development of the productive forces. But the process of disintegration of old production relations and the emergence of new production relations cannot be a smooth one. The transformation of old relations of production and the establishment and perfecting of new relations of production are often realized only through revolutionary struggles. Therefore, if one wants to understand how old relations of production are transformed, and new relations of production established and perfected, it is not enough to study this solely in terms of the contradictions between the relations of production and the productive forces. The relations between the superstructure and the economic base must also be investigated.

The superstructure refers to the national government, army, law, and other political institutions, and their corresponding ideological forms, such as philosophy, literature, and fine arts. The economic base consists of the relations of production. "The sum total of these relations of production constitutes the economic structure of society, the real foundation, on which rises a legal and political superstructure and to which correspond definite forms of social consciousness."[7] This statement by Marx scientifically explains the relation between the superstructure and the economic base.

In the contradiction between the superstructure and the economic base, the latter, in general, plays the principal and decisive role. The economic base determines the superstructure. With change in the economic base, "the entire immense superstructure is more or less rapidly transformed."[8] This is to say, when the old economic base disintegrates, the superstructure built upon this foundation must also disintegrate. But the superstructure does not disintegrate at the same rate as does the base. Even after the reactionary state machinery has been transformed and the old economic base replaced, the overthrown reactionary classes do not willingly quit the stage of history. They inevitably engage in prolonged and desperate struggles with the advanced classes in the political, ideological, and cultural spheres. In particular, the old ideological forms associated with the overthrown classes remain for a long time.

The superstructure is determined by the economic base. Once the superstructure is established, it exerts a tremendous reaction on the economic base. Stalin pointed out: "[The superstructure] . . . actively assists its base to take shape and consolidate itself, and does its utmost to help the new system to finish off and eliminate the old base and the old classes."[9] This explains why the superstructure always serves its economic base. The socialist superstructure serves its socialist economic base, and the capitalist superstructure serves its capitalist economic base.

In capitalist society, with the intensification of the contradiction between socialized production and private ownership of the means of production, there is an urgent objective need to replace capitalist private ownership with socialist public ownership. But the bourgeoisie controls the reactionary state machinery and uses it to maintain and defend the capitalist economic base. If the proletariat does not first smash the capitalist state machinery, it is impossible to destroy the capitalist economic system. The new and old revisionists' claim that "capitalism can peacefully grow into socialism" is a pack of lies.

In socialist society, the superstructure and the economic base are basically compatible. But due to the existence of the bourgeoisie and its ideological forms, the existence of certain bureaucratic styles of work in the state organs, and the existence of defects in certain parts of the state system, the consolidation, improvement, and further development of the socialist economic base are hindered or undermined. We must make the socialist superstructure better serve the socialist economic base. We must firmly grasp the struggle in the superstructure and carry the socialist revolution in the superstructure through to the end.

Political economy touches upon the most practical and immediate interests of various classes and strata. It explains the most acute and intense problems of class struggle. Marxist political economy, like Marxist philosophy, openly proclaims that it is in the service of proletarian politics. Political economy is a science that concerns itself with class struggle.

Political economy is the theoretical basis upon which the Party formulates its basic line

Marxist political economy came into being with the emergence of the modern proletariat and advanced productive forces, particularly large-scale industry. Marx participated in the class struggles of his time. He used revolutionary materialist dialectics to analyze capitalist society. He revealed the secrets of how the capitalists exploited the workers and scientifically disclosed the contradictions between socialized production and capitalist ownership. These contradictions were manifested as acute antagonisms between the proletariat and the bourgeoisie. With the daily development of the contradictions of capitalist society, the proletariat, the gravediggers of the capitalist system, grew in strength. "The knell of capitalist private property sounds. The expropriators are expropriated."[10] From this flowed the revolutionary and scientific conclusion that the capitalist system would inevitably be replaced by the

7

socialist system, and the bourgeois dictatorship by the proletarian dictatorship. "Marx deduces the inevitability of the transformation of capitalist society into socialist society wholly and exclusively from the economic law of the development of contemporary society."[11] Thus, Marxist political economy, along with Marxist philosophy and scientific socialism, became the theoretical basis enabling the proletarian political party to formulate its basic line. On the theoretical basis of Marxism and under capitalist conditions, the proletarian revolutionary leaders of the proletariat formulated for the proletarian party the basic political line of using revolutionary violence to seize political power. They guided the proletariat to struggle for the complete overthrow of the bourgeoisie and all exploiting classes, the replacement of bourgeois dictatorship by proletarian dictatorship, the triumph of socialism over capitalism, and the ultimate achievement of communism.

In socialist society, Marxist political economy still provides the theoretical basis for the proletarian party to formulate its basic line. Chairman Mao has penetratingly analyzed the contradictions between the socialist relations of production and the productive forces, and between the superstructure and the economic base, and revealed the protracted and complex nature of the struggle between the two classes and between the two lines in the socialist period. On this theoretical basis, he further formulated the basic line for our Party for the entire socialist period. This basic line teaches us: "Socialist society covers a considerably long historical period. Throughout this historical period, there are classes, class contradictions and class struggle, there is the struggle between the socialist road and the capitalist road, there is the danger of capitalist restoration and there is the threat of subversion and aggression by imperialism and social-imperialism. These contradictions can be resolved only by depending on the theory of continued revolution under the dictatorship of the proletariat and on practice under its guidance."[12] The Party's basic line guides the Chinese people, enabling them to persist in continuing the revolution under the dictatorship of the proletariat, to struggle for the consolidation of the dictatorship of the proletariat, the prevention of capitalist restoration, and the construction of socialism, and to struggle for the magnificent ideal of the worldwide realization of communism.

Chairman Mao has pointed out: "In a word, China is a socialist country. Before liberation she was much the same as a capitalist country. Even now she practices an eight-grade wage system, distribution according to work, and exchange through money, and in all this differs very little from the old society. What is different is that the system of ownership has been changed."[13] Chairman Mao has also pointed out: "Our country at present practices a commodity system, the wage system is unequal, too, as in the eight-grade wage scale, and so forth. Under the dictatorship of the proletariat such things can only be restricted. Therefore, if people like Lin Piao come to power, it will be quite easy for them to rig up the capitalist system. That is why we should do more reading of Marxist-Leninist works."[14] The bourgeois rights embodied in the commodity system and the principle of distribution according to work provide an important economic foundation out of and upon which capitalism and new bourgeois elements are engendered. Grasping the profound character of this question has important implications in persevering in exercising all-round dictatorship over the bourgeoisie. These are all questions in the realm of political economy. By studying some political economy, we can deepen our understanding of the Party's basic line and raise our consciousness so that we can better implement it.

Marxist political economy stands in opposition to all bourgeois and revisionist political economy; it developed through the process of challenging bourgeois and revisionist political economy. Studying Marxist political economy helps us to distinguish between Marxism and revisionism, between socialism and capitalism, and between the proletariat and the bourgeoisie. It will also enable us to correct deviations and heighten our ideological awareness.

In summary, we must study some political economy if we want to defeat anti-Party, anti-Marxist ideology, truly persevere in exercising all-round dictatorship over the bourgeoisie, thoroughly implement the Party's basic line, and continue to score new and greater victories in the great socialist revolution and the cause of socialist construction.

Combine theory with practice to learn political economy well

Political economy is an application of, and demonstrates the validity of, dialectical materialism and historical materialism. In studying political economy, we must follow the guidance of dialectical materialism and

9

historical materialism. The dialectical method "regards every historically developed social form as in fluid movement, and therefore takes into account its transient nature not less than its momentary existence; because it lets nothing impose upon it, and is in its essence critical and revolutionary."[15] This proletarian world outlook is in direct opposition to idealism and metaphysics. Only by grasping dialectical and historical materialism and using them to observe and analyze the laws of motion of capitalist society and economy can we understand why capitalism is bound to perish and socialism bound to triumph. And only by using dialectical and historical materialism to observe and analyze the laws of motion of socialist society and economy can we understand the protracted and complex nature of class struggle and line struggle in socialist society, and only then can we understand the general trend of historical development from socialism to communism, which is independent of human will. This will strengthen our resolve to struggle for the ultimate victory of the cause of communism—with full determination and fearing neither difficulty nor sacrifice.

In studying political economy, we must insist on the revolutionary style of learning which combines theory with practice. Chairman Mao teaches us: "It is necessary to master Marxist theory and apply it, master it for the sole purpose of applying it."[16] To combine theory and practice is a question of whether one has a revolutionary style of study, of whether one has party spirit. We must combine study of political economy with criticism of revisionism, with criticism of the reactionary fallacies peddled by Liu Shao-chi, Lin Piao, and similar swindlers, with the three great revolutionary movements of class struggle, the struggle for production, and scientific experiment, and with the transformation of world outlook. Chairman Mao has pointed out: "Lenin said that 'small production engenders capitalism and the bourgeoisie continuously, daily, hourly, spontaneously, and on a mass scale.' They are also engendered among a part of the working class and of the Party membership. Both within the ranks of the proletariat and among the personnel of state and other organs there are people who take to the bourgeois style of life."[17] We should use Marxist political economy to consciously combat the "bourgeois style" and to wage a persistent struggle against capitalist forces and the bourgeoisie.

Is it difficult to learn Marxist political economy? Yes. In the preface to the first edition of *Capital*, Marx said: "Everything starts out difficult.

Every science is this way." In the concrete analysis of objective phenomena, Marxist political economy penetrates beneath the surface, grasps the essence, and undertakes scientific abstraction. Thus, when we start, we often come across some terms and concepts which are difficult to understand. But Marxist political economy was written for the proletariat and deals with the theory of proletarian revolution. If we seriously study it, then we can gradually come to understand it. "'Nothing in the world is difficult for one who sets one's mind to it.' To cross the threshold is not difficult, and mastery, too, is possible provided one sets one's mind to the task and is good at learning."[18]

Marx once pointed out: "There is no royal road to science, and only those who do not dread the fatiguing climb of its steep paths have a chance of gaining its luminous summits."[19] The revolutionary leaders of the proletariat devoted their entire lives to founding and developing Marxist theory. Following their shining examples and diligently reading works by Marx, Lenin, and Chairman Mao, we should struggle to study and master this Marxist theoretical weapon—for the socialist revolution and socialist construction, and for the achievement of communism worldwide.

Major Study References

Marx, "Preface to *A Contribution to the Critique of Political Economy,*" *Selected Works of Marx and Engels,* volume 1

Engels, *Anti-Duhring,* part 2, chapter 1

Lenin, "Karl Marx," *Collected Works,* volume 21

Mao, "On Contradiction," section 4, *Selected Works,* volume 1

Mao, "On the Correct Handling of Contradictions Among the People," section 1, *Selected Readings*

Notes

1. Quoted in Chang Chun-chiao, "On Exercising All-Round Dictatorship Over the Bourgeoisie," Peking Review No. 14, 4 April 1975; reprinted in Raymond Lotta, ed., *And Mao Makes Five* (Chicago: Banner Press, 1978), p. 209.
2. Frederick Engels, "Karl Marx, *A Contribution to the Critique of Political Economy,*" in Karl Marx and Frederick Engels, *Selected*

Works (Moscow: Progress Publishers, 1969 [volumes 1 and 2], 1970 [volume 3]), volume 1, p. 514. (Hereafter, this collection is referred to as *MESW.*)

3. Mao Tsetung, "On Practice," in *Selected Works (SW)* (Peking: Foreign Languages Press, 1967 [volumes 1, 2, and 3], 1969 [volume 4]), volume 1, p. 295. (Hereafter, this collection is referred to as *SW.*)

4. Karl Marx, *Wage, Labor and Capital* (Peking: Foreign Languages Press, 1978), p. 29.

5. Mao, "On Protracted War," *SW* 2, p. 143.

6. Mao, "The Bankruptcy of the Idealist Conception of History," *SW* 4, p. 454.

7. Marx, "Preface to *A Contribution to the Critique of Political Economy*," *MESW* 1, p. 503.

8. Ibid., p. 504.

9. J.V. Stalin, *Marxism and Problems of Linguistics* (Peking: Foreign Languages Press, 1972), p. 5.

10. Marx, *Capital* (New York: International Publishers, 1967), volume 1, p. 715.

11. V.I. Lenin, "Karl Marx," in *Collected Works (CW)* (Moscow: Progress Publishers, various dates [date will follow volume number in first citation for each volume]), volume 21 (1974), p. 71.

12. Communist Party of China (CPC), "Constitution of the Communist Party of China," in *The Tenth National Congress of the Communist Party of China (Documents)* (Peking: Foreign Languages Press, 1973), p. 62.

13. Quoted in Chang Chun-chiao, "Exercising All-Round Dictatorship," in Lotta, *And Mao Makes Five*, p. 211.

14. Ibid., p. 214.

15. Marx, "Afterword to the Second German Edition of *Capital*," *Capital* 1, p. 29.

16. Mao, "Rectify the Party's Style of Work," *SW* 3, p. 38.

17. Quoted in Chang Chun-chiao, "Exercising All-Round Dictatorship," in Lotta, *And Mao Makes Five*, p. 209.

18. Mao, "Problems of Strategy in China's Revolutionary War," *SW* 1, p. 190.

19. Marx, "Preface to the French Edition of *Capital*," *Capital* 1, p. 30.

2

SOCIALIST SOCIETY USHERS IN A NEW ERA IN HUMAN HISTORY

Socialist Society and the Dictatorship of the Proletariat

In the middle of the nineteenth century, Marx and Engels, the teachers of the world proletarian revolution, analyzed the emergence, development, and decline of capitalist relations of production and reached the scientific conclusion that the proletariat would certainly overthrow the bourgeoisie and all exploiting classes, that proletarian dictatorship would certainly replace bourgeois dictatorship, that socialism would certainly replace capitalism, and that communism would certainly be realized in the end. They called on the proletariat of the world to unite with the broad laboring masses and take up arms to struggle fearlessly for the destruction of the bourgeois state machinery, the establishment of the dictatorship of the proletariat, and the achievement of socialism and communism. In the past hundred years and more, the proletariat of the world, fearing no sacrifice, has marched forward unwaveringly under the brilliant guidance of Marxism. The international proletariat has turned the scientific socialist ideal into a reality that illumines a large area of the world. "The socialist system will eventually replace the capitalist system; this is an objective law independent of man's will."[1] The socialist society under proletarian dictatorship, established through violent revolution, is a fundamental negation of the exploitative capitalist system and all exploitative systems. It ushers in a new era of human history.

PROLETARIAN REVOLUTION AND THE DICTATORSHIP OF THE PROLETARIAT ARE THE PREREQUISITES FOR THE EMERGENCE OF SOCIALIST RELATIONS OF PRODUCTION

Socialist relations of production cannot emerge within capitalist society

The transition from one form of society to another in human history is impelled by the fundamental contradiction in society, namely, the contradiction between the relations of production and the forces of production, and between the superstructure and the economic base. Marx pointed out: "At a certain stage of their development, the material productive forces of society come in conflict with the existing relations of production, or—what is but a legal expression for the same thing—with the property relations within which they have been at work hitherto. From forms of development of the productive forces these relations turn into their fetters. Then begins an epoch of social revolution. With the change of the economic foundation the entire immense superstructure is more or less rapidly transformed . . . and new, higher relations of production never appear before the material conditions of their existence have matured in the womb of the old society itself."[2] The material conditions for socialist relations of production—socialized production and the proletariat acting as the gravediggers of capitalism—steadily develop under capitalist conditions. When capitalism develops into imperialism, the death knell of capitalism is sounded, and the time for proletarian socialist revolution has come.

In human history, slavery, feudalism, and capitalism are all exploitative systems based on private ownership of the means of production. The transitions from slavery to feudalism to capitalism always take the form of a new system of private ownership replacing an old system of private ownership. Under these conditions, new relations of production can gradually emerge and develop in the old society. For example, capitalist relations of production emerged gradually towards the end of feudal society. But even under these conditions, in order for a new system of private ownership to become the dominant economic basis of society, it must rely on the newly emerging exploiting class, which represents this new system of private ownership, to launch revolu-

14

tions, seize political power, and engage in life-and-death class struggle. This is a time-tested law.

Socialist relations of production are relations of production based on public ownership. They cannot possibly emerge within capitalist society. The socialist system of public ownership stands in fundamental opposition to the system of capitalist ownership in which the means of production are privately owned. To implement socialist public ownership of the means of production implies the expropriation of the bourgeoisie's means of production. This cannot be carried out in capitalist society under bourgeois dictatorship. The bourgeois state machinery and its whole superstructure exist for the protection of the system of capitalist private ownership. The bourgeoisie will never allow socialist relations of production to take shape within the capitalist society. All fallacious arguments that "capitalism can peacefully evolve into socialism," championed by new and old revisionists, are totally contrary to the facts. These "theories" serve to preserve the capitalist system and to prevent the proletariat from rising up and rebelling. With the development of capitalism, the path to complete and revolutionary societal transformation is clear: *"The proletariat seizes state power and to begin with transforms the means of production into state property."*[3]

The fundamental issue of revolution is political power. Chairman Mao pointed out: "Political power grows out of the barrel of a gun."[4] Only by overthrowing the bourgeois state machinery and establishing proletarian dictatorship through revolutionary violence can the proletariat institute socialist nationalization of the capitalist economy and socialist transformation of the individual economy and establish and develop production relations based on socialist public ownership. Thus, proletarian revolution and proletarian dictatorship become the prerequisites for the emergence of socialist relations of production.

The Paris Commune of 1871 was the historic first, great attempt made by the proletariat to overthrow the capitalist system with revolutionary violence. Although the Paris Commune failed, the principles of the commune lived on. The experience of the Paris Commune demonstrated that the proletariat must destroy the bourgeois state machinery, that is to say, "the working class cannot simply lay hold of the ready-made State machinery, and wield it for its own purposes."[5]

15

Lenin's leadership in the October Revolution was a brilliant application of the Marxist theory of violent revolution. The experience of the October Revolution demonstrated that in the period of imperialism and proletarian revolution, as long as there is a proletariat of some size, as long as there are masses suffering oppression, and as long as there is a relatively mature proletarian party which is able to combine a Marxist line with revolutionary practice in that country and which is able to correctly lead the proletariat, the poor, and the suffering peasants by uniting all forces that can be united to wage a persistent struggle against the class enemy, it is possible to overthrow bourgeois rule through armed revolution, even in the most backward capitalist country, and thereby establish a socialist state under proletarian dictatorship.

The cannon fired in the October Revolution brought the Chinese people Marxism-Leninism. The great Chairman Mao formulated a general line for China's new democratic revolution by combining the universal truth of Marxism-Leninism with China's revolutionary situation. The general line was: "The revolution against imperialism, feudalism and bureaucrat capitalism [will be] waged by the broad masses of the people under the leadership of the proletariat."[6] Under the guidance of this revolutionary line, the path of establishing base areas in the countryside and the rural areas and laying siege to, and finally seizing, the urban areas was followed. After a prolonged period of revolutionary war, the Chinese people overthrew the reactionary rule of imperialism, feudalism, and bureaucrat capitalism, destroyed the old state machinery, and established the People's Republic of China under a people's democratic dictatorship, a specific form of the dictatorship of the proletariat. The birth of the People's Republic of China was the greatest world-historical event since the October Revolution.

The experience of the Chinese revolution demonstrates that, in the period of imperialism and proletarian revolution, if the proletariat of the colonial and semicolonial countries seriously combines the universal truth of Marxism-Leninism with concrete revolutionary practice in those countries, assumes firm leadership of the democratic revolution, and leads the people to victory in this revolution, it is entirely possible to enter the stage of socialist revolution immediately after completing the anti-imperialist and antifeudal tasks.

The triumphs of the October Revolution and the socialist revolution in China are the great victories of the Marxist theory of armed revolution. New and old revisionists constantly and maliciously attack armed revolutions. They espouse the fallacy of "peaceful transition," which is nothing but a refurbished version of the "benevolence" preached by the philosopher Confucius, a spokesman for the then decadent slave-owning class in China. Confucius's "benevolence" has never been benevolent at all, and the bourgeoisie has always used reactionary force to suppress the proletariat. The so-called "way of loyalty and trust" was a hoax perpetrated by the exploiting class to sap the fighting will of the laboring people. That veritable present-day disciple of Confucius, Lin Piao, even picked up such dust-covered weapons as "one who wields virtue prospers, one who wields force perishes," vainly attempting to restrict the freedom of the proletariat and to oppose the use of revolutionary violence against the reactionary class. With respect to the fallacy of "peaceful transition" and the opposition to revolutionary violence consistently pushed by domestic and foreign revisionists, Chairman Mao solemnly pointed out: "The seizure of power by armed force, the settlement of the issue by war, is the central task and the highest form of revolution. This Marxist-Leninist principle of revolution holds good universally, for China and for all other countries."[7] This is a universal law of proletarian revolution.

The crux of the "theory of the productive forces" is its opposition to proletarian revolution and proletarian dictatorship

The most fundamental betrayal of Marxism by the new and old revisionists is their opposition to proletarian revolution and proletarian dictatorship. The tattered banner they often hoist in opposition to proletarian revolution and proletarian dictatorship is the reactionary "theory of the productive forces" [or the "productivity first" theory].

The revisionists Bernstein and Kautsky of the Second International tried very hard to promote the idea that, by virtue of the development of the productive forces, capitalist countries with highly developed industrial economies would "gradually evolve" towards socialism. In these countries, it was therefore unnecessary to resort to violent revolution. The corollary was that in capitalist countries with underdeveloped industries, in the colonies, and in the dependent countries it was necessary first to "develop" the productive forces, since, [it was alleged,] without highly developed productive forces, the proletariat could not wage revolution. This was an early version of the "theory of the productive forces" in the international communist movement. This erroneous theory treated social transformation purely as an issue of the development of the productive forces. It completely ignored that the relations of production react back upon the development of the productive forces, and that the superstructure reacts back upon the economic base. It ignored the principle of historical materialism that in class society social transformation can be realized only through fierce class struggle.

The founders of Marxism dealt a firm blow to the revisionists' "theory of the productive forces." Engels pointed out: "According to the materialist conception of history, the *ultimately* determining element in history is the production and reproduction of real life. More than this neither Marx nor I have ever asserted. Hence if somebody twists this into saying that the economic element is the *only* determining one, he transforms that proposition into a meaningless, abstract, senseless phrase."[8]

In the course of the proletarian revolution in Russia, people like Trotsky and Bukharin again picked up this shopworn "theory of the productive forces" in a futile attempt to oppose the Russian proletariat's triumphant advance against the capitalist system. They insisted that economically backward Russia was not qualified to establish a socialist system. This type of nonsense was roundly criticized by Lenin. Lenin asked: "Why cannot we begin by first achieving the prerequisites for that definite level of culture in a revolutionary way, and *then*, with the aid of the workers' and peasants' government and the Soviet system, proceed to overtake the other nations?"[9]

In the course of the Chinese revolution, leaders of the revisionist line, like Chen Tu-hsiu, borrowed the reactionary "theory of the productive forces" from the revisionists of the Second International and the Trotskyites. They said that China's economy was backward and that the proletariat could seize political power only after capitalism was highly developed. This theory in effect negated the need for revolution in China and would have kept China in her semicolonial and semifeudal state. Chairman Mao countered this position with this observation: "In the absence of political reforms all the productive forces are being ruined, and this is true both of agriculture and of industry."[10] Referring to the semicolonial and semifeudal character of China's old society, Chairman Mao pointed out that China's revolution must proceed in two steps. The first step is the new democratic revolution. The second step is the socialist revolution. These are two distinct yet interrelated revolutionary processes. The democratic revolution is the necessary preparation for the socialist revolution. The socialist revolution is an inevitable trend of the democratic revolution. This totally and thoroughly demolishes the conspiracy of people like Chen Tu-hsiu who unsuccessfully attempted to stem the rolling torrent of the Chinese people's revolution by resorting to the reactionary "theory of the productive forces."

Chairman Mao said: "True, the productive forces, practice, and the economic base generally play the principal and decisive role; whoever denies this is not a materialist. But it must also be admitted that in certain conditions, such aspects as the relations of production, theory and the superstructure in turn manifest themselves in the principal and decisive role."[11] The history of the international communist movement shows that the line of demarcation between Marxism and revisionism in the proletarian struggle for political power lies in whether one persists in upholding the theory of the dialectical unity between productive forces and the relations of production and between the economic base and the superstructure, or whether one pushes the reactionary "theory of the productive forces."

SOCIALIST SOCIETY IS A FAIRLY LONG HISTORICAL PERIOD

Socialist society is a period of struggle between declining capitalism and rising communism

What kind of a society is the socialist society established through proletarian revolution? What are its basic characteristics?

Marx pointed out: "Between capitalist and communist society lies the period of the revolutionary transformation of the one into the other. There corresponds to this also a political transition period in which the state can be nothing but *the revolutionary dictatorship of the proletariat.*"[12] The period described by Marx as "a period of revolutionary transformation of the one into the other" and "a political transition period" is the historical period of socialism. The society in this period is socialist society under the dictatorship of the proletariat.

In socialist society, the system of public ownership of the means of production replaces the system of private ownership. The laboring people control the lifelines of the socialist economy and become the masters of society. Marxist ideological education gradually liberates millions of laboring people from the influence of the old society so that they can advance along the socialist and communist paths. From this aspect, socialist society already contains some elements of communist society. But socialist society is merely a preliminary stage of communist society, not a completely communist society. Just as Marx pointed out: "What we have to deal with here is a communist society, not as it has *developed* on its own foundations, but, on the contrary, just as it *emerges* from capitalist society; which is thus in every respect, economically, morally, and intellectually, still stamped with the birth marks of the old society from whose womb it emerges."[13] Chairman Mao, referring to the socialist system, said: "In a word, China is a socialist country. Before liberation she was much the same as a capitalist country. Even now she practices an eight-grade wage system, distribution according to work and exchange through money, and in all this differs very little from the old society. What is different is that the system of ownership has changed." Chairman Mao pointed out: "Our country at present practices a commodity system, the wage system is unequal, too, as in the eight-grade wage scale, and so forth. Under the dictatorship of the proletariat such things can only be restricted."

The scientific analysis of socialist society by the revolutionary teachers shows that in various spheres of socialist society there still exist capitalist traditions and birthmarks. The bourgeoisie and all exploiting classes have been overthrown, but these classes and their influence on economics, politics, and ideology will continue to exist for a long time. The differences between worker and peasant, town and country, and mental and manual labor, which are left over from the old society, will continue to exist for a long time, as will bourgeois right. In short, the soil that engenders capitalism and new bourgeois elements will continue to exist for a long time. Consequently, the entire historical period of socialism "has to be a period of struggle between dying capitalism and nascent communism."[14]

The very nature and characteristics of socialist society determine that socialist society will not be a short and transient period of transition, but will extend over a fairly long historical period.

Before the socialist revolution, the revolutions to replace slavery with feudalism and feudalism with capitalism merely represented the replacement of an old exploitative system by a new exploitative system. The proletarian socialist revolution is fundamentally different. It must thoroughly abolish all exploitative systems among people. It must abolish class distinctions generally, abolish all the relations of production on which they rest, abolish all the social relations that correspond to these relations of production, and revolutionize all the ideas that result from these social relations, thereby making it impossible for the bourgeoisie to exist or for a new bourgeoisie to arise. Hence, this revolution is richer, wider, and more complex than any other revolution in history. The goal of communism can be realized in the end only through prolonged struggle and by creating favorable conditions step-by-step.

To eliminate classes, socialist society must make a thorough and clean break with all influences and traditions of private ownership and of the old society. The legacy of Confucius, who stubbornly defended slavery in China more than two thousand years ago, has been used by the exploiting classes of various historical periods to consolidate their reactionary rule. Today, the reactionary thought of Confucius is still used by the bourgeoisie and revisionists as an ideological weapon to restore capitalism. It is a protracted and complex task to solve the issue of whether socialism or capitalism will win out in the sphere of political ideology. Chairman Mao pointed out: "There must also be a thorough socialist revolution on the political and ideological fronts. Here a very long period of time is needed to decide 'who will win' in the struggle between socialism and capitalism. Several decades won't do it; success requires anywhere from one to several centuries."[15]

"The final victory of a socialist country not only requires the efforts of the proletariat and the broad masses of the people at home, but also involves the victory of the world revolution and the abolition of the system of exploitation of man by man over the whole globe, upon which all mankind will be emancipated."[16] We are still in the period of imperialism and proletarian revolution. The final triumph of the socialist revolution will be won only after a series of difficult, complex, and protracted class struggles in the world.

Correctly understanding the nature and characteristics of socialist society, correctly understanding that socialist society is a fairly long historical period, and drawing a clear distinction between scientific socialism and all kinds of phony socialism have great significance for the success of the proletariat of all countries in making socialist revolution and struggling to prevent capitalist restoration after the victory of the revolution. The victory of socialism in large areas of the world will force its enemies to disguise themselves as socialists. They will hoist various "socialist" banners to deceive the world and win fame for themselves. In the contemporary period, there is the "developed socialism" served up by Brezhnev, the "real socialism" peddled by Lin Piao, and so forth. People like Brezhnev vainly hope to hide under the cloak of "developed socialism" in order to intensify the exploitation and oppression of the laboring people in their own country as part of their unscrupulous restoration of capitalism. Abroad, they step up aggression and expansion in their futile attempt to achieve world supremacy. The so-called "developed socialism" is a new form of bureaucrat-monopoly capitalism, that is, social-imperialism. The "real socialism" peddled by people like Lin Piao was merely a disguise. His reactionary program was Confucius's "restraining oneself and restoring the rites." He clamored that "of all things, this is the most important." His intention was to sabotage China's socialist system under the dictatorship of the proletariat and to restore capitalism. The so-called "real socialism" was in fact real capitalism. This company of renegades sought to mix the genuine with the sham in order to paralyze the revolutionary spirit of the broad masses of people. But Marxist scientific socialism cannot be faked. Once a comparison is made with the nature and characteristics of socialist society as explained by Marxism, it becomes easy to expose the various brands of sham socialism.

The theory of the basic contradictions in socialist society is the theoretical basis for continuing the revolution under the dictatorship of the proletariat

After proletarian dictatorship was established in China, Chairman Mao laid down a general line for the Party in the transition period: "Bring about, step by step and over a fairly long period, the socialist industrialization of China and the socialist transformation of agriculture, handicrafts and capitalist industry and commerce by the state."[17] According to this general line, China had basically completed the socialist transformation of the system of ownership of the means of production in 1956. Does this mean then that after the basic completion of the socialist transformation of the system of ownership of the means of production socialist society ceases being an historical process of the motion of contradictions? What are the basic contradictions in socialist society? Are these contradictions mainly manifested in the contradiction and the struggle between the proletariat and the bourgeoisie? It is exactly in answer to these questions that there exist fundamental differences between Marxism and modern revisionism.

The Soviet revisionist renegade clique flatly denies that contradictions exist in socialist society from beginning to end. It flatly denies that these contradictions are mainly manifested in the struggle between the proletariat and the bourgeoisie. It flatly denies that it is precisely the unity and struggle between opposites that propels the development of socialist society. By denying all of this, the Soviet revisionist clique aims to conceal its high crime of totally restoring capitalism and implementing fascist dictatorship. Liu Shao-chi, Lin Piao, and company followed in the footsteps of the Soviet revisionists. After the great victory achieved in China's socialist transformation of the system of ownership of the means of production, they fabricated the nonsense that "there was a contradiction between the advanced socialist system and the backward social productive forces." They unsuccessfully attempted to use this nonexistent "contradiction" to negate the ever-present contradiction between the relations and forces of production, between the superstructure and the economic base. To cover up their conspiracy to restore capitalism in China, they denied that the principal contradiction in Chinese society was the contradiction between the working class and the bourgeoisie.

Confronted by this revisionist countercurrent, Chairman Mao has advanced the great theory of the basic contradictions in socialist society, based on the fundamental principles of Marxism and the accumulated experience of the international communist movement. Chairman Mao pointed out that the universal law of the unity and struggle between opposites in nature, human society, and human thought is equally applicable to socialist society. "The basic contradictions in socialist society are still those between the relations of production and the productive forces and between the superstructure and the economic base."[18] Chairman Mao's theory of the basic contradictions in socialist society represents a continuation, a defense, and a further development of Marxism-Leninism. It has dealt a fatal blow to modern revisionism and is a powerful weapon for the proletariat and the broad laboring people.

The socialist relations of production correspond to the development of the productive forces. This permits the productive forces to develop rapidly, at a speed that was not possible in the old society. The state system and law under proletarian dictatorship, and other elements of the superstructure, such as socialist ideology, which are guided by Marxism, also conform to the socialist economic base, namely socialist relations of production. This is the fundamental aspect. But there is another aspect. Not only is there correspondence between the relations of production and the productive forces, and between the superstructure and the economic base, there is also contradiction. The correspondence and contradiction of the various aspects of the basic contradictions of socialist society propel socialist society forward.

In order to correctly understand the contradiction between the relations of production and the productive forces under socialism, it is necessary to make a concrete analysis of the relations of production in socialist society.

For a certain period of time in socialist society, there still exist nonsocialist relations of production. In regard to the ownership system, for example, the joint state-private enterprises in China were basically socialist in nature. But the capitalist could still obtain interest at a fixed rate. In other words, exploitation and remnants of capitalist private ownership still existed. After the fixed interest was abolished, there were still remnants of individual economy in the urban and rural areas for a fairly long period of time. In regard to mutual relations between people, opposition between classes representing the capitalist relations of production and the laboring people still existed. In regard to the distribution of personal consumption goods, high salaries were still paid to the capitalist and bourgeois experts whose services were retained for a period of time. These high salaries did not embody the socialist principle of from each according to one's ability and to each according to one's work, but were in fact a form of buying them out. All these nonsocialist relations of production were in conflict not only with the development of the productive forces but also with socialist relations of production. In the process of development of socialist construction, these nonsocialist relations of production must be transformed step by step.

On the other hand, the socialist relations of production themselves also undergo a process of development from a less mature to a more mature state. In socialist society, "communism *cannot* as yet be fully ripe economically and entirely free from traditions or traces of capitalism."[19] The establishment of the system of socialist public ownership was a fundamental negation of the system of private ownership. But this does not imply that the issue of ownership is completely settled; bourgeois right has not been abolished entirely in the sphere of ownership. Furthermore, owing to the practice of the commodity system, exchange through money, distribution according to work, and the existence of basic differences between workers and peasants, town and country, and mental and manual labor, bourgeois right still exists to a serious extent in the mutual relations between people, and holds a dominant position in distribution. This kind of bourgeois right in the historical period of socialism cannot be entirely abolished, and in certain aspects it is still allowed to exist legally and is protected by the state. It can only be restricted under the dictatorship of the proletariat, which actively creates the conditions for the elimination of bourgeois right from the stage of history.

At the same time, with the rapid development of the productive forces, there arise conditions in which some aspects of socialist production relations are no longer compatible with the development of the productive forces, and they must be adjusted and improved in a timely manner.

But, in the final analysis, the central problem of perfecting socialist relations of production cannot but be a process of struggle in which the rising communist factors gradually triumph over the declining capitalist traditions and influences.

To understand the contradiction between the superstructure and the economic base under socialism, it is also necessary to conduct a concrete analysis of the superstructure in socialist society. To begin with, in socialist society there still exist the ideologies of the bourgeoisie and other exploiting classes. Furthermore, the existence of certain representatives of the bourgeoisie in the state organizations, certain bureaucratic styles of work, and certain defects in the state system are all in conflict with the socialist economic base. Only by continually resolving such contradictions can the superstructure further meet the need to consolidate and develop the socialist economic base.

The basic contradictions in socialist society are fundamentally different in their nature and conditions from the contradictions between the relations of production and the forces of production, and between the superstructure and the economic base, in the old society. The basic contradictions of capitalist society are manifested as violent antagonisms and upheavals. These contradictions can only be resolved through violent revolution by the proletariat, the overthrow of the bourgeois dictatorship, and the elimination of capitalist relations of production. The contradictions between the socialist relations of production and the productive forces and between the socialist superstructure and the economic base are an entirely different matter. Viewed from the perspective of the objective law of historical development of human society, the process of the ceaseless emergence and resolution of these contradictions is also the process of transition from socialist society to communist society. In this process, workers, peasants, and other laboring people, who are the ruling class, are not overthrown by any opposition power. They still remain the masters of society. The system of public ownership is not destroyed, but is developed to a higher stage. In this sense, the contradictions of socialist society "are not antagonistic and can be resolved one after another by the socialist system itself."[20]

The correspondence and contradiction between the relations of production and the productive forces, and between the superstructure and the economic base, in socialist society constitute a ceaseless dialectical process of development which propels socialist society forward towards communist society. Of course, the motion of socialist society, like that of other historical epochs of human society, cannot avoid temporary twists and turns in the course of its development. There had been the restoration of the class of slavemasters in feudal society, there had been restoration of the feudal dynasty in capitalist society, and there had also been restoration of capitalism in socialist society, of which the restoration of capitalism in the Soviet Union is a concrete example. Historical development proceeds through many twists and turns. But the counterrevolutionary restoration of the reactionary classes is a desperate attempt before death that runs counter to the law of development of social history, and cannot last for too long.

It is certain that the Soviet Union will return to the Marxist-Leninist road in the future.

Chairman Mao's theory of the basic contradictions in socialist society is the theoretical basis for continuing the revolution under the dictatorship of the proletariat. Chairman Mao pointed out: "In China, although in the main socialist transformation has been completed . . . , there are still remnants of the overthrown landlord and comprador classes, there is still a bourgeoisie, and the remolding of the petty bourgeoisie has only just started. . . . The class struggle between the proletariat and the bourgeoisie, the class struggle between the different political forces, and the class struggle in the ideological field between the proletariat and the bourgeoisie will continue to be long and tortuous and at times will even become very acute."[21] This was the thesis, drawn clearly for the first time in the historical theory and practice of the international communist movement: After the socialist transformation of the ownership system of the means of production is basically completed, there still exist classes and class struggle; the proletariat must continue the revolution and wage the socialist revolution on the political, economic, ideological, and cultural battlefronts to the very end.

Keep firmly to the basic line of the Party for the entire historical period of socialism

Chairman Mao teaches us that "everything depends on whether or not the ideological and political line is correct." To persevere in continuing the revolution under the dictatorship of the proletariat, the proletariat needs a correct line.

Based on a detailed analysis of the basic contradictions in socialist society and his theory of continuing the revolution under the dictatorship of the proletariat, Chairman Mao formulated for our Party a basic line for the socialist transition period: "Socialist society covers a considerably long historical period. In the historical period of socialism, there are still classes, class contradictions and class struggle, there is the struggle between the socialist road and the capitalist road, and there is the danger of capitalist restoration. We must recognize the protracted and complex nature of this struggle. We must heighten our vigilance. We must conduct socialist education. We must correctly understand and handle class contradictions and class struggle, distinguish the

27

contradictions between ourselves and the enemy from those among the people and handle them correctly. Otherwise a socialist country like ours will turn into its opposite and degenerate, and a capitalist restoration will take place. From now on we must remind ourselves of this every year, every month and every day so that we can retain a rather sober understanding of this problem and have a Marxist-Leninist line."[22] This proletarian revolutionary line formulated by Chairman Mao reveals the objective laws governing class struggle in the socialist period and is the only correct line for achieving the basic program of the Party. This basic line is a brilliant beacon for the whole party, the whole country, and the whole people. It illumines the historical path of continuing the revolution under the dictatorship of the proletariat.

The protracted nature of class struggle in socialist society is the inevitable reflection of the struggle between rising communist factors and declining capitalist traditions and influences on class relations. The overthrown exploiting classes still survive and continue to challenge the proletariat, making every bid to recover their lost "paradise." Because the soil and conditions that breed capitalism still exist in socialist society, new bourgeois elements will be engendered batch after batch. Chairman Mao pointed out: "Lenin said that 'small production engenders capitalism and the bourgeoisie continuously, daily, hourly, spontaneously, and on a mass scale.' They are also engendered among a part of the working class and of the Party membership. Both within the ranks of the proletariat and among the personnel of state and other organs there are people who take to the bourgeois style of life." The existence of bourgeois influence, and of the influence of revisionism, constitutes the political and ideological source of the new bourgeois elements. And the existence of bourgeois right provides an important economic foundation for their emergence. At the same time, international imperialism and social-imperialism always try hard to convert socialist countries into capitalist countries or even into colonial or semicolonial countries. International class struggle will inevitably be reflected in the socialist countries.

The proletariat and the broad laboring people under its leadership are the representatives of socialist relations of production. They keep firmly to the socialist road and to the Marxist theory of uninterrupted revolution and its development through stages. They restrict bourgeois right and they promote the continued consolidation and perfecting of the socialist relations of production and the superstructure. The bourgeoisie and its agents inside the Communist Party are the representatives of capitalist relations of production.* They insist on taking the capitalist road and always try hard to consolidate and expand bourgeois right and to transform socialist relations of production into capitalist relations of production. Therefore, throughout the entire historical period of socialism, there is struggle between the proletariat and the bourgeoisie and between the socialist and the capitalist roads. This is an objective law independent of human will. In a word, struggles are inevitable; though people may want to avoid them, it is not possible. The proletariat can only gain victory by creating and seizing upon favorable conditions through struggle.

Chairman Mao said: "Why did Lenin speak of exercising dictatorship over the bourgeoisie? It is essential to get this question clear. Lack of clarity on this question will lead to revisionism. This should be made known to the whole nation." Chairman Mao's directive has great immediate practical and long-range importance for consolidating the dictatorship of the proletariat, preventing capitalist restoration, constructing socialism, and achieving communism. Only by exercising all-round dictatorship over the bourgeoisie, in all stages of revolutionary development and in all spheres, and by creating the conditions in which it will be impossible for the bourgeoisie and all exploiting classes to exist or for a new bourgeoisie to arise, can the proletariat accomplish the historical task of proletarian dictatorship and realize the great ideal of communism.

Class struggle in socialist society develops in a wavelike motion, sometimes rising high and sometimes subsiding. This is due to differences in the conditions of class struggle and not to whether there is class struggle or not. The history of socialist society tells us that class enemies and all monsters and freaks will show themselves. Chairman Mao pointed out: "Great disorder across the land leads to great order. And so once again every seven or eight years. Monsters and demons will jump out themselves. Determined by their own class nature, they are bound to jump out."[23] The law of class struggle finds expression in a major struggle every few years. Only after repeated tests of strength will the forces of the reactionary classes become weaker and weaker

---

* For the further development of Mao's theory of the new bourgeoisie, and what had been learned through the class struggle in post-1949 China, see the appendix to Chapter 4.

and will the proletariat be able to finally fulfill the great historical mission of eliminating the bourgeoisie and all other exploiting classes.

Class struggle in society is of necessity reflected in the Party and is manifested as a struggle between the two lines inside the Party. The basic Party line tells us that the struggle against revisionism is a long-term struggle. The struggle between our Party and the four anti-Party cliques headed by Kao Kang, Jao Shu-shih, Peng Te-huai, Liu Shao-chi, and Lin Piao was a struggle against revisionism. Chairman Mao personally launched and led the Great Proletarian Cultural Revolution. It was a great revolution in the superstructure, a great political revolution under the conditions of the dictatorship of the proletariat. It could also be called "the second revolution" of China. In the Great Proletarian Cultural Revolution, Chairman Mao led the whole Party, the whole armed forces, and the whole people to destroy the two bourgeois headquarters commanded by Liu Shao-chi and Lin Piao. This bunch of renegades and traitors conspired to usurp the supreme power of the Party and the state and sought to fundamentally transform the basic Party line and its basic policies for the entire historical period of socialism in order to convert the Marxist-Leninist Party into a revisionist fascist party, to sabotage the dictatorship of the proletariat, and to restore capitalism. The substance of their revisionist line is extreme rightism. Their counterrevolutionary conspiracy has been crushed by the hundreds of millions of revolutionary people of China. The Great Proletarian Cultural Revolution has won a great victory. Revolution is still developing and struggle is still continuing. The struggle between the two lines inside the Party, which is a reflection of class struggle, will exist throughout the historical period of socialism. Chairman Mao pointed out: "The current Great Cultural Revolution is only the first one, and we are to carry out many later ones. The victory of a revolution can only be decided after a long historical period. It is likely that capitalism may be restored any time if we do not have our work done well. Members of the whole Party and people of the whole country should not think that three or four Great Cultural Revolutions are sufficient to bring peace to the nation. You must be always on guard and never for a moment slacken your vigilance."[24]

SOCIALIST SOCIETY CONSTITUTES THE BEGINNING OF PEOPLE CONSCIOUSLY MAKING HISTORY

The great soaring leap in the history of human development

The proletariat and the laboring people continue the revolution under the dictatorship of the proletariat in order to make the superstructure serve the socialist economic base, to make the relations of production conform to the development of the productive forces, and to consciously transform society and nature in accordance with the economic laws of socialism. This is a giant stride in human history.

There are several thousand years of written human history. But before the birth of socialist society, this long period of history was but a "prehistory" in the development of human society. The producers were enslaved not only by nature but also by the means of production which they themselves created. "It is not the producers who dominate the means of production, but the means of production which dominate the producers."[25] That is to say, the exploiting class, which controlled the basic means of production and thus state political power, viciously oppressed and exploited the broad laboring people and reduced them to a dark and miserable existence. The proletarian socialist revolution is like spring thunder and has shaken human history. It has brought an end to this "prehistory" and has ushered in a new era in which people consciously make history.

The material basis for this great leap in human history lies in the transformation of private ownership of the means of production into socialist public ownership after the proletariat and the laboring people have seized political power. In socialist society, public ownership of the means of production enables the laboring people, who are the majority of the people, to become masters of the state and enterprises. Only when the laboring people have become the masters of social relations can they become the masters of nature and consciously transform the world and make history under the guidance of Marxism.

Certainly, compared with an advanced communist society, socialist society is only the beginning of an era in which people consciously make history. In addition to the limitations imposed by the level of development of the productive forces and by the conditions of our knowledge of the physical world, the main obstacle lies in the continuing existence in socialist society of the bourgeoisie and its ideological influence, of the differences between worker and peasant, town and country, and mental and manual labor, and of the soil breeding capitalism. Therefore, although the proletariat and the broad laboring people control state political power and the basic means of production, their conscious activities in transforming the world and making history are still restricted by history. Nevertheless, "the important thing is that the ice has been broken; the road is open, the way has been shown."[26] The proletariat will ultimately enter the communist new world along the socialist road.

Bring the initiating role of the superstructure fully into play, consciously make use of objective laws

In socialist society, people begin to consciously make their own history. This does not mean that people can make history at will. It simply means that for the first time people of the entire society can consciously identify and make use of objective economic laws to serve the interests of the proletariat and the broad laboring people.

"Freedom is the understanding of necessity *and* the transformation of necessity."[27] Economic laws are objective laws governing the development of social economy and are not subject to change according to human will. People cannot "transform" or "create" objective laws. But people are not entirely helpless before objective laws. In socialist society, people can correctly identify them, utilize and rely on them, and channel the destructive forces of certain laws, or restrict their scope of operation. On the other hand, a larger scope of operation is given to laws that are constructive and which serve the purpose of transforming the objective world.

Under different social systems, the forms of expression of economic laws have different characteristics. In capitalist society, owing to private ownership of the means of production, production is carried out under blind competition and chaotic conditions. Therefore, economic laws always assume an external, alien form in capitalist society. Socialist society is based on public ownership of the means of production. The laboring people are the masters of social economic relations. This makes it possible for people to consciously master and apply economic laws. Just as Engels once prophesied: "The laws of man's own social activity, which have hitherto confronted him as external laws of nature dominating him, will then be applied by man with full knowledge and hence be dominated by him."[28]

The establishment of a system of public ownership of the means of production makes it possible for people to identify and consciously act in accordance with economic laws. But to turn this possibility into reality, struggle is inevitable. The efforts of the proletariat to act in accordance with economic laws of society, and to accelerate the transformation of socialist society into communist society, will certainly meet with violent resistance from the bourgeoisie and other decadent social forces, and especially with interference and sabotage from the revisionist line. The process of conscious application of socialist economic laws is the process of struggle between the proletariat and the bourgeoisie, between the Marxist line and the revisionist line. At the same time, people must also resolve "the contradiction between the objective laws of economic development of a socialist society and our subjective understanding of them" in practice.[29] This represents another process. It is necessary to start from practice, conduct investigation and research, go from no experience to experience and from a little experience to a lot of experience, and gradually overcome spontaneity and raise consciousness. This process of understanding cannot be divorced from the process of transformation of people's world outlook. People with the proletarian world outlook can more correctly identify the laws of development governing socialist economy. Those stubbornly clinging to the bourgeois outlook can never correctly identify the laws of development governing socialist economy. Therefore, this process of understanding is also a process of destroying the bourgeois world outlook and establishing the proletarian world outlook. Those viewpoints which regard the conscious application of economic laws in socialist society as an easy matter that requires neither hard work nor overcoming resistance and interference from the bourgeoisie and the revisionist line, nor struggle between the two world outlooks, are wrong. These viewpoints advocate, "let nature take its own course," or "let us extinguish class struggle."

In socialist society, in order to consciously apply objective economic laws, it is necessary to give full scope to the active and initiating role of the superstructure.

The immense capability of the socialist superstructure is manifested first and foremost in the leadership of the proletarian political party. The proletarian political party is established in accord with Marxist revolutionary theory and revolutionary style. It is good at comprehending the objective laws governing historical development, assimilating the wisdom of the masses, grasping the general trend of historical development, and formulating correct theory, programs, lines, and general and specific policies based on actual conditions in the various stages of social development. These correct theories, programs, lines, and general and specific policies come from the masses and return to the masses, leading them to victory in their struggle. The Communist Party of China uses Marxism-Leninism-Mao Tsetung Thought as the theoretical basis guiding its thinking. The reason that the Party's theory of revolution, especially its theory of continuing the revolution under the dictatorship of the proletariat, and the Marxist line and general and specific policies formulated by the proletarian political party can be so invincible is that those theories correctly reflect the objective laws governing the economic development of society. "Without a revolutionary theory there can be no revolutionary movement."[30] It is therefore important to seriously study the Marxist theory of continuing the revolution under the dictatorship of the proletariat as a guide to correctly identify, and act in accordance with, the economic laws governing socialist society.

In the final analysis, Party leadership is leadership by the Marxist line. Only by grasping revolution in the superstructure, including the ideological sphere, and making sure that the ideological and political lines are correct, can a Marxist party lead the proletarian revolutionary cause from victory to still greater victory.

The state political power of the dictatorship of the proletariat under the leadership of the Marxist-Leninist Party is a powerful tool of class struggle in the hands of the proletariat that can be used to continuously defeat the bourgeoisie, restrict bourgeois right, and eliminate the soil that engenders capitalism. It plays an immense role in guaranteeing the thorough implementation of the basic Party line and in organizing and leading the socialist economy. By exercising its own state political power, the proletariat can unfold socialist revolution on the economic battlefront, establish and develop socialist relations of production, plan, organize, and lead the whole national economy, develop social productive forces, and unleash socialist revolution on the political, ideological, and cultural battlefronts in order to consolidate the socialist economic base by steadily perfecting the socialist superstructure.

Continuing the revolution under the dictatorship of the proletariat means giving full play to this initiating role of the state political power of the proletarian dictatorship. These conditions cannot be created under bourgeois dictatorship. It is true that the bourgeoisie for a certain time following the seizure of political power also used its state power to consolidate and promote capitalist relations of production. But as these relations became increasingly moribund, the bourgeois state lost its revolutionary role and became a fetter on change in relations of production and the development of the productive forces. As far as the socialist revolution is concerned, the seizure of political power by the proletariat is merely the beginning of revolution. With the development of the productive forces, socialist relations of production undergo an historical process by which the new supersedes the old. The state political power under proletarian dictatorship, promoting such renewal and transformation and propelling the development of the productive forces, is, in the end, the most powerful weapon with which the proletariat continues socialist revolution. With this weapon, the proletariat can now crush the resistance of the bourgeoisie and other reactionary forces, unite the whole laboring people around itself, triumphantly unfold the three great revolutionary movements of class struggle, the struggle for production, and scientific experiment, and promote the steady consolidation and perfecting of the socialist economic base and superstructure so that socialist society can advance along the path charted by the basic Party line until the achievement of the highest ideal, communism.

Major Study References

Marx, *Critique of the Gotha Programme*
Lenin, "Economics and Politics in the Era of the Dictatorship of the Proletariat," *Collected Works*, volume 30
Mao, "On the Correct Handling of Contradictions Among the People," *Selected Readings*

Notes

1. Mao Tsetung, "Speech at the Meeting of the Supreme Soviet of the U.S.S.R. in Celebration of the 40th Anniversary of the Great October Socialist Revolution," cited in *Quotations from Chairman Mao Tsetung* (Peking: Foreign Languages Press, 1966), p. 14. (Hereafter, this source is referred to as *The Red Book*.)
2. Marx, "Preface to *A Contribution to the Critique of Political Economy*," *MESW* 1, pp. 503-504.
3. Engels, *Anti-Duhring* (Peking: Foreign Languages Press, 1976), p. 362.
4. Mao, "Problems of War and Strategy," *SW* 2, p. 224.
5. Marx, *The Civil War in France* (Peking: Foreign Languages Press, 1974), p. 64.
6. Mao, "Speech at a Conference of Cadres in the Shansi-Suiyuan Liberated Area," *SW* 4, p. 238.
7. Mao, "Problems of War and Strategy," p. 219.
8. Engels, "To J. Bloch in Konigsberg (September 21-22, 1890)," *MESW* 3, p. 487.
9. Lenin, "Our Revolution," *CW* 33 (1973), pp. 478-79.
10. Mao, "On Coalition Government," *SW* 3, p. 252.
11. Mao, "On Contradiction," *SW* 1, p. 336.
12. Marx, *Critique of the Gotha Programme* (Peking: Foreign Languages Press, 1972), pp. 27-28.
13. Ibid., p. 15.
14. Lenin, "Economics and Politics in the Era of the Dictatorship of the Proletariat," *CW* 30 (1974), p. 107.
15. Communist Party of China (CPC), "Khrushchev's Phony Communism and its Historical Lessons for the World," in *The Polemic on the General Line of the International Communist Movement* (Peking: Foreign Languages Press, 1965), pp. 471-72.
16. Mao, quoted in CPC, *Important Documents on the Great Proletarian Cultural Revolution in China* (Peking: Foreign Languages Press, 1970), p. xi.
17. Mao, quoted in "Commemorate the 50th Anniversary of the Communist Party of China," *Peking Review* No. 27, 1971.

18. Mao, "On the Correct Handling of Contradictions Among the People," in *Selected Readings from the Works of Mao Tsetung (SR)* (Peking: Foreign Languages Press, 1971), pp. 443-44.
19. Lenin, *The State and Revolution* (Peking: Foreign Languages Press, 1973), p. 117.
20. Mao, "Correct Handling of Contradictions," p. 443.
21. Ibid., pp. 463-64.
22. Mao, quoted in *Important Documents*, pp. ix-x.
23. Mao, quoted in Wang Hung-wen, "Report on the Revision of the Party Constitution," in *Tenth Party Congress Documents* (Peking: Foreign Languages Press, 1973); reprinted in Lotta, *And Mao Makes Five*, p. 96.
24. Mao, quoted in Wang Hung-wen, "Report to the Central Study Class," in Lotta, *And Mao Makes Five*, p. 57.
25. Engels, *Anti-Duhring*, p. 378.
26. Lenin, "Fourth Anniversary of the October Revolution," *CW* 33, p. 57.
27. Mao, "Talk on Questions of Philosophy," in Stuart Schram, ed., *Chairman Mao Talks to the People* (New York: Pantheon, 1974), p. 228.
28. Engels, *Anti-Duhring*, pp. 366-67.
29. Mao, "Correct Handling of Contradictions," p. 477.
30. Lenin, *What Is To Be Done?* (Peking: Foreign Languages Press, 1975), p. 28.

3

THE SOCIALIST SYSTEM OF PUBLIC OWNERSHIP IS THE FOUNDATION FOR SOCIALIST RELATIONS OF PRODUCTION

The Socialist System of Ownership by the Whole People and Collective Ownership by Working People

After the proletariat seizes political power, in order to eliminate the sources of capitalism and all other exploitative systems and to establish a socialist economic foundation, it is necessary to transform, step by step, the system of private ownership of the means of production into a socialist system of public ownership. This is an important step in consolidating the dictatorship of the proletariat and defeating capitalism with socialism.

THE SOCIALIST SYSTEM OF OWNERSHIP BY THE WHOLE PEOPLE IS THE PRINCIPAL ECONOMIC FOUNDATION OF THE DICTATORSHIP OF THE PROLETARIAT

The proletariat and working people must control the means of production

In the past several thousand years, the fundamental reason for the exploitation and oppression of the laboring people by the slave owner, the feudal landlord, and the capitalist was the fact that the means of production were not in the hands of the laboring people. "The subjugation of a man to menial service in all its forms presupposes that the subjugator has at his disposal the means of labour through which alone he can employ the person placed in bondage, and in the case of slavery, in addition, the means of subsistence which enable him to keep the slave alive."[1] Successive generations of laboring people launched various forms of struggle, as they attempted to take the means of production into their own hands, but for historical reasons, all these attempts failed. In capitalist society, the proletariat, nurtured and tempered by capitalist large-scale industry, emerged as a social force. This class lost all control over the means of production; aside from the chains on their necks, the workers had absolutely nothing else. With the increasing intensification of the contradiction between the private character of capitalist ownership of the means of production and the social character of production, the possibility for the proletariat to control the means of production developed.

However, the exploiting classes are never willing to give up exploitation. They not only used the state machinery to protect their private ownership of the means of production but also concocted all sorts of fallacies in the ideological realm. For example, they said that the poverty of the worker was due to the rapid increase in population, the lack of a "just and reasonable principle of distribution," and so forth, attempting to deceive and dupe the laboring people so they would not touch bourgeois ownership and wrest control of the means of production. The revolutionary teachers of the proletariat denounced these fallacies. They pointed out that the root cause of the exploitation and enslavement of the laboring people lay in the fact that the means of production were not in the hands of the laboring people but were instead in the hands of the exploiting class.

The first sentence in the "Gotha Program," reflecting the influence of Ferdinand Lassalle on the German workers' movement of the 1870s, stated: "Labor is the source of all wealth and culture." On the surface, "labor" was accorded a very high position. But Marx at once saw the theoretical error of this statement. He pointed out that labor could create wealth and culture only in combination with the means of production. Without the means of production and without ownership of the means of production, what would happen to labor? Marx incisively pointed out: "The man who possesses no other property than his labour power must, in all conditions of society and culture, be the slave of other men who have made themselves the owners of the objective conditions of labour. He can work only with their permis-

40

sion, hence live only with their permission."[2] The proletariat must replace the system of private ownership under capitalism by the system of public ownership under socialism before it can free itself. This insight of Marxism has theoretically and politically demolished the exploiting class's insane capitalist conspiracy to monopolize forever the means of production and to exploit and enslave the laboring people. It indicates the correct orientation of struggle for the proletariat.

The development of capitalist society makes it possible for the proletariat and the laboring people to collectively own the means of production. To fully realize this possibility is a fairly long historical process. The proletariat must first smash the bourgeois state machinery and establish a proletarian dictatorship before it can "eliminate the cause of poverty and sow seeds of wealth," that is, transform the system of private ownership of the means of production into a system of public ownership and take the means of production into its own hands. This is the necessary starting point from which all exploitative systems will be fundamentally negated and from which the proletariat and the laboring people will be liberated economically and proceed along the socialist road to common abundance. On this road there will still be plenty of struggles. Only by persistently and firmly holding the fate of the socialist economy in its own hands can the proletariat create favorable material conditions for the elimination of all classes and class differences and realize the lofty ideal of communism. Once political power and the means of production are lost, and once control over the state machinery and economic lifelines is usurped by the bourgeoisie and its agents in the Party, the socialist economy will degenerate and the proletariat and the laboring people will once again become "shivering and hungry slaves." This possibility exists throughout the entire historical period of socialism.

Confiscation and buying out are ways to establish the system of socialist state ownership

More than a hundred years ago, Marx and Engels pointed out that after the proletariat seizes political power, it "will use its political supremacy to wrest, by degrees, all capital from the bourgeoisie, to centralize all instruments of production in the hands of the State, *i.e.*, of the proletariat organized as the ruling class."[3]

41

Highly socialized productive forces objectively require a social center to centrally coordinate all the economic departments and enterprises. In capitalist society, this objective requirement is difficult to realize. In socialist society, this social center is the socialist state under the dictatorship of the proletariat. Only by first establishing this state, representing all the laboring people, and the socialist system of ownership by the whole people of the means of production can the laboring people firmly maintain their hold over the socialist economic lifelines and can the exploitative capitalist system be basically eliminated.

By what means, then, can the proletariat transform the bourgeois ownership of the means of production into a socialist system of ownership by the whole people? According to the experience of the international communist movement and the Chinese experience, after the proletariat seizes political power, big enterprises are immediately socialized, while medium and small enterprises are gradually transformed.

In general, after the proletariat seizes political power, it confronts a situation in which big, medium, and small capital coexist. Big capital represents the most reactionary production relations; it controls the lifeblood of the national economy and seriously impedes the development of social productive forces. It is also the main economic prop of bourgeois reactionary rule. Immediately after the seizure of political power, if the proletariat fails to secure control over the national economy and lets the big capitalists take it over, it can never consolidate its power. In summing up the experience and brilliant achievements of the Paris Commune, Lenin pointed out that one of the two mistakes that proved fatal to the outcome of the struggle was the failure of the proletariat to seize the big enterprises like the Bank of France, which was the vital nerve center of the national economy. Therefore, big capital must be immediately confiscated by the socialist state.

Big capital in old China was bureaucrat capital. This was the comprador and feudal state monopoly capital owned by the bureaucrat bourgeoisie headed by Chiang Kai-shek. Chairman Mao made a penetrating analysis of the reactionary nature of this capital, pointing out: "During their twenty-year rule, the four big families, Chiang, Soong, Kung, and Chen, have piled up enormous fortunes valued at ten to twenty thousand million U.S. dollars and monopolized the economic lifelines of the whole country. This monopoly capital, combined with state power, has become state monopoly capitalism. This monopoly capitalism, closely tied up with foreign imperialism, the domestic land-lord class and the old-type rich peasants, has become comprador, feudal, state monopoly capitalism."[4] In light of the reactionary nature of bureaucrat capital, our Party, early in the process of the democratic revolution, clearly stipulated the policy of confiscating bureaucrat capital and "[transferring it] to the people's republic led by the proletariat."[5] This confiscation of bureaucrat capital was achieved in a step-by-step way upon victory of the war of liberation. The confiscation of bureaucrat capital, which accounted for 80 percent of the fixed capital assets in China's manufacturing and transportation industries before Liberation, eliminated the major portion of China's capitalist economy and put the proletarian political power in control of the lifeblood of the national economy. The economic basis of socialism was thus established, creating favorable conditions for the development of the socialist revolution and socialist construction.

After the proletariat seizes political power, confiscates big capital, and establishes a socialist economic foundation, it is possible to gradually subject medium and small capital to socialist transformation through the policy of buying out this capital and to transform the capitalist system of ownership of the means of production into a socialist system of ownership by the whole people. The class nature of medium and small capital is the same as that of big capital. They are all enmeshed in the capitalist exploitation of the laboring people; they have interests contrary to those of the laboring masses and are the objects of socialist revolution. However, there are some differences between them. While medium and small capital often have the strong desire to develop capitalism, they can, at the same time, also be compelled into accepting compensation for their assets by the proletariat under certain conditions. Marxism believes that "under certain conditions the workers would certainly not refuse to buy out the bourgeoisie."[6] Once the proletariat has seized political power and secured control over the lifeblood of the national economy, it will be advantageous to the proletariat if these capitalists can be compelled to accept a policy of being bought out by the proletariat and transform their capitalist enterprises into socialist enterprises.

In China, the national bourgeoisie owning medium and small capital assumed a dual character. In the period of democratic revolution, it assumed a revolutionary character as well as a compromising character. In the period of socialist revolution, it can be compelled into accepting socialist transformation, but it also has the strong reactionary desire to develop capitalism. The industrial and commercial enterprises operated by this class played a dual role in the rehabilitation of China's national economy. They played a positive role in increasing production, expanding economic exchanges between the urban and rural areas, and maintaining employment, thus contributing to the national economy and to people's livelihoods. But they also exploited the workers and did anything for profit, thus playing a negative role in socialist reconstruction and the improvement of people's livelihoods. In view of the dual character of the national bourgeoisie and the dual role of the national capitalist economy, our Party formulated a policy to utilize, restrict, and transform national capitalist manufacturing and commercial enterprises. This meant making use of their positive role which was beneficial to the national economy and the livelihood of the people, restricting their negative aspect detrimental to the national economy and the livelihood of the people, and gradually transforming them into a part of the socialist state economy.

The socialist transformation of capitalist manufacturing and commercial enterprises in China was conducted through various forms of state capitalism. This state capitalism was "capitalism which [could be] restrained, . . . the limits of which [could be] fixed"[7] by the state under the dictatorship of the proletariat. In manufacturing, elementary state capitalism consisted of processing, ordering, unified procurements, and contract-marketing;[*] in commerce, it consisted of purchasing and distribution by commission. In this form, the capitalist economy could be restricted to a certain extent, both in its orientation of production and operation and in the degree of exploitation. Even so, this form did not change the nature of ownership and control over the means of production by the capitalist; nor could it fundamentally resolve the antagonistic contradiction of the capitalist relations of production obstructing the development of the productive forces. With the development of China's social productive forces, what was objectively required was to turn elementary state capitalism into advanced state

---

[*] Small and medium capitalist enterprises were supplied with raw materials and given contracts to produce finished goods for the state. In this way, control was exerted over them.

capitalism, namely, joint state-private operation. In joint state-private enterprises, the state sent cadres to do leadership work. They managed the enterprise in accordance with state plans and by relying on the working masses. This, in effect, forced the capitalist to give up his control of the means of production in the enterprises. The exploitation of labor by capital was severely restricted. In China's practice, this advanced form of state capitalism was divided into two stages: joint state-private operation in individual enterprises and then joint state-private operation in whole industries. In the stage of joint operation in individual enterprises, the capitalist participated in profit distribution according to his share in the total capital of the enterprise. The profit obtained by the capitalist increased with the development of production. This was unfavorable to the full mobilization of labor enthusiasm and to the accumulation of funds by the state. After an entire industry was put under joint state-private operation, the capitalist was allowed to receive only a fixed dividend, that is, fixed interest (about 5 percent per annum) for a certain period of years. This rate was fixed according to the total value of his fixed assets before joint state-private joint operation was introduced. Thus, the capitalist's right of ownership of the means of production was expressed exclusively by a fixed dividend according to the size of his shares. Such joint state-private enterprises were basically socialist in nature. At the end of the period in which fixed interest was payable to the capitalist as stipulated by the state, the state decided to stop paying interest. Thus the state-private enterprises became enterprises under the full-fledged socialist system of ownership by the whole people.

Under the dictatorship of the proletariat, there is a difference between the transformation of medium and small capital and that of big capital. But this does not imply the absence of class struggle. In fact, acute class struggle between the proletariat and the bourgeoisie runs through the entire process of the socialist transformation of capitalist industry and commerce. This struggle is manifested as a struggle between restriction and counterrestriction, transformation and counter-transformation. In the spring of 1950, it was necessary to wage struggle against speculative activities in order to stabilize prices. In 1951, there was the "Five Antis" struggle—anti-bribery, tax evasion, theft of state property, shoddy workmanship and inferior materials, and theft of state economic secrets. In 1957, there was a struggle against the frantic attacks from the rightists. These were acute class struggles. These class struggles were also reflected in the Party itself as struggles between the two lines. Revisionists like Liu Shao-chi repeatedly peddled the nonsense that capitalist "exploitation has merit" and opposed the socialist transformation of capitalist industry and commerce in an attempt to preserve capitalist influence. Under the leadership of the Party Central Committee headed by Chairman Mao, the conspiracies of these renegades were crushed in time, their revisionist lines criticized, and victory in the socialist transformation of capitalist industry and commerce finally secured. This demonstrated that only by firmly adhering to the struggle of the proletariat against the bourgeoisie, the Marxist line against the revisionist line, and effectively defeating a handful of reactionary capitalists and their agents in the Party who opposed the socialist revolution, and who were hostile to and sabotaged socialist construction, could the national bourgeoisie be compelled to gradually accept socialist transformation.

The socialist system of ownership by the whole people possesses immense superiority

The replacement of capitalist private ownership by socialist ownership by the whole people represents a revolutionary leap in production relations. The system of socialist ownership by the whole people is a system of public ownership in which both the means of production and products of labor are owned by the proletarian state representing the whole laboring people. The appearance of the system of socialist ownership by the whole people shows that the liberated laboring people have not only become the ruling class of society but have also been transformed from wage slaves of the capitalists into masters of socialist production.

In China, the scope of socialist ownership by the whole people includes mineral deposits, rivers, and territorial waters; forests, virgin land, and other natural resources placed under the jurisdiction of the state by law; and enterprises such as railways, postal and communications services, banks, state-run factories, farms, and commerce. As the representative of the whole laboring people, the state owns the means of production and sees to it that they are allocated rationally and in a unified manner. This creates a new situation in which, for the first time in our country's history, the national economy is systematically guided and developed, thus paving the way for the development of social productive forces.

The system of socialist ownership by the whole people is a system of socialist public ownership that conforms to the highly social nature of production. In modern industry, departments and enterprises are interconnected and interdependent. They are integral and organic components of social production as a whole. The appearance of the socialist system of ownership by the whole people is an inevitable result of the contradiction between highly socialized productive forces and capitalist private ownership in modern industry. Only with socialist ownership by the whole people can the contradiction between the social nature of production and the private ownership of the means of production in capitalist society, and the contradiction between the organized nature of production in individual enterprises and the anarchy of production in society as a whole, be resolved. Only on this basis can the squandering and destruction of productive forces and products characteristic of the capitalist system, along with the extravagance and waste of the bourgeoisie and its political representatives, be eliminated, thereby promoting the more rapid development of the productive forces.

The state economy based on the socialist system of ownership by the whole people controls the lifeblood of the national economy. The state economy includes the modern industries and transport. State-operated industries furnish large quantities of machines, materials, equipment, fuels, and motor power to promote technical improvement in various departments of the national economy. They furnish large quantities of tractors, harvesters, transport equipment, electricity, fuels, chemical fertilizers, and pesticides to promote agricultural mechanization. They also accumulate vast funds for economic, cultural, and defense construction. The socialist state economy occupies a leading role in the national economy as a whole. It is the material base from which the state pursues socialist revolution and construction. The socialist transformation of agriculture, handicrafts, and capitalist industry and commerce in China was realized under the leadership and guidance of the state economy. The consolidation and development of the collective economy was also linked to the leading role of the state economy upon the basic completion of socialist transformation. The socialist state economy is a strong material force for consolidating the dictatorship of the proletariat.

In agriculture, the segment of the economy that falls under the system of socialist ownership by the whole people is mainly the state farm. In China, the state farm assumes some roles different from those of the collective economy: (1) In addition to funds accumulated by the farm itself, investment can also, when necessary, come directly from the state to accelerate agricultural mechanization, thus permitting the state farm to play a leading role and to be a model. (2) The state farm is an important base for the state to conduct agricultural scientific experiments. Scientific experiments that require more specialized research personnel, more funds, and a long period of time to obtain useful results often cannot be conducted by the collective economy in the countryside, because of manpower, material, and financial constraints. The state farm, on the other hand, can concentrate manpower, material resources, and funds under a unified plan in order to conduct various scientific experiments and to disseminate the useful results—superior strains and advanced experience—to agricultural people's communes in good time. (3) The state farm is superior to the collective economy in the large-scale reclamation of virgin land, development of forests, and lumbering.

Socialist ownership by the whole people is a form of socialist ownership with a high degree of public ownership, and the direction of its development is towards growing into a system of communist ownership by the whole people. From the standpoint of public ownership of the means of production by the working people as a whole, this form of ownership already has a communist element. But socialist ownership by the whole people is a system that has barely emerged from the womb of the old society, and hence cannot but carry with it the traditions and birthmarks of the old society. First off, the system of socialist ownership by the whole people is still a form of ownership closely bound up with classes and class struggle. The term "by the whole people" is shorthand for "the laboring people as a whole," and this system of socialist ownership serves only the proletariat and laboring people. Second, socialist ownership by the whole people of necessity takes the form of socialist state ownership, and the socialist state, as pointed out by Lenin, is, in a certain sense, a "bourgeois state without the bourgeoisie." This is so because the state must still protect bourgeois right.* Third, socialist

---

* "The proletarian state recognizes bourgeois right, allows it to be retained, defends it, and compels people to abide by it (of course restricting it at the same time). In this sense, the state of the dictatorship of the proletariat plays that part of the role performed by the bourgeois state." (*Peking Review*, 14 November 1975 (46), p. 23)

ownership by the whole people is bound up with the commodity system, exchange through money, and distribution according to work; and equal rights within the commodity system, in the process of exchange through money and distribution according to work, are still bourgeois rights. These phenomena stress that there are no grounds to view the system of socialist ownership by the whole people as the purest. Only when socialist ownership by the whole people develops further into a system of communist ownership by the whole people can society rid itself of the stamp of classes and the traditions and birthmarks of capitalism.

Once the system of socialist ownership by the whole people has been established, there is still a long process of consolidating and continuously improving it. Whether socialist ownership by the whole people progresses or retrogresses is one of the central issues in the struggle between the two classes, the two roads, and the two lines in the socialist period.

THERE WILL BE NO CONSOLIDATION OF SOCIALISM WITHOUT SOCIALIZATION OF AGRICULTURE

It is necessary to subject the small peasant economy to socialist transformation

After the proletariat seizes political power, it not only faces a highly socialized capitalist economy. It also often faces extensive systems of private economy based on ownership by the individual laborer. Its components can be found in agriculture, the handicraft industry, transportation, and commerce but they are most numerous and widespread in agriculture. Those participating in this individual economic activity are individual laborers. The individual household is a unit of production and operation. Although the individual laborers participating in these economic activities own some means of production, the amount is very small and their lot is an uncertain one; they can be reduced to bankruptcy at any moment by the capitalist economy. When the proletariat overthrows bourgeois rule and establishes a system of socialist ownership by the whole people of the means of production, can systems of individual economy be allowed to continue their operation? No. Chairman Mao said, "Without socialization of agriculture, there can

49

be no complete, consolidated socialism."[8] What we have to analyze here is the issue of what road systems of individual economy in agriculture should follow under conditions of socialism, since the road followed by individual economy in agriculture is also in principle the road followed by other systems of individual economy, such as individual handicraft industry.

The system of socialist ownership by the whole people established by the proletariat after the seizure of political power is the main economic foundation of the state system under the dictatorship of the proletariat. But the small peasant economy based on individual labor and ownership is in conflict with the system of socialist public ownership and with the superstructure of the dictatorship of the proletariat. This is because the small peasant economy based on private ownership is a hotbed of capitalism. It will certainly polarize the peasantry into a majority of poor peasants and farm laborers and a minority of rich peasants, who constitute the bourgeoisie in the countryside. Lenin pointed out, "Small production *engenders* capitalism and the bourgeoisie continuously, daily, hourly, spontaneously, and on a mass scale."[9]

China's people's democratic revolution was a great victory in thoroughly transforming the land system, confiscating land from the feudal class and distributing it to the peasants, and eliminating the feudal ownership system, thus enabling the broad masses of peasants to liberate themselves from feudalism. But after land reform, there is still a question of where the individual peasants should go. Should they follow the capitalist road or the socialist road? Within a few years after China's land reform, spontaneous capitalist tendencies developed steadily. New rich peasants appeared everywhere, and many better-off middle peasants tried very hard to become rich peasants. Many poor peasants were still suffering from poverty because of insufficient means of production. Many of them were in debt. Some had to sell or rent their land. The emergence of these conditions underscored the fact that if, after land reform, the proletariat did not immediately lead the broad masses of peasants to take the socialist road and subject the small peasant economy to socialist transformation in good time but rather let it polarize, then those upper middle peasants bent on taking the capitalist road would grow further and further removed from the interests of the working class, while those peasants who had recently lost their land again and were still beset by poverty would protest that the proletariat did not rescue them and help them solve their problems. Thus the worker-peasant alliance established on the basis of land reform would face the danger of collapse. Such a situation would also threaten the dictatorship of the proletariat and the consolidation of the socialist economic base.

After land reform, the small peasant economy based on private ownership played a certain role in reviving and developing agricultural production. But this economy was, after all, predicated on backward relations of production. Individual and scattered operation made it impossible to adopt advanced techniques and modern farm tools, rendered the small peasant economy helpless in the face of natural calamities, and made it impossible to sustain expanded reproduction. Therefore, the small peasant economy proved incapable of satisfying the socialist economy's demand for commodity food grain, industrial raw materials, and increased labor power; nor could it provide a large domestic market for industrial development. The small peasant economy was thus in sharp conflict with socialist industrialization. To resolve this contradiction, it was necessary for the proletariat to take appropriate measures to lead the scattered and backward small peasant economy on to the socialist road.

How can the small peasant economy be led on to the socialist road?

Getting organized is the necessary road for the socialist transformation of the small peasant economy

The peasant is a laborer and an ally of the proletariat. The means of production owned privately by the individual peasant cannot be expropriated. Engels once pointed out: "When we are in possession of state power we shall not even think of forcibly expropriating the small peasants (regardless of whether with or without compensation), as we shall have to do in the case of the big landowners. Our task relative to the small peasant consists, in the first place, in effecting a transition of his private enterprise and private possession to cooperative ones, not forcibly but by dint of example and the proffer of social assistance for this purpose."[10] This is to say, agricultural cooperativization is realized by getting organized. "This is the only road to liberation for the people, the only road from poverty to prosperity. . . . "[11] In China, the broad masses of poor and lower-middle peasants were quite receptive to socialist transformation. There was great enthusiasm for the socialist road. Some of the upper-middle peasants were skeptical of the socialist road, while the landlords and rich peasants tried hard to sabotage it. Therefore, on the question of whether agricultural cooperativization should begin to be implemented, there existed, from the very beginning, a serious struggle between the socialist and capitalist roads. This struggle was reflected in the Party itself as a serious struggle between the two lines.

The Liu Shao-chi and Chen Po-ta clique, representing the interests of the bourgeoisie and the rich peasants, proposed a revisionist line of "mechanization first, cooperativization later." They attacked ferociously, arguing that to undertake cooperativization before mechanization was "erroneous, dangerous, and illusory agricultural socialism," in a futile attempt to lead the individualistic economy on to the evil road of capitalism. To counter the fallacies peddled by Liu Shao-chi and company, Chairman Mao pointed out, "In agriculture, with conditions as they are in our country cooperation must precede the use of big machinery (in capitalist countries agriculture develops in a capitalist way)."[12] The Party Central Committee headed by Chairman Mao resolutely defended the interests of the proletariat and the poor and lower-middle peasants. It analyzed the actual conditions of China's countryside and formulated a basic Party line for agriculture: the first step was to implement agricultural collectivization, and the second step was to achieve agricultural mechanization on the basis of agricultural collectivization. This was a Marxist line. Chairman Mao's revolutionary line was thoroughly implemented. In the process of agricultural cooperativization, the whole Party relied firmly on the poor and lower-middle peasants to unite solidly with other middle peasants in order to wage a resolute struggle against the landlords and the rich peasants and rebuke the revisionist line of the Liu Shao-chi clique. As a result, agricultural cooperativization was triumphantly achieved in a very short time.

The process of China's socialist transformation of agriculture was one of motion of contradictions between the relations of production and the productive forces in the countryside. The process of transformation went through three stages, proceeding step by step, one after another. In the beginning, mutual-aid teams with certain socialist elements were organized in order to train the peasants in collective labor and demonstrate that their production would increase faster this way than through the practice of individual operations. But there was a contradiction between group labor and scattered operation in the mutual-aid team. Had this contradiction not been resolved, it would have been difficult to further tap the superior potential of "getting organized." At that time and in the light of local circumstances, the peasants were led to organize primitive agricultural production cooperatives of a semisocialist nature. In these primitive cooperatives, privately owned land was jointly operated by the cooperative, while privately-owned livestock and large farm tools were jointly used by the cooperative, in this way resolving the contradiction between group labor and scattered operation in the mutual-aid team. Production was further promoted. But the primitive cooperative still retained "land dividends" and certain remuneration for the use of privately-owned livestock and large farm tools. Private ownership of the means of production had not been abolished. There still existed a contradiction between joint operation and collective labor, on the one hand, and the private ownership of land and other means of production, on the other. Had this contradiction not been resolved, the activism of the broad poor and lower-middle peasants would not have been fully unleashed. At that time, based on concrete conditions, the Party once again led the peasants to form completely socialist, advanced agricultural production cooperatives. On the basis of the system of collective ownership of the means of production by the working people, the advanced cooperative implemented the socialist principle of "from each according to one's ability and to each according to one's work." It was a completely socialist collective economy. The policy of proceeding phase by phase according to actual circumstances was instrumental in gradually accustoming the peasants to collective labor and collective operation, getting them to relinquish the concept of private ownership, and arousing their socialist enthusiasm so that they would willingly join the cooperative. As a result, during the entire process of cooperativization, not only was agricultural production not reduced but it increased year after year, fully demonstrating the incomparable correctness of Chairman Mao's revolutionary line.

After completing land reform, the socialist transformation of agriculture in China's vast countryside was basically completed in less than four years. Agricultural cooperativization was achieved and the vast system of individual ownership was transformed into a system of socialist collective ownership by working people. The achievement of agricultural cooperativization further liberated the productive forces, strengthened the socialist stronghold of the proletariat in the vast countryside, consolidated the worker-peasant alliance, and consolidated the dictatorship of the proletariat. The implications of this were profound.

China's rural people's commune is an important development in the system of collective ownership

After the establishment of the system of socialist collective ownership by working people, there followed a process of gradual development and improvement. With the development of the productive forces and the heightening of socialist consciousness of the laboring masses, small collectives developed into bigger collectives, and collectives with a lower degree of public ownership developed into collectives with a higher degree of public ownership. This is an objective law. In 1958, under the guidance of the Party's General Line for Socialist Construction, given impetus by the Great Leap Forward, and in accord with the need for developing the productive forces in the countryside, China's rural people's commune rose over the vast horizon of East Asia like an early rising sun. The broad masses of poor and lower-middle peasants dearly loved the people's commune. They wrote numerous folk songs praising its birth. One of them went as follows:

> Individual operation is like a single plank bridge,
> It rocks three times with every step;
> Mutual aid is like a stone bridge,
> That does not stand up well to wind and rain;
> The iron bridge is not bad,
> But it cannot handle heavy traffic;
> The people's commune is a golden bridge,
> That leads the way to Heaven.

The scale of the people's commune was one per *hsiang,* and the commune was formed by merging several advanced agricultural production cooperatives in a *hsiang.** The commune is an organization com-

---

* Hsiang was an administrative unit at the township level, made up of one or several villages.

bining administration with production and includes the worker, the peasant (including those in forestry, livestock husbandry, sidelines, and fishery), the trader, the student, and the soldier. It is the basic unit of China's socialist society in the countryside. It is also a basic unit of China's government in the countryside. For a fairly long historical period to come, it will be the collective economic organization of socialism based on mutual aid and benefit. However, when the advanced agricultural cooperative developed into the people's commune, both the scale of operation and the share of the means of production owned by the public were increased. Its characteristic was "big and public." This was an important development in China's system of socialist collective ownership by the working people.

At the present stage, the economic system of collective ownership in the rural people's communes generally takes the form of "three-level ownership with the production team at the basic level." In the three-level system of ownership, collective ownership at the commune and brigade levels is partial. It is the production team that is the basic accounting unit in the people's commune. It exercises its own independent accounting functions and is responsible for all its profit and loss. It directly organizes production and decides the distribution of income. The reason for this is that agricultural production at the present stage still basically depends on manual labor and draft animals. Although the degree of agricultural mechanization has steadily increased after the establishment of the people's commune, manual labor remains dominant in the countryside as a whole. At the present stage, it is generally appropriate to have twenty to thirty households in a production team, forming a basic accounting unit. This is a favorable condition for organizing production and distribution, strengthening management, mobilizing the socialist activism of the broad numbers of commune members, arousing them to be more concerned with the collective, and strengthening the supervision of cadres. Above the production team, there are the collective economies of the brigade and the commune. The degree of socialization at these two levels is comparatively high, and with the development of the collective economy it becomes financially possible to purchase large- and medium-size farm machinery, to engage in farm land construction such as water conservation, to run small factories and mining enterprises, and, at key points, to assist weak production teams, in order to hasten the development of the collective economy. These activities are too big for the production team to carry out. The people's commune is an integral and indivisible unit organized on the basis of the system of collective ownership and economic accounting at three levels. The system of three-level collective ownership is exceedingly flexible for coping with the different conditions existing in the country-side and with the diverse demands thrown up by the developing rural productive forces; it is therefore conducive to the rapid development of social productivity.

Provided that the development and predominance of the collective economy of the people's commune are ensured and well taken care of first, commune members are permitted and encouraged to use their free time and holidays to farm small plots for their personal needs and to engage in limited household sideline production. The right of commune households to retain and farm private plots and to engage in family side occupations is a remnant of the small private economy. But under socialism, these activities are adjuncts to and subordinate to the socialist economy based on socialist ownership by the whole people and socialist collective ownership by working people. For a period of time during the socialist transition, such farming and sideline production can play a certain role in allowing the labor power of the country-side to be more fully utilized, the social product to be increased, the livelihood of the commune members to be improved, and the amount and variety of goods at the rural trade fairs to be enhanced. But such remnants of the system of small private ownership are, at the same time, definitely soil that engenders capitalism, and therefore leadership must be strengthened to restrict their negative role.

The system of collective ownership in China's rural people's commune, generally taking the form of "three-level ownership with the production team at the basic level," will remain as it is for years to come. However, with the gradual improvement of various conditions (for example, with a higher degree of agricultural mechanization, a smaller income gap among production teams, and the gradual heightening of commune members' socialist consciousness), China's rural people's commune will gradually pass from the current system of ownership based on the production team to a future system of ownership based on the brigade and the commune, and then from there, step by step, to a system of socialist ownership by the whole people. This will be a long process of gradual development.

Like the system of collective ownership in agriculture, the system of collective ownership of the handicraft industry also involves a long process of passing from small collectives to large collectives, and then from large collectives to a system of socialist ownership by the whole people.

The development of the system of collective ownership from the small to the large, from the low to the high, and from socialist collective ownership to socialist ownership by the whole people is all based on the step-by-step improvement of the productive forces and the gradual heightening of socialist consciousness among the people. It would be a mistake to attempt to change the situation too quickly, when the necessary conditions do not exist. It would also be a mistake to be content with the status quo, when the necessary conditions do exist. These two tendencies will dampen the socialist enthusiasm of the masses and are unfavorable to the development of the productive forces. These tendencies may even impede the development of the productive forces. In the process of transforming the advanced agricultural production cooperative to the rural people's commune in China, these two tendencies did in fact exist. The appearance of the people's commune is a natural result of economic and political development in China and is completely in line with objective laws. But revisionists like Liu Shao-chi maliciously attacked the formation of the people's commune as "premature and a big mess." When the powerful tide of the people's commune overwhelmed the countercurrent they had stirred up, they then clamored for "a leap toward communism," fanning a wind of "communization" in a futile attempt to sabotage the people's commune. From now on, there will be struggle between the two classes, the two roads, and the two lines in the process of development of the rural economy based on socialist collective ownership by working people. This is inevitable and not in the least surprising.

Although socialist collective ownership by working people and socialist ownership by the whole people are two kinds of socialist public ownership, there are important differences between them. The means of production of the collective economy are not the public property of the working people of the whole country but are the public property of the working people of particular units of the collective economy. Therefore, manpower, materials, and financial resources cannot be transferred between the state and collective sectors without compensation, nor can resources be transferred between the various units of the collective economy without compensation.

Socialist collective ownership by working people is a form of socialist ownership that has a lower degree of public ownership and that has more birthmarks of the old society. Within particular units of the collective economy, ownership of the means of production among people is equal [land, tools, etc., are collectively owned by all the people of the unit]. But among the various units of the collective economy, there is inequality in ownership of the means of production. Among different production brigades of the people's communes in our countryside, not only are there differences in the amount of land owned but also, owing to differences in soil fertility and geographic location, there will be differences in incomes, this despite the fact that they may be contributing equal amounts of labor. Thus, for different communes, different production brigades of the same commune, and different production teams of the same brigade, the value of work points will be different.* These phenomena show that, within the confines of collective ownership, bourgeois right still has not been totally abolished and that the consolidation and perfecting of socialist collective ownership remains a huge and difficult task.

THE SYSTEM OF SOCIALIST PUBLIC OWNERSHIP IS CONSOLIDATED AND DEVELOPED THROUGH STRUGGLE

The serious lesson of the restoration of capitalism in the Soviet Union

Since the Khrushchev-Brezhnev renegade clique restored bourgeois dictatorship, the system of socialist public ownership established under the dictatorship of the proletariat has been completely transformed into a new system of ownership by the bureaucrat-monopoly bourgeoisie. This is a serious lesson.

Marxism tells us that the nature of the system of ownership of the means of production is ultimately determined by which social group owns the means of production and which social groups they serve. How is this to be understood? In *Capital,* Marx had quoted Aristotle's

---

* Work points were the standard by which collective members were remunerated for their labor. This is discussed in greater detail in Chapter 11.

remark that "'the master proves himself such not by obtaining slaves but in employing slaves.'" Marx then went on: "The capitalist proves himself not by ownership of capital which gives him power to buy labor power but in using laborers, nowadays wage laborers, in the production process."[13]

Today, a glimpse at the way the Soviet proletariat and laboring people are "used in the production process" will reveal the essence of Soviet revisionism, namely that Brezhnev and his associates, under the cloak of socialist public ownership, have usurped control over the Soviet people's means of production and that these means of production serve the interests of a bureaucrat-monopoly bourgeoisie. Indeed, it is precisely by forcing the Soviet laboring people to be used as wage laborers in the production process that the Soviet revisionists prove themselves to be a bureaucrat-monopoly bourgeoisie.

In the Regulations Governing the Socialist State-operated Production Enterprises, the Soviet revisionists stipulate: "The authority over production and management shall be exercised by the manager (administrator or director) in conjunction with other responsible personnel designated in accordance with the division of their duties." The manager of the enterprise has the authority to determine the structure and personnel of the enterprise; to recruit or dismiss employees; to grant awards or mete out penalties; to fix wage scales and bonuses; to sell, rent, or lease the means of production of the enterprise; and to appropriate various "economic incentive funds," which, according to the regulations of the Soviet revisionist leadership, have been reserved for the enterprise's own allocation.

The Soviet revisionist "Regulations Governing the Model Collective Farms" stipulate that the chairman of the collective farm possesses the authority to rent, lease, or transfer the land owned by the state; to appropriate farm funds, or even to freely buy or sell the means of production, such as agricultural machines; and to decide the labor remuneration and bonuses of the farm members, hire outside people to work at the farm, and so forth. These "managers," or "farm chairmen," have this and that power. What powers do the laboring people have? None. Their rights of ownership to the means of production have all been expropriated by the bureaucrat-monopoly bourgeoisie, which has reduced the laboring people of the Soviet Union to wage laborers "in the production process." According to Soviet revisionist magazines, the monthly piecework wages of a lathe operator in a state enterprise in the Soviet Union are as low as 50 to 60 rubles. Medium-level wages are 70 to 80 rubles. But what the manager, plant director, and other bourgeois elements get in the form of wages, bonuses, subsidies, and other "legal" means is more than ten times, or even several tens of times, that of the worker. The net monthly income of an ordinary farmer is less than 60 rubles. But the monthly income of a farm chairman is generally about 300 rubles. Some salaries exceed 1,000 rubles. One old Soviet worker with more than thirty years of experience said: "We have a lot of millionaires here. They are different from us not only in standard of living but also in language." A manager of the construction trust of the Soviet revisionist Ministry of Agriculture frantically exclaimed: "The trust is my home. I am the master. I do what I like." The kind of tree determines the kind of flower, and the kind of class determines the kind of talk. The bureaucrat-monopoly bourgeoisie has become the lords in production; like the capitalists, they "do what they like." On the other hand, the broad masses of laboring people have been reduced to wage laborers in production; they are enslaved, exploited, and suffering miserably.

It is a fact, a shocking fact, that the system of socialist public ownership of the Soviet Union has completely degenerated. This proves that after the system of socialist public ownership is established, the issue of ownership has not yet been fully settled. Moreover, the system of ownership will not automatically be consolidated and perfected; there will be a protracted process of struggle.

The system of ownership is not a matter of things, it is a social relation bound up with things. On the one hand, the establishment of the system of socialist public ownership means that the laboring people have broken the chain of private ownership and have begun to become the masters of the means of production of the society. The relation between the proletariat and laboring people and all the exploiting classes has been reversed: it has become the relation in which the previously exploited are ruling over and remolding all members of the exploiting classes. On the other hand, it must also be recognized that bourgeois right has not been entirely abolished in the system of ownership. Moreover, we must see that both ownership by the whole people and collective ownership involve the question of leadership, that is, the question of which class holds the ownership in fact and not just in name. In these kinds of social relations, the proletariat and laboring people want to consolidate the fruits of appropriation, to strengthen their rule over and remolding of the members of the exploiting classes, and through the process of restricting the bourgeois rights that still have not been entirely abolished in the system of socialist ownership and gradually eliminating the traditions and birthmarks of the old society, to consolidate and continuously perfect the system of socialist ownership. As regards social relations, the bourgeoisie and all exploiting classes resist being ruled over and remolded. They try to utilize and expand the traditions and birthmarks of the old society that still exist within the system of socialist ownership, and they will attempt to expand the bourgeois rights that have not been entirely abolished and restore those that have already been abolished. In this way, they will bring about the steady erosion and sabotage of the system of socialist public ownership and its eventual transformation into a system of capitalist private ownership.

The contradictions and struggles between the proletariat and the bourgeoisie around the question of ownership are multifaceted. But they mainly find expression in the struggle for leadership over the economy that is based on socialist public ownership. Whoever seizes leadership becomes the de facto master of the relations of ownership. Once leadership falls into the hands of the bourgeoisie or its agents, the system of socialist public ownership not only cannot be consolidated or improved but will certainly degenerate. It is exactly because a handful of persons in power in the Soviet Union taking the capitalist road has seized leadership of an economy based on a system of socialist public ownership that this system has been transformed into a system of ownership of the bureaucrat-monopoly bourgeoisie. As a result, the proletariat and the laboring people of the Soviet Union have been transformed from masters of a system of socialist public ownership into slaves of an ownership system of the bureaucrat-monopoly bourgeoisie. Since the Khrushchev-Brezhnev renegade clique usurped the supreme power of the Party and state of the Soviet Union, capitalism has been completely restored.

Struggle for the consolidation and development of socialist public ownership

After the establishment of socialist public ownership, the issue of ownership has not yet been fully settled. There still exist the two possibilities: advancing towards communism, or retreating back to capitalism. The proletariat and the broad masses of laboring people face the historical task of constantly struggling for the consolidation and development of the system of socialist public ownership.

To consolidate and develop the system of socialist public ownership, it is necessary first of all to ensure that leadership of the socialist economy is in the hands of genuine Marxists and the broad laboring masses. Just as with other questions, in analyzing the question of ownership, it is necessary not only to examine its form but also its actual content. One must see: To whom do the means of production of the enterprise actually belong? Who actually controls them? Whose interests are actually served by these means of production? This is manifested and concentrated in the question of which class wields [the power of] leadership in the enterprise.

The system of socialist public ownership demonstrates that the proletariat and the laboring people are the masters of the means of production. But how can one decide whether the proletariat and the laboring people are in fact masters of the means of production? That depends on their role in the production process. In socialist society, the laborers participate in the production process as masters. They create wealth for society through conscious labor. Then who organizes this production process? Ultimately, it should be the laborers themselves. Naturally, this does not mean that all the laborers directly organize and manage production. The broad masses of laborers appoint representatives through the state and the collective, or they elect representatives to organize production. But here a problem arises: if the broad masses of laborers delegate to their representatives the power to organize production, can these representatives represent the interests of the proletariat and the laboring people in organizing production? After the laborer has delegated his or her power to organize production to a representative, is there any power left to the individual laborer? This problem is, again, related to the big problem of which class actually owns the means of production, to the question of whether the system of public ownership of the means of production is moving forward or backward. In today's Soviet Union, those who lead and organize production do not represent the interests of the proletariat and the laboring people at all; rather, they represent the interests of the bureaucrat-monopoly bourgeoisie. State monopoly capitalism has become the economic basis of Soviet society. This is a big historical retrogression.

Under the dictatorship of the proletariat in China, the struggle between the two classes over the leadership of the socialist enterprise is also very sharp. Chairman Mao pointed out at the First Plenary Session of the Ninth Central Committee of the Party: "Apparently, we couldn't do without the Great Proletarian Cultural Revolution, for our base was not solid. From my observations, I am afraid that in a fairly large majority of factories—I don't mean all or the overwhelming majority—leadership was not in the hands of real Marxists and the masses of workers. Not that there were no good people in the leadership of the factories. There were. There were good people among the secretaries, deputy branch secretaries, and members of Party committees and among the Party branch secretaries. But they followed that line of Liu Shao-chi's, just resorting to material incentive, putting profit in command, and instead of promoting proletarian politics, handing out bonuses, and so forth." "But there are indeed bad people in the factories." "This shows that the revolution is still unfinished."[14] When the leadership of socialist economy is in the hands of genuine Marxists, they can represent the interests of the workers, the poor and lower-middle peasants, and all laboring masses in owning and dominating the means of production, and in restricting those bourgeois rights in the sphere of ownership that have not been completely abolished, in order to consolidate and push forward the development of socialist public ownership. If leadership of the socialist economy is usurped by those in power taking the capitalist road, they will turn the responsibility of serving the people that is given to them by the Party and the state into special privileges serving their own private interests and gain. They will utilize the traditions and birthmarks of the old society that still exist in the socialist economy to restore those bourgeois rights in the system of ownership that have already been abolished and to erode the system of socialist public ownership. "Lessons from history are noteworthy." The Tenth National Party Congress summed up rich experience and lessons and clearly pointed out: "We should strengthen the leadership given to primary organizations in order to ensure that leadership there is truly in the hands of Marxists and in the hands of workers, poor and lower-middle peasants and other working people, and that the task of consolidating the dictatorship of the proletariat is fulfilled in every primary organization."[15] This is of decisive importance in consolidating and developing the system of socialist public ownership.

To ensure that the leadership of the enterprise under the state economy and the collective economy is in the hands of genuine Marxists, the proletariat and the laboring people must engage in a resolute struggle with the renegades, secret agents, and capitalist roaders who have usurped leadership and win it back. This type of struggle cannot be resolved with one Great Cultural Revolution. In their futile attempts at restoration, the bourgeoisie will stop at nothing to usurp the leadership of the state and the collective economy. At the same time, the representatives (cadres at various levels) of the proletariat and the laboring people who control the leadership of the state and the collective economy must further transform their world outlook and try hard to become Marxists, so that they can truly represent the interests of the proletariat and the laboring people. If they do not work hard in this direction, it is possible that in the process of organizing production they may, under the influence of the bourgeois world outlook, go against the interests of the proletariat and the laboring people. Some people are interested in material incentives, profit, and restrictive measures in running and managing the socialist economy. In other words, they do not treat the laboring people as the masters of the socialist enterprise. This will inevitably impede and weaken the system of socialist public ownership. If this tendency goes unchecked, the system of socialist public ownership will degenerate. In the Great Proletarian Cultural Revolution, the broad masses and cadres criticized and repudiated this tendency. But under certain conditions, things that have been criticized and repudiated can appear again. At the beginning of 1974, some of the workers in the No. 5 Loading and Unloading District of the Shanghai Harbor Affairs Bureau posted a big-character poster entitled "Be Masters of the Wharf, Not Slaves to Tonnage." It pointed out: "The leadership does not treat the workers as masters of the wharf. Instead they are treated as the slaves of tonnage. This is a reflection of the revisionist line in running an enterprise." These words strike at the heart of what it means to consolidate and develop socialist public ownership and are of universal practical significance.

If the leadership of the state economy and the collective economy is really to be in the hands of genuine Marxists, it must also really be in the hands of the workers, poor and lower-middle peasants, and other laboring masses. These two aspects are inseparable. Since the laboring masses are the masters of the socialist economy, it does not mean that they no longer have the right to intervene once leadership has been delegated to a few representatives. The revisionist "system of one-man management," championed by the Soviet revisionists, is an institutionalization of this viewpoint. Facts have demonstrated that this is chloroform spread by the bourgeoisie and its agents in order to usurp leadership. Engels once pointed out: "The running of industry by individuals inevitably leads to private ownership."[16] If the leadership of the enterprise under socialist ownership is not in the hands of the workers, poor and lower-middle peasants, and other laborers, the revisionist system of "one-man management" will take hold. Under the revisionist system of "one-man management," the laboring masses are in effect separated from the means of production. They simply receive orders from the "head" of the enterprise. Without leadership over the enterprise, they are no longer masters of the enterprise. If this develops, they will be treated as pure labor power in the production process by the "head" of the enterprise. The laboring masses will no longer have the right to question whether a particular production process serves the interests of the proletariat and the laboring people. In this way, socialist enterprises will gradually slide into the mudhole of capitalism. But when leadership of the enterprise is really in the hands of genuine Marxists and the workers, poor and lower-middle peasants, and other laboring masses, the position of the laboring masses as masters of the enterprise will surely be guaranteed. As masters, they will unleash socialist activism. If some bad people have usurped leadership of the enterprise, the laboring masses would take it back under the Party's leadership. This has been proven more than once by the practice of China's socialist revolution, especially since the Great Proletarian Cultural Revolution. It will be proven again.

The crux of judging who controls the leadership of the socialist economy lies in what line is being implemented by the departments of the enterprise in charge of production operation or economic management. The revisionist line always goes against the interests of the proletariat and the laboring people. It fosters material incentives, profit, and restrictive measures. On the other hand, following socialist principles, the Marxist line always insists that revolution command production and that operation management be strengthened by relying on the masses as the masters. Therefore, firmly adhering to the Marxist line, and criticizing and repudiating the revisionist line, is the ultimate guarantee for consolidating and developing the system of socialist public ownership.

To consolidate and develop the system of socialist public ownership, it is necessary to restrict bourgeois right under the dictatorship of the proletariat. In socialist society, bourgeois right in the sphere of ownership has not been completely abolished. It is necessary to divide one into two in treating these bourgeois rights in socialist society: while there is a need to affirm their historical role, allowing them to exist, there is also a need to restrict them, not allowing them to develop and expand. If these bourgeois rights are not restricted under the dictatorship of the proletariat, but rather expanded, they will ultimately cause the system of ownership of enterprises to change its nature, and cause socialist enterprises to degenerate into capitalist enterprises.

To consolidate and develop socialist public ownership, it is also necessary to implement various policies of the Party. For example, it is necessary to correctly handle the relations between the center and the locality in order to have two kinds of initiative within the economy under the system of socialist ownership by the whole people. It is necessary to correctly handle the relations between the state and the enterprise so that the enterprise can fully take the initiative in operation and management under the unified leadership of the state. Also, in the collective economy of the rural people's commune, it is necessary to correctly implement the basic system of ownership, which at the present stage takes the form of "three-level ownership with the production team at the basic level," in order to mobilize the socialist activism of the three-level collective economy of the commune, the brigade, and the production team. While acknowledging the existence of differences among teams, among brigades, and among communes, we must strive to create favorable conditions, that is, we must narrow such differences in order to follow the socialist path to common abundance.

To consolidate and develop the system of socialist public ownership, socialist education must be strengthened. Socialist public ownership is built on the basis of eliminating private ownership. But "remnants of old ideas reflecting the old system remain in people's minds for a long time, and they do not easily give way."[17] These remnants of the old ideology, based on the old system of private ownership, including the ideology of bourgeois right, are manifested in many realms and are in conflict with the system of socialist public ownership. Only by strengthening education in ideological and political line, constantly heightening the political consciousness of the cadres and broad masses, and firmly establishing the proletarian world outlook can the consolidation and development of the system of socialist public ownership be effectively promoted.

To consolidate and develop the system of socialist public ownership, it is also necessary to energetically develop social productive forces. The system of socialist public ownership creates favorable conditions for the development of social productive forces, while the further development of social productive forces must provide a material basis for the further consolidation and development of the system of socialist public ownership. The acceleration of socialist industrialization will strengthen the socialist state economy. The acceleration of agricultural mechanization and the constant development of agricultural productive forces will strengthen the collective economy and thus promote the further consolidation and development of collective ownership. Therefore, resolutely implementing the policy to "grasp revolution, promote production" and developing the socialist economy with greater, faster, better, and more economical results are important conditions for the consolidation and development of the system of socialist public ownership.

The process of consolidating and developing socialist public ownership is a protracted process of struggle between the two classes, the two roads, and the two lines. This is a long-term struggle. Arduous tasks lie before us, and we must fight with all our strength!

Notes

1. Engels, *Anti-Duhring*, p. 205.
2. Marx, *Critique of the Gotha Programme*, p. 9.
3. Marx and Engels, *Manifesto of the Communist Party* (Peking: Foreign Languages Press, 1973), p. 59. Hereafter, references to this work are cited as *Communist Manifesto.*
4. Mao, "The Present Situation and Our Tasks," *SW* 4, p. 167.
5. Mao, "Report to the Second Plenum of the Seventh Central Committee of the Communist Party of China," *SW* 4, p. 367.
6. Lenin, "'Left-Wing' Childishness and the Petty-Bourgeois Mentality," *CW* 27 (1974), p. 343.
7. Lenin, "Political Report of the Central Committee of the R.C.P.(B.), March 27, 1922," *CW* 33, p. 278.
8. Mao, "On the People's Democratic Dictatorship," *SW* 4, p. 419.
9. Lenin, *Left-Wing Communism, An Infantile Disorder* (Peking: Foreign Languages Press, 1965), p. 6.
10. Engels, "The Peasant Question in France and Germany," *MESW* 3, p. 470.
11. Mao, "Get Organized," *SW* 3, p. 157.
12. Mao, "On the Question of Agricultural Co-operation," *SR*, p. 406.
13. Marx, *Capital* 3, pp. 384-85.
14. Mao, quoted in Chang Chun-chiao, "Exercising All-Round Dictatorship," in Lotta, *And Mao Makes Five*, p. 213.
15. CPC, *Tenth Party Congress Documents*, p. 35.
16. Engels, "Principles of Communism," *SW* 1, p. 88.
17. Mao, cited in *The Red Book*, p. 33.

4

ESTABLISH MUTUAL RELATIONS BETWEEN PEOPLE ACCORDING TO SOCIALIST PRINCIPLES

The Position and Mutual Relations of People in Socialist Production

The position and mutual relations of people in production are an important component of the relations of production. After the establishment of socialist public ownership, it is very important to forge mutual relations of people in production that are compatible with this form of ownership. If this middle link of the relations of production is grasped and constantly improved, the system of socialist public ownership and its relations of distribution will continue to consolidate and develop further.

THE POSITION AND MUTUAL RELATIONS OF PEOPLE IN PRODUCTION HAVE UNDERGONE A FUNDAMENTAL CHANGE

The system of socialist public ownership is the precondition for the establishment of socialist mutual relations

In history, the position and mutual relations of people in production have always been determined by the system of ownership of the means of production. The system of slave ownership determined the relationship between the slave owner and his slaves. The system of ownership of the feudal lords determined the relationship between the landlord and the peasant. The system of ownership of the capitalist determined the relationship between the capitalist and the worker. In slave and feudal societies, the mutual relations between people in production are a nakedly unequal relationship: the relations of exploiting and being exploited, of oppressing and being oppressed, are very transparent. But as between the capitalists and workers in capitalist society, the relations of exploiting and being exploited, of ruling and being ruled, are concealed by the false appearance of equality. Besides, these relations often involve goods and are manifested as relations between goods. For a long time, bourgeois economists have written books and concocted theories about relations between things in an attempt to conceal the reality of class antagonisms between people. "Where the bourgeois economists saw a relation between things (the exchange of one commodity for another) Marx revealed a *relation between people.*"[1] "Economics deals not with things but with relations between persons, and, in the last resort, between classes."[2]

The mutual relations between people in socialist production are established only after the proletariat and the broad masses of laboring people overthrow the bourgeois state machinery with violence and establish the dictatorship of the proletariat and the system of socialist public ownership of the means of production.

In socialist society, the relationship which existed in the old society between the ruling and the ruled—with the working class and the broad mass of peasants on one side and the bourgeoisie, the landlords, and the rich peasants on the other—has been reversed. This reversal has as its precondition the transformation of the system of private ownership of the means of production into the system of socialist public ownership. The establishment of the system of socialist public ownership is a coercive economic measure. In this system, the exploiting class is deprived of its means of exploiting the laboring people and is forced to accept transformation by the proletariat and the broad masses of laboring people. On the other hand, with the establishment of the system of socialist public ownership, the proletariat and the broad masses of laboring people, once slaves in the old society, become masters of the new society. From here on, the proletariat and the laboring people are in the ruling position in the socialist production process, while the bourgeoisie and all exploiting classes are in the position of being ruled. Socialist mutual relations are to be established and developed on this basis.

The system of socialist public ownership enables the laboring people to rise from the position of being oppressed and ruled in social production to the position of ruling. It is the greatest change of mutual relations between people in production since the appearance of the slave system several thousand years ago. From the aspect that the laborers have become the masters of social production, mutual social relations already contain a communist element. But as is also the case with socialist ownership and socialist relations of distribution, the socialist relations between people have yet to rid themselves of the traditions and birthmarks of the old society. Even among the laboring people, bourgeois right—equality on the surface but inequality in actual fact—still exists to a serious extent. This is so because in socialist social production, even though the laboring people all are in the position of being the masters, there still exist important differences: between worker and peasant there exist differences in working conditions and material/cultural/living standards and among the laboring people there still exists the division of labor between mental and manual labor (generally, the mental laborer has better working conditions and living standards than the manual laborer). Furthermore, the economic relations between industry and agriculture, and between town and country, still require the support of commodity exchange, while the relations of cooperation between state enterprises still follow the principle of equal exchange. These are all expressions of bourgeois right in the spheres of production and exchange, and these phenomena are all rooted in the three major differences[*] and the old social division of labor that is bound up with them.

The struggle between restriction and counterrestriction of bourgeois right as regards mutual relations is an important component of the struggle between the two classes, the two roads, and the two lines in the socialist period. During the entire historical period of socialism, the proletariat and the broad masses of laboring people will try hard to defend and consolidate their ruling position in socialist production, and to restrict bourgeois right, so as to consolidate and perfect socialist mutual relations. The bourgeoisie and all exploiting classes will never forget their past position of dominance over the laboring people, the

---

[*] The three major differences refer to the differences between industry and agriculture, town and country, and mental and manual labor.

"good old days" when they could reap without work. They will attempt to free themselves from the position of being ruled and remolded, and will try hard to expand bourgeois right and to restore the capitalist mutual relations. Lin Piao's espousal of Confucius's extremely reactionary political proposal to "revive states that are extinct, restore families that have lost their positions, and call to office those who have fallen into obscurity" was a conspiracy to rehabilitate all fallen exploiting classes, to overthrow the laboring people as the new masters, and to restore capitalist mutual relations. Therefore, the process of consolidating and developing socialist mutual relations is essentially a process of struggle between the proletariat and the bourgeoisie.

Socialist mutual relations still bear the stamp of class

In class society, mutual relations between people exist ultimately as relations between classes. How then are the mutual relations between people in socialist production manifested as class relations?

To better understand the class relations in socialist production, it is necessary to briefly retrace the class relations in semicolonial and semifeudal China.

The economic base of old China gave rise to the following classes: the proletariat, the peasantry, the urban petty bourgeoisie, the national bourgeoisie, the bureaucrat bourgeoisie, and the landlords. At that time, the position of and interrelations among these classes could be characterized in the following way. The landlords and the bureaucrat bourgeoisie who controlled the major means of production and the reactionary state machinery, and who colluded with imperialism, occupied a dominant position in social production. They relentlessly exploited and oppressed the proletariat, the peasantry, and the urban petty bourgeoisie. The national bourgeoisie also owned a large quantity of the means of production. On the one hand, they were connected in the overall process of production with imperialism, the landlords, and the bureaucrat bourgeoisie; they shared in the exploitation of the proletariat and the laboring people. On the other hand, they were hemmed in and stifled by the landlords and the bureaucrat bourgeoisie. The proletariat and the broad masses of poor peasants were in a helpless position in social production, subject to triple oppression and exploitation from the imperialists, the feudal forces, and the bourgeoisie.

"Overthrowing the old social system and establishing a new one, the system of socialism, is a great struggle, a great change in the social system and in men's relations with each other."[3] When China entered the historical period of socialist revolution, with the socialist transformation of agriculture, handicraft industry, and capitalist industry and commerce basically achieved, and as socialist public ownership of the means of production became the sole economic foundation, "class relations [were] changing throughout the country."[4] The landlords and the bureaucrat bourgeoisie had already been overthrown and were in the position of being ruled and transformed through social production. The means of production belonging to the national bourgeoisie had already passed into the hands of the proletariat and the laboring people as a whole. Having lost their controlling position in enterprises, the national bourgeoisie had to accept education and transformation from the working class. The peasants (including individual handicraftsmen) had been transformed from individual producers into collective laborers and, with the working class, became masters of the socialist economy. The urban petty bourgeoisie had been assimilated into socialist production relations through the process of socialist transformation. The working class had become the leading class in the country, controlling the lifeblood of the socialist economy and occupying a leading position in the whole process of social production. The old classes of the semicolonial and semifeudal society still existed, but the relations among these classes had undergone fundamental change.

Revisionists from Khrushchev and Brezhnev to Liu Shao-chi and Lin Piao and their associates peddle the doctrine that when the system of socialist public ownership becomes the sole economic foundation, all exploiting classes vanish. Consequently, the relations of production, which include relations between people, lose their class character, and the mutual relations between people become relations among so-called "comrades, friends, and brothers." This fallacy runs totally counter to Marxism and flies in the face of the reality of socialist society.

In socialist society, although the exploiting class has lost its means of production, it still exists as a class. After socialist transformation of ownership of the means of production is basically accomplished, the existence of classes is bound up with people's economic relations prior to socialist transformation and their political stands in the struggle between the socialist and capitalist roads. Moreover, and of great importance, the continuing existence of the three great differences and the continuing existence of bourgeois right, the soil that nurtures capitalism and from which new bourgeois elements are engendered, means that classes will exist for a long time. In fact, after the land reform and socialist transformation of the means of production have basically been accomplished, not only do the landlords and the bourgeoisie still exist, but within the laboring classes new bourgeois elements are constantly being engendered. Lenin once pointed out: "In order to abolish classes completely, it is not enough to overthrow the exploiters, the landowners and capitalists, not enough to abolish *their* rights of ownership; it is necessary also to abolish *all* private ownership of the means of production, it is necessary to abolish the distinction between town and country, as well as the distinction between manual workers and brain workers. This requires a very long period of time."[5]

Although some people concede that there are still exploiting classes in socialist society, they refuse to admit that these classes survive within socialist relations of production. After overthrowing the exploiting classes, the proletariat still needs to transform, step by step, the great majority of members of these classes into self-supporting laborers. For this to happen, it is impossible to seal them off in a vacuum; it is necessary to put them to work in the socialist state and collective enterprises so that they can receive supervision from and undergo transformation by the proletariat and the poor and lower-middle peasants. These relations, whereby the proletariat rules and transforms the members of the exploiting classes, are an essential part of the basic content of the mutual relations between people in socialist society. To think that socialist relations of production do not manifest themselves as relations in which the working class and the laboring people rule and transform the exploiting classes will lead to the revisionist conclusion that socialist relations of production are independent of classes. Some people think that since we all earn our living through labor, everyone is the same, and that, therefore, classes no longer exist. This erroneous concept is closely related to the theoretical negation of the class nature of socialist relations of production.

In the conditions of China, there exist two exploiting classes and two laboring classes. The two exploiting classes are the remnants of the landlord and comprador classes and the bourgeoisie and their affiliated intellectuals. The two laboring classes are the working class and the collective peasants and their affiliated laboring intellectuals. The mutual relations in socialist production are mainly the relations among and within these four classes. The relations among these four classes are not of equal importance. Throughout the entire historical period of socialism, the principal contradiction is between the proletariat and the bourgeoisie. The relationship between the ruling proletariat and the dominated bourgeoisie is the basic class relationship in socialist society. Mutual relations between people in production are inevitably governed, regulated, and influenced by this relationship. Modern revisionists gloss over the class nature of mutual relations between people in production. They loudly proclaim that the mutual relations between people are all relations among "comrades, friends, and brothers." The Lin Piao clique trumpeted such slogans as "while the two struggles turn all people into enemies, the two peaces turn all people into friends" and "within the four seas all are brothers." How absurd! Anyone who has been exposed to Marxism-Leninism knows that there are no relations among "comrades, friends, and brothers" that are independent of classes in a class society. The hatred of the proletariat for the bourgeoisie originated in the exploitation and oppression of the proletariat by the bourgeoisie. "There is absolutely no such thing in the world as love or hatred without reason or cause."[6] These two classes can never be "friends," not to mention "brothers." Is it conceivable that the proletariat and the laboring people will relinquish their rule and become "brothers" and "friends" of the bourgeoisie? The intention of the modern revisionists in espousing these fallacies is to defend the bourgeoisie, deceive the laboring people, and conceal their conspiracy to transform the socialist mutual relations into capitalist mutual relations in order to restore capitalism.[7]

In socialist production, the two exploiting classes are now in the position of being ruled. In China's conditions, these two classes are handled differently. The contradiction between the landlord and comprador classes and the people is handled as a contradiction between the enemy and the people, while that between the national bourgeoisie and the people is handled as a contradiction among the people. These two exploiting classes are forced to accept transformation by different methods, but their relations with the worker and the peasant are still based on class opposition. In socialist production, the laboring people, occupying a dominant position, are the masters in the socialist relations of production. Through persistent and resolute struggle, the working class and the poor and lower-middle peasants will gradually transform the majority of these two exploiting classes into self-supporting laborers after a long period of reeducation through labor.

The working class and the toiling people had the same painful experience of exploitation and oppression in the old society. Under socialism, employing the means of production owned by the state or by the collective, they all work, though in different roles, for the new society. They shoulder the common burden of reforming the exploiting class and share the same goal—to fight for the ideal of communism. Therefore, their basic interests are the same. In socialist production, the relations among the workers, the peasants, and the intellectuals that attach themselves to them, and the relations within each of the three groups, constitute daily developing relations among revolutionary comrades who share the same basic interests. This is a fundamental point which determines the socialist nature of the relations among the laboring people.

But is there a "state in which there are no differences" and no contradictions of any kind in the relations among the laboring people in socialist production? No! In socialist production, not only are there contradictions among the laboring people, but these contradictions will inevitably assume the character of class contradictions. This is due not only to the existence of the differences between worker and peasant, town and country, and mental and manual labor; it is also the case that the two laboring classes, workers and peasants, are still bound together by two different kinds of socialist ownership. Furthermore, the differences between the intelligentsia and the worker-peasant masses also assume the character of class difference. At the same time, class struggles between the proletariat and the bourgeoisie will inevitably be reflected among the laboring people. All issues of right and wrong, revolutionary and conservative, and advanced and backward bear the stamp of class. They are governed, regulated, and influenced by the contradiction between the proletariat and the bourgeoisie, which is the principal contradiction in society. The contradictions among the people will also reflect, to varying degrees, the contradictions and struggles between the socialist road and the capitalist road. Therefore, in the final analysis, the mutual relations among the laboring people are class relations.*

The immensely active role of mutual relations

Mutual relations between people in production are based on a corresponding system of ownership of the means of production. But mutual relations also play an immensely active role with respect to the two other aspects of the relations of production, namely, the form of ownership of the means of production and its corresponding relations of distribution.

The function of the mutual relations between people in production as regards the two other aspects of the relations of production was very apparent in the historical period preceding the emergence of socialist society. For example, in order to establish and consolidate the system of capitalist ownership and its relations of distribution, the bourgeoisie had to establish mutual relations between people based on capitalist principles, that is, relations in which the bourgeoisie ruled the worker. In refuting the reactionary arguments of the defenders of the American slave system who had claimed that [the work of supervision and management] "justified" exploitation and oppression, Marx pointed out, "Now, the wage-laborer, like the slave, must have a master who puts him to work and rules over him."[8] If the capitalists and their agents did not wield absolute powers of domination over the worker and if they could not compel the worker to work according to their will, then capitalist exploitation would not materialize and the system of capitalist ownership and capitalist relations of distribution, in which "the laborer does not reap and the reaper does not labor," could never be consolidated and developed. Therefore, the bourgeoisie pays a great deal of attention to the establishment and con-

---

* The revolutionary forces grouped around Mao continued to deepen the analysis of the nature of class relations and the sources and centers of power of a new bourgeoisie under socialism. See the appendix to this chapter and the Introduction for further discussion.

solidation of the subordinate position of the worker to capital, in order to consolidate and develop capitalist ownership and distribution.

In socialist society, the transformation of mutual relations is also an important link in the transformation of the relations of production. When this link is grasped and continually improved, the implications are enormous for consolidating and perfecting the system of socialist ownership and the relations of socialist distribution, and consequently for promoting the development of social productive forces.

The historical experience of the dictatorship of the proletariat, nationally and internationally, tells us that whether the socialist system progresses or retrogresses is tightly bound up with whether or not the mutual relations between people can be adjusted. When bourgeois right is restricted under the conditions of proletarian dictatorship, and the communist elements are promoted, making it possible to gradually establish mutual relations between people on the basis of socialist principles, the activism and creativity of the laborers can be more fully developed, the socialist orientation of enterprises can be more solidly ensured, the system of socialist ownership can be further consolidated, and the relations of distribution can be further perfected. When bourgeois right is strengthened and expanded, giving free play to capitalist money relations, capitalist labor relations, and capitalist relations of competition, and making it possible for bourgeois elements to violate and sabotage socialist mutual relations, the position of the masses as masters will be threatened and their socialist activism will be suppressed and inhibited. As a result, socialist ownership and relations of distribution will be damaged—indeed, they may even degenerate and change their nature.

Mutual relations, gradually established on the basis of public ownership of the means of production and in accordance with socialist principles, are not confined to one enterprise. They encompass all enterprises, all economic sectors, the system of ownership by the whole people, and the system of collective ownership. Mutual relations between people are manifested in interenterprise activities, such as cooperation in production and exchanges of advanced experience and advanced technology. The development of such mutual links and exchanges in production, involving coordinated leadership and planning among enterprises and sectors, embodies the superiority of the system of socialist public ownership. But cooperation among socialist enterprises must often take the form of commodity exchange and comply with the principle of equal exchange—wherein lies bourgeois right and the soil that engenders capitalism. Only by restricting this kind of bourgeois right under the dictatorship of the proletariat can the proletariat promote the consolidation and development of socialist ownership, fully mobilize the forces of various economic sectors, fully tap production potentialities, and promote the rapid development of social productive forces.

The step-by-step improvement of mutual relations is of great importance with respect to the consolidation of the relations of production and the development of social productive forces. It deserves our full attention. After the establishment of the system of socialist public ownership, the issue of mutual relations must be continually and painstakingly resolved.

CONSOLIDATE AND DEVELOP SOCIALIST MUTUAL RELATIONS IN THE COURSE OF STRUGGLE

Develop relations of mutual support and mutual promotion between industry and agriculture

Viewed from the perspective of social production as a whole, rather than from the standpoint of a particular enterprise, mutual relations are primarily manifested as relations between industry and agriculture. Industry and agriculture are the two basic sectors of material production. Socialist ownership by the whole people, which is dominant in industry, and socialist collective ownership by working people, which is dominant in agriculture, are two kinds of socialist ownership. From the standpoint of class relations, this economic structure is a relationship between worker and peasant. This class relationship is fundamentally different from the relationship between the laboring class and the exploiting class: it is the relation of a worker-peasant alliance in which basic interests are identical and leadership is in the hands of the working class.

After basic victory in the sphere of ownership had been won in China's socialist revolution, Chairman Mao pointed out: "Relations between production and exchange in accordance with socialist principles are still being gradually established in various departments of our economy and more and more appropriate forms are being sought."[9] The interrelations among various economic sectors are primarily interrelations between industry and agriculture and, consequently, interrelations between worker and peasant. The worker and the peasant are both masters of the means of production. The worker labors in enterprises under the system of ownership by the whole people. The peasant labors in enterprises under collective ownership. The worker and the peasant must trade with each other so that social production can be carried on.

In socialist society, the worker and the peasant constitute an industrial army in socialist construction. Their relationship as revolutionary comrades in production is a daily developing one of mutual support and mutual promotion based on the system of socialist public ownership. In the production and exchange processes, the worker produces various agricultural machines, chemical fertilizers, insecticides, and industrial products for daily use in the countryside in support of the development of agricultural production and the improvement of the livelihood of the peasant. The peasant produces food grain, raw materials, and various agricultural and sideline products. Furthermore, in line with the rate of growth of labor productivity in agriculture, the peasant supplies an appropriate amount of labor power in support of the development of industrial production, satisfies the material requirements of industrial production, and helps ensure the livelihood of the urban population. Under the leadership of the working class, mutual support and mutual promotion between the worker and the peasant are in accord with the basic interests of these two classes and constitute a powerful force for consolidating the worker-peasant alliance and promoting socialist economic development.

In addition to the direct contribution to state accumulation of finances through tax payments,* the exchange activities between worker and peasant under the two kinds of socialist ownership primarily take the form of commodity exchanges of industrial and agricultural products. Therefore, even though their basic interests are the same, there may also arise some contradictions relating to matters of quantity, variety, quality, and price in industrial and agricultural product exchanges, as well as contradictions relating to the proportions of agricultural output to be marketed and to be retained by the peasant and the tax burdens on the peasant.

The relations between worker and peasant in socialist production are governed, regulated, and influenced by the principal contradiction

* An agricultural tax levied on the normal yield of land in the collective economy and industrial taxes applied to enterprises in the state economy contributed to state revenues. There was no personal income tax in revolutionary China.

between the proletariat and the bourgeoisie. The working class (through the Communist Party) must lead the peasant to establish, consolidate, and develop the socialist collective economy, to restrict bourgeois right in commodity exchange, to consolidate the worker-peasant alliance, and to consolidate the dictatorship of the proletariat. The bourgeoisie always tries hard to expand bourgeois right in commodity exchange, to induce the peasant to take the capitalist road, to undermine the worker-peasant alliance, and to overthrow the dictatorship of the proletariat. Therefore, the process of developing worker-peasant relations in socialist production cannot but be the process of struggle between the proletariat and the bourgeoisie. So, in handling the exchange of industrial and agricultural products, we cannot only see the relations between things; more important, we need to see the relations of worker and peasant and see the struggle of the proletariat and the bourgeoisie to win over the peasantry. The proletariat must ceaselessly conduct socialist education among the peasant masses, criticize revisionism, criticize capitalist tendencies, and lead them firmly in taking the socialist road. At the same time, the proletariat must also practice strict socialist management over the exchange activities between these two big sectors, that is, industry and agriculture. The proletariat must pay special attention to capitalist forces in the city and countryside that are using the channels of commodity production and exchange through money to connive together, to sabotage the socialist economy, and to undermine the worker-peasant alliance. The new bourgeois elements and those who want to use bourgeois right to develop capitalism must be hit hard in accordance with the party's policies.

Promote the "Lung-chiang style,"* develop relations of socialist cooperation

Another important aspect of mutual relations between people in socialist production involves the relations among enterprises, among sectors, and among regions. These relations are mainly manifested as relations of socialist cooperation among enterprises, sectors, and regions.

Marx said: "When numerous laborers work together side by side, whether in one and the same process, or in different but connected

---

* Lung-chiang was a model brigade in Fukien province. Its collective efforts to battle floods were chronicled in the model revolutionary opera "Song of Lung-chiang."

processes, they are said to cooperate, or to work in cooperation."[10] The character and scope of this sort of cooperation will vary greatly according to different relations of production.

Under conditions of capitalist private ownership of the means of production, cooperation in capitalist production is mainly confined to the narrow scope of one enterprise or one monopoly capitalist group. At the level of capitalist society as a whole, it is impossible to develop systematic cooperation among the various sectors of production and various enterprises divided by private ownership. Even certain relations of cooperation established through contracts are extremely unstable and are often disrupted.

Socialist cooperation based on public ownership of the means of production can be developed not only within one enterprise but also in a planned and organized manner over the whole of society—among different enterprises, sectors, and regions. "When one plant participates, a hundred plants cooperate. When each plant makes one, a hundred plants form into a production line." Socialist cooperation creates a new productive force. Such cooperation is conducive to the development of "one specialty and many abilities" in enterprises, thus further contributing to increasing labor productivity. It is conducive to concentrating manpower, material resources, and finances to complete production and construction projects which one enterprise, one sector, or one region could not undertake or complete alone. It is conducive to concentrating strength for a short period to overcome weak links in the development of the national economy, thus stimulating rapid development of the whole national economy.

While promoting the communist style, it is also necessary to adhere to socialist principles. These are the principles that developing socialist cooperation must follow. There are no basic conflicts of interest among the constituent parts of the socialist economy. Socialist cooperation requires that proletarian politics be put in command. It requires the breaking down of boundaries among enterprises, among sectors, and among regions, concern for the whole situation, growth in the face of difficulties, and consideration for other people. Socialist cooperation also requires strict compliance with supply contracts, cooperative coordination so that plan assignments can be completed, and adoption of effective measures to guarantee the completion of assignments in accordance with stipulated variety, specifications, quality, quantity, and schedule. These cooperative relations are fundamentally opposed to capitalist mutual relations based on mutual deception, competition, and capitalist departmentalism. However, these relations of cooperation can only take shape and develop step-by-step through struggle. This is so for two basic reasons. First, owing to the existence of the commodity system, cooperation among enterprises, among departments, and among regions is by necessity bound up with exchange through money, and must take place in accordance with the principles of exchange of equivalents; hence, objectively, there exists the boundary of "you and me." Second, and relatedly, departmentalism, an ideological reflection of the system of private ownership, will exist, in varying degrees, in socialist society for a long time to come. "Lack of consideration for the whole and complete indifference to other departments, localities and people are characteristics of a selfish departmentalist."[11] For these two reasons, the following erroneous concepts and actions will invariably assert themselves in socialist cooperative relations: reckoning economic accounts at the expense of political accounts; paying attention only to partial interests and not to overall interests, even to the extent of benefiting oneself at the expense of others; disregarding the state's unified economic plan by cutting corners; and so forth. The appearance of these problems in forging socialist cooperation is a reflection of the struggle between the two classes, the two roads, and the two lines. The process of development of socialist cooperation is a process of struggle against bourgeois influences, especially bourgeois departmentalism.

The *Charter of the Anshan Iron and Steel Company* is a compass for handling mutual relations within enterprises

The socialist enterprises (in industry, agriculture, communications and transportation, commerce, and all production and circulation departments) are the basic units of human material production and exchange. Within these enterprises, there exist a multiplicity of mutual relations between people in production. With regard to the laboring people, mutual relations are chiefly of two categories: there are the relations between leadership and the masses, and there are the relations between management personnel and technicians (mental laborers), on the one hand, and the workers and the peasants (manual laborers), on the other. The correct handling of these two categories of mutual relations involves creating "a political situation in which there are both centralism and democracy, both discipline and freedom, both unity of will and personal ease of mind and liveliness."[12] This is an important issue in consolidating and developing socialist relations of production and in improving socialist enterprise management. (In enterprises, there are also the relations between the worker-peasant laboring people and the two exploiting classes. These relations have already been analyzed.)

The socialist enterprise is an enterprise of the working class and the laboring people. The working class and the laboring people are responsible for leading the enterprise through their representatives. Thus arises the issue of the relations between the leadership and the masses. Although the leadership personnel and the masses in the enterprise hold different jobs, socialist public ownership of the means of production demands that they be "comrades-in-arms in the same trench" who share the heavy duty of properly managing the enterprise and who labor for a common revolutionary goal. Workers on the Shanghai wharfs put it nicely: "Though jobs are different in revolution, our thinking must be in unison." These words point the way to improving the relations between the leadership and the masses in the socialist enterprises.

In enterprises, it is also necessary to have some people in charge of various management and technical jobs. And thus arises the issue of the relations between the management personnel and technicians and the worker-peasant laboring masses. There are two categories of China's management personnel and technicians. One consists of management personnel and technicians left over from the old society. With the exception of a few reactionaries who are hostile to socialist society, the great majority of them love their country, love our People's Republic, and are willing to serve the people and the socialist state. Another category consists of those intellectuals trained by the proletariat through struggle and through the development of socialist revolution and socialist construction. Though some of them may have been poisoned by the revisionist line in education, and their world outlook must still be continually transformed, the great majority are willing to integrate with the worker-peasant masses and make contributions to the socialist and communist cause. Therefore, in socialist society, the relations between leadership and the masses, and between management personnel and technicians and the worker-peasant masses, are also daily developing relations among revolutionary comrades who share common interests.

But the division of labor in socialist enterprises between the leadership and the masses, and between the management personnel and technicians and the direct producers, still reflects the division of labor of the old society and is a manifestation of the still-existing differences between mental and manual labor. After the establishment of the system of public ownership of the means of production, all laborers become masters of enterprises. But those who are carrying out specialized leadership and management functions are mainly mental laborers, divorced from production, while the broad masses are mainly physical laborers. Lenin described the opposition between mental and manual labor as "one of the principal sources of modern *social* inequality."[13] Even though socialist society has eliminated the antagonism between mental and manual labor, it still reproduces the basic differences between mental and manual labor, and it is inevitable that the mutual relations between people carry with them bourgeois right.

Under these conditions, if the leadership, management, and technical personnel responsible for organizing and guiding production do not regularly participate in collective productive labor, they will become divorced from the laboring masses and subject to the corrosive influence of bourgeois thinking, and will develop contradictions with the laboring masses. These contradictions often reflect, to varying degrees, the contradictions between the proletariat and the bourgeoisie. For example, some leadership cadre, management personnel, and technicians under the ideological sway of bourgeois right neither treat the masses nor regard themselves with the correct attitude. They think that "the leadership is brighter" and do not treat the worker-peasant masses as masters of the enterprise. They resort to restrictive measures and seek to convert relations among revolutionary comrades into relations of domination and subordination. These are all manifestations of the lingering poison of the revisionist line and reflect, to varying degrees, the contradictions and struggles between the bourgeoisie and the proletariat. If these contradictions are allowed to develop, and bourgeois right is not restricted but allowed to expand, then socialist mutual relations will degenerate into capitalist relations, and socialist enterprises will gradually change color.

The *Charter of the Anshan Iron and Steel Company,* formulated personally by Chairman Mao, and his series of instructions, such as "Management Is Also Socialist Education,"[14] constitute the compass for restricting bourgeois right, eradicating the ideology of bourgeois right, gradually narrowing the basic differences between mental and manual labor, and correctly handling the mutual relations between people in socialist enterprises. The basic spirit of the *Anshan Charter* is to keep proletarian politics firmly in command; strengthen Party leadership; launch vigorous mass movements; institute "the two participations, one reform, and three-in-one combination" (cadre participation in manual labor and worker participation in management, reform of irrational and outdated rules and regulations, and establishment of three-in-one combinations of workers, leading cadres, and technical personnel); and go full steam ahead with technical innovations and technical revolution. Keeping proletarian politics firmly in command and strengthening Party leadership are basic principles for the correct handling of mutual relations. Under the guidance of these principles, the determined and thoroughgoing implementation of the "two participations, one reform, and three-in-one combination" will allow the relations between the leadership and the masses and between the managerial and technical personnel and the worker-peasant laboring masses to develop steadily as relations of revolutionary comrades.

The participation of cadres in productive labor is a major measure of fundamental importance under the socialist system. It is also an important element of the proper handling of socialist mutual relations. Chairman Mao pointed out: "It is necessary to maintain the system of cadre participation in collective productive labor. The cadres of our Party and state are ordinary workers and not overlords sitting on the backs of the people. By taking part in collective productive labor, the cadres maintain extensive, constant and close ties with the working people. This is a major measure of fundamental importance for a socialist system; it helps to overcome bureaucracy and to prevent revisionism and dogmatism."[15] Chairman Mao expounded this infallible truth on the basis of summing up the historical experience and lessons of the international communist movement. Those cadres who can voluntarily and regularly participate in collective productive labor are generally more conscious in restricting bourgeois right and have a higher degree of self-awareness. They show concern and affection for the masses, humbly listen to the call of the masses, are receptive to criticism and supervision from the masses, and can keep firmly to the socialist orientation of the enterprise. They are more familiar with production conditions and seldom blindly issue orders. There is a song that some women textile workers sing that describes the transformation of a leadership cadre in their factory after she participated in collective productive labor: "In the past, she never visited the workshop; now she comes to the side of the machine to ask for advice. In the past, things were delayed; now they are solved immediately. In the past, only big reports were issued; now she says what she thinks in the workshop. In the past, she was called a petty bureaucrat; now she is treated like a sister." The fact is that this kind of leadership and the same kind of managerial and technical personnel are welcomed by the masses. Even if there are contradictions between them, they can be correctly resolved in good time.

The participation of the worker-peasant masses in management is a requirement of socialist relations of production. It is the masses' right under the socialist system. Only by insisting on worker-peasant participation in management can the position of the laboring masses as masters in the enterprises be defended and consolidated. The belief that only a few bourgeois "experts" and "authorities" can manage enterprises, and that they must be relied on while the worker-peasant masses must be suppressed, will surely undermine socialist mutual relations and lead, ultimately, to the degeneration of socialist enterprises. In order to perfect socialist mutual relations and consolidate and develop socialist public ownership, "we must at all costs break the old, *absurd,* savage, despicable and disgusting prejudice that only the so-called 'upper classes,' only the rich, and those who have gone through the school of the rich, are capable of administering the state and directing the organizational development of socialist society." [16]

Participation of the masses in management primarily refers to the participation of the direct producers, the worker-peasant masses, in management. The masses who participate in enterprise management must not only direct production, technical innovation and revolution, and accounting; more important, they must also aid and supervise the cadres in thoroughly implementing the Party line and its general and specific policies. In the Great Proletarian Cultural Revolution, the workers employed the "four big weapons" of big contending [outpourings of opinion], big blossoming [airing views fully], big-character posters, and big debates in order to take part in the management of the enterprises. The representatives of the worker-peasant masses participated directly in the work of the revolutionary committees that manage enterprises. They were not divorced from production, but they still performed their supervisory work. This is a new development in the participation of the masses in management.

The implementation of the "three-in-one combination" of the masses, the cadres, and the technicians in the struggle for production and scientific experiment is a means of solving major technical problems of production. It is not only conducive to stimulating technical innovation on a mass basis but also conducive to accustoming the intellectuals to labor and the worker-peasant masses to systematic knowledge—thus narrowing the basic differences between mental and manual labor, and further perfecting and developing socialist mutual relations.

The reform of irrational and outdated rules, regulations, and systems in enterprise management is another aspect of the unceasing adjustment and transformation of socialist mutual relations. Any kind of social production will require certain regulations and systems.* But the type of regulations and systems instituted is determined by the production relations in society. Lenin sharply pointed this out with respect to enterprise management in capitalist society, "in whose interest it is to administer while plundering and to plunder while administering."[17] The regulations and systems of capitalist enterprise aim at one thing only: how to better restrict the freedom of the worker and how to extract more surplus value from the worker. The endless rules and regulations in capitalist enterprise are all designed to safeguard, and are bounded by, capitalist relations of production. Under socialism, "systems have to be favorable to the masses."[18] This is the most fundamental difference between socialist regulations and systems and capitalist regulations and systems. To say that systems must be favorable to the masses means that such systems have to be favorable to the masses' role as masters, to the improvement and development of mutual rela-

---

* Systems refer to systems of management and production control and the corresponding chains of responsibility and operational rules.

tions between people in the enterprise, to the exercise of socialist initiative by the masses, and to the development of the three revolutionary movements of class struggle, the struggle for production, and scientific experiment. Regulations and systems which are favorable to the masses will certainly be favorable to the development of production as they will unleash the activism of the masses. Under the influence of the revisionist line of Liu Shao-chi and Lin Piao, the regulations and systems of some enterprises often restricted the masses. The criticism of the workers was that "there are too many rules and regulations and they are created either for the purpose of punishment or coercion." Under good leadership, the masses should be mobilized to carefully revise the rules and regulations that are irrational, restrictive, and detrimental to production, and that sow discord and alienation among workers. Meanwhile, on the basis of the experience acquired in practice, a new set of healthy and rational systems and regulations which correspond to the requirements of socialist mutual relations and the development of the productive forces should be established.

The immense influence of the superstructure on the formation of mutual relations

People's position in production and the nature of their mutual relations in production are determined by the system of ownership of the means of production. But the superstructure also reacts on the position and mutual relations of people in production, influencing both their form and development. In fact, without the active role of the superstructure, the position and mutual relations of people in production will not be able to cohere, to consolidate, and to develop. The ruling class of any society invariably uses the power of the superstructure to safeguard, by all means at its disposal, the system of ownership that has been established and to consolidate and develop the position and mutual relations of people in production and the corresponding relations of distribution. This is a general law.

Take capitalist society. The bourgeoisie of any capitalist country uses the power of the superstructure to establish and extend by force its domination of wage labor as expressed in the capital-labor relationship. Marx pointed out that to establish and extend the domination of capital over labor, the newly emerging bourgeoisie "wants and uses the power of the state."[19] From the end of the fifteenth century to the first half of the nineteenth century, the bourgeoisie in England resorted to violent measures, the most prominent of which was the "enclosure movement,"[20] to evict a large number of poor peasants from the English countryside. These now destitute and uprooted peasants drifted into the urban areas only to become objects of domination by capital. However, the peasants who migrated to the urban areas often preferred to become tramps rather than to surrender to the arbitrary rule of capital over labor. To coerce these ruined peasants into the factory, the British bourgeoisie passed punitive laws against vagabonds and tramps; they were "whipped, branded, tortured by laws grotesquely terrible, into the discipline necessary for the wage system."[21] Look how cruel were the means used by the bourgeoisie to establish and develop mutual relations between people in which capital dominated labor.

This relationship of domination by capital over labor was established through force, and it is a relationship that can only be destroyed by force. In socialist countries under proletarian dictatorship, this relationship was destroyed precisely by means of force.

Because socialist relations of production can only be established under the dictatorship of the proletariat, the reaction of the socialist superstructure on the socialist economic base is especially apparent. Socialist mutual relations are determined by the system of socialist public ownership. They are also formed and subject to development under the immense influence of the socialist superstructure. If we thought that socialist mutual relations would automatically take shape and develop with the mere establishment of socialist public ownership, we would be seriously mistaken.

In the realm of socialist mutual relations, the relationship of the working class and other laboring people to the bourgeoisie and other exploiting classes is one of ruler to ruled, transformer to transformed. Given their class nature, the exploiters will not voluntarily accept the position of being ruled and transformed. The proletariat is capable of compelling some of them into accepting socialist transformation because it controls the powerful state machinery. Without state power as a precondition, the rule over, and the transformation of, the bourgeoisie is impossible.

As far as the relations among the laboring people are concerned, if their mutual relations as revolutionary comrades are to develop steadily in accordance with socialist principles, it is necessary to rely on, and grasp the role of, the socialist superstructure. The socialist superstructure enables us to educate and transform ourselves so that we can free ourselves from the influence of reactionaries at home and abroad. Chairman Mao pointed out: "The people's state protects the people. Only when the people have such a state can they educate and remold themselves by democratic methods on a country-wide scale, with everyone taking part, and shake off the influence of domestic and foreign reactionaries."[22] Only by persisting in waging socialist revolution in the superstructure, using proletarian ideology to gradually overcome bourgeois ideology, and by ceaselessly uprooting capitalist traditions and influences in the sphere of mutual relations between people can revolutionary and comradely relations among the laboring people steadily develop. Only on this basis can the way be cleared for the formation and development of the mutual relations of socialist production.

To sum up, the process of formation and development of socialist mutual relations is a prolonged process of political and ideological struggle between the two classes. To safeguard and develop socialist mutual relations, the proletariat must firmly adhere to the basic Party line for the entire historical period of socialism. After a basic victory has been won in the socialist revolution in the sphere of ownership of the means of production, the proletariat must continue to penetratingly carry out socialist revolution in the political and ideological spheres, root out bourgeois ideology and foster proletarian ideology, and fight self and criticize revisionism. This is a fundamental issue for the consolidation and perfecting of socialist mutual relations. If we thought that after the establishment of the system of socialist public ownership the exploiting classes would somehow vanish, and if we departed from the fundamental standpoint of the proletariat's opposition to the bourgeoisie in explaining socialist mutual relations, then our thinking would run counter to the basic line of the Party and we would fall prey to the "dying out of class struggle" argument. If we did not insist on carrying out socialist revolution in the superstructure and if we allowed bourgeois ideology to run rampant, then socialist mutual relations would degenerate into capitalist mutual relations, and the system of socialist public ownership would disintegrate. The restoration of capitalism in the Soviet Union teaches us, by way of negative example, to understand the scientific truth of Marxism in this regard.

91

Major Study References

Mao, "On the Correct Handling of Contradictions Among the People," *SR*

Mao, "Speech at the Chinese Communist Party's National Conference on Propaganda Work," *SR*

Notes

1. Lenin, "The Three Sources and Three Component Parts of Marxism," in *CW* 19 (1973), p. 26.
2. Engels, "Karl Marx, *A Contribution to the Critique of Political Economy*," in *MESW* 1, p. 514.
3. Mao, "Speech at the Chinese Communist Party's National Conference on Propaganda Work," in *SR*, p. 481.
4. Ibid., p. 480.
5. Lenin, "A Great Beginning," in *CW* 29 (1974), p. 421.
6. Mao, "Talks at the Yenan Forum on Literature and Art," in *SW* 3, p. 90.
7. Many contemporary Soviet revisionist cultural works reveal the essence of the "comrades, friends, and brothers" fallacy championed by Soviet revisionism. For example, in a play entitled "The Outsider," the major character, a Soviet revisionist Party member and an engineer of a certain enterprise, went to a foundry to transform its "backward appearance." He arrogantly roared to the workers: "We are the leaders. Our hands do not do anything. We work with words and our brains." He ordered the foremen to keep a close watch on the workers, to "keep an eye on them and grab them by their throats." "Whoever disobeys an order should be punished by deducting half of his bonus." "Hit them with rubles." In the Soviet Union, the laboring people are subject to cruel exploitation and oppression from a new bureaucrat-monopoly bourgeoisie. This is what is meant when the Soviet revisionists trumpet relations of "comrades, friends, and brothers."
8. Marx, *Capital* 3, p. 386.
9. Mao, "Correct Handling of Contradictions," in *SR*, p. 445.
10. Marx, *Capital* 1, p. 308.
11. Mao, "Rectify the Party's Style of Work," in *SW* 3, p. 46.

12. Mao, noted in *Tenth Party Congress Documents*, p. 55.
13. Lenin, *State and Revolution*, p. 114.
14. Mao, quoted in Writing Group of the Kirin Revolutionary Committee, "Socialist Construction and Class Struggle in the Field of Economics," *Peking Review*, 17 April 1970 (No. 16), p. 10.
15. Mao, quoted in CPC, "Khrushchev's Phony Communism," in *Polemic*, p. 474.
16. Lenin, "How to Organize Competition?", in *CW* 26 (1972), p. 409.
17. Ibid.
18. Mao, quoted in *Renmin Ribao (People's Daily)*, 31 May 1972.
19. Marx, *Capital* 1, p. 698.
20. The "enclosure movement" was one of the important means of primitive capitalist accumulation. At the end of the fifteenth century, the emergence of England's wool-spinning industry had the effect of pushing wool prices ever upward. Sheep farming became a very profitable business. The landed aristocracy and the bourgeoisie of England colluded to forcibly evict the peasant from the land, and then enclosed it to raise sheep. Houses within the enclosure were totally destroyed. The peasants were made homeless and reduced to being beggars and tramps. In the eighteenth century, the British bourgeois government, by means of a series of "enclosure acts" concocted by the Parliament, supported the violent plundering of the peasant by the bourgeoisie. The peasants continually resisted and started many rebellions against the enclosure movement.
21. Marx, *Capital* 1, p. 688.
22. Mao, "On the People's Democratic Dictatorship," in *SW* 4, p. 418.

Appendix

CAPITALIST-ROADERS ARE
THE BOURGEOISIE INSIDE THE PARTY*

by Fang Kang

In the great struggle to criticize Teng Hsiao-ping [Deng Xiaoping] and beat back the Right deviationist wind to reverse correct verdicts, Chairman Mao has pointed out: "With the socialist revolution they themselves come under fire. At the time of the co-operative transformation of agriculture there were people in the Party who opposed it, and when it comes to criticizing bourgeois right, they resent it. You are making the socialist revolution, and yet don't know where the bourgeoisie is. It is right in the Communist Party—those in power taking the capitalist road. The capitalist-roaders are still on the capitalist road." This scientific thesis has incisively laid bare the bourgeois essence of the capitalist-roaders in the Party, further indicated the main target of the revolutionary struggle throughout the historical period of socialism, and defended and developed the great Marxist-Leninist theory on class struggle and the dictatorship of the proletariat. It is a powerful ideological weapon for us to persist in continuing the revolution under the dictatorship of the proletariat and to combat and prevent revisionism.

---

* This article was not part of *The Shanghai Textbook*. It is excerpted from *Peking Review* (14), 18 June 1976.

An Important Feature of Class Struggle in the Historical Period of Socialism

The emergence of capitalist-roaders—the bourgeoisie inside the Party—is an important feature of class struggle in the historical period of socialism and is closely linked with the change in class relations under the dictatorship of the proletariat. In the period of democratic revolution, the principal contradiction in our society was the contradiction between the proletariat and the masses of the people on the one hand and imperialism, feudalism and bureaucrat-capitalism on the other. At that time, there were also opportunists, revisionists and chieftains of the various opportunist lines inside the Party; they were agents of the bourgeoisie and other exploiting classes in the Party, but for the bourgeoisie as a whole, they were merely its appendages. Since the landlord and comprador-capitalist classes held the reins of government at that time, the nucleus and the main force of the bourgeoisie, its headquarters and its chief political representatives were outside and not inside the Party.

After great victory had been won in the new-democratic revolution, the rule of imperialism, feudalism and bureaucrat-capitalism was overthrown and the proletariat led the people of the whole country in seizing the political power of the state. Since then China has entered the historical period of socialist revolution and the contradiction between the proletariat and the bourgeoisie has become the principal contradiction in society. Since our Party has become the ruling party, the struggle between Chairman Mao's proletarian revolutionary line and the bourgeois and revisionist line determines not only the nature of our Party but also the character and prospects of our country as a whole. From that time on, our struggle against the bourgeoisie both inside and outside the Party has gradually developed in depth in all spheres, centering around the basic question of whether or not to carry out the socialist revolution. The *san fan* and *wu fan* movements,* the socialist transformation of the ownership of the means of production and the

---

* These were two movements carried out between December 1951 and June 1952. The first was the anti-"three evils," aimed at corruption, waste, and bureaucracy in the Communist Party and government organs. The second was the anti-"five evils" movement aimed at corruption and intrigue by the national capitalists.

anti-Rightist struggle* were all major struggles between the proletariat and the bourgeoisie since the founding of New China. In these struggles, the bourgeoisie outside the Party still had some strength to engage in a trial of strength with the proletariat and was still able to nominate its own protagonists; but even then a complicated situation had already developed in which the bourgeoisie inside and outside the Party responded to and colluded with each other. In their unbridled attacks on the Party, the bourgeoisie and other exploiting classes outside the Party had the support of the bourgeoisie inside the Party and banked on its help. Through the two-line struggle in the Party, we brought to light the activities of the bourgeoisie inside the Party against the socialist revolution and criticized its revisionist line, thereby ensuring the victories of the various major campaigns in the socialist transformation.

With the continuous deepening of the socialist revolution, the bourgeoisie outside the Party which is in a position of being ruled has lost its means of production economically and met with one defeat after another on the political and ideological fronts; consequently, its strength has been gradually weakened. If during the bourgeois Rightists' attack on the Party they still had the so-called "Chang-Lo alliance"** playing the commander's role, then after the anti-Rightist struggle it has become much more difficult for the bourgeoisie outside the Party to openly muster its forces to wage an all-round struggle against the proletariat, subvert the dictatorship of the proletariat and restore capitalism.

The principal contradiction in the entire historical period of socialism is the contradiction between the proletariat and the bourgeoisie. With the balance of class forces having undergone a change, the class struggle between the proletariat and the bourgeoisie finds expression in the Party in an increasingly profound and acute way. Thus the capitalist-roaders emerge in the Party as the force at the core of the bourgeoisie as a whole and become the main danger in subverting the pro-

---

*   In 1957, the Chinese Communist Party waged struggle against "bourgeois rightists" outside the Party who took advantage of the Party's rectification movement at the time to launch major attacks on the socialist system.

**   Chang Po-chun and Lo Lung-chi were non-Party ministers in the Chinese government associated with the bourgeois rightist forces outside the Party. They had plotted to topple the Communist Party and overthrow proletarian rule.

letarian dictatorship and restoring capitalism. While carrying out the socialist revolution, we must not only see that the old bourgeoisie and its intellectuals still exist in society and that large numbers of the petty bourgeoisie are still in the course of remoulding their ideology, but we must be especially aware of the bourgeoisie hidden inside the Party, that is, those Party persons in power taking the capitalist road. Only by waging a resolute struggle against the capitalist-roaders in the Party like Liu Shao-chi, Lin Piao and Teng Hsiao-ping and persisting in directing our revolution at the bourgeoisie inside the Party can victory be ensured in the struggle against the bourgeoisie and the capitalist forces in society at large; only thus can it be said that the main target of the socialist revolution has been really grasped. Anyone who fails to understand that the bourgeoisie is right in the Communist Party is not a sober-minded proletarian revolutionary.

In summing up the historical experience of the Paris Commune, Engels pointed out that after the establishment of the dictatorship of the proletariat, it is necessary to guard "against this transformation of the state and the organs of the state from servants of society into masters of society" "in pursuance of their own special interests." (Introduction by Frederick Engels to Karl Marx's *The Civil War in France*. [Peking: Foreign Languages Press, 1974], p. 15.) After the victory of the October Revolution, Lenin analysed the actual social conditions in the Soviet Union and clearly pointed out that a new bourgeoisie existed in the country and that it was arising from among the Soviet government employees and the small producers. In the light of the historical lesson of how the Soviet Union has turned revisionist and the practical experience in exercising the dictatorship of the proletariat in China, Chairman Mao has put forward the brilliant thesis that the bourgeoisie "is right in the Communist Party—those in power taking the capitalist road." This is an important development of Marxism-Leninism. Over the last 20 years and more following the founding of the People's Republic of China, Chairman Mao has not only made a profound analysis of the bourgeoisie inside the Party from a theoretical angle, but has also in practice led us in carrying out repeated struggles against it. The chieftains of the revisionist line Kao Kang, Peng Teh-huai, Liu Shao-chi, Lin Piao and Teng Hsiao-ping were all commanders of the bourgeoisie inside the Party, and the several major two-line struggles in the socialist period have been struggles waged by the proletariat against the bourgeoisie inside the Party with them as the ringleaders. It is precisely in the course of these struggles that our socialist system of the dictatorship of the proletariat has been continually consolidated and developed.

Class Nature of Capitalist-Roaders

Chairman Mao has pointed out in his *Analysis of the Classes in Chinese Society*: "To distinguish real friends from real enemies, we must make a general analysis of the economic status of the various classes in Chinese society and of their respective attitudes toward the revolution." It is, therefore, extremely necessary for us to apply the Marxist scientific method to reveal, both politically and economically, the bourgeois nature of the capitalist-roaders so that we can clearly see that the bourgeoisie is right in the Communist Party.

The most essential political characteristic of the capitalist-roaders in the Party is that they push the revisionist line and cling to the capitalist road. In analysing them, we must first and foremost grasp this characteristic and, from the viewpoint of political line, get a clear understanding of their essence. It is on the basis of a common effort to push the revisionist line that the capitalist-roaders form a political faction in the Party in a vain attempt to restore capitalism. And the chieftains of the revisionist line that emerged on many occasions in the past were all general representatives of this line. These chieftains, like Liu Shao-chi, Lin Piao and Teng Hsiao-ping, all held a very large portion of the Party and state power, so they were in a position to recruit deserters and renegades, form cliques to pursue their own selfish interests and set up bourgeois headquarters, turn the instruments of the dictatorship of the proletariat into those of the dictatorship of the bourgeoisie, and hoodwink for a time a number of people who lack an understanding of the real situation and do not have a high level of consciousness, inveigling them into following their revisionist line. They were more ruthless and dangerous than the bourgeoisie outside the Party in their efforts to restore capitalism. The revisionist line pushed by the capitalist-roaders in the Party represents in a concentrated way the interests of the old and new bourgeoisie and all other exploiting classes, and this determines the bourgeois nature of the capitalist-roaders. The socialist period is "a period of struggle between moribund capitalism and nascent communism." (Lenin: *Economics and Politics in the Era of the Dictatorship of the Proletariat.*) It is beyond doubt that the capitalist-roaders as the bourgeoisie inside the Party are part of the declining bourgeoisie as a whole. Precisely because the bourgeoisie is a moribund and decadent class, its reactionary nature is all the more pronounced. "The rise to power of revisionism means the rise to power of the bourgeoisie." (Mao, quoted in Wang Hung-wen, "Report on the Revision of the Party Constitution," 10th Party Congress [1973], in Lotta, *And Mao Makes 5*, p. 96.) Bent on practising revisionism, Lin Piao went so far as to cook up the *Outline of Project "571"* and to launch a counter-revolutionary armed coup d'etat, while Teng Hsiao-ping who persisted in practising revisionism caused the counter-revolutionary political riot like the incident at Tien An Men Square. These soul-stirring facts of class struggle have bared in an extremely sharp and clear-cut manner the reactionary nature of the bourgeoisie inside the Party.

Economically, the reason why the capitalist-roaders are the bourgeoisie inside the Party is that they represent the decadent capitalist relations of production. In the socialist period, the proletariat wants to constantly transform those parts of the superstructure and the relations of production which are not in harmony with the socialist economic base and the productive forces and carry the socialist revolution through to the end. The capitalist-roaders in the Party, however, do everything possible to preserve those parts of the superstructure and the relations of production which hamper the development of the socialist economic base and the productive forces; their vain attempt is to restore capitalism.

If we examine the position of the capitalist-roaders in the Party in the relations of social production by following Lenin's teaching on the meaning of classes as expounded in his *A Great Beginning* and Chairman Mao's analysis in *On the Correct Handling of Contradictions Among the People* regarding classes and class struggle in socialist society after the basic completion of the socialist transformation of the ownership of the means of production, we will get a fairly clear understanding of their bourgeois nature. We can see from real life that once the leadership in certain units or departments was controlled by capitalist-roaders like Liu Shao-chi, Lin Piao and Teng Hsiao-ping, they would use the power in their hands to energetically push the revisionist line and turn the socialist mutual relations among people into capitalist relations between employers and employees; they would use legal and numerous illegal means to expand bourgeois right with respect to distribution and appropriate the fruits of other people's labour without compensation; and they would also take advantage of their position and power to dispose of state- or collectively-owned means of production and consumption, with the result that socialist ownership exists only in name but is actually turned into capitalist ownership under the control of the capitalist-roaders. In the final analysis, the revisionist line pushed by Liu Shao-chi, Lin Piao and Teng Hsiao-ping was designed to preserve the decadent and declining capitalist relations of production, to "cling to the bourgeois ideology of oppression and exploitation of the proletariat and to the capitalist system" and to serve the economic interests of the bourgeoisie as a whole, so as to drag our country back to those dark days of the semi-colonial and semi-feudal old China.*

Class and Historical Roots of the Emergence of Capitalist-Roaders

The emergence of capitalist-roaders—the bourgeoisie inside the Party—in the socialist period is by no means accidental but has deep class and historical roots. In the struggle to repulse the Right deviationist attempt to reverse correct verdicts, Chairman Mao has pointed out: "After the democratic revolution the workers and the poor and lower-middle peasants did not stand still, they want revolution. On the other hand, a number of Party members do not want to go forward; some have moved backward and opposed the revolution. Why? Because they have become high officials and want to protect the interests of high officials." This instruction of Chairman Mao's has stung the capitalist-roaders in the Party to the quick. The switchover from the democratic

---

* "The power to allocate and manage the means of production and the power to distribute products are expressed in a concentrated way as the power of political leadership. . . . As individuals, they [capitalist-roaders] may not necessarily own capital, run factories and operate banks like former capitalists, but their political line which energetically upholds the capitalist relations of production reflects in a concentrated way the economic interests and political aspirations of the bourgeoisie as a whole." (Chuang Lan, "Capitalist-Roaders Are the Representatives of the Capitalist Relations of Production," in Lotta, *And Mao Makes 5*, pp. 368, 371.)

101

revolution to the socialist revolution is a fundamental change in the course of which division is bound to take place within the revolutionary ranks. The workers and poor and lower-middle peasants want revolution and Chairman Mao's revolutionary line reflects their demand and guides the whole Party and the people throughout the country to continue to make the socialist revolution, but a number of people in the Party who cling to bourgeois democratic ideas and refuse to remould themselves do not want to go forward. In the eyes of these people, imperialism, feudalism and bureaucrat-capitalism, which were like three big mountains weighing down on the Chinese people, were overthrown while they themselves had gained enormous political and material benefits, and that meant the end of the revolution. Some of them whose revolutionary will had sagged failed to keep pace with the times; some others clung to the reactionary bourgeois stand and, in order to protect their own interests which are, in essence, those of the bourgeoisie as a whole, came out into the open to oppose the proletarian socialist revolution and the dictatorship of the proletariat, in a vain attempt to turn back the wheel of history and restore capitalism, and these people are none other than those Party persons in power taking the capitalist road. The arch unrepentant capitalist-roader in the Party Teng Hsiao-ping is just such a person, and turning from a bourgeois democrat into a capitalist-roader is the course he actually followed.

An important reason why the capitalist-roaders oppose the socialist revolution is that they are against restricting bourgeois right. Chairman Mao has pointed out: "Lenin spoke of building a bourgeois state without capitalists to safeguard bourgeois right. We ourselves have built just such a state, not much different from the old society: there are ranks and grades, eight grades of wages, distribution according to work, and exchange of equal values." Bourgeois right is inevitable in the socialist period and this birthmark left over from the old society cannot be eliminated overnight. But it must be restricted under the dictatorship of the proletariat, otherwise it would lead to capitalist restoration. Bourgeois right is an important economic basis for engendering the new bourgeoisie. Some people in the Party whose world outlook has not been thoroughly remoulded and who try hard to strengthen and expand bourgeois right are bound to turn step by step into capitalist-roaders, or members of the bourgeoisie. To expand bourgeois right is, in essence, to safeguard the interests of the bourgeoisie as a whole and to reinforce the social basis for restoring capitalism. That Teng Hsiao-ping was so resentful and panic-stricken when he heard that bourgeois right was being criticized was because bourgeois right is the lifeblood of the bourgeoisie inside the Party, and any restriction of bourgeois right means directing the revolution against it.

In the socialist period, what attitude one takes toward bourgeois right—to restrict it or expand it—is an important criterion for distinguishing whether one is continuing the revolution or is standing still or even opposing the revolution. On this issue, our struggle against the capitalist-roaders in the Party—a struggle between restriction and counter-restriction—will continue for a long time to come.

5

DEVELOP SOCIALIST PRODUCTION WITH GREATER, FASTER, BETTER, AND MORE ECONOMICAL RESULTS

The Nature and Goal of Socialist Production and the Means of Achieving This Goal

The establishment of the system of socialist public ownership has led to a fundamental change in the social relations of people in the production, exchange, and distribution processes. To begin with, the nature of social production has changed. And the goal of social production and the means to attain the goal of social production have also changed. Thus, the development of socialist production follows laws that are different from the laws of capitalist production. Only by correctly understanding and making use of these laws can socialist production be developed with greater, faster, better, and more economical results.

SOCIALIST PUBLIC OWNERSHIP HAS FUNDAMENTALLY CHANGED THE NATURE OF SOCIAL PRODUCTION

The socialist labor product is both direct social product and commodity

Production of material wealth is a necessary condition for the survival and development of human society. Under different social and economic systems, however, social products possess different characteristics.

Under the system of private ownership of the means of production, production is a private affair. The product belongs to the individual producer. Therefore, production is always directly manifested as private production. The product is also directly manifested as a private product. When this product is not produced for the consumption of the producer but is instead intended for exchange, then it becomes a commodity. The private product as commodity also possesses a social nature. But this social nature is concealed by the system of private ownership and cannot be directly expressed. Only through exchange, wherein the produced commodity has proven to meet the needs of society, can the social nature of the product be validated. In capitalist society, all products are both private products and commodities. Capitalist production is the most developed form of private commodity production.

In socialist China, after the socialist transformation of the system of ownership of the means of production had been basically completed, the whole of social production (with the exception of a small amount of land retained by commune members to farm for their personal needs and family sidelines operated by members of the rural collective economy) has been constituted on the foundation of a system of public ownership of the means of production. Taken as a whole, the production of the state economy and the collective economy, based on socialist public ownership and organized in accordance with countrywide planning, is aimed at directly meeting the needs of society, namely, directly meeting the needs of the proletariat and the laboring people as a whole. This kind of production is fundamentally different from capitalist private production. Viewed from its principal aspect, it has become direct social production. The products of labor are also socially useful from the start, and therefore they are no longer private products but rather direct social products. Needless to say, the labor that is engaged in direct social production to create direct social products is no longer private labor but rather direct social labor. Engels once observed, "From the moment society enters into possession of the means of production and uses them in direct association for production, the labor of each individual, however varied its specifically useful character, becomes social labor straight away and directly."[1]

Historically, in the process of development of human society, direct social production had once existed. This was in the primitive commune. At that time, "the members of the community were directly associated for production."[2] They labored together and distributed products to the members according to custom and need. This was a kind of direct social production based on a system of public ownership by the clan commune. It appeared under conditions in which the level of productive forces was low and the social division of labor under-developed. It was a primitive public ownership economy without commodity production and exchange.

Socialist direct social production is large-scale social production based on a division of labor and a mode of cooperation involving millions, tens of millions, hundreds of millions of people. From the point of view of the development of human society, socialist direct social production is a higher form of direct social production than that which existed under conditions of primitive communism. But compared with the future communist direct social production, socialist direct social production remains an immature form of direct social production; it has not yet rid itself of the traditions and birthmarks of the old society, nor has it freed itself from commodity production.

In the fairly long historical period of socialist society, the socialist system of public ownership consists of two kinds of socialist public ownership—and socialist production is conducted on the basis of these two forms of ownership. Products are owned, respectively, by the socialist state and by various units and enterprises under the collective ownership system. This determines that while socialist production is direct social production, it cannot but be commodity production. To attain normal economic relations between the state and collective sectors of the system of socialist public ownership and between industry and agriculture, and to facilitate the consolidation of the worker-peasant alliance, it is necessary to retain and suitably develop commodity production and exchange for a fairly long period of time. This cannot be changed at will. Lenin pointed out, "Commodity exchange is a test of the relationship between industry and agriculture."[3]

In analyzing the primitive origins of the commodity, Marx had already pointed out: "So soon, however, as products once become commodities in the external relations of a community, they also, by reaction, become so in its internal intercourse."[4] The "community" to which Marx referred is primitive communism. But this reasoning is also applicable to the socialist economy. The socialist economy is an integrated whole; the commodity relations between two kinds of socialist public ownership cannot but be reflected in the exchange relations within the system of socialist ownership by the whole people itself. At the same time, in consequence of the existing level of social productivity, and in order to strengthen the management responsibility of enterprises, material conditions demand that the state enterprises maintain their relative independence of operation and management. Hence, even though various state enterprises all are in the same family and all belong to the same owners, it still holds that when these enterprises mutually require the products of others, these products cannot be transferred without being paid for. The same family needs to be treated as two different families, still needs to be treated like different owners being paid according to price. Thus, in socialist society the commodity system is not only practiced between units of the state and the collective sectors (based on two kinds of socialist public ownership) but is also practiced within the state enterprise sector itself.

In socialist society, it is still necessary to maintain commodity production. But because this is commodity production bound up with direct social production, established on the foundation of socialist public ownership, it is quite different from commodity production that has existed historically. This commodity production has the following characteristics:

(1) It is conducted to directly meet social needs and is mainly manifested in the exchange relations between the worker and the peasant, the two great laboring classes.

(2) In contrast to unorganized and unplanned capitalist commodity production, socialist commodity production is conducted in a planned manner under the guidance of state planning.

(3) Compared with capitalist society, the scope of commodities is greatly reduced in socialist society. Labor power is no longer a commodity. Land, mineral resources, and other natural resources are no longer commodities either.

In sum, socialist society is a transitional society between capitalist society, where commodity production has developed to its peak, and communist society, where commodity production will have withered away. The commodity relations of socialist society already display in embryo the characteristics of the withering away of the commodity system. (This will be analyzed in more detail in chapter 9.)

Since socialist products are both direct social products and commodities, categories related to commodity production and circulation—such as use value and exchange value, concrete and abstract labor, money and price, and so forth—will certainly exist. To negate the necessity of maintaining commodity production in socialist society and to attempt to abolish commodity production prematurely are quite obviously erroneous. Chen Po-ta, a renegade and Trotskyite, clamored for the abolition of commodity production and exchange during the period of the rapid development of China's rural people's commune movement, this in a futile attempt to lead revolution and economic construction astray. Chairman Mao saw through this conspiracy in time and engaged him in a resolute struggle. In the resolutions of the Sixth Plenum of the Eighth Central Committee of the Chinese Communist Party, personally convened and chaired by Chairman Mao, it was pointed out: "This way of thinking which attempts to prematurely abolish commodity production and exchange, prematurely negate the constructive role of commodities, value, money, and price is detrimental to developing socialist construction and is therefore incorrect."[5] Socialist commodity production must not only be retained but must also be developed to consolidate the economic link between China's industry and agriculture and between urban and rural areas for the purpose of promoting the development of socialist construction.

But, on the other hand, it must also be recognized that socialist commodity production, while it differs from private commodity production, remains commodity production. It is still the case that the characteristics of commodity production, and the categories associated with it, are generated by the socialist system of public ownership of the means of production. As to commodity production itself in socialist society, it is not that much different from that of the old society. Concretely:

(1) In socialist society, the commodity still has use value and value, that is, a dual nature; hence, socialist enterprises, whether they operate within the sphere of collective ownership or the sphere of ownership by the whole people, must still take into account value [output value, cost, profit, and so forth], as well as use value.

(2) In socialist society, the economic law of commodity production is still the law of value; the value of the

commodity is still determined by the socially necessary labor time required to produce it; hence, the production unit whose individual labor time is lower than the socially necessary labor time will be able to receive higher income, and those production units whose individual labor time is higher than the socially necessary labor time can only receive lower income, perhaps even suffer a loss.

(3) In socialist society, owing to the existence of commodity production, money will continue to function as the general equivalent, and the value of commodities still needs to be expressed in terms of money, *i.e.*, expressed as price; hence, the price of commodities will still deviate from the values of commodities, allowing different commodity producers who expend equal amounts of labor to receive unequal amounts of income.

The phenomena described above reveal that socialist commodity production involves bourgeois right (equality on the surface but inequality in actual fact). These kinds of bourgeois rights in the field of commodity production are the soil that engender capitalism and bourgeois elements, and they must be restricted under the dictatorship of the proletariat. The proletariat wants to use commodity production to promote socialist construction, while the bourgeoisie wants to use commodity production to restore capitalism. In the three years of natural calamities (1960-62), the Liu Shao-chi clique unscrupulously advocated the extension of privately retained plots, the unregulated development of the free market, and a system of "internal responsibility for profit and loss" in the state economy. Their intention was to expand bourgeois right in commodity production in order to erode and break up the socialist economy and to restore the capitalist system. Chairman Mao was the first to discover this evil design of the Liu Shao-chi clique. He led the whole Party to criticize and repudiate the revisionist line carried out by the Liu Shao-chi clique, and to work out and take up a series of policies and plans restricting bourgeois rights in commodity production, which achieved very good results. But owing to the protracted and complex nature of class struggle, this struggle between restriction and counterrestriction, far from ceasing after several rounds of struggle, will continue for a long time.

Socialist production is a unity of the labor process and the value-creation process

The duality of socialist products is reflected in the duality of the production process that generates these products. As production for direct social products, socialist production is a direct social labor process that creates in a planned manner various use values that satisfy the needs of the proletariat and the masses of laboring people. As commodity production, the labor of the producer not only creates concrete use values but also creates exchange values. The socialist production process is a unity of this direct social labor process and the value-creation process. Thus, the characteristics of socialist production can only be determined with reference to the characteristics of the direct social labor process and the value-creation process.

If we abstract the labor process from specific social conditions and examine it from the standpoint of the functions performed by the various primary factors of production, we find that the labor process is merely a means through which the people who possess labor power incorporate it into materials, creating desired products—it is a purposeful activity for creating use value, a process of material transformation between people and nature. However, all production processes are carried out under definite social conditions. Therefore, labor processes reflect the relations not only between people and nature but also among people. If we examine the labor process from this standpoint, it becomes clear that there is a fundamental difference between the labor process under socialism and the labor process under capitalism.

The labor process under the capitalist system is a process in which the capitalist consumes labor power. Chief among its characteristics is the fact that the worker labors under the supervision of the capitalist while the products of that labor belong to the capitalist. Which is to say, labor under the capitalist system is hired labor, slave labor . . . backbreaking labor performed by the exploited. Under the socialist system, for the first time the laboring people become masters of the state and the enterprise. Consequently, there appear in the socialist labor process new characteristics that are without historical precedent. Lenin said: "Every factory from which the capitalist has been ejected, or in which he has at least been curbed by genuine workers' control, every village from which the landowning exploiter has been smoked

111

out and his land confiscated has only now become a field in which the working man can reveal his talents, unbend his back a little, rise to his full height, and feel that he is a human being. For the first time after centuries of working for others, of forced labor for the exploiter, it has become possible to *work for oneself* and moreover to employ all the achievements of modern technology and culture in one's work."[6] The socialist labor process is a process in which the worker, the peasant, and other laborers create material wealth for the laboring class itself. Chief among its characteristics is the fact that the laboring people, as their own masters, are engaged in organized and planned labor in socialist production. The entire labor product is distributed by the laboring class itself. Therefore, the socialist labor process is a planned labor process, not subject to exploitation; it is a voluntary and conscious labor process of the laboring people aimed at the creation of social wealth. It is a direct social labor process.

However, socialist society is a society with classes. In addition to the laboring class, there are the exploiting classes. The former exploiters must also labor in the socialist society in which consumption depends on labor. Supervised labor is imposed on the landlords, the rich peasants, and members of other antagonistic classes. The bourgeois elements are allowed to reform through labor in the enterprise. The treatment accorded these two exploiting classes is different, because the nature of their contradictions with the laboring people is different. But as exploiters, their labor necessarily carries with it varying degrees of compulsion. Naturally, the compulsion imposed on the exploiter by the laborer is fundamentally different from the compulsion imposed by the exploiter on the laborer. In the past, the exploiter compelled the laborer to labor in order to extract surplus value from the laborer. Now the laborer compels the exploiter to labor in order to transform him into a new person. Therefore, the socialist labor process is also a process for reforming the exploiter. This is to say, the socialist labor process does not merely involve material transformation between people and nature but also involves social and class reform.

As far as the laboring people are concerned, the socialist labor process still carries with it traditions and influences of the old society. This is because the old social division of labor inherited from capitalist society can only be eliminated gradually, through the entire historical period of socialism. The position of the laboring people in socialist production cannot but be restricted and affected by the old social division of labor: some people are primarily engaged in mental labor, while others are primarily engaged in manual labor; some people occupy a position of leadership and management in production, while others occupy the position of direct producers. The antagonistic opposition between mental and manual labor is one of the most important sources of inequality in capitalist society. Socialist society has overcome this antagonism. But there still exists a fundamental difference between mental and manual labor, a difference that can also become antagonistic under certain conditions. The Soviet Union, under the rule of the Brezhnev renegade clique, is ruled by a bureaucrat monopoly bourgeoisie, a handful of "people using their brains," including Party bureaucrats, intellectual aristocrats, and technical bureaucrats. Therefore, the process by which the laboring people come to be the masters of society and enterprise in socialist society is a long process of struggle. It is not only a process of struggle with the bourgeoisie and its agents in the Party, it is also a process in which favorable conditions are created to gradually eliminate the basic differences between mental and manual labor. In the socialist period, although all the laboring people are free from exploitation, labor has still not become life's prime want for all the laborers. The traditions and influences of the old society continue to leave their mark on labor and can only be swept away, once and for all, in the highest stage of communism.

These characteristics of the socialist labor process are also reflected in the value-creation process.

Every commodity embodies the duality of labor: concrete labor creates use value, while abstract labor creates value. Value reflects certain social relations. Under different social and economic conditions, the social relations reflected by value are different, and so too does this apply to the formation of value.

Under the conditions of a simple commodity economy, the peasant or handicraftsman produces by using his or her own means of production. Labor products and their values naturally belong to the producer. After the commodity is sold, the producer gets back the value of the means of production used up in the production process. But the producer also realizes the new value created by his or her own labor. This new value compensates for the value of the means of subsistence required for the reproduction of labor power. In such a way, the production process can continue on the scale of simple reproduction. Marx called the value-formation process under simple commodity production the simple value-formation process.

Under capitalism, the aim of commodity production undertaken by the capitalist is to extract surplus value from the worker. Through the production and sale of commodities, the capitalist gets back the value of the means of production used up in the production process. At the same time, the new value created by the labor of the worker not only compensates for the variable capital advanced by the capitalist to purchase labor power but also creates a surplus. This surplus is the surplus value extracted by the capitalist. Marx called the value-formation process in capitalist production the value-expansion process. This value-expansion process reflects the exploitative relations between capital and hired labor.

In the socialist production process, the labor of the laborer, as concrete labor, transfers and preserves the value of the means of production used up in the production process. As abstract labor, it creates new value. Should this new value created by the producer belong entirely to the producer himself? No. To realize socialist expanded reproduction and to satisfy the diverse common needs of the laborers, society must control various social funds. These social funds can only come from the new value created by the producer. If the newly created value belonged entirely to the direct producer, then the socialist economy would not be able to carry on expanded reproduction. It could only maintain simple reproduction. The common needs of the laborers could not be satisfied either. Therefore, in socialist society, the new value created by the producer must be divided into two parts. One part is at the disposal of the producer himself. It constitutes the personal consumption fund of the producer and is used to satisfy the personal living requirements of the producer. Another part constitutes various social funds: this social net income is at the disposal of society and is used to further develop socialist production and to satisfy the various common needs of the masses of laboring people. Actually, this situation shows that in socialist society the labor of the producer is also divided into two parts. One part can be designated as the labor that constitutes the social fund, the other part can be designated as the labor that constitutes the personal consumption fund for the producer.

114

The differentiation of the new value created by the producer into the labor remuneration fund and the social fund under the socialist system is fundamentally different from the differentiation of the new value created by the worker into wages and surplus value under the capitalist system. Under the capitalist system, labor power is a commodity and is subject to the law of value. Wage means the price of labor power. No matter how large the newly created value, the part that belongs to the individual worker is only equal to the value of those means of consumption necessary for the reproduction of labor power. The rest, that is, surplus value, is not only appropriated by the capitalist but used as a means to increase the exploitation of the worker. Under the socialist system, labor power is no longer a commodity. The laborer is no longer exploited. All of the value created by the producer is at the service of the laboring class. As producer, part of the new value created by the laborer has to be deducted and placed at the disposal of society as social funds. As part of the laboring people, the producer is fully entitled to enjoy the social welfare made possible by the social funds. The distribution of newly created value into the personal consumption fund for the producer and the social fund at the disposal of society is regulated by an overall consideration of the common and the individual interests, and the long-term and the short-term interests, of the laboring people.

Consequently, the value-formation process under the socialist system is different not only from the simple value-formation process in simple commodity production but also from the value-expansion process in capitalist production. It is a particular and unique process of value-creation reflecting socialist relations of production. The socialist production process is a unity of this direct social labor process and the value-creation process.

THE FUNDAMENTAL ECONOMIC LAW OF SOCIALISM EMBODIES THE MOST FUNDAMENTAL RELATIONS OF SOCIALIST PRODUCTION

The aim of socialist production is to satisfy the ever-increasing needs of the state and the people

If socialist production is a unity of the direct social labor process and the value-creation process, what then is the principal aspect of this contradiction?

The principal aspect of a contradiction in social production embodies the objective aim of this social production and reflects the most fundamental relations of this social production. It is independent of people's will and is ultimately determined by the nature of the ownership of the means of production. Social production has to serve the interests of the class which owns the means of production.

Under the system of capitalist ownership of the means of production, the labor process also creates use values. But this is not the aim of capitalist production. The capitalist operates factories in order to exploit the worker and obtain profit through the value-expansion process. Value expansion is the principal aspect of capitalist production. It embodies the most fundamental relations of capitalist production. Marx pointed out, "The aim of capital is not to minister to certain wants, but to produce profit."[7] "Capital and its self-expansion appear as the starting and the closing point, the motive and the purpose of production."[8]

The system of socialist public ownership of the means of production enables the laboring people to become the masters of production. Social production must serve the needs of the laboring people as a whole. Therefore, a direct social labor process that creates use values in a planned manner to satisfy the needs of the laboring people is the principal aspect of socialist production. It embodies the objective aim of socialist production and the most fundamental relations of socialist production. The value-creation process is subordinate to the direct social labor process that creates use values.

In the socialist production process, it is entirely necessary to calculate labor expenditure and profit and loss. But what and how much to produce cannot be determined by the magnitude of output value and the magnitude of profit. What and how much to produce should be based instead on the needs of the masses of laboring people. Whatever is urgently needed by the laboring people should be produced in greater quantity with the greatest possible effort, even at the risk of temporary losses. On the other hand, anything that is not urgently required by the laboring people, even if it yields high output value and high profits, cannot be indiscriminately produced in great quantity. The reason the socialist enterprise must calculate labor expenditure and profit and loss is not only so that it can reduce production costs in order to reimburse value [expenditure] but also to provide an ever-increasing social fund for developing production at a high speed and increasing the supply of social product. The subordination of the value-creation process to the direct social labor process is aimed, in the final analysis, at creating an ever-increasing quantity of social wealth to satisfy the needs of the laboring people as a whole. Before the victory of the October Revolution, Lenin pointed out that in socialist society, "the wealth created by the common labor will go to benefit, not a handful of rich men, but all those who work."[9]

The purpose of socialist production is to satisfy the needs of the laboring people as a whole. But the long-term interests of the laboring people and their overall interests can only be reflected and expressed through the state system under the dictatorship of the proletariat. Therefore, the aim of socialist production can also be described as the satisfaction of the ever-increasing needs of the socialist state and the people. These needs are multifaceted. To develop their intellectual and physical well-being, and their moral sense of right and wrong, there is a need for the proletariat and the laboring people to continously raise the level of their material and cultural life. There is also a need, since classes, class contradictions, class struggle, the danger of capitalist restoration, and the threat of sabotage and aggression from imperialism and' social imperialism still exist in socialist society, for the socialist country to consolidate proletarian dictatorship and strengthen national defense. And since the proletariat can emancipate itself, once and for all, only by emancipating all of humanity, the socialist country must fulfill its internationalist duties and support the revolutionary struggles of the peoples of the world. Therefore, the aim of socialist production is to raise the level of the material and cultural life of the proletariat and the laboring people, consolidate the dictatorship of the proletariat, strengthen national defense, and support the revolutionary struggles of the peoples of the world. In the final analysis, socialist production is aimed at eliminating classes and realizing communism.

The great strategic policy formulated by Chairman Mao to "be prepared against war, be prepared against natural disasters, and do everything for the people" fully embodies the objective aim of socialist production and indicates a correct direction for the development of China's socialist production and the whole national economy. Under the guidance of Chairman Mao's proletarian revolutionary line, and his general and specific policies, China's socialist production develops vigorously. The level of the people's material and cultural life is increasing all the time. The dictatorship of the proletariat is being continuously strengthened and consolidated. Within our capabilities, we have given aid to the cause of world revolution.

In the Soviet Union under the rule of the Brezhnev renegade clique, the law of surplus value governs social production. The aim of production is to pursue profit and to guarantee that the largest possible amount of surplus value is extracted from the laboring people of the Soviet Union by the bureaucrat-monopoly bourgeoisie. On the one hand, the Soviet revisionist renegade clique rants and raves that "the most important summary indicator of an enterprise's productive activity is profit and the rate of profit," and continually calls on enterprises "to struggle to raise profit." But, on the other hand, in order to deceive the masses, this clique still morbidly clings to the signboard of pseudo-socialism, trying hard to distort the aim of socialist production. It typically proclaims that "the highest purpose is to raise people's welfare," or that "everybody will have enough food, clothing, shoes, housing, and books. We call this communism." This renegade clique deceives the masses with the sweet talk of bourgeois welfarism, the purpose of which is to make people forget class struggle and revolution in order to facilitate the restoration of capitalism. In the Soviet Union, the only people who eat well, dress well, and are properly sheltered are the bureaucrat-monopoly bourgeoisie and the revisionist intellectual aristocracy under their wing. The broad laboring people have again fallen into the abyss of exploitation and suffering.

Grasp revolution, promote production

The principal aspect of the socialist production process—the most essential thing that determines socialist production—is the satisfaction of the ever-increasing needs of the state and the people. To serve this aim, social production must be developed so as to increase total social output. Marx and Engels pointed out in the *Communist Manifesto* that after the proletariat has overthrown bourgeois rule, it will use its political rule to expropriate the capitalist. "It will use its political supremacy to wrest, by degrees, all capital from the bourgeoisie, to centralize all instruments of production in the hands of the State, *i.e.*, of the proletariat organized as the ruling class; and to increase the total of productive forces as rapidly as possible."[10] When China was faced with the transition from the new democratic revolution to the socialist revolution, and when the emphasis of Party work shifted from the rural areas to the urban areas, Chairman Mao also earnestly taught us to pay attention to the rehabilitation and development of production, saying, "From the very first day we take over a city, we should direct our attention to restoring and developing its production."[11]

There are generally two ways of developing social production and increasing total social output. One is to increase the labor force in production as the population increases. In general, this may increase the total social output, but it cannot increase per capita output. Another way is to increase labor productivity. This not only increases total social output but also increases per capita output. From the long-range perspective, the major way to develop socialist production can only be by increasing labor productivity. When he discussed the significance of increasing labor productivity, Lenin said, "Only by increasing production and raising labor productivity will Soviet Russia be in a state to win."[12] He also said, "Productivity of labor is the most important, the principal thing for the victory of the new social system."[13]

How then can labor productivity be increased so as to develop socialist production?

Marxism holds that the productive forces develop under the constraint and impetus of the relations of production. In class society, production is always carried out under definite class relations. Even though changes and developments in social production always begin with changes and advances in the productive forces, major advances in the productive forces always occur after major transformations in the relations of production. In the early stages of capitalist development, it proved necessary to have a bourgeois revolution, in order that capitalist relations of production could become the principal economic base of society, before it became possible for major advances in the productive forces to take place. In socialist society, it is also only after the establishment of the dictatorship of the proletariat, the in-depth unfolding of socialist revolution, and the carrying out of socialist nationalization and agricultural collectivization, thereby establishing socialist relations of production as the sole economic foundation of society, that major advances in the productive forces can take place.

When the socialist transformation of the system of ownership of the means of production is basically completed, revolution is not yet finished. In the realm of production relations, only by consolidating socialist relations of production, corresponding to the development of productive forces, and by adjusting or transforming in a timely way those parts of the relations of production that conflict with the development of the productive forces, can socialist production be continously and rapidly developed.

Advances in science and technology and innovations in production tools play a big role in developing production and raising labor productivity. But "it is people, not things, that are decisive."[14] Science and technology are discovered by people, and production tools are created by people. "Of all things in the world, people are the most precious. Under the leadership of the Communist Party, as long as there are people, every kind of miracle can be performed."[15] The broad masses of China put it well: "Fear not the lack of machines; fear only the lack of determination. With one red heart and two hands, everything can be produced through self-reliance."

The socialist activism of the broad masses must be aroused through the political and ideological work of the Party. Only by grasping the key link of political and ideological work—mobilizing the masses to take up and discuss major national issues, criticizing and repudiating revisionism, the reactionary outlooks of Confucius and Mencius and the world outlooks of all the exploiting classes, and, most fundamentally, raising the consciousness of the broad masses on questions of class and two-line struggle—can socialist production be continuously and rapidly developed.

Therefore, in socialist society, the ultimate way to develop production and increase labor productivity is to persist in continuing the revolution under the dictatorship of the proletariat. After the proletariat seizes political power, only by wielding the socialist superstructure to unfold in-depth socialist revolution on the political, economic, and ideological battlefronts, under the guidance of the Party's correct line and with the aid of state power under proletarian dictatorship, can the sabotage and obstruction of the bourgeoisie, and capitalist influence in general, be swept away and destroyed. Only then can socialist relations of production be consolidated and improved and can all positive factors be mobilized to promote the development of socialist production at high speed. The policy "grasp revolution and promote production" formulated by Chairman Mao correctly reflects the requirements of the objective laws governing the motion of the basic contradictions of socialist society. This policy teaches us that proletarian politics must command all economic work and that revolution must guide and propel production. Only in this way can China's socialist production be guaranteed to advance with big strides in the correct direction.

The modern-day revisionists have always used the reactionary "theory of the productive forces" to oppose continued revolution under the dictatorship of the proletariat. The renegade cliques of Liu Shao-chi and Lin Piao always opposed revolution under the pretext of developing production. They even attributed the development of production wholly to the development of science and technology and the improvement of production tools to reliance on bourgeois experts. The revisionist line pushed by the cliques of Liu Shao-chi and Lin Piao has been overthrown, but the lingering poison of this "theory of the productive forces" has not been completely swept away and has to be criticized and repudiated repeatedly.

The fundamental economic law of socialism determines all major aspects of development of the socialist economy

The objective aim of social production and the means to realize it express the basic direction of development of social production and embody the requirements of the economic laws of society. Different social and economic systems have different aims of production and different means to achieve them. Consequently, there are different fundamental economic laws. The aim of socialist production is to satisfy the ever-increasing needs of the state and the people. This aim is attained by means of propelling the development of technology and production through revolution. Therefore, to sum up briefly, the major characteristics and requirements of the fundamental economic law of socialism are: to opportunely adjust and transform the relations of production and the superstructure; to steadily raise the level of technology; to develop socialist production with greater, faster, better, and more economical results; to satisfy the ever-increasing needs of the state and the people, and create the material conditions for the ultimate elimination of classes and the realization of communism.

121

The fundamental economic law of socialism determines all major aspects of development of the socialist economy and the basic content of socialist production, exchange, distribution, and consumption.

As far as production is concerned, what and how much to produce, and how production should be arranged in socialist society, must obey the requirements of the fundamental economic law of socialism. In drawing up plans, the socialist country specifies the variety, quantity, and arrangement of production in keeping with this law, so that the development of socialist production can be conducive to consolidating the dictatorship of the proletariat, strengthening national defense, supporting the revolutionary struggles of the peoples of the world, and steadily raising the level of material and cultural life of the laboring people.

Socialist exchange must also obey the requirements of the fundamental economic law of socialism. In determining the proportions of exports and imports to domestic production and consumption, the proportions between military and civilian use, the proportions between supply to the rural areas and supply to the urban areas, and the prices of products, the first thing that the socialist country considers is not how much money can be made or how much the profit is. The first thing it considers is whether the arrangement is favorable to raising the level of material and cultural life of the laboring people, consolidating the worker-peasant alliance, strengthening national defense, and supporting the revolutionary struggles of the peoples of the world.

The fundamental economic law of socialism also determines socialist distribution and consumption. In the distribution of national income and personal consumption goods, the socialist state must obey the requirements of the fundamental economic law of socialism. For example, the determination of the proper ratio between accumulation and consumption, as well as the level of wages, must take into account both the long-term and immediate, and the collective and individual, interests of the proletariat and laboring people. Similarly, socialist consumption, whether it be collective or individual consumption, must be favorable to improving the material and cultural life of the proletariat and laboring people, revolutionizing people's thought, fostering new socialist ideological standards of behavior, consolidating the dictatorship of the proletariat, and accelerating socialist construction.

In summary, the fundamental economic law of socialism embodies the most essential links between socialist production, exchange, distribution, and consumption. It determines the ultimate direction of development of the socialist economy. The correct understanding and use of the fundamental economic law of socialism can raise our consciousness, help us overcome spontaneity in our work, and enable us to advance with big strides in the correct socialist direction.

THE HIGH-SPEED DEVELOPMENT OF SOCIALIST PRODUCTION IS A UNITY OF OBJECTIVE POSSIBILITY AND SUBJECTIVE INITIATIVE

The socialist system enables production to develop at speeds unattainable in the old society

The aim of socialist production is to satisfy the ever-increasing needs of the state and the people. The degree of satisfaction of these needs is closely related to the speed with which production develops. The consolidation of national defense in the socialist country, the development of cultural, educational, and health facilities and activities in socialist society, the improvement of the material and cultural life of the people, and aid to the cause of world revolution all require rapid development of socialist production to create their material preconditions. Also, because imperialist rule is generally overthrown at its weakest link, the first countries in which socialist revolution is successful are likely to have a relatively weak industrial base. This creates an even greater necessity for high-speed development of socialist construction.

Under the socialist system, it is not only necessary but possible to have rapid development of production. Chairman Mao pointed out: "In saying that socialist relations of production are better suited to the development of the productive forces than are the old relations of production, we mean that they permit the productive forces to develop at a speed unattainable in the old society, so that production can expand steadily to meet the constantly growing needs of the people step by step."[16] Therefore, rapid development of socialist production is not a mere hope but is based on objective possibility inherent within socialist relations of production. It is a manifestation of the superiority of the socialist system.

Can socialist relations of production propel production and the whole national economy to develop at high speed?

First of all, the socialist system provides wide-ranging possibilities to unleash the activism and creativity of the laboring people in the production process. Under the socialist system, the proletariat and the laboring people are no longer wage slaves selling their labor power. They have freed themselves from enslavement and exploitation and have become masters of the new society. They no longer perform hard labor for any exploiter but instead work for the interests of their own class. Labor has become a glorious and great vocation. This change in the position of the laboring people in social production allows them to begin to really concern themselves with production as masters and to exercise their inexhaustible talents. People with the ability to labor are the most important factor in production. Socialist relations of production can propel the development of production at a high speed primarily because the activism and creative talents of the laboring masses, suppressed under the capitalist system, are now liberated.

Second, the socialist system eliminates the immense waste of manpower, material resources, and finances that is inevitable under the competitive and chaotic conditions of capitalism. The socialist country can fully and rationally utilize labor and material resources by drawing up a unified plan to direct the development of the whole national economy. Facilities and natural resources can be used in a planned and rational manner; and labor power can be trained and allocated in a planned and rational manner.

Third, the socialist revolution has eliminated the system of man exploiting man and has made it possible to use that part of the wealth which was formerly used by a handful of members of exploiting classes for parasitic consumption to improve the livelihood of the laboring people and to develop socialist production.

Fourth, the socialist system has cleared a wide road for the rapid development of science and technology. Under the capitalist system, new technology is used only when it can bring more profit to the capitalist. New technology that has already been adopted is monopolized by the capitalist as "trade secrets." This inevitably restricts the development of new technology. Under the socialist system, new technology is adopted for the purpose of economizing on labor expenditure in production. It is also adopted for the purpose of reducing labor intensity and improving working conditions. Therefore, the development of science and technology becomes a conscious demand of the laboring people. Furthermore, the advanced experience in technical innovations of any one socialist enterprise is the common property of the laboring people. It can be more quickly adopted by other enterprises after it is summed up and disseminated.

Fifth, the socialist system has eliminated the contradiction between increases in production capacity and the relative decrease of mass purchasing power that is peculiar to capitalism. This is so because, with the development of socialist production, the consumption level of the proletariat and the laboring people steadily increases while the scale of national construction steadily expands. Economic crises due to overproduction never occur. This clears away artificial obstacles to the rapid development of production.

Although the objective possibility exists within the socialist system for the rapid development of production, there also exist some factors that undermine and inhibit the rapid development of production. Examples are the sabotage activities of the bourgeoisie and its agents, obstruction deriving from the continuing influence of the petty bourgeoisie, the ravages brought about by natural calamities, and so forth. In addition to the objective existence of these social and natural factors, there are also subjective factors related to the proletariat itself. Along the path in unfolding socialist revolution and socialist construction, the proletariat will certainly be faced with new situations and new problems. In order to understand the objective laws of the new situations and to find correct methods to solve the new problems, a period of time is needed to accumulate experience. Socialist construction should not be expected to proceed smoothly; it can only advance in a wavelike manner. To turn the objective possibility of high-speed socialist construction into a reality, our subjective efforts are required. Here a Marxist line which correctly reflects objective law plays a determining role. If the line is correct, the potential of the socialist system to promote the rapid development of social production can be realized. If the line is incorrect, or the correct line is interfered with by the revisionist line, high-speed socialist construction will be obstructed and undermined.

The General Line is a compass for building socialism with greater, faster, better, and more economical results

After summing up domestic and international experiences and lessons in socialist construction, Chairman Mao in 1958 formulated the General Line "go all out, aim high, and build socialism with greater, faster, better, and more economical results." It is a Marxist line that fully taps the superiority of the socialist system, fully unleashes the subjective initiative of people, and seeks to build socialism with greater, faster, better, and more economical results.

The General Line for socialist construction requires the unification of greater, faster, better, and more economical results in building socialism. "Greater" refers to the quantity of products, "faster" refers to time, "better" refers to quality, and "more economical" refers to less labor expenditure. The requirements of greater, faster, better, and more economical results are mutually reinforcing as well as interdependent. If we pay attention only to greater and faster results at the expense of better and more economical results, the result will be poor quality and high costs. In the long run and overall, the effect will not really be greater and faster results but rather lesser and slower results. If we pay attention only to better and more economical results at the expense of greater and faster results, although product quality may be high, there will not be enough produced. The speed of construction will be too slow to satisfy the needs of the state and the people. Only if we can build socialism with greater, faster, better, and more economical results can there be truly rapid development and can the ever-increasing needs of the state and the people be satisfied to the greatest extent possible. The General Line for socialist construction, and a whole series of "walking-on-two-legs" policies formulated by Chairman Mao, enable industry and agriculture, heavy and light industry, large-scale, medium, and small-scale industry, production by foreign and indigenous methods, etc., to complement and promote each other, thus ensuring the balanced development of the various sectors of China's socialist national economy. This General Line correctly reflects both the objective requirements of the fundamental economic law of socialism, the law of rapid development of socialist production and the law of planned development of the national economy, and the revolutionary will of the people of the whole country, who demand a rapid change in the backward status of the country.

How can greater, faster, better, and more economical results be achieved and lesser, slower, worse, and more expensive results be avoided in socialist construction? The key lies in fully mobilizing the masses in building socialism. The general line for socialist construction emphasizes the combination of Party leadership and the broad people; it is a new development of the Party's mass line on socialist construction. Marxism has long held that "history is *nothing but* the activity of man pursuing his aims."[17] Chairman Mao teaches, "The people, and the people alone, are the motive force of world history."[18] Chairman Mao pointed out more than once that the masses have to be relied upon to seize political power and build socialism. The Lin Piao clique, loyal disciples of Confucius, slandered the masses in every conceivable way. They boasted that their "brains are not those of the ordinary peasant, nor those of the ordinary worker." They tried hard to peddle the Confucian nonsense that "only the most intelligent and the most ignorant are not subject to change," fully exposing their position as diehard enemies of the people. Numerous facts demonstrate that the lowest are the most intelligent and the highest and most noble are the most ignorant. Only by fully trusting the masses, relying on the masses, respecting the innovative spirit of the masses, mobilizing all positive factors, uniting all people that can be united, and, as much as possible, transforming negative factors into positive ones can socialist revolution be victoriously unfolded on the political, economic, ideological, and cultural battlefronts and can socialist production and scientific, cultural, and educational undertakings be developed with greater, faster, better, and more economical results.

"Going all out and aiming high" refers to the spiritual condition and subjective initiative of people. Thus the General Line gives prominence to putting proletarian politics in command and emphasizes the role of the revolutionary enthusiasm and creativeness of the masses in socialist construction. The Party's task in socialist construction is to grasp the key link of political-ideological work, raise the socialist consciousness of the people, help the masses to master the Party's Marxist line and general and specific policies, and mobilize and organize the broad masses to struggle for the great cause of building socialism. Chairman Mao teaches us: "Social wealth is created by the worker, the peasant, and the educated. As long as these people control their destiny, have a Marxist-Leninist line, and solve problems with a constructive attitude rather than avoiding them, any difficulty in the human world is solvable."[19] Once the broad revolutionary masses have mastered the Party's Marxist line, their immense revolutionary zeal will be aroused and will become a powerful material force for creating miracles in the human world. The Great Leap Forward in China's national economy emerged because of this.

Achieve a great leap forward in the national economy through independence and self-reliance

Under the guidance of the General Line, "Go all out, aim high, and build socialism with greater, faster, better, and more economical results," the working class and all the laboring people of China are high-spirited and combat-ready. Their revolutionary spirit of daring to think, speak, and act is sky-high. The upsurge in socialist emulation, campaigns to compare with, learn from, and catch up to the advanced, while helping the backward, is rising to ever-greater heights. The correct leadership of the Party's Marxist line enables China's national economy to develop vigorously through independence and self-reliance. A great leap forward situation has appeared.

Under the oppression and enslavement of imperialism, feudalism, and bureaucrat capitalism, the broad laboring people of old China were in the grips of tremendous hardship and suffering. The national economy was at a standstill. For a long time, many industrial products for daily use were all imported from foreign countries. A box of now commonplace matches was called "foreign fire," machine-woven fabrics were called "foreign cloth," and nails were called "foreign nails." There were also "foreign umbrellas," "foreign oil," and so forth. Foreign goods flooded the domestic market, driving out the products of China's domestic industries. This was what was left behind by old China.

Since liberation, under the wise leadership of the Chinese Communist Party, the heroic Chinese working class and laboring people have stood up and are determined to transform the backward old China and construct a prosperous and strong socialist new China. The basic completion of socialist revolution in the system of ownership of the means of production and the proclamation of the Party's General Line for socialist construction greatly propel the development of socialist construction. Amid the seething national upsurge of the Great Leap Forward, Chairman Mao pointed out: "We cannot follow the old paths of technical development of every other country in the world, and crawl step by step behind the others'. We must smash conventions, do our utmost to adopt advanced techniques, and within not too long a period of history, build China into a modern powerful socialist state. When we talk of a Great Leap Forward we mean just this."[20]

Under the guidance of the Marxist line formulated by Chairman Mao and under the guidance of the policy of national construction on the basis of independence and self-reliance, the people of the whole country have developed their own independent, integrated industrial system. Not only is the light industry sector turning out a full range of products and components, it is producing enough so that China can both maintain its self-reliance and engage in export. The old days when the streets were full of imported goods are completely gone. China's own machine-building industry, metallurgical industry, chemical industry, scientific instruments and measuring tools industry, and electronics industry were quickly established and have developed rapidly. In the developmental process of socialist industry, the lopsided concentration of industry in the coastal provinces that existed in old China has been changed. New industrial bases in the interior have been built, thus gradually rationalizing the location of production capacities and meeting the needs of China's economic construction and national defense construction. In the practice of the three great revolutionary movements [class struggle, the struggle for production, and scientific experiment], new scientific and technical manpower has rapidly expanded, and the level of science and technology is rising steadily. Many large pieces of precision equipment and major projects can now be designed and manufactured by us without outside help. On this basis, China has exploded atomic and hydrogen bombs and launched man-made satellites. China was the first country in the world to successfully synthesize insulin, thereby making an important contribution to the study of the origin of life. China was the first country in the world to successfully manufacture a double internal water-cooling turbogenerator. Under the guidance of Mao Tse-tung Thought, the Chinese people have broken through scientific and technological barriers, one after another, and have set new records by leaps and bounds. With the soaring leap in the development of industry, science, and technology, China's agricultural mechanization is also rapidly pushing ahead. Significant achievements have been won in China's farmland water control construction, and the acreage under effective irrigation has greatly expanded. The "eight-character charter" of soil, fertilizer, water, seeds, close planting, plant protection, and field management for higher agricultural output has been widely practiced.

In the course of China's socialist construction, a certain "pause" once appeared for some time in some sectors as a result of the sabotage and interference of the revisionist line pushed by the Liu Shao-chi and Lin Piao cliques. This was a manifestation of the struggle between the two classes and the struggle between the two lines in the process of socialist construction. It is a struggle between progress and retrogression. Judging from the whole process and from the whole situation since the establishment of the People's Republic, China's national economy has been developing by leaps and bounds under the guidance of the dominant Marxist line formulated by Chairman Mao. From 1949 to 1973, the total value of our country's agricultural production has increased 1.8 times, the value of light industrial production has increased 12.8 times, and the value of heavy industrial production has increased 59 times. Along with the development of industrial and agricultural production, China's communications and transportation, its commerce, banking, and finance, and its cultural and educational endeavors have also rapidly advanced. The level of material and cultural life of the people has also been raised substantially. These indisputable facts cannot be denied by anyone. The Lin Piao clique attempted unsuccessfully to negate the brilliant achievements scored by the Chinese people under the radiance of the General Line by slanderously declaring that "the national economy is stagnant." This merely further exposed their position as agents of imperialism, revisionism, and reaction, their hatred for socialism, and their wolfish ambition to restore capitalism.

The brilliance of the Party's basic line for the entire historical period of socialism and the General Line for socialist construction illumines our big strides forward. Our great socialist motherland is prospering and progressing. When we look to the future, we feel confident and vigorous. What the Western bourgeoisie failed to do, the Eastern proletariat must and can achieve!

Major Study References

Lenin, "Once Again on the Trade Unions, the Current Situation, and the Mistakes of Trotsky and Bukharin," *CW* 31
J.V. Stalin, *Economic Problems of Socialism*
Mao, "We Must Learn to Do Economic Work," *SW* 3

Notes

1. Engels, *Anti-Duhring*, pp. 401-02.
2. Ibid., p. 401.
3. Lenin, "Instructions of the Council of Labor and Defense to Local Soviet Bodies," *CW* 32 (1973), p. 384.
4. Marx, *Capital* 1, p. 91.
5. From "Resolutions on Some Questions Concerning the Peoples Communes, Adopted by the 8th Central Committee of the Party at its 6th Plenary Session on December 10, 1958." This text with a slightly different translation can be found in *Communist China, 1955-9: Policy Documents with Analysis* (Cambridge: Harvard University Press, 1962), p. 497.
6. Lenin, "How to Organize Competition?", *CW* 26, p. 407.
7. Marx, *Capital* 3, p. 256.
8. Ibid., p. 250.
9. Lenin, "May Day," *CW* 7 (1961), p. 199.
10. Marx and Engels, *Communist Manifesto*, p. 59.
11. Mao, "Report to the 2nd Plenum of the 7th Central Committee of the CPC," *SW* 4, p. 365.
12. Lenin, "The Eighth All-Russia Congress of Soviets," *CW* 31 (1974), p. 501.
13. Lenin, "A Great Beginning," *CW* 29, p. 427.
14. Mao, "On Protracted War," *SW* 2, p. 143.
15. Mao, "The Bankruptcy of the Idealist Conception of History," *SW* 4, p. 454.
16. Mao, "Correct Handling of Contradictions," *SR*, p. 444.
17. Marx, *The Holy Family* (Moscow: Progress Publishers, 1975), p. 110.

18. Mao, "On Coalition Government," *SW* 3, p. 207.
19. Mao, cited in *The Red Book*, p. 198.
20. Mao, "China's Great Leap Forward," in Schram, *Chairman Mao Talks to the People*, p. 231.

6

THE SOCIALIST ECONOMY
IS A PLANNED ECONOMY

Planned and Proportionate
Development of the National Economy

Any form of social production must solve the problem of regulating and distributing social labor, that is, allocating both manpower (living labor) and material power (materialized labor) to the various sectors and branches of production. The regulation of social labor and production follows certain laws. Correctly identifying and making use of the economic laws regulating socialist production, and differentiating them from the economic laws regulating capitalist production, is very important if we are to develop socialist production with greater, faster, better, and more economical results.

THE LAW OF PLANNED DEVELOPMENT*
REGULATES SOCIALIST PRODUCTION

The law of planned development is the opposite of the
law of competition and the anarchy of production

In any large-scale social production, there exist close relations of mutual dependence among various branches of production. For example, the

---

* In other Chinese texts and commentaries of the period, this law was sometimes referred to as the law of planned and proportionate development.

textile industry needs agriculture to supply cotton and the machine-building industry to supply spinning and weaving machines; the machine-building industry needs the iron and steel industry to supply a variety of rolled steel; and the iron and steel industry needs the coal industry to supply raw coal and the machine-building industry to supply excavation equipment, smelting equipment, rolling equipment, and so forth. All these industrial and mining enterprises need agriculture to supply the means of subsistence, the power industry to supply electricity, and the communications and transportation departments to transport raw materials and finished goods for them. These relations of mutual dependence among the various branches of production and among enterprises demand that they maintain proper proportions among themselves and supply what they produce to others to satisfy each other's needs. Otherwise, social production will be obstructed or even disrupted.

Capitalist society is a society with a high degree of social production. But it is impossible under capitalist conditions to allocate social labor in society as a whole in a planned way. The aim of capitalist production is not the satisfaction of social needs but the expansion of value in order to obtain profit. To go after bigger profits, the capitalists engage in life-and-death struggles among themselves. Like flies chasing after filth, the capitalist shifts his capital around in response to the spontaneous movements of market prices, expanding commodity production first in this and then in that sector. Under these conditions, the required proportional relations among the branches of production are often violated. Only after spontaneous adjustments, through the destruction of production capacities, can the violated proportional relations be temporarily restored. Lenin's statement that "for capitalism *there must be a crisis* so as to create a *constantly disturbed* proportion"[1] exactly describes this situation.

With the replacement of the capitalist system by the socialist system, economic conditions are fundamentally changed. Socialist production is based on a system of public ownership of the means of production, and its aim is to satisfy the needs of the socialist state and the laboring people as a whole. Under the socialist system, on the one hand, social production is further developed. It is all the more necessary to allocate social labor according to certain proportions and to maintain a proper balance among various branches of production. On the other hand, the system of socialist public ownership of the means of production turns the laboring people into the masters of production. Their basic interests are identical. This eliminates the conflicts of interest among the various branches and enterprises that are inherent in capitalism. Thus, the socialist state, which represents the interests of the proletariat and the laboring people as a whole, can allocate labor power and the means of production among the various sectors of the national economy—under a unified plan in accordance with the needs of the state and the people. This enables the various sectors of the national economy to develop in a balanced and proportionate manner. It is exactly these economic conditions underlying socialist production that eliminate the law of competition and the anarchy of production from the historical stage. These conditions also give rise to a new economic law, namely, the law of planned development of the national economy, which regulates social production and the development of the whole national economy. These inevitable changes consequent upon the replacement of capitalism by socialism were foreseen scientifically by Engels. He had pointed out, "The seizure of the means of production by society eliminates commodity production and with it the domination of the product over the producer. The anarchy within social production is replaced by consciously planned organization."[2]

The planned economy demonstrates the superiority of the socialist system

The replacement of competition and the anarchy of production by planned development of the national economy is an important aspect of the superiority of socialism over capitalism.

The socialist planned economy marks the beginning of people consciously making their own history. In capitalist society, characterized by competition and anarchy of production, things rule people, rather than people ruling things. The laborers cannot control their own fate, nor can the capitalists free themselves from the blind operation of these objective economic laws working behind people's backs. In socialist society, the system of public ownership of the means of production has been realized; the laboring people have become masters of society. They control their own fate and consciously begin to make use of objective law to make their own history. This conscious activity, this conscious making of history, is manifested in the process of practice as the step-by-step identification of objective laws, the formulation of plans, based on objective laws, to transform nature and society, and the achievement of anticipated results through organized activity. Chairman Mao hailed the conscious activity of China's laboring people by which they transform the world under the leadership of the Party, pointing out: "Human development has been going on for hundreds of thousands of years. But in China, the conditions for a planned development of her own economy and culture have been obtained just now. With these conditions, the face of China will change year after year. There will be a greater change every five years. An even greater change will occur after several five-year periods."[3]

The socialist planned economy possesses great superiority over the economy of capitalist competition and its anarchy of production. But this does not mean that it can guarantee that the proportional relations among the various sectors of production will be maintained in a state of absolute balance all the time. There is nothing in the world that can develop in an absolutely balanced manner. Balance is only temporary and relative, whereas imbalance is permanent and absolute. In the developmental process of the socialist economy, owing to the obstruction and disruption of bourgeois and revisionist lines, owing to the ever-changing conditions as between the advanced and the backward among various enterprises, various sectors, and various regions, owing to changes in natural conditions, and owing to the limits of people's understanding of objective things, there will still regularly arise situations in which balance and proportionate relations are upset. But, in socialist society, this kind of imbalance in the various sectors of production can be continually overcome through people's conscious activities and through regulation by the socialist state plan. Compared with the blind groping associated with capitalist competition and anarchy of production, the continual overcoming of imbalance, and the establishment of relative balance through regulation by plans, makes it possible to avoid the enormous waste of human and material resources and funds characteristic of capitalist society. And thus it becomes possible to achieve a more rational and a fuller utilization of social labor and to guarantee rapid development of socialist production.

Chairman Mao pointed out: "A constant process of readjustment through state planning is needed to deal with the contradiction between production and the needs of society, which will long remain as an objective reality. Every year our country draws up an economic plan in order to establish a proper ratio between accumulation and consumption and achieve a balance between production and needs. Balance is nothing but a temporary, relative unity of opposites. By the end of each year, this balance, taken as a whole, is upset by the struggle of opposites; the unity undergoes a change, balance becomes imbalance, unity becomes disunity, and once again it is necessary to work out a balance and unity for the next year."[4] Those viewpoints that regard the planned development of the socialist economy as being absolutely balanced development and free from contradictions are metaphysical. The correct attitude should be to conduct scientific analysis of imbalances in the national economy to discover their different conditions and to prescribe treatment accordingly. After the appearance of imbalance, we must treat it with a constructive attitude. We cannot rigidly pull down the high to suit the low. Instead, we must in good time pull up the backward sectors to establish a new balance according to the needs and possibilities. Thus, the change from balance to imbalance and from imbalance to balance in the developmental process of the socialist economy implies the breaking down of the old proportional relations and the establishment of new proportional relations at a higher level of development. This is a concrete manifestation of the superiority of the socialist economy.

The proportional relations in the national economy must be handled correctly

The socialist economy requires people to regulate the various, mutually-dependent sectors of the national economy with plans so as to ensure proportionate development. What then are the objective proportional relations among the various sectors of the national economy?

Proportional relations in the national economy are numerous and complex. The main proportional relations are as follows:

First, the proportions between agriculture and industry. Agriculture and industry are the two basic, mutually-dependent sectors of production. The staff and workers of the industrial sector require agriculture to supply them with food grains and various nonstaple foods. Light industry requires agriculture to supply it with raw materials. Both light and heavy industry need the agricultural sector as an important market for their products. On the other hand, the rural population needs industry to supply industrial products for daily use. Agricultural production needs industry to supply it with chemical fertilizers, insecticide, agricultural machinery, electricity, and other means of production. The agricultural sector also needs industry and the urban population as a market for that portion of the agricultural product not retained by the agricultural sector. Because there exist these mutually-dependent relations between agriculture and industry, and because the relations between industry and agriculture are, in essence, relations between worker and peasant and between socialist ownership by the whole people and socialist collective ownership, a key issue in the planned development of the national economy is the maintenance of a proper proportion between industry and agriculture, so that they can support one another in the developmental process of the socialist economy. (This issue will be discussed in greater detail in the next chapter.)

Second, the proportions within agriculture. These include the proportions among crop growing, forestry, animal husbandry, sideline production, and fishery, as well as the proportions among food grain, cotton, vegetable oil, bast fibers, silk, tea, sugar, vegetables, fruit, herbal medicines, and miscellaneous foodstuffs within crop-growing itself. Taking agricultural production as a whole, the production of food grains occupies the most important position. Chairman Mao taught us to "store grain everywhere." With grain in our hands, we won't panic. If the production of grain is no good, it not only affects the development of agriculture itself but also will affect the development of industry and the whole national economy. Since the production of grain occupies such an important position, food grains must be insisted upon as the key link in handling the proportional relations within agriculture. The development of cash crops, forestry, animal husbandry, sideline production, and fishery cannot be divorced from the key link of food grains. However, this does not imply that the development of other items of agricultural production can be neglected. Take forestry. It not only directly supplies products to society but also serves an important function in conserving water and soil. "Without trees on the mountain, water and soil cannot be retained; having a lot of trees on the mountain is as good as building dams." The importance of forestry to agricultural development can thus be seen. The development of animal husbandry, sideline production, fishery, and cash crops cannot be neglected either. The development of forestry, animal husbandry, sideline production, and fishery is vital to national construction and people's living standards. These activities can also promote the further development of food grain production by accumulating funds and increasing fertilizers. The policy of "taking grain as the key link and ensuring an all-round development," formulated by Chairman Mao, pointed a direction for the correct handling of the proportional relations within agriculture. Provided that food grains are taken as the key link, this policy requires that the characteristics of different regions be considered and that an overall arrangement for agriculture, forestry, animal husbandry, sideline production, and fishery, as well as food grain, cotton, oil, bast fibers, silk, tea, and so forth, be worked out so that they can support one another and develop as a whole.

Third, the proportions within industry. These include the proportions between light and heavy industry, the raw materials industry and the processing industry, national defense industry and basic industry, as well as the proportions between major machines and minor machines and between whole machines and spare parts within various industries. The proportional relations within industry are even more complex than the proportional relations within agriculture. But in the complex relations, there is still a key link. This key link is steel. With steel, we can make machines, and with machines, we can develop various industries. This key role of steel in industry reflects a major aspect of the proportional relations within industry and illustrates that the development of the various sectors of industry must be based on the development of the iron and steel industry. In addition, other proportional relations must also be correctly handled. In the relationship between heavy and light industry, we must not neglect light industry when we give priority to the development of heavy industry. In the relationship between the raw materials industry and the processing industry, the leading aspect of the contradiction is the raw materials industry. To develop the raw materials industry, especially the mining industry, which is of decisive significance in the raw materials industry, it is important to unfold socialist construction through independence and self-reliance and to maintain a balance between the raw materials industry and the processing industry. In the relationship between national defense industry and basic industry, priority must be given to the development of the basic industries. Without the development of such basic industries as the metallurgical, chemical, machine-building, electronics, and measuring instruments industries, the national defense industry cannot go very far. Only by closely linking the development of the defense industry with the development of basic industry and by maintaining a relative balance between defense industry and basic industry can the defense industry and industry as a whole be developed faster. In the relationships between major and minor machines and between complete machines and spare parts within industry, it must be noted that without the complement of minor machines, major machines simply cannot operate. With complete machines but without spare parts, complete machines have to stop operation once some parts are worn out. Therefore, we must overcome the erroneous tendency of emphasizing major machines at the expense of minor machines and complete machines at the expense of spare parts, the erroneous thinking of "only wanting to be a leading character, not a supporting character," in order to maintain a proper proportion.

The proportional relations within industry, within agriculture, and between agriculture and industry are three very important proportional relations in the whole national economy. This is because, among the economic links of production, exchange, distribution, and consumption, production is the determining link. And agriculture and industry are also basic sectors of production. Agriculture and light industry basically produce means of consumption. And heavy industry basically produces means of production. Once these three proportional relations are properly handled, the proportional relation between the two departments of social production (industries of means of production and industries of means of consumption) is basically arranged.

Fourth, the proportions between industrial and agricultural production and the communications and transport industry. Marx classified the transport industry as the fourth sphere of material production, following the extractive industry, agriculture, and manufacture. Large-scale social production requires that the various sectors and enterprises expeditiously receive their supply of raw materials, processed materials, and fuel and that they expeditiously ship their products to points of consumption. Planned production needs planned transport to tightly coordinate with it. Without corresponding development in communications and transport, industrial and agricultural production will be greatly hindered.

Fifth, the proportion between cultural and educational construction and economic construction. Cultural and educational construction serve economic construction. Economic construction also promotes and delimits the development of cultural and educational undertakings. To construct a socialist country with modern agriculture, industry, and national defense, the development of modern science and culture is indispensable. The development of economic construction requires a corresponding development of cultural and educational construction in order to facilitate the continuing supply of educated laborers with socialist consciousness.

Sixth, the proportions between increases in production and the development of cultural and educational undertakings, on the one hand, and population growth, on the other. A planned development of material production and of culture and education objectively requires a planned population growth, that is, family planning. Family planning is not only a basic precondition for the reproduction of labor power, it is also a necessary condition for a planned arrangement of people's livelihood, the protection of the health of the mother and the baby, and planned development of socialist construction. Blind population growth will certainly interfere with planned and proportionate development of the national economy. In capitalist society, population growth is as chaotic as the production of things; family planning applied over the whole society is inconceivable. Only under conditions in which the proletariat and the laboring people are the masters does it become possible to simultaneously plan the regulation of population growth and the regulation of goods production. Family planning is a result of having the proletariat control its own destiny and is a manifestation of the superiority of the socialist system.

Seventh, the proportional relations between accumulation and consumption. Because socialist products possess varying degrees of commodity characteristics, there exists, in addition to the above-mentioned, primarily material proportional relations, a proportional relation, based on value, between accumulation and consumption. If this proportional relation is not properly handled, the development of the whole national economy will be hindered. (This problem will be discussed in greater detail in chapter 10.)

Finally, the proportional relations among various regions, namely, the rational distribution of production capacities. Socialist society develops out of capitalist society, and the distribution of production capacities in capitalist society, effected within the framework of competition and the anarchy of production, embodies many irrational factors. Take the example of the early period after liberation in China. The total value of industrial production in the seven provinces and two municipalities along China's coast accounted for more than 70 percent of the total value of national industrial production. Eighty percent of iron and steel production capacity was distributed along the coast. There was almost no iron and steel industry in Inner Mongolia, the northwest, or the southwest, where material reserves were abundant. In the textile industry, more than 80 percent of the spindles and more than 90 percent of the weaving machines were distributed along the coast. There were very few textile factories in the cotton-producing area and the interior. Therefore, after the proletariat seized political power, it faced the task of geographically reallocating production capacities. A rational geographic distribution of production capacities must be such that it is: favorable to consolidating the dictatorship of the proletariat and to consolidating and strengthening national defense against possible aggression and threats from imperialism; favorable to narrowing the differences between town and country; favorable to strengthening the unity among the laboring people of various nationalities; favorable to utilizing various resources in the most rational manner; and favorable to building socialism with greater, faster, better, and more economical results. The key issue in the rational distribution of production capacities is to achieve "industry . . . dispersed over the whole country in the way best adapted to its own development and to the maintenance and development of the other elements of production."[5] In the more than twenty years after the establishment of the People's Republic and under the guidance of Chairman Mao's theory on the correct handling of the relations between coastal industry and interior industry, China's industry in the interior has developed rapidly. The newly established industrial bases are beginning to take shape. Former industrial bases in the provinces and municipalities along the coast have also been fully utilized and rationally developed.

THE LAW OF VALUE STILL INFLUENCES SOCIALIST PRODUCTION

Planning is primary, price is secondary

Socialist production is, to a certain extent, both direct social production and also commodity production. Commodity production has its own laws of operation: "Wherever commodities and commodity production exist, there the law of value must also exist."[6] Thus, both the law of planned development of the national economy and the law of value act on socialist production.

The substance of the law of value is:

(1) the value of commodities is determined by the socially necessary labor time expended on their production;

(2) commodity exchange must be based on the principle of equivalent values.

What the law of value embodies is bourgeois right, the basic content of which in socialist society is not that much different from what it was in the old society. But under different social economic systems, the law of value will assume different forms and exert different effects on production.

Under the capitalist system, social production is carried on under competitive and anarchic conditions of production. The price of commodities fluctuates with the change in the supply-demand relationship. Sometimes it is higher than the production price and sometimes lower. When the price is higher than the production price, profit is higher than the average profit. When the capitalist sees this opportunity for higher profit, he will rush in to invest his capital in those more profitable sectors. In the opposite situation, capital will be withdrawn. It is under these blind conditions that social production develops. These conditions demonstrate that the law of value under the capitalist system is manifested as an alien force working behind people's backs and is the overall regulator of social production.

Under the socialist system, social production is carried on in a planned manner. Prices are based on values and are determined by the state in a unified manner. Prices no longer fluctuate with changes in supply-demand relationships. The law of value is no longer an alien force ruling over people. Basically speaking, it is consciously utilized by people to serve socialist construction. Furthermore, the effects of the law of value on social production have also been greatly restricted. Their concrete manifestations are as follows:

First, production in the socialist state enterprise is not subject to fluctuations according to the level of prices and the magnitude of profit. Production is not regulated by the law of value, but rather by the national economic plan formulated according to the requirements of the fundamental economic law of socialism [the satisfaction of the ever-increasing needs of the state and the people] and the law of planned development of the national economy. Based on the needs of the state and the people, the state plan stipulates what and how much to produce, and the state enterprise must thoroughly carry this out. The enterprise must produce according to the plan regardless of profit. Any loss is then made up by planned subsidies. If the leadership of an enterprise disobeys the stipulations of the plan and on its own expands production of highly profitable products, it will violate the requirements of the fundamental economic law of socialism and the law of planned development of the national economy and go astray on the capitalist road.

Second, production in socialist rural collective enterprises is also carried out under the guidance of the state plan. Unlike the state enterprise, the collective enterprise is an economic unit responsible for its own profits and losses. The level of product prices and the magnitude of income directly influence the accumulation of the collective and the income of its members. Other conditions being equal, the collective enterprise generally tends to produce more of those products which have low costs and which command high income. In this respect, the law of value influences the production of the collective enterprise more than is the case with production in the state enterprise. However, the area sown for food grains, cotton, vegetable oil, and other major crops is stipulated by the state plan. The collective economy cannot arbitrarily expand the sown area of those crops commanding a higher income. It can only increase the yield per-unit-area of these crops within the sown area specified by the state through more intensive farming, more fertilizers, and better management. Therefore, with regard to the production of major products in the rural collective economy, the regulating role of decisive importance is still played by the law of planned development of the national economy. The law of value merely plays a secondary role. Only for products which are not important to the state and the people, those not included in the state plan or procured through contracts, are the level of prices and the magnitude of income of greater importance. Products which command higher revenue develop easily, while products which command lower revenue develop only with great difficulty. The law of value performs a regulating role to a certain extent with regard to these products.

As far as the whole of socialist production is concerned, planning is primary and price is secondary. That is to say, in the allocation of social labor among various production sectors, what and how much to produce are regulated by the state plan, which reflects the requirements of the fundamental economic law of socialism and the law of planned development of the national economy. The state plan plays a primary and decisive role. The law of value is still useful, but it plays only a secondary and supportive role.

While there is a need to utilize, there is also a need to restrict

Under conditions of socialist public ownership, the law of value has a two-fold effect on socialist production: on the one hand, if utilized correctly, it can have the effect of actively promoting the development of production; on the other hand, as the law of commodity production, it is, in the final analysis, a remnant of private economy. As long as the law of value exists, bourgeois right will also exist, and will bring danger and harm to socialist production. Hence, the socialist state must be extremely careful in utilizing the law of value, and must research, study, and sum up experiences. Only in this way can we make use of its positive effects on socialist production, while at the same time we restrict its negative, destructive effects.

In the process of development of socialist production, the direction of effects exerted by the law of value and the law of planned development of the national economy is sometimes the same. For example, the law of planned development of the national economy requires the acceleration of production of certain cash crops to meet the demand for raw materials, due to rapid development of some light industries. The prices of these cash crops can also guarantee a reasonable income to the agricultural collective economy. Under these conditions, the state plan's requirements for increased production are the same as the requirements of the agricultural collective economy for increased production and increased income. The plan for increased production can generally be fulfilled or overfulfilled. However, the direction of the effects exerted by these two laws can be different. With regard to the comparative price relations between food grain crops and cash crops, and among various cash crops within agricultural production, the prices of some cash crops can bring a relatively higher income to the collective economy than the prices of other cash crops. If the law of value is permitted to freely influence production, it will be detrimental to the requirement of the national economic plan that there be an overall increase in production of all crops (though in varying degrees for different crops).

Thus we can see that when the effects of the two laws are identical, the law of value plays a constructive role in the process of fulfilling the state plan. But when the effects of the two laws are different, the law of value, if not handled well, disrupts the fulfillment of the state plan and plays a negative role. What has been described as conscious utilization of the law of value means that the role of the law of value must be comprehensively understood and that through political and ideological work, arrangement of the state plan, and price policy, the positive role of the law of value must be utilized and its negative role restricted so that its effects on socialist production will be conducive to fulfilling the state plan. Our Party and government have consistently emphasized socialist education of the peasant and planned leadership of agricultural production. At the same time, they have also paid attention to the rational arrangement of the purchase prices of agricultural and sideline products and to the comparative price relations among various agricultural and sideline products. They have struggled hard to be able both to satisfy the state's need for agricultural and sideline products and to promote the development of commune and brigade production and the increase of the commune members' income, thus correctly handling the interests of the state, the collective, and the individual.

The conscious utilization of the law of value by the socialist country in order to promote socialist production is also manifested in its use in the system of economic accounting as a means of implementing the policy of running an enterprise with diligence and frugality. Based on the requirement of the law of value, the socialist country charges the same price for the same products according to the average social expenditure of labor in producing the product. But since conditions in production technology and levels of management and operation will differ, the individual labor expended on the same product in different enterprises may differ. The individual labor expenditure in enterprises which are experienced in mobilizing the masses, constantly updating production technology, and lowering costs by careful and detailed calculation may be lower than the average social expenditure of labor. They can thus fulfill and overfulfill the plan targets assigned by the state and occupy an advanced position. Conversely, enterprises which are careless, wasteful, conservative, and inefficient in mobilizing the masses to transform their backward technological conditions may have individual labor expenditures which are higher than the social average. They cannot fulfill the plan targets assigned to them by the state and occupy a backward position. Therefore, the unified prices set by the socialist state, making use of the law of value, are conducive to exposing the contradictions of various enterprises in operation and management and aid in detecting disparities between the advanced and the backward. Thus, assorted enterprises can be pressed to constantly improve their operation and management, lower their production costs, and implement the policy of running an enterprise with diligence and frugality. But, as the state wants to use the law of value in its application to the management of state enterprises by means of the economic accounting system, it must use the economic categories of value, price, profit, etc. Thus, there will inevitably arise situations where price and value deviate from each other. And thus, under the influence of bourgeois thinking, some enterprises might use the bourgeois right embodied in the law of value, disregarding the needs of the state and the people, to produce high-priced, high-profit products, thereby violating the requirement of the fundamental socialist economic law and the law of planned development of the national economy. Such negative effects exerted by the law of value on the production of the state enterprises must be severely restricted.

To correctly apply the law of value, we then have to: follow the requirements of the law of value to set prices rationally; utilize the influence and effects of the law of value to organize production rationally; calculate precisely the volume of production and tap and utilize production potentialities based on actual conditions; and constantly improve production methods, lower production costs, and implement economic accounting. These positive functions reveal that the law of value is a great school. Stalin observed: "It is a good practical school which accelerates the development of our executive personnel and their growth into genuine leaders of socialist production at the present stage of development."[7]

In socialist society, the proletariat wants to make use of the law of value to promote the development of socialist construction while the bourgeoisie tries hard to use the law of value to set up free markets and disrupt socialist construction. The Liu Shao-chi and Lin Piao cliques tried hard to exaggerate the role of the law of value. They emphasized the "almighty nature" of the law of value and advocated the law of value as regulator of social production. In restoring capitalism, the Soviet revisionist, renegade clique has flagrantly used the law of value as "an objective regulator of socialist social production." It has also launched a "new economic system" centering on putting profit in command and adopting material incentives in accordance with this revisionist theory. Even though the measures taken by the domestic and foreign revisionists are sometimes different, their purpose is the same, namely, to disrupt socialist construction and restore capitalism. The experience reflected in the struggles between the two lines with respect to the question of the law of value tells us that it is necessary to draw a line of demarcation between Marxism and revisionism and firmly adhere to the socialist road if the law of value is to correctly serve socialist production. We should never be careless, otherwise we will lose our way.

THE NATIONAL ECONOMIC PLAN MUST CORRECTLY REFLECT OBJECTIVE LAWS

Work on the national economic plan must reflect the requirements of objective laws

The law of planned development of the national economy and the law of value are both objective economic laws in socialist society. The roles of these laws are realized basically through their conscious application. The national economic plan of the socialist state is a form of

148

conscious application of these laws. Work on the national economic plan includes research, formulation, implementation, inspection, adjustment, and summation. Without the work on the national economic plan, it is impossible to realize proportionate development of the socialist national economy. Of course, even if people do not consciously apply them, the law of planned development of the national economy and the law of value will eventually prevail. For example, if the economic leadership organs did not seriously investigate and study, did not respect the objective requirements of the law of planned development, or if they formulated the proportions carelessly or formulated the price plan without considering the requirements of the law of value (setting prices arbitrarily such that the socially necessary expenditure of some branches of production was not compensated, with the result that production could not continue), then various dislocations would appear in mutually-dependent branches of social production. These phenomena would teach people by negative example to respect these laws and to take account of the requirements of these laws by strengthening and improving work on the national economic plan.

An important link in the work on the national economic plan is the formulation of plans. Plans are formulated by people and are products of ideology. Ideology is a reflection of reality and also reacts back on reality. A correct plan promotes rapid development of the socialist economy. An incorrect plan hinders the development of the socialist economy.

If the national economic plan is to be correct, it is necessary first of all for people to identify and grasp the objective requirements of the law of planned development, in all its aspects, in the process of formulating the plan. Its requirements must be reflected in their thinking. This is by no means easy. In socialist society, the bourgeoisie and all exploiting classes work overtime to disrupt and interfere with the planned development of the national economy and make it difficult for the proletariat to understand this law. Lin Piao and company had argued that planning is just a lot of "idle talk" and that if you want to get the right proportions, "just go out and do it,"* aiming to confuse matters and sabotage socialist construction. Besides, the whole national economy is a complex entity full of contradictions. Imbalances crop

---

* This is evidently a reference to a pragmatic and unprincipled approach to planning work, which would basically deny the scope of planned economy.

up and then get resolved . . . only to crop up again. Objective conditions are changing all the time; hence, people must go through a learning process in order to grasp objective laws. But this is definitely not to say that the proportional relations in the national economy cannot be identified. Provided that we constantly sum up experience, penetratingly investigate and study, seriously analyze, rely on the masses, and do meticulous work, it is entirely possible to gradually identify the law of planned development and bring the national economic plan more into conformity with the requirements of this law.

The law of planned development of the national economy merely requires that harmonious, proportional relations be maintained among interdependent sectors in the development process. It does not indicate the direction and duties of socialist economic development. It is the fundamental economic law of socialism—the satisfaction of the ever-increasing needs of the state and people—that indicates the essential direction and duties of socialist economic development. Therefore, an accurate national economic plan must correctly reflect not only the requirements of the law of planned development but also the requirements of the fundamental economic law of socialism in its various aspects. The national economic plan, which reflects the requirements of these objective laws, embodies the interests of the proletariat and the laboring people as a whole. It is the Party program for economic construction and must be treated seriously and implemented resolutely.

Overall* balance is the basic method in planning work

In the work on the national economic plan, it is important to master overall balance. Overall balance is not balance within individual sectors. It is balance in agriculture, balance in industry, and balance between industry and agriculture. Overall balance is the basic method in a planned economy.

The task of overall balance lies mainly in the arrangement of proportional relations in the national economy. In accordance with the major tasks of the state in the planning period, the state properly

---

* This may also be understood as integrated (that is, intersectoral and interregional) balance.

allocates labor, material resources, and finance to various sectors of the national economy and establishes a balance between social production and social needs—so that the growth of production of the means of production corresponds to the needs of the ever-developing socialist production, and so that the growth of production in the means of consumption corresponds to the needs arising from the gradual improvement of the people's livelihood.

The process of overall balance is a process of exposing, analyzing, and resolving contradictions. To do a good job in overall balance, we must handle contradictions with a positive attitude, energetically promote production of means of production temporarily in short supply, and accelerate the development of key sectors in the national economy that are temporarily backward so that a new balance can be established on a new and higher level. Only in this way can national defense construction, general economic construction, and the needs of the people's livelihood be better safeguarded. To oppose Chairman Mao's proletarian revolutionary line, the Liu Shao-chi clique sometimes suggested so-called "short-run balance" and practiced passive balance in a big way to pull down the high to suit the low.[8]*

Sometimes they set targets so high that they were not feasible. When these targets could not be reached, they resorted to "total retreats." They pushed a Right opportunist line in planning work that was "Left" in form but Right in essence.

Overall balance is the establishment of a balance in the whole national economy. But it is not an even application of force without

---

* The Maoists did not see balance as a static relationship between economic variables. They conceived of it as a dynamic phenomenon in which, as the text emphasizes, balance gives way to imbalance which in turn gives way to a new balance. "Passive" and "short-run" balance were attempts to achieve formal balance; a premium was placed on equilibrium at every phase of development. The criticism by the Maoists was that the quest for such temporary or "short-run" balance would contribute to greater imbalances in the long run. This view of balance would stifle and restrict the dynamic elements of the different levels of the national economy, drag down the advanced, and squash local initiative. For the Maoists, the way to adjust for imbalances induced by rapid and uneven growth and to overcome various bottlenecks and shortfalls was to encourage the backward to catch up with the advanced and to encourage all levels of the economy to dig deeper into their own production potentialities and to mobilize local resources—this was "active" balance. The theory of "passive balance" was used by rightist forces to denigrate mass movements to build local industries, which were seen as "irregular" and likely to cause "disturbances of balance."

differentiating what is more and what is less important. If two hands had to catch ten fish at one time, the result would be that no fish could be caught. In the complex proportional relations of the whole national economy, there are the principal and the secondary, the dominant and the subordinate. To achieve overall balance, we must differentiate the more and less important and make sure to take care of the key points. We must first guarantee that the needs of the leading links and the key sectors in the development of the national economy be met. In formulating a plan for capital construction, the principle of concentrating forces to fight a battle of annihilation must be implemented. If we start from departmentalism, pay no attention to what is more important and what is less important, concentrate on too many items, and spread the limited labor power, material resources, and funds thinly over a long battlefront, then our forces will be dispersed, and the early completion and operation of many key items will inevitably be affected. Of course, safeguarding the key points does not mean neglecting ordinary things. There are close relations of mutual dependence between the key points and ordinary things. Ordinary things will not develop properly if we neglect the key points. But if we neglect ordinary things, the development of the key points will also be affected. Therefore, provided that we take care of the key points, we must also pay attention to ordinary things. We must start from the whole and consider all vertical and horizontal relations in order to avoid the error of one-sidedness.

In the work of overall balancing, attention must be paid to the balance of labor, materials, and funds. People are the most important factor of the productive forces; so of the three, the balance of labor must be arranged first. In conformity with the principle that agriculture is the foundation of the national economy, sufficient labor must first be secured for agriculture. Laborers will be transferred from agriculture to industry, or other sectors of the national economy, only when the development of agricultural production and agricultural mechanization enables the rural areas to succeed in providing surplus labor power and more marketable grain and commodity crops. If we depart from this prerequisite and transfer too much labor power from agriculture, the overall balance will be disrupted, and this would be unfavorable to the rapid, planned, and proportionate development of the national economy.

There is an inevitable process of the emergence of imbalances and the establishment of new balances among the various sectors of the national economy. To guarantee proportionate development among various sectors, it is necessary to establish and maintain a certain amount of material reserves. The amount of material reserves of various kinds must be appropriate. If the reserves are too low, they cannot satisfy the needs for filling the gap between two relative balances. As a result, some sectors will have to work below capacity because of a shortage in certain material resources, and this will affect the rapid development of the national economy as a whole. If the material reserves are so high as to exceed the need for filling a temporary shortage, then material resources which could have been used for current production will not be available, and this will also adversely affect the rapid development of the national economy.

Follow the basic principles of planning work

To do a good job in planning work, in addition to using the basic method of overall balance, it is also necessary to observe some basic principles derived from the practical experience of planning work.

Planning work must give full play to both central and local initiative and must combine centralized and unified leadership with local initiative.

To formulate and implement a unified national economic plan, it is necessary to have a highly centralized and unified leadership. In national economic planning work, there can be no unified national economic plan if there is no centralized and unified leadership; the viewpoint of the whole situation must be promoted and excessive decentralization, under which every local unit can make its own plans, must be opposed. However, socialist centralized leadership is built on a wide foundation of democracy. Centralized leadership must be combined with local initiative. In formulating a national economic plan, the central departments concerned must find out what local opinion is, consult with local units, and formulate plans with local units. In implementing the plan, it is also necessary to allow exceptions for local conditions. These exceptions are not excuses for creating independent kingdoms but are necessary allowances that suit the interests of the whole, permit full tapping of production potentialities according to local conditions, and better facilitate the fulfillment of the national economic plan. As for the system of planning work, it is necessary to implement a system combining unified planning with level-to-level administration. Chairman Mao pointed out in the period of the founding of the People's Republic of China: "What should be unified must be unified. Excessive decentralization, with each doing what they separately think 'best', cannot be permitted. But it is necessary to combine unification with local adaptations."[9] Later, Chairman Mao taught us more than once to rely on local initiative more often in handling the relations between the center and the localities. The local units should be encouraged to do more things under centralized and unified planning. Following Chairman Mao's teachings, the broad people of the country criticized and repudiated the "dictatorship by regulations" pushed by the Liu Shao-chi clique that stifled local initiative, and they better exercised both central and local initiative in the work of planning and management, thus promoting the rapid, planned, and proportionate development of China's socialist economy.

Chairman Mao remarked, "When the plan is being formulated, it is necessary to mobilize the masses and to leave leeway."[10] This is a very important principle in national economic planning work.

In socialist construction, the mass line must be followed whatever the work may be. Mass movements must be vigorously launched. Planning work must also follow the mass line. The masses must be mobilized to discuss lines, expose contradictions, uncover disparities, and accelerate changes. If the plan targets are not discussed by the masses, they are the ideas of the cadre. Only after the plans are discussed by the masses do they become the plans of the masses. Only then will the plan targets be both advanced and attainable and will the enthusiasm of the broad masses be fully aroused.

Plan targets should be advanced. Only an advanced plan can embody the superiority of the socialist system, and only an advanced plan can heighten morale. To formulate an advanced plan, it is necessary to struggle with conservative thought. Some people clearly realize there is immense production potential, but they set the plan targets very low. All they care about is to be able to fulfill the plan comfortably. The process of formulating a plan is also a process of struggle between advanced and conservative thought.

Plan targets should be advanced. But this does not mean that the higher the targets, the better. Plan targets that are too high to be practicable not only will fail to unleash the enthusiasm of the masses but will dampen it. Advanced plan targets must have a scientific basis; they

154

must be attainable and practicable. Chairman Mao said: "No one should go off into wild flights of fancy, or make plans of action unwarranted by the objective situation, or stretch for the impossible."[11] Plan targets that are objectively possible should not be set too high. Leave some leeway. Practical experience demonstrates that plan targets which are not set too high and which enable the plan to be overfulfilled through the efforts of the masses are more favorable to unleashing the enthusiasm of the masses.

It is necessary to combine long-range plans (plans covering five years, ten years, twenty years) with short-range plans (annual plans, quarterly plans, and monthly plans) in national economic planning. If long-range plans are not set, it is difficult to arrange capital construction. Long-term plans embody long-term targets. They encourage people to raise their sights and to exert themselves. The worker comrades put it well: "Without big targets in our minds, even one simple straw is heavy enough to bend our backs. With big targets in our minds, even Mount Tai will not bend our backs." But long-term plans require that short-term plans materialize, that they are grasped, and that they serve the purpose of comparison and inspection so that the fulfillment of long-term plans will not fall short.

The planning work for an economy under socialist collective ownership has its own characteristics. An economy under collective ownership must obey the leadership of a unified state plan. But it can retain a higher degree of flexibility and independence provided that the unified state plan and state policies and laws are not violated. This allows the initiative and enthusiasm of the collective economy in socialist production to be brought into fuller play through local adaptations, enabling the collective economy to develop in step with the state economy.

155

Major Study References

Engels, *Anti-Duhring*, part 3, chapter 2
Stalin, *Economic Problems of Socialism*
Mao, "Correct Handling of Contradictions," section 1

Notes

1. Lenin, "Uncritical Criticism," *CW* 3, p. 618.
2. Engels, *Anti-Duhring*, p. 366.
3. Mao Tsetung, "Comments on 'A Long-Range Plan of the Red Star Collective Team,' " in *Socialist Upsurge in China's Countryside*, originally published in 1956 and for which Mao wrote the preface and editor's notes. A slightly different English translation can be found in a reprinted *Socialist Upsurge in China's Countryside* (Peking: Foreign Languages Press, 1978), p. 437.
4. Mao, "Correct Handling of Contradictions," *SR*, p. 446.
5. Engels, *Anti-Duhring*, p. 385.
6. Stalin, *Economic Problems of Socialism*, p. 18.
7. Ibid., p. 19.
8. When means of production were in temporary short supply, "short-run" and "passive" balancing was a method [criticized in the text] to cope with such shortages.
9. Mao Tsetung, from "Directive Issued at the Fourth Meeting of the CPGC," published in *People's Daily*, 4 December 1949. A slightly different translation can be found in Michael Kau and John Leung, eds., *The Writings of Mao Zedong*, 1949-76, vol. 1 (Armonk, N.Y.: M.E. Sharpe, 1986), pp. 46-47.
10. Quoted in "Grasp Revolution, Promote Production, and Win New Victories on the Industrial Front," *Peking Review*, 28 February 1969 (9), p. 6.
11. Mao, cited in *The Red Book*, p. 223.

7

WE MUST RELY ON AGRICULTURE AS THE FOUNDATION AND INDUSTRY AS THE LEADING FACTOR IN DEVELOPING THE NATIONAL ECONOMY

The Interrelationship Between Socialist Agriculture and Industry

Agriculture and industry are the two major sectors of material production in the socialist national economy. Correctly understanding the importance and role of these two sectors in the national economy and correctly handling their relations are essential if we are to consolidate and develop the worker-peasant alliance and promote rapid and planned development of the socialist national economy.

AGRICULTURE IS THE FOUNDATION OF THE NATIONAL ECONOMY

We must rely on agriculture as the foundation in developing the national economy

To live, to produce, and to engage in cultural and social activities, people must first solve the problem of eating. Agricultural production is a precondition for the survival of human beings and for all productive activities. Agriculture (including gathering, planting, hunting, fishing, and animal husbandry) was the only sector of production in the early stages of human society. Because labor productivity was so exceedingly low in this epoch of human history, as a matter of sheer survival, it was necessary that all available labor of the primitive commune engage in agricultural activities. Only when labor productivity in agriculture developed to the degree that a portion of the labor force could grow agricultural products in sufficient quantity to support all the members of society could labor be freed up to engage in other activities. Thus, the handicraft industry separated off from agriculture to become an independent branch of production; commerce emerged, and so did branches of human activity that were concerned with intellectual production, such as culture and education. The higher the labor productivity was in agriculture, the more developed were the branches outside of agriculture concerned with material and intellectual production. Marx observed, "The less time the society requires to produce wheat, cattle, etc., the more time it wins for other production, material or mental."[1] He also pointed out, "This natural productivity of agricultural labor . . . is the basis of all surplus labor."[2] In essence, agriculture is the basis of human survival and the basis for the independent existence and further development of the other branches of the national economy. This is an economic law applicable to all historical periods in human society.

The role of agriculture as the foundation of the national economy is more pronounced in socialist society than in any previous society. In capitalist society, the objective law of agriculture as the foundation of the national economy plays its role under competition and the anarchy of production. Some imperialist countries whose domestic agriculture was underdeveloped plundered their colonies and semicolonies for agricultural products by paying low prices to satisfy the developmental requirements of monopoly capital. In those countries, it was not domestic agriculture but foreign agriculture that served as a foundation of the national economy. In socialist society, it is not permissible to plunder the agriculture of backward countries. Even if exchanges are made according to equal values, it is still not permissible to rely on foreign countries for food, or to develop the socialist economy on the basis of foreign agriculture. To do so would be contrary to the principles of independence and self-reliance. In organizing the development of the national economy, the socialist country must consciously apply the objective law of agriculture as the foundation of the national economy.

In concrete terms, the primary reason that the development of the socialist national economy must rely on agriculture as the foundation is that the development of the various branches of the socialist economy depends on agriculture to provide means of subsistence. Regardless of the enterprise—be it in industry, transportation, or education—the bottom line is that agriculture has to provide a certain amount of commodities and grain.

Another reason that agriculture is the foundation for developing the socialist national economy is the fact that it is the source of industrial raw materials (with the exception of a portion of supply that comes from industry itself). For light industry in particular, raw materials are by and large provided by agriculture. At present, approximately 70 percent of the raw materials for our light industry is provided by agriculture. Heavy industry also requires certain agricultural products as inputs. If agriculture could not increase its supply of raw materials, industrial development would be gravely affected. Chairman Mao pointed out: "Light industry is closely related to agriculture. Without agriculture there can be no light industry."[3] Agriculture is directly related to industrial development, particularly that of light industry.

Another reason why agriculture is the foundation for developing the socialist national economy is the fact that the rural areas constitute a vast market for industrial products. The rural population, accounting for approximately 80 percent of the total population, forms a major market for industry. The more developed agricultural production is, the more commodity grains and industrial raw materials will be produced, and the higher will be the peasants' purchasing power. The peasants' need for both light and heavy industrial products is always growing. Soon after the victorious implementation of China's cooperativization, Chairman Mao observed: "It is not yet so clearly understood that agriculture provides heavy industry with an important market. This fact, however, will be more readily appreciated as gradual progress in the technical improvement and modernization of agriculture calls for more and more machinery, fertilizer, water conservancy and electric power projects, and transport facilities for the farms, as well as fuel and building materials for the rural consumers."[4]

Another reason why agriculture must be relied on as the foundation in developing the socialist national economy is the fact that agriculture is the main reservoir of labor power for industry and other sectors of the national economy. To develop socialist industry, commerce, and transportation, additional labor is required. It is not enough that we exert efforts to raise labor productivity in these sectors in order to free up the labor force thus saved for new needs; additional labor must also come from outside these sectors, partly from the urban areas and partly from the rural areas. Chairman Mao pointed out, "It is the peasants who are the source of China's industrial workers."[5] However, the share of the rural population that can be transferred as labor force to support the needs of other sectors of the national economy is not determined by these developmental needs as such but by the level of development of agricultural production, by how much agricultural labor productivity can be increased. Only under the conditions that agricultural labor productivity is being constantly raised and the output of agricultural and sideline products is constantly increasing is it possible to transfer an appropriate amount of labor power out of agriculture to support the development of other sectors of the national economy.

There is yet another reason why agriculture must be relied on as the foundation in developing the socialist national economy. Agriculture is an important source of the accumulation funds of the state. In addition to directly providing the state with funds through agricultural taxes, agriculture indirectly increases socialist accumulation by supplying agricultural products to light industry as raw materials. Therefore, the development of agriculture also assumes significance by increasing state revenue, expanding the accumulation fund, and supporting socialist construction.

Viewed from the above aspects, the importance and role of agriculture in the national economy determine that the development of the national economy cannot be separated from the development of agriculture. If agriculture is not properly developed, other sectors of the national economy will not do well either. The experience of China's socialist construction has demonstrated that if there is a bumper harvest in a particular year, the development of the national economy will accelerate in the same year or in the following one. Conversely, if there is a lean year, the development of the national economy will slow down in the same year or the next one. This should tell us that in socialist construction the principle of relying on agriculture as the foundation for developing the national economy must firmly take hold.

The fundamental way out for agriculture lies in mechanization

Agriculture is the foundation of the national economy. In order to develop the national economy, we must treat the development of agriculture as a leading priority. Only when agriculture is developed as the foundation of the national economy can light industry, heavy industry, and other economic, cultural, and educational undertakings be developed.

How can agriculture be developed? The socialist country cannot achieve agricultural mechanization before agricultural collectivization. Agricultural collectivization must precede the use of large machines. But after the collectivization of agriculture is accomplished, it is very important to achieve agricultural mechanization on the basis of agricultural collectivization. On the eve of China's upsurge in agricultural cooperation, Chairman Mao had already pointed out that China's countryside required not only the realization of social reform—the conversion of the system of individual ownership to one of collective ownership—but also the realization of technical innovation—the conversion of hand labor to mechanical production.

"The social and economic physiognomy of China will not undergo a complete change until the socialist transformation of the social and economic system is accomplished and until, in the technical field, machinery is used, wherever possible, in every branch of production and in every place."[6] After the victorious accomplishment of China's agricultural collectivization and the establishment of the rural people's communes, Chairman Mao opportunely proposed the grand task of steadily realizing agricultural mechanization. He clearly pointed out, "The fundamental way out for agriculture lies in mechanization." By giving full play to the stimulating role of socialist relations of production, and with the support of socialist industry, especially heavy industry, the pace of agricultural mechanization will be quickened.

Before liberation, old China was a very backward agricultural country. In 1949, the food grain output of the whole country amounted to only 216.2 billion *jin*.* After liberation, when socialist relations of production were established and developed in the rural areas through agricultural collectivization and the people's communes, agricultural production developed substantially. The output of food grain in 1971 reached 492 billion *jin*, more than twice the amount of 1949. But the level of mechanization in China's agriculture is still not high. Agricultural labor productivity remains relatively low. Compared with other countries where the level of agricultural mechanization is fairly advanced, China's agricultural production is still in a relatively backward state. This condition is not in line with the development of China's industry and other sectors of the national economy. Therefore, it is necessary to go further with agricultural mechanization and promote rapid development of agricultural production on the basis of continuously consolidating and developing socialist relations of production in the rural areas.

When machines are used in plowing, seeding, harvesting, and transportation, agricultural labor productivity will be raised tens and hundreds of times. Plowing by hand, a veteran worker can only plow one *mu*** a day. With an ox, it is possible to plow four *mu* a day. With a medium or large tractor, several tens to several hundreds of *mu* can be plowed in a day, effectively raising agricultural labor productivity by tens to hundreds of times. The labor power saved through agricultural mechanization can be used to increase production, both intensively and extensively, by raising the yield per unit-area and promoting the overall development of agriculture, forestry, animal husbandry, sideline production, and fishery. The labor power saved can also be used to support the development needs of other sectors of the national economy.

The realization of agricultural mechanization can also help bolster China's capacity to combat natural calamities and help lessen its dependence on the weather for food. With China's vast territory and many rivers, some drought and flooding will occur every year. But with electrically-powered drainage and irrigation equipment, water can be more effectively controlled. The resulting reduction in damage due to possible droughts or floods will guarantee a steady and high yield in agricultural production. The poor and lower-middle peasants put it

---

* One *jin* is equivalent to 0.5 kilograms or 1.1 pounds.
** One *mu* is equivalent to 1/15 hectare, or 0.16 acres.

well: "The sound of machines in the river brings joy to the crops in the field. With no fear of drought and flooding, good harvests and high yields are guaranteed."

Under the guidance of Chairman Mao's proletarian revolutionary line, and especially after the Great Proletarian Cultural Revolution, there has been rapid development in China's agricultural mechanization. Comparing 1973 with 1965, electricity consumption in the rural areas increased 2.8 times, use of chemical fertilizers increased 1.9 times, ownership of large and medium tractors increased 2.2 times, and ownership of hand-held tractors increased 75-fold. In this same period, of the total farmland, the area actually plowed by mechanized means increased by about 70 percent. Electric drainage and irrigation equipment increased 2.8 times. Over 90 percent of the counties in the country have repair shops for agricultural machinery. With the step-by-step achievement of agricultural mechanization in China, the drought control and drainage capacity of agriculture will increase, the people's ability to combat natural calamities will be strengthened, and the steady growth of agricultural production will be more assured. From this we can see that the further achievement of agricultural mechanization, on the basis of agricultural collectivization, is a necessary path for developing agricultural productive forces.

Besides facilitating the development of agricultural productive forces, agricultural mechanization will also react powerfully on the development of heavy industry, especially the machine-building, chemical, electric power, and fuel industries. Agricultural mechanization will also create favorable conditions for narrowing the differences between industry and agriculture, town and country, and mental and manual labor, thus further consolidating the worker-peasant alliance.

In the process of gradually realizing agricultural mechanization, the material basis of the collective economy will grow daily, and the three-level ownership system of the rural people's commune will be further consolidated and developed. The experience of agricultural mechanization has demonstrated that large- and medium-sized agricultural machines can be effectively utilized only if they are owned by the commune and the production brigade. Consequently, with the development of agricultural mechanization, the scale and role of the collective economy at the commune and brigade levels will gradually expand, and the superiority of the people's commune will be further revealed.

The poor and lower-middle peasants will love the people's commune all the more and will be all the more resolute in following the socialist road. The poor and lower-middle peasants used vivid language to depict the necessity of agricultural mechanization: "The people's commune is full of strength. The collective economy blooms with a red flower. With agricultural mechanization, even a class-twelve typhoon will fail to overpower us."

In agriculture, learn from Tachai

Agricultural mechanization will be gradually achieved on the basis of collectivization—this is an inevitable trend of development of socialist agriculture. But agricultural mechanization must be under the command of revolutionization. Chairman Mao teaches us, "Once the correct ideas characteristic of the advanced class are grasped by the masses, these ideas turn into a material force which changes society and changes the world."[7] When the broad masses of poor and lower-middle peasants, who are the masters of socialist agriculture, study Marxism-Leninism-Mao Tsetung Thought and master Chairman Mao's line and general and specific policies, they acquire indomitable strength and become powerful enough to tame mountains and harness rivers. They can transform unfavorable natural conditions into favorable ones, transform low yields into high yields, advance from a condition of owning no agricultural machines to owning various agricultural machines, and realize the potential of agricultural mechanization. This is how the Tachai Production Brigade of Tachai Commune in Hsiyang County, Shansi Province, was transformed.

The Tachai Production Brigade is situated in the Taihang Mountains. Before agricultural collectivization, it was a poor mountainous area with plenty of rocks and little soil. The poor and lower-middle peasants of Tachai described it this way: "The mountain is high, and rocks are plentiful. When you go outside, you have to clamber up slopes. There are less than 3.5 *mu* of land for each family. Natural disasters are commonplace." When the elementary cooperative was started in 1953, the average per-*mu* yield of food grain was 250 *jin*. In the process of developing from the elementary cooperative to the advanced cooperative and then to the people's commune, the Party branch of Tachai Production Brigade firmly adhered to the principle of putting proletarian politics in command. It issued the slogan "transform the people, transform the land, and transform the yield," used Mao Tsetung Thought to educate the cadres and the masses, and carried out a big transformation in agricultural production through an ideological revolution among the people. The cadres and the masses of Tachai Brigade smashed the sabotage of the landlord, the rich peasant, the counterrevolutionary, and the bad elements, and resisted interference from the revisionist line pushed by the Liu Shao-chi and Lin Piao cliques. Under the guidance of Chairman Mao's great policy of self-reliance through arduous struggle, Tachai Brigade engaged in capital construction for water control and transformed the "three lost fields," in which water, fertilizers, and soil were lost because of poor construction, into "three retained fields," in which water, fertilizers, and soil were retained after the fields had been leveled and terraced. The average per-*mu* yield of food grain in Tachai Brigade was gradually raised from 250 *jin* in 1953 to 543 *jin* in 1958, 802 *jin* in 1964, and 1,096 *jin* in 1967. Simultaneous with the rapid growth of food grain production, Tachai Brigade achieved all-round development of agriculture, forestry, animal husbandry, and sideline production. In this process of "transforming the people, transforming the land, and transforming the yield," the Party branch of Tachai Brigade also led the commune members to use their own hands to combine indigenous and foreign technology to substantially push forward the mechanization of plowing, cultivating, threshing, transporting, and processing food grain and fodder, and to advance on the road of putting mechanization under the command of revolution. The heroic attitude of the poor and lower-middle peasants to fight nature and farm for revolution is a powerful criticism and repudiation of the reactionary fallacies of Lin Piao who slandered the worker-peasant laboring people, saying, "All they think about is how to make money, get rice, oil, salt, sauce, vinegar, and firewood, and take care of their wives and children," and of Confucius who preached that "the little people can only be persuaded by self-interest."

The Tachai Brigade is a model of how to develop socialist agriculture in accordance with Chairman Mao's proletarian revolutionary line. The fundamental experience of the Tachai Brigade lies in conducting the three great revolutionary movements of class struggle, the struggle for production, and scientific experiment, firmly adhering to the principle of putting proletarian politics and Mao Tsetung Thought in command, and maintaining the spirit of self-reliance and hard work and the communist style of loving the state and loving the collective. The most essential thing is to educate the peasants in Marxism-Leninism-Mao Tsetung Thought, to consciously implement the basic line of the Party, and to consolidate and strengthen the dictatorship of the proletariat over the bourgeoisie. "In agriculture, learn from Tachai" is a great call from Chairman Mao. Countless examples have shown that in agriculture, whether to learn from Tachai or not makes a big difference.

Owing to the interference and sabotage of Liu Shao-chi's revisionist line before the Great Proletarian Cultural Revolution, Hsiyang County, where Tachai Brigade is located, did not unfold the mass movement of learning from Tachai. Its agricultural production developed very slowly. The total output of food grain in the county as a whole hovered around 70 to 80 million *jin*. The annual maximum sale of food grain to the state was only 7 million *jin*. The Great Proletarian Cultural Revolution transformed the outlook of Hsiyang County. Starting in 1967, the whole county vigorously unfolded the mass movement of learning from Tachai. It also resisted the interference and sabotage of Lin Piao's revisionist line. The people of the whole county fought heaven and earth, transformed mountains and rivers, and greatly transformed the land acreage of Hsiyang County. Agricultural production developed rapidly. The output of food grain doubled in three years and tripled in five years. The total output of food grain in 1971 reached 240 million *jin*, three times greater than the peak output before the Great Proletarian Cultural Revolution. Commodity food grain sold to the state reached 80 million *jin*, a more than ten-fold increase over the record harvest achieved before the Great Proletarian Cultural Revolution.

The experience of Hsiyang County's learning from Tachai demonstrates that when the masses are armed with Mao Tsetung Thought, they can overcome any difficulties and can perform any miracle in the human world. Vigorously unfolding the mass movement of learning from Tachai and letting the Tachai flower bloom all over the country will certainly accelerate the development of agricultural production, further consolidate the socialist base in the rural areas, and permit agriculture to play a greater role as the foundation of the national economy.

166

All trades and industries must
support agriculture with their efforts

Agriculture is the foundation of the national economy. Agricultural production influences the development of the whole socialist national economy. If agriculture is not properly developed, other trades and industries cannot hope to develop either. If agriculture is properly developed, everything else will do well too. The development of socialist agriculture is related to all trades and industries. All trades and industries must attach great importance to the support of agriculture and must actively perform the job of supporting agriculture. The industrial sectors must, above all, regard the support of agriculture and the promotion of agricultural mechanization as a major task. They must resolutely orient their work toward the objective of treating agriculture as the foundation. Small local industries such as iron and steel, machine building, chemical fertilizer, and cement must all the more firmly adhere to the correct orientation of serving agricultural production.

The support of agriculture by all trades and industries is an important characteristic of the socialist economy. In capitalist society, industry exploits agriculture, and the urban areas plunder the rural areas. Therefore, the relationship between the industrial capitalist and the laboring peasant is one of class antagonism. In the socialist economy, after the urban and rural areas have undergone socialist transformation, and on the basis of the system of socialist public ownership, the antagonism between the urban and rural areas and between industry and agriculture is eliminated. But there are still two forms of socialist public ownership. And because the economic, cultural, and technological level of the rural areas is still below that of the urban areas, there remain basic differences between them. The great program of the proletariat to build socialism and communism requires that, in the process of continuously developing agricultural production and carrying forward with social reform and technical innovation in agriculture, these basic differences be gradually narrowed and finally eliminated. Therefore, in developing the socialist economy, it is an objective necessity that all trades and industries lend their support to agriculture and to raising the economic, cultural, and technical level of the rural areas. The proletarian party calls on all trades and industries to firmly embrace the principle of treating agriculture as the foundation of the national economy and to render their assistance to developing socialist agriculture from all sides and aspects.

Out of their need to restore capitalism, the bourgeoisie and its agents inside the proletarian party not only will not narrow the differences between the urban and the rural areas but will introduce the capitalist method of letting industry exploit agriculture and letting the urban areas plunder the rural areas. The process of capitalist restoration in the Soviet Union is also the process of intensifying control and exploitation of the rural areas by the bureaucrat-monopoly bourgeoisie headed by Brezhnev. The revisionist line of "emphasizing industry at the expense of agriculture" and "squeezing agriculture to benefit industry," advocated by the Liu Shao-chi clique, was also a line that sought to widen the differences between town and country and between industry and agriculture and, ultimately, to restore capitalism.

It is not an easy job to imbue people with the idea of treating agriculture as the foundation and of resolutely implementing the policy of having all trades and industries support agriculture. Under the influence of the revisionist line, people often develop the idea of upgrading industry and downgrading agriculture. After agriculture has reaped bumper harvests for several years in succession, the idea of treating agriculture as the foundation loses ground in people's minds. They pay lip service to "agriculture, light industry, heavy industry" but act according to "heavy industry, light industry, agriculture." The tendency to neglect agriculture in the allocation of funds and the supply of material goods is obvious. These conditions demonstrate that to foster the principle of agriculture as the foundation, it is necessary to seriously study Chairman's Mao's theories about the interrelations between agriculture and industry, to seriously study the general policy of developing the national economy with "agriculture as the foundation and industry as the leading factor," and to further criticize and repudiate the various reactionary fallacies of modern revisionism that preach disdain for agriculture.

Under the guidance of Chairman Mao's revolutionary line, tens of millions of educated youths in China have answered his great call that "educated youths must go to the villages and receive reeducation from the poor and lower-middle peasants" and have gone to the rural areas and mountainous areas to fight in the forefront of agricultural production. This is a social revolution that changes the established customs of society and a strategic measure for training a large number of successors to the proletarian revolutionary cause. Confucius, the spokesman for the declining slave-owning class, greatly despised agricultural labor. His student Fan Chih asked him how to grow crops and vegetables. He scolded him for being "a small man." Lin Piao, the faithful disciple of Confucius, inherited this reactionary idea completely. He maliciously attacked the policy of sending educated youths to the rural and mountainous areas, branding it as "equivalent to disguised labor reform." All exploiting classes despise both agriculture and the peasants. The hopeless intention of these classes is to ride as long as they can on the shoulders of the laboring people and exploit them. Chairman Mao thoroughly criticized and repudiated the reactionary ideas of people like Confucius. He pointed out that the "political orientation and...methods of work [of the revolutionary youth] are correct," that is, studying revolutionary theories, participating in production, and joining the worker-peasant masses. The rural areas are wide open. It is extremely important for the maturation of the educated youths themselves, the construction of a new socialist countryside, the criticism of Lin Piao and Confucius, and the narrowing of the basic differences between the worker and the peasant, and between mental and manual labor, that the educated youths go to the countryside to accept re-education from the poor and lower-middle peasants, participate in class struggle, the struggle for production, and scientific experiment in the countryside, and be exposed to various experiences and tests.

INDUSTRY IS THE LEADING FACTOR IN THE SOCIALIST ECONOMY

Give full play to the role of industry as the leading factor

Agriculture is the foundation of the national economy. Industry is the leading factor of the national economy. Industry not only produces the means of consumption but also produces the means of production. The revolutionization of the means of production plays a significant role in the development of social production. Viewed historically, the evolution from bone implements to metal tools, and from metal tools to all kinds of machines can be seen to be as not only so many milestones in human history but also as benchmarks of the various economic epochs of human society. The leading role of industry in the national economy means that the development of industry will certainly bring forth advanced tools for the many sectors of the national economy, promote technical innovations in the national economy, and consequently increase labor productivity and social production.

Industry is divided into light industry and heavy industry. Light industry is primarily concerned with producing means of consumption. Heavy industry is primarily concerned with producing capital goods and manufacturing means of production. If industry is to play the role as the leading factor in the national economy, it is necessary to give full scope to heavy industry, precisely because it produces means of production. In socialist society, taking industry as the leading factor means primarily taking heavy industry as the leading factor. The role of heavy industry can be described as follows: to provide various modern agricultural machines, motor power, chemical fertilizers, pesticides, and other means of production for agriculture; to produce various light industrial machines and light industrial raw materials and to promote technical innovation and labor productivity in light industry so that light industry can provide ever-richer and more varied industrial products for daily use; and to provide modern equipment for transportation, construction, and national defense industries, in order to promote technical innovation and development in these fields. From all of this, we can see that the role of heavy industry as the leading factor is not only manifested as the necessary condition for achieving agricultural mechanization; it is also manifested as a necessary condition for promoting technical innovation for the national economy as a whole and for consolidating national defense, guaranteeing national security, strengthening proletarian dictatorship, and supporting world revolution. Just as Chairman Mao pointed out, "Without industry there can be no solid national defense, no well-being for the people, no prosperity or strength for the nation."[9] Industry is the leading factor in the national economy, and this is determined by its important role as described above.

If the role of industry as the leading factor is primarily fulfilled by heavy industry, this does not mean that light industry is unimportant. Although light industry does not generally produce production tools, it is still an important sector of the socialist national economy. It is basically a sector connected with the production of the means of consumption. Like agriculture, it is an indispensable sector for the reproduction of labor power. Light industry is a necessary complement to agriculture. It processes agricultural and sideline products, produces various and necessary consumer goods for the laboring people of the urban and rural areas, and assists agriculture to better play its role as the foundation of the national economy. Compared with heavy industry, light industry is characterized by small investment and quick returns. Light industry contributes to the accumulation fund of the state and is an important source of funds for the expansion of heavy industry. Chairman Mao paid special attention to the position and role of light industry in the national economy: "As agriculture and light industry develop, heavy industry, assured of its market and funds, will grow faster."[10] Chairman Mao clearly pointed out that the development of heavy industry depends not only on agriculture but also on light industry. He emphasized the important role of light industry, something which people easily forget.

Achieve socialist industrialization in a step-by-step way

The important role of industry in the national economy objectively requires the socialist country to pay attention to the development of socialist industry. For countries in which industrial development is relatively backward, an important task facing the proletariat after it seizes political power is to rapidly develop modern industry, realize socialist industrialization, and turn the originally economically backward country into a strong socialist country with modern agriculture, modern industry, modern national defense, and modern science and technology.

In addition to more fully bringing into play the role of industry as the leading factor, and thus guaranteeing the independence of the national economy and consolidating national defense, the realization of socialist industrialization has more far-reaching significance. The step-by-step achievement of socialist industrialization will certainly increase the proportion of the economy under state ownership and strengthen the leading role of the state economy in the whole national economy. The development of socialist industrialization will accelerate the development of industry in areas where industry was formerly backward and change the irrational distribution of industries. At the same time, the ranks of the working class will expand, which will be favorable to strengthening the leadership of the working class over the whole country. Socialist industrialization will also certainly accelerate agricultural mechanization and bolster industry's capacity to support agriculture, in this way creating favorable conditions for gradually narrowing the differences between town and country and between worker and peasant. Exactly because the realization of socialist industrialization has such significance, Chairman Mao, in personally directing the formulation of the Party's General Line in the 1953 transition period, stipulated that step-by-step socialist industrialization is an important task which the whole Party and the whole people should strive to fulfill.

Old China was a semicolonial and semifeudal country. Under the oppression of imperialism, feudalism, and bureaucrat capitalism, production was extremely backward. There were very few modern industries. And those modern industries that did exist were primarily the light industries, particularly textiles. When the country was liberated in 1949, the annual output of steel was only 158,000 tons. There was not much heavy industrial production.

Faced with this "poor and blank" condition inherited from old China, the rapid achievement of industrialization was a very pressing problem for the Chinese proletariat, which now wielded political power. During the past twenty years or more, under the brilliant leadership of Chairman Mao, significant measures have been taken to accelerate the process of socialist industrialization.

To achieve socialist industrialization in China, it is necessary to build a complete socialist industrial system which combines large, medium, and small enterprises, which are distributed geographically in a comparatively rational manner, and in which the iron and steel and the machine-building industries are at the core. This national industrial system is built on the foundation of industrial systems in the various provinces and coordinating regions.* Once modern industrial systems that are complete and relatively independent but which all vary according to local conditions have been established in a planned and step-by-step manner

---

* For most of the period between the 1950s and the publication of the *Textbook*, China had 29 provincial-level administrative divisions (21 provinces, 3 municipalities, and 5 autonomous regions). These entities were grouped in 1957-58 into 7 larger units, called coordinating, or economic cooperation, regions.

in every coordinating region and within the framework of many provinces, the formation of the national industrial system will have an even stronger foundation.

How will socialist industrialization be achieved? Chairman Mao pointed out to us: "In discussing our path to industrialization, I am here concerned principally with the relationship between the growth of heavy industry, light industry and agriculture."[11] To achieve socialist industrialization, it is of course necessary to give priority to developing heavy industry, but that does not mean that agriculture and light industry can be ignored. Chairman Mao pointed out: "It must be affirmed that heavy industry is the core of China's economic construction. At the same time, full attention must be paid to the development of agriculture and light industry."[12] Based on the interrelations among agriculture, light industry, and heavy industry, Chairman Mao formulated a revolutionary line to achieve socialist industrialization with greater, faster, better, and more economical results, namely, to develop heavy industry by developing more light industry and agriculture. Through this method, agriculture and light industry have developed. They not only can provide ever-greater amounts of the means of livelihood and improve people's lives; agriculture and light industry can also solve the problem of accumulating funds and providing markets for heavy industry, thus insuring more stable and reliable development of heavy industry. In the long run, this approach will actually promote greater and better development of heavy industry.

In opposition to Chairman Mao's revolutionary line was the revisionist line of the Liu Shao-chi and Lin Piao cliques. They advocated developing heavy industry at the expense of agriculture and light industry, that is, fewer, slower, and poorer results at higher costs. Because it neglects the development of agriculture and light industry, this line of lopsidedly developing heavy industry does not ensure the living standards of the broad masses and will certainly result in discontent among the people as well as the improper development of heavy industry.

Under the guidance of Chairman Mao's revolutionary line, the revisionist line of Liu Shao-chi and Lin Piao has been criticized and repudiated, independence and self-reliance have been persisted in, the interrelations among agriculture, light industry, and heavy industry have been correctly handled, brilliant results have been achieved in China's socialist industrialization, and the rudiments of an independent and modern industrial system have been developed.

On Chairman Mao's instructions, Premier Chou En-lai had proposed in the report of the Fourth National People's Congress on the work of the government that "we might envisage the development of our national economy in two stages beginning from the Third Five-Year Plan: The first stage is to build an independent and relatively comprehensive industrial and economic system in fifteen years, that is, before 1980; the second stage is to accomplish the comprehensive modernization of agriculture, industry, national defense, and science and technology before the end of this century, so that our national economy will be advancing in the front ranks of the world."[13] Our socialist industrialization has achieved great successes. But compared to the long-term and great goal of socialist revolution and construction, we still have a fairly long way to go. We must continue to advance along the road of socialist industrialization charted by Chairman Mao, carry on the struggle, and build a powerful socialist country in the some twenty years before the end of this century.

In industry, learn from Taching

The process of socialist industrialization is a process of intense struggle between the two classes, the two roads, and the two lines. In the process of leading China to accomplish socialist industrialization, Chairman Mao scientifically charted a road for socialist industrialization based on the interrelations among agriculture, light industry, and heavy industry. But in addition to this, he also advanced policies such as independence, self-reliance, arduous struggle, and "smashing foreign conventions and following our own road to develop industry." This was a sharp criticism and repudiation of the line of "servility to things foreign" and "trailing behind at a snail's pace" advocated by the Liu Shao-chi and Lin Piao cliques. Following Chairman Mao's teaching, China's working class displayed the revolutionary spirit of daring to think, daring to speak up, and daring to act, and gave impetus to the rapid development of China's industrial construction. The Taching Oil Field is an industrial model for building socialism with greater, faster, better, and more economical results. In the struggle between the two lines, it firmly adhered to Chairman Mao's proletarian revolutionary line.

The new Taching Oil Field was formerly a barren plain. When several hundreds of thousands of staff and workers arrived there in 1960 to construct the oil field, it was "a blue sky above and a grass plain below." The weather was cold and the ground was frozen. There were no houses, no beds, no cooking equipment. Production conditions were also very difficult. Several dozens of giant drilling machines were soon set up on the grass plain. But the equipment was incomplete, there were not enough trucks or cranes, and there were no highways. Roads were muddy. Water and electricity supplies were grossly inadequate. Under such difficult conditions, the heroic Taching workers raised the battle cry "Conquer the big oil field, and drive the imperialists, revisionists, and reactionaries nuts," persisted in putting proletarian politics in command, and diligently studied Chairman Mao's works, particularly "On Practice" and "On Contradiction." They armed themselves with Marxism-Leninism-Mao Tsetung Thought, raised high the banner of "The Charter of the Anshan Iron and Steel Company," fought heaven and earth, fought class enemies, and displayed the revolutionary spirit of self-reliance and arduous struggle. In just a little over three years, a big, first-class oil field had been established in China. China has been basically self-sufficient in oil products since 1963. The Taching workers also conducted a large amount of scientific research and solved several important technical problems related to prospecting and refining that are of worldwide significance. Following Chairman Mao's teaching on running an enterprise with diligence and thrift, the total state investment was recovered in 1963. On the eve of May Day 1974, the funds accumulated by Taching for the state amounted to eleven times the state investment, achieving greater, faster, better, and more economical results. Even more important, the Taching Oil Field has trained a worker battalion that has class consciousness, drive, a good style of work, organization, and discipline, and that can endure hardship and fight hard battles. It is this contingent of revolutionized workers that has enabled the Taching Oil Field to continually and rapidly develop. Taching represents a great victory for Chairman Mao's proletarian revolutionary line.

The Taching Oil Field is a red banner on China's socialist industrial front. "In industry, learn from Taching" is Chairman Mao's great call. There is a basic similarity between the Taching Oil Field and the Tachai Brigade. Comrade Chou En-lai pointed out in his Political

Report to the Tenth Party Congress: "One basic experience from our socialist construction over more than two decades is to rely on the masses. In order to learn from Taching in industry and to learn from Tachai in agriculture, we must persist in putting proletarian politics in command, vigorously launch mass movements, and give full scope to the enthusiasm, wisdom, and creativeness of the masses." In learning from Taching, just as in learning from Tachai, of fundamental importance is putting proletarian politics in command, thoroughly implementing the basic line of the Party, and keeping firmly to the socialist orientation. The experience of Taching demonstrated that educating people with Marxism-Leninism-Mao Tsetung Thought and forging a workers' contingent is the most basic element in socialist enterprise construction. With such a battalion of iron and steel armed with Mao Tsetung Thought, there is no fear of hardship or difficulties. The harder it is, the further the contingent will advance, overcoming all difficulties in order to build socialist industries with greater, faster, better, and more economical results. People like Lin Piao slandered the working class as being merely interested in "matters of livelihood." The Taching experience is a slap in their faces. In building socialist industry, whether the political and ideological education of the staff and workers is given priority, whether we trust the masses, whether we dare to mobilize the masses, whether we insist on following the mass line, and whether the road of self-reliance and arduous struggle is followed are important indicators of whether the banner of "In industry, learn from Taching" is truly upheld and whether Chairman Mao's revolutionary line has been truly put into practice.

Chairman Mao's call "In industry, learn from Taching" pointed the direction for China's industrial development. It greatly aroused the working class of China to be self-reliant, to strive hard, and to rapidly transform the face of China's industry. The deep unfolding of the mass movement to "Learn from Taching in industry" will certainly accelerate the pace of China's socialist industrialization and build China into a great socialist country with modern agriculture, modern industry, modern national defense, and modern science and technology.

CORRECTLY HANDLING THE RELATION BETWEEN INDUSTRY AND AGRICULTURE, CONSOLIDATING THE WORKER-PEASANT ALLIANCE

The industry-agriculture linkage in socialist society has a dual character

Marx and Engels set forth that after seizing power, one of the major tasks that the proletariat must accomplish under its dictatorship is the "combination of agriculture with manufacturing industries; gradual abolition of the distinction between town and country."[14] With the achievement of socialist public ownership, socialist society eliminates the antagonistic contradiction characteristic of capitalist society whereby industry exploits agriculture and town plunders country. But the differences between industry and agriculture, and between town and country, still exist. Thus, the linkage between industry and agriculture in socialist society possesses a dual character peculiar to the transitional period from capitalism to communism.

In the history of human society, the connections between agriculture and industry have taken many forms. In the primitive commune economy, handicraft production, such as spinning and weaving and tool- and utensil-making, were carried out as sideline activities of agriculture. This constituted a kind of primitive linkage between industry and agriculture. Alongside the development of social productive forces, there also developed a more complex social division of labor; private ownership was introduced, and the ties between handicrafts and agriculture were severed. From this point on, the linkage between agriculture and industry started to take a circular form of exchange through money. This form of linkage between industry and agriculture, involving exchange through money, has reached its highest development under the capitalist system. However, exchange through money enabled the bourgeoisie to expand the "price scissors" between industrial and agricultural products,* thereby exacerbating the antagonistic contradiction between industry and agriculture and between town and country. But this only hastens the process by which capitalism turns

---

* That is, pushing up the prices of industrial goods and keeping down the prices of agricultural goods.

into its opposite. Marx pointed out: "Capitalist production . . . at the same time . . . creates the material conditions for a higher synthesis in the future, viz., the union of agriculture and industry on the basis of the more perfected forms they have each acquired."[15] The new, "higher synthesis" of agriculture and industry of which Marx speaks, and that now becomes possible with the abolition of the capitalist system, is the direct linkage in production between industry and agriculture, built on the foundation of the system of public ownership of the means of production and under the guidance of unified planning of society.

In socialist society, with the achievement of the socialist transformation of the system of ownership of the means of production and with the implementation by the state of planned regulation of industrial and agricultural production, that new form of linkage between industry and agriculture that Marx foresaw begins to take shape. The socialist state links industry and agriculture in the realm of production through national economic planning. It ensures that socialist agriculture produces food grains in a planned way and that agriculture provides nonstaple food and material demanded by the development of industry. The socialist state ensures that socialist industry produces in a planned way all kinds of daily industrial products demanded by rural villages, along with chemical fertilizers, pesticides, and all kinds of agricultural machinery and equipment demanded by the development of agriculture. Such planned linkages between industry and agriculture in the realm of production present a new relation of mutual support and mutual promotion between industry and agriculture. From this aspect of things, the linkage between socialist agriculture and industry already has a communist element.

But, on the other hand, owing to the still-existing differences between industry and agriculture and between town and country, and owing to the fact that socialist industry is mainly built on the foundation of the system of ownership by the whole people, while socialist agriculture is built mainly on the foundation of the system of collective ownership, and that, therefore, the planned linkage between industry and agriculture in the realm of production can only be realized through exchange through money, bourgeois right is an inevitable aspect of the ties between industry and agriculture. From this aspect of things, there still exist remnants of the old society in the relations between agriculture and industry in socialist society.

The dual character of the linkage between industry and agriculture in socialist society demands that we pay attention to two aspects of work in handling the relations between industry and agriculture. On one hand, and this is the principal aspect, we must do well in planning the linkages between industrial and agricultural production, ensuring that industrial production and agricultural production be brought into the orbit of state planning, and never allow capitalist liberalization in production. On the other hand, commodity exchange between industry and agriculture must be organized well. Even though this is the secondary aspect, it would be wrong to pay little attention to it. Since the linkage of socialist industry and agriculture is a linkage under the commodity system, the law of value must operate. Correctly utilizing the categories of commodity, value, money, price, etc.; correctly handling problems in the exchange of industrial and agricultural products in accordance with socialist principles; gradually narrowing the "price scissors" between industrial and agricultural products; properly arranging the relative prices of various agricultural and sideline products that the state acquires from agriculture—all these factors play an active role in linking up socialist agriculture and industry. At the same time, it must be seen that in the process of linking up socialist agriculture and industry, the struggle between the proletariat and the bourgeoisie is very sharp. The linking up of industry and agriculture requires the use of commodity and money relations, where commodity and money relations are precisely the soil breeding new bourgeois elements. Due to bourgeois influence, the existence of bourgeois right, the force of habit of small producers, it is inevitable that, batch after batch, new bourgeois elements will be engendered. The new and old bourgeois elements always want to use the commodity and money relations between industry and agriculture to speculate and make huge profits. These kinds of capitalist activities must be hit at; bourgeois right in the process of linking up industry and agriculture must be restricted; the spontaneous tendencies of small producers must be criticized. Only in this way can the linkage of industry and agriculture be gradually rid of the traces of the old society, and advance in the direction of communism.

The essence of linking up industry and agriculture is a question of worker-peasant alliance

The question of linking socialist agriculture and industry is not only a question of the proportional relations between these two sectors of material production; it is also a question of the interrelations between two big laboring classes of workers and peasants, which is to say, it is a question of the worker-peasant alliance.

Under the socialist system, the basic interests of the worker and the peasant are identical. Under the leadership of the working class, the worker-peasant alliance, an alliance of mutual support and promotion, is established for the purpose of waging a common struggle to build socialism and to achieve communism. But certain differences still exist between town and country and between worker and peasant with respect to economics, culture, technology, and material livelihood. These differences are the remnants of the old society. To allow these differences to continue to exist for a long time, much less to expand, and not to create conditions for narrowing and eliminating these differences can only be detrimental to the consolidation of the worker-peasant alliance.

In his analysis of the relations between the leading class and the class which is led, Chairman Mao pointed out:

> "The leading class and the leading party must fulfill two conditions in order to exercise their leadership of the classes, strata, political parties and people's organizations which are being led:
>
> "(a) Lead those who are led (allies) to wage resolute struggles against the common enemy and achieve victories;
>
> "(b) Bring material benefits to those who are led or at least not damage their interests and at the same time give them political education."[16]

After the working class has seized political power, led the peasants to overthrow the landlord class, and accomplished land reform and agricultural collectivization, it is still necessary to lead the peasants to fight a determined battle against the class enemy in the rural areas, to conduct socialist education to help them further realize agricultural mechanization on the basis of collectivization, to raise their material and cultural living standards gradually on the basis of the development of production, and to lead them to resolutely follow the socialist road. In this way, the differences between town and country can be narrowed and the worker-peasant alliance can be further consolidated.

Therefore, the question of linking industry and agriculture is fundamentally a question of correctly handling the relations between the worker and the peasant. The essence of this problem is the issue of consolidating the leadership of the working class, consolidating the alliance between worker and peasant, and seeing to it that the working class wages struggle with the bourgeoisie for the allegiance of the peasants—all this is a new issue of class struggle under the socialist system. Chairman Mao's theory of the interrelations among agriculture, light industry, and heavy industry, the general policy of developing the national economy with "agriculture as the foundation and industry as the leading factor," and the arrangement of the national economic plan according to the order of agriculture, light industry, and heavy industry charted the path for solving these problems.

Major Study References

Marx, *Capital* 3, chapter 37
Mao, "Correct Handling of Contradictions," sections 3 and 12

Notes

1. Marx, *Grundrisse,* trans. Martin Nicolaus (New York: Vintage, 1973), p. 172.
2. Marx, *Capital* 3, p. 632.
3. Mao, "Correct Handling of Contradictions," *SR*, p. 476.
4. Ibid.
5. Mao, "On Coalition Government," *SW* 3, p. 250.
6. Mao, "On Question of Agricultural Co-operation," *SR,* p. 413.
7. Mao, "Where Do Correct Ideas Come From?," *SR*, p. 502.
8. Mao, "The Orientation of the Youth Movement," *SW* 2, p. 248.
9. Mao, "On Coalition Government," *SW* 3, p. 252.
10. Mao, "Correct Handling of Contradictions," *SR*, p. 476.
11. Ibid.

12. Ibid.
13. Chou Enlai, "Report on the Work of the Government," in *Documents of the First Session of the Fourth National People's Congress of the PRC* (Peking: Foreign Language Press, 1975), p. 55.
14. Marx and Engels, *Communist Manifesto*, p. 60.
15. Marx, *Capital* 1, p. 474.
16. Mao, "On Some Important Problems of the Party's Present Policy," *SW* 4, pp. 187-88.

8

FRUGALITY IS AN IMPORTANT
PRINCIPLE IN THE SOCIALIST ECONOMY

Practice Frugality and Economic Accounting

Socialist production is at once a process of the planned allocation of labor time and the striving to economize on labor time. Practicing frugality and economic accounting in all enterprises and in the management of the national economy as a whole are essential conditions for building socialism with greater, faster, better, and more economical results.

FRUGALITY IS A NECESSITY IN
SOCIALIST ECONOMIC DEVELOPMENT

The significance of frugality to
socialist economic development

What frugality means here is economizing on manpower, materials, and funds. Economizing on manpower means saving living labor; economizing on materials means saving materialized labor; and economizing on funds means saving living and materialized labor manifested in currency circulation. Therefore, all frugality is in fact economizing on living and materialized labor, or economization of labor time.

In socialist society, economy of labor time assumes immense importance. Marx pointed out: "Economy of time, to this all economy ultimately reduces itself. Society likewise has to distribute its time in a purposeful way, in order to achieve a production adequate to its overall needs; just as the individual has to distribute his time correctly in order

183

to achieve knowledge in proper proportions or in order to satisfy the various demands on his activity. Thus, economy of time, along with the planned distribution of labor time among the various branches of production, remains the first economic law on the basis of communal production. It becomes law, therefore, to an even higher degree."[1]

The aim of socialist production is to meet the needs of the state and the people. In order to produce the maximum possible amount of use value with the minimum amount of labor expenditure, it is necessary to economize on labor time and to allocate labor time in a planned way over the whole of society. These are basic means for guaranteeing, to the greatest extent, the satisfaction of the ever-increasing needs of the state and the people. Practicing frugality thus corresponds to the objective requirements of the fundamental economic law of socialism. To violate the law of frugality is to violate the basic requirements of socialist economic development and to violate the basic interests of the proletariat and the laboring people. Therefore, whether frugality is enforced is primarily an issue of whether the objective laws of socialist economy are accepted and whether the basic interests of the proletariat and the laboring people are valued.

Practicing strict economy is an important means of increasing accumulation through self-reliance in the socialist country. To engage in large-scale economic construction, the socialist country requires a large amount of funds. Where do the funds come from? Unlike capitalist-imperialism and social-imperialism, the socialist country cannot exploit its own people, engage in external aggression and plunder, demand war damages, or sell national resources to develop its economy. The socialist country can only rely on the diligent labor of its laboring people and on internal frugality for accumulation. On the one hand, the production unit saves as much manpower, materials, and funds as possible, rationally allocates funds, and steadily expands the scale of production. On the other hand, nonproduction units, such as state organs, military units, schools, and people's organizations, must economize and eliminate waste in order to minimize the share of nonproduction expenditure in the state budget. In this way, a large amount of funds can be accumulated for economic construction. The socialist country must practice strict economy and combat waste in order to accelerate socialist construction and better satisfy the ever-increasing needs of the state and the people.

Frugality is especially important to China's socialist construction. China is not only a big country, it is also an economically backward and poor country, a developing country. Chairman Mao pointed out: "We want to carry on large-scale construction, but our country is still very poor—herein lies a contradiction. One way of resolving it is to make a sustained effort to practice strict economy in every field."[2] Therefore, Chairman Mao called upon the whole people: "To run factories with diligence and economy, to run shops with diligence and to run all state enterprises and cooperative enterprises with diligence and economy, and to run all other enterprises with diligence and thrift. The principle of diligence and economy must be applied to everything. This, then, is the principle of frugality."[3] The broad workers and poor and lower-middle peasants fighting on the front lines of production pay close attention to Chairman Mao's instructions. They understand the great significance of frugality. The laboring masses put it nicely, "Diligence without economy means pure waste of effort." Only through diligence and thrift can the laboring masses create wealth and play the greatest possible role and can China soon be developed into a big and strong socialist country. At the same time, our country must fulfill internationalist obligations abroad. Only by saving more domestically, can we contribute more to world revolution.

Chairman Mao pointed out: "All the 600 million people of our country . . . must strive for increased production and economy, and against extravagance and waste. This is of prime importance not only economically, but politically as well."[4] Diligence and frugality have always been the virtue of the proletariat and the laboring people. Under the guidance of Chairman Mao's revolutionary line, the broad masses of China practice diligence and frugality. It has developed into a common habit. Ostentatious display and waste are the poison of the bourgeoisie and all exploiting classes. Extravagance and waste are part of the very nature of the exploiting class. Like their master Confucius, the Liu Shao-chi and Lin Piao cliques were composed of people who "never worked with their four limbs and who could not distinguish the five cereals." They hated Chairman Mao's policy of "building up the country through diligence and frugality." In construction work, they went after "the big, the foreign, and the glamorous" projects. In resource management, they resorted to what was described as "generous budget and generous expenditure." In operations and management, they went so far as to argue that "we needn't worry about money escaping abroad, even if accounts aren't reckoned for three years." Their criminal design was to corrode the outlook of those in the revolutionary ranks who were irresolute, to waste national resources, to undermine socialism, to sabotage proletarian dictatorship, and to restore capitalism. Therefore, by practicing strict economy and combating waste, we will not only be accelerating socialist construction but will also be striking a powerful political blow against people like Liu Shao-chi and Lin Piao. This orientation also stands as a thorough criticism and repudiation of traditional concepts and conventional wisdom. We must consciously resist the corrosion and attacks of bourgeois ideology and uphold the glorious tradition of the proletariat, that is, we must establish new enterprises with ardor and practice diligence and strict economy. "We must help all our young people to understand that ours is still a very poor country, that we cannot change this situation radically in a short time, and that only through the united efforts of our younger generation and all our people, working with their own hands, can China be made strong and prosperous within a period of several decades."[5]

The socialist system opens a broad avenue to frugality

The development of socialist revolution and construction objectively demands that we practice strict economy; at the same time, the socialist system also opens a broad avenue to frugality. In socialist society, the laboring people have become masters. The ultimate purpose of saving as much manpower, material resources, and funds as possible— in order to provide more accumulation for the state and the collective and to facilitate expanded reproduction—is to satisfy the needs of the proletariat and the people. Hence, practicing strict economy is consistent with the fundamental interests of the working people, and, therefore, frugality can become the conscious activity of the broad laboring people. Once the socialist enthusiasm of the masses has been aroused, all methods for frugality are employed: warehouses and storehouses are inventoried to tap potential material resources; technical innovations are made in a big way to tap the potential of unused equipment; labor organization and methods of operation are improved to tap labor potential; and campaigns of multipurpose utilization are launched in order to turn "waste" into valuable items and to transform "the useless" into the useful. For example, the main plant of Northeast Pharmaceuticals mobilized the masses to launch such a campaign of multipurpose utilization. The laboring masses and technicians taxed their brains to find ways to use "solid waste," "fluid waste," and "gaseous waste." As a result, many new products were added. The main distillery in Peking formerly produced only liquor. After launching a mass movement to increase production and practice strict economy, many important products were produced from the "three wastes" of the plant. It developed into a diversified enterprise, turning out a great variety of products. The broad laboring masses are concerned with frugality and practice it in thousands of ways. This is not possible in capitalist society. Under capitalism, the capitalist practices frugality in his own enterprise. The purpose is to maximize costs and extract maximum surplus value. The essence of frugality is to increase the exploitation of hired labor. Marx pointed out: "Capitalist production, when considered in isolation from the process of circulation and the excesses of competition, is very economical with the materialized labor incorporated in commodities. Yet, more than any other mode of production, it squanders human lives, or living labor, and not only blood and flesh, but also nerve and brain."[6] The laboring masses are extremely resentful of the so-called frugality practiced by the capitalist and will resolutely resist and rebel against it.

Under the conditions of socialist public ownership, the law of frugality not only plays a role within various enterprises; more important, it plays a role in the national economy as a whole. The socialist economy is a planned economy. "[Labor-time's] apportionment in accordance with a definite social plan maintains the proper proportion between the different kinds of work to be done and the various wants of the community."[7] The socialist country can, through the national economic plan, rationally utilize manpower, material resources, and funds, centrally organize production and circulation, unfold socialist cooperation over the whole country, and combine the frugality of individual enterprises with the frugality of the whole society. Under capitalism, owing to competition among enterprises and the anarchy of social production, it is basically not possible to practice strict economy in a systematic manner throughout the whole society. This is especially so because of the serious waste of manpower, material resources, and funds associated with the periodic occurrence of business cycles. Marx pointed out: "The capitalist mode of production, while on the one hand, enforcing economy in each individual business, on the other hand, begets, by its anarchical system of competition, the most outrageous squandering of labor-power and of the social means of production."[8]

Even though the socialist system has opened a broad avenue to frugality, if the possibility of practicing strict economy is to be turned into reality, we must strengthen the education of the masses and cadres in ideological and political line, unceasingly unfold struggle against waste, and foster the idea of building up the country through diligence, frugality, and arduous struggle. On the other hand, we must also combine ideological and political work with complex economic work and establish rational systems of rules and regulations to conduct such work. Strengthening economic accounting in the various enterprises and in the national economy as a whole and running socialist enterprises on the basis of economic accounting are a very important means by which the principle of frugality is being practiced.

ECONOMIC ACCOUNTING IS AN IMPORTANT MEANS TO DEVELOP THE SOCIALIST ECONOMY WITH GREATER, FASTER, BETTER, AND MORE ECONOMICAL RESULTS

Use economic accounting to achieve greater, faster, better, and more economical results

Economic accounting involves the activities of recording, calculating, analyzing, and comparing productive consumption* and productive results in the production (or management) process. This is commonly referred to as bookkeeping or balancing the books. In the struggle for production, people learned a long time ago the importance of using economic accounting. In the primitive commune of India there was a bookkeeper to record agricultural accounts and all events connected with them.[9] Marx borrowed the story, popular among bourgeois economists, of Robinson Crusoe, who lived on an isolated island, to explain

---

* Productive or industrial consumption refers to the use (consumption) of machinery, raw materials, semi-finished goods, etc., in the production process.

the necessity of bookkeeping in the production process: "Moderate though he be, yet some few wants he has to satisfy, and must therefore do a little useful work of various sorts, such as making tools and furniture, taming goats, fishing and hunting. . . . Necessity itself compels him to apportion his time accurately between his different kinds of work. . . . His stock-book contains a list of the objects of utility that belong to him, of the operations necessary for their production; and lastly, of the labor time that definite quantities of those objects have, on an average, cost him."[10] The more socialized the production process becomes, the greater the necessity for economic accounting. "Book keeping . . . is . . . more necessary in capitalist production than in the scattered production of handicraft and peasant economy, more necessary in collective production than in capitalist production."[11]

Under different social systems, the form, content, and social consequences of economic accounting are different. In capitalist society, the capitalist uses economic accounting to extract the greatest possible amount of surplus value with the smallest possible amount of capital. The stricter this economic accounting, the more capital is saved, the crueler is the exploitation of hired labor, and the poorer do the laboring people become. In socialist society economic accounting no longer reflects capitalist relations of production. Rather, it reflects socialist relations of production. By promoting economy of time, socialist economic accounting also promotes the uninterrupted growth of socialist production, and can thereby better satisfy the ever-growing needs of the state and the people.

Socialist economic accounting, as an important means of enforcing strict economy, demands all-round frugality. And it demands that the all-round development of the socialist economy with greater, faster, better, and more economical results be treated as a unified whole. In production, if we practice frugality, reduce the consumption of raw materials, fuel, and labor, and thereby lower costs, then we can use the same amount of labor, material resources, and funds to produce more products. Improving on the design of products and projects, and cutting out unnecessary work procedures and crafts, can shorten the time required for turning out products and completing construction projects, reduce the consumption of living labor and materialized labor, and accelerate production and construction. The rational selection of raw materials and the substitution of cheaper and better quality raw materials for more expensive and poorer quality raw materials can lower production costs and raise the quality of products and projects. Therefore, there exists an objective unity as regards achieving greater, faster, better, and more economical results. We should not treat these elements as if they stood absolutely opposed to one another. Yet, by the same token, there is also an aspect of contradiction in achieving greater, faster, better, and more economical results. If we ignore the contradictions among these elements, and one-sidedly pursue saving—which will in the end affect the quality of products and projects—then the results not only won't be greater, faster, and better, but in fact won't even be more economical; instead, there will be great waste.

The laboring masses are the masters of economic accounting

Socialist economic accounting is an important means of enforcing strict economy and developing the socialist economy with greater, faster, better, and more economical results. But it can only be realized by relying on the conscious activism of the broad laboring masses. This is an entirely different situation from that of capitalist economic accounting. Because economic accounting in the capitalist enterprise serves the bourgeoisie, and is fundamentally opposed to the interests of the laboring people, economic accounting is the business of only a few experts employed by the bourgeoisie. Socialist economic accounting serves the interests of the laboring people and is in line with their basic interests. Therefore, economic accounting in the socialist enterprise is not merely the work of experts but is also an economic activity involving the conscious participation of the laboring masses.

The socialist system requires as a necessary condition and furnishes as an objective possibility the combining of economic accounting by experts with economic accounting by the laboring masses. China's experience demonstrates that in order to do a good job in economic accounting, the masses must participate. Economic accounting by experts must be based on mass accounting. Because the broad laboring masses have rich practical experience gained from fighting long and hard on the production battlefront, they are familiar with their own production conditions. They know clearly where waste exists and where frugality can be further increased. They know very well how to improve techniques to raise efficiency, and how to calculate labor costs, material resources, and funds in order to achieve greater, faster, better, and more economical results. Group accounting, organizations for economic supervision, and conferences to analyze economic activities in China's socialist enterprises are some of the better forms of economic accounting that have resulted from the masses taking control of financial management and from various combinations of the laboring masses and the experts. In the socialist enterprise, the masses, as their own masters, participate in group accounting, analysis of economic activities, and financial management. Thus, economic accounting not only plays a greater role in promoting greater, faster, better, and more economical results; it also presses the leading personnel and the broad cadres to act in accordance with the Party's line and its general and specific policies so that the enterprise will advance along the socialist road.

In socialist economic accounting, it is quite necessary to utilize experts. Keeping in touch with the various workshops and departments in the enterprise allows the experts to become more familiar with the situation of the whole enterprise and facilitates leadership and organization of many and varied economic activities. But this is not enough. The experts must also go down to the front lines of production, fully rely on the masses, strengthen investigation and research, respect the creativeness of the masses, and promptly solve problems of economic accounting that arise out of the production process. Only in this way can they play their proper role.

THE SYSTEM OF ECONOMIC ACCOUNTING IS A MANAGEMENT SYSTEM OF THE SOCIALIST ENTERPRISE

The system of economic accounting embodies the relations between the state and state enterprises and the relations among state enterprises

After the socialist country establishes a socialist state economy, how should the state enterprise be managed?

The state economy is the property of the laboring people as a whole. The socialist state controls and manages the state economy as the representative of the laboring people as a whole. The socialist state fixes production and operational plan assignments for the state enterprise and centrally allocates the output and earnings of the state enterprise to meet the needs of the state and the people. Does state management of the state economy therefore imply that there is no relative economic independence in the many state enterprises? Does this mean that all means of production and funds for workers and staff are provided free to the state enterprise, that all products of the state enterprise are passed on to the state without compensation, and that there is no independent accounting of profit or loss in the state enterprise? This kind of enterprise management system, called the free supply system, does in fact have a history. During the 1918 to 1920 period in the Soviet Union, this system of state enterprise management was adopted, and it was necessary under the special historical conditions of war communism. But it is not practicable under the general conditions of building socialism. The absence of independent accounting of profit and loss under a free supply system would make it difficult to detect where inefficiencies or waste existed in the process of production and operation. Consequently, conditions would not be favorable to mobilizing the working personnel of the state enterprises to take operational responsibility for running these enterprises, and conditions would not be favorable to realizing the principle of frugality.

Then is it permissible to let state enterprises take independent responsibility for their own profits and losses? This is even less practicable. If this system were implemented, the system of socialist ownership by the whole people would exist only in name and would degenerate into a system of enterprise ownership, into a system of small group ownership, and ultimately into a system of capitalist private ownership.

In socialist society, the economic management of enterprises by the state objectively requires a system along the lines of the system of economic accounting. What is the economic accounting system? In simple terms, it is an economic management system which guarantees the central leadership of the state but which at the same time permits the relatively independent operation of enterprises.

As early as 1942, Chairman Mao raised the principle of "centralization in leadership, and decentralization in management" in his directive to establish an economic accounting system in all sectors of the state economy. Centralized leadership means planned management of state enterprises in accordance with centralized lines, directives, and policies. In the light of concrete conditions, enterprises are assigned various production targets including variety, quantity, quality, output value, labor productivity, costs, and profits to be turned over to the state. The enterprise must be held accountable to the state plan and must fulfill the various targets assigned by the state. Decentralized management means that the state allots a certain amount of funds to the state enterprise to use, according to its production and operational requirements, and that the enterprise will organize its production, supply, and marketing activities—but on the basis of the plan assignment given it by the state. Every state enterprise possesses a certain relative independence of operation. Each enterprise must conduct independent calculations, figuring out its own gains and losses, and each uses its own enterprise income to cover expenses and to furnish accumulation for the state. Decentralized management under centralized state leadership requires, on the one hand, that the state enterprise improve management of production and operation, strengthen economic accounting, and guarantee the fulfillment of the state plan. On the other hand, the state must create the requisite conditions such that the state enterprise can improve production and operation. For example, production plans must be promptly announced and the supply of raw materials and broad socialist cooperation must be properly organized. The management of the state enterprise by the state through the economic accounting system guarantees centralized leadership by the state over state enterprises and also facilitates the exercise of socialist operational initiative by the enterprise. This arrangement both avoids excessive control, which may be unfavorable to enterprise economic accounting, and prevents excessive enterprise independence, which may lead to the capitalist tendency of free operation.

Under the system of economic accounting, the economic relations among state enterprises take the form of joint cooperation and independent accounting. State enterprises are the property of the proletariat and the entire laboring people. They are mutually linked not only by the social division of labor but also by the fact that they belong to the same owners and are objectively required to coordinate and closely cooperate on their own initiative. These enterprises are fundamentally different from capitalist enterprises based on the system of private ownership. However, under the conditions of implementing the economic accounting system, state enterprises are also units with relatively independent management. Therefore, when manpower, material resources, and funds are exchanged among state enterprises, it is not only necessary to promote the cooperative style of communism; it is also necessary to observe the principle of exchange of equal value and to keep books and settle accounts so that economic effects can be calculated.

Under the conditions of the economic accounting system, the above-mentioned relations between the state and state enterprises and among state enterprises enable hundreds of thousands of state enterprises to both closely cooperate and organize production in a coordinated way as an organic whole and to fully exercise their individual management responsibility and initiative. Lenin once pointed out: "Trusts and factories have been founded on a self-supporting basis precisely in order that they themselves should be responsible and, moreover, fully responsible, for their enterprises working without a deficit."[12] Some people wonder: since all state enterprises are state property, why is it necessary to have such a refined accounting system for them? This idea, which negates the system of economic accounting, violates the socialist principle of frugality. In socialist society, the expansion of production and the practice of strict economy depend primarily on the Party's ideological and political work, on its ability to raise the consciousness of the cadres and the masses. But it is also necessary to establish a system of responsibility with respect to operation and management. If the system of economic accounting were not implemented, conditions would not be favorable for strengthening the operational responsibility of the management personnel, and substantial waste of manpower, material resources, and funds would result.

Strengthen management with the system of economic accounting in the rural people's communes

The implementation of management by means of economic accounting is necessary not only in the state economy but is also absolutely necessary in the collective economy. The means of production and products within the economy of socialist collective ownership by working people belong to each individual collective economic organization. Each collective economic organization is an accounting unit. It organizes production under the direction of the state plan and sells commodities according to prices set by the state. It operates independently and is responsible for its own profits and losses. Production and income distribution are carried on within the collective. At the same time, funds for accumulation are provided to the state through taxes. The socialist national economy is a unified whole. The unified national economic plan drawn up by the state encompasses the collective economy as well as the state economy. To implement management with the appropriate system of economic accounting in the collective economy and to promote the strengthening of economic accounting by each unit of the collective economy will benefit the development of the national economy as a whole as well as the consolidation and development of the collective economy.

China's socialist economy under the system of collective ownership by working people exists in agriculture, industry (including the handicraft industry), transportation, and commerce. But it is most important in agriculture. Here we are mainly concerned with the problem of strengthening management by means of the economic accounting system in the collective economy of the rural people's commune.

China's rural people's commune at present uses the system of three-level ownership of the commune, the production brigade, and the production team. The commune, the brigade, and the production team are all accounting units that operate independently and that are responsible for their profits and losses. Financial transactions among the communes, production brigades, and production teams, as well as the allocation of material resources and labor power, must be based on the principle of "exchange of equivalents on a voluntary and mutually beneficial basis."

In the economy of the rural people's commune under the system of collective ownership, management by means of the economic accounting system is implemented in commune-operated enterprises by the commune and in brigade-operated enterprises by the brigade. The commune and the brigade exercise unified leadership over their respective enterprises, allocate a certain amount of funds to each enterprise, demand that they use these funds in a responsible way to fulfill the production plan assignments given to them by the state, the commune, and the brigade, and require them to meet their expenses with their incomes and fulfill or overfulfill the accumulation assignments set by the commune and the brigade. With the development of commune- and brigade-operated enterprises and with the development of the collective economy at various levels, more and more units within the people's commune are adopting management by the economic accounting system, and management by the economic accounting system must be further strengthened.

The production team is a basic accounting unit that operates independently. The collective fund of the production team is not allotted by the production brigade or the commune. It comes from the contribution and accumulation of the production team members. The commune and the brigade should lead, help, and support the production team to develop the collective economy. They cannot use the funds of the production team to develop the commune or brigade economies. Between the production brigade and the production team, there does not exist a relationship of management by the economic accounting system. This is to say, the production brigade is not ultimately responsible for profits or losses incurred by the production team. The teams themselves are responsible for their own profits and losses.

Although there does not exist a relationship of management by the economic accounting system as between the commune, the production brigade, and the production team, the production team must also adopt economic accounting. Economic accounting in the production team consists primarily of calculating the annual consumption of materialized and living labor in production, reckoning annual income and expenses, reducing expenses and costs, avoiding unproductive labor and other such expenditures, and firmly opposing extravagance and waste. Especially important is the establishment of a sound system of financial management. All financial expenditures must be subject to the required approval procedure. Democracy in financial matters must be practiced. All incoming and outgoing items must be announced monthly to the members. People must have separate responsibilities for food grain, material resources, money, and accounts to prevent excessive consumption, theft, and losses. Once economic accounting is strengthened and the system of financial management is improved, production costs can be reduced, the accumulation of production funds and members' income can be increased, and the broad members will love the collective economy all the more and will struggle for further consolidation and development of the collective economy and oppose spontaneous capitalist tendencies.

Correctly handle the contradiction between calculation in use value and calculation in value

The state economy and collective economy that practice management by means of economic accounting all need to compare and calculate productive consumption and productive results of their production processes. The socialist production process is both a direct social labor process and a value-creation process. As a direct social labor process, the laborers create, according to plans, various use values that suit and satisfy the needs of the state and the people; as a value-creation process, the laborers also create new value, besides transferring the old value of the means of production and raw materials to products. Hence, calculation in use value [materials consumed and material output] or use value accounting, and calculation in value (or value accounting) constitute the two aspects of socialist economic accounting.

Calculation in use value and calculation in value have aspects both of unity as well as contradiction. Use value is the material carrier of value. For products of a given variety and specification, it is generally the case that the achievement of greater output volume and higher quality yields greater value. Hence, generally speaking, if the enterprise overall fulfills the use value targets fixed by the state with regard to product variety, specifications, output, and quality, etc., then it can also fulfill the value targets of output value, surrendered profits [turned over to the state], etc. This is the aspect of unity between calculation in use value and calculation in value. But calculation in use value and calculation in value are, after all, two different kinds of calculation conducted from two different angles; hence, they must also have the aspect of contradiction. The value targets assigned by the state to the enterprise, such as output value, surrendered profits, etc., are combined targets [expressed in monetary and price magnitudes]. On the other hand, the use value targets assigned by the state to the enterprise, such as variety, output volume, etc., are stipulated as discrete targets. When the enterprise overall fulfills the value targets of output value, surrendered profits, etc., that does not necessarily mean

197

that it has fulfilled the use value targets of variety, output, etc. Thus the contradiction often faced by the enterprise in the process of conducting economic accounting is between calculation in use value and calculation in value.

In order to handle correctly the contradiction between calculation in use value and calculation in value, we must first of all have a correct understanding of the nature of value categories in socialist economic accounting.

Capital funds, production costs, profits, and other value categories in the system of socialist economic accounting are linked with socialist public ownership; hence, they reflect specific relations of production and are different from capital, production costs, profits, and other value categories in the system of capitalist economic accounting. Under capitalism, capital is value that generates surplus value, and the value category reflects the exploitative relations of capital over hired labor. Capital funds in the socialist state enterprise are that part of the accumulated state wealth used for production and operation. The use of these funds by the enterprise in production and operational activities follows the requirements of the fundamental socialist economic law of the satisfaction of the ever-increasing needs of the state and the people and serves expanded reproduction. The rational use of capital funds has tremendous significance in developing the socialist economy.

Cost in a capitalist enterprise is the consumption of capital; cost reduction in a capitalist enterprise means capital saving and intensification of the exploitation of labor. Cost in a socialist enterprise is the expense incurred in the production of a certain quantity of products. Because enterprises under the system of economic accounting depend on income from the sale of products to cover expenses and to obtain profits, the continual reduction of production costs means the continual saving of labor time and the raising of labor productivity. The state or the collective can thus accumulate more, and, as a result, more products can be produced to satisfy the needs of the state and the people.

Capitalist profits consist of transformed surplus value expropriated by the capitalist. Profits in socialist enterprises are the net social income created by the laboring masses. These profits are centralized in the hands of the state in the two forms of surrendered profits and taxes, and are mainly used to expand socialist production and to improve the people's livelihoods and living standards.*

Profits in the socialist economy can also be looked at from the perspective of the national economy as a whole. Under certain conditions, the socialist state can allow some enterprises to just break even or even to operate at a loss. For example, in order to bring about a rational distribution of industrial capacity throughout the country, local industries in the interior are developed. Some individual enterprises among them may not be making profits for a period of time owing to unfavorable conditions. Yet the state still supports their development. Or, to take another example, some enterprises producing certain industrial products—especially new products, new materials, and products which support agriculture—may sustain losses over a certain period of time. But, in the interests of the national economy as a whole and the consolidation of the worker-peasant alliance, temporary planned losses are allowed. This kind of profit, examined from the standpoint of the overall interests of the national economy as a whole, is called "higher-level profit" [or "higher-level gain"]. And this kind of

---

* In this section of the text, where socialist profit is contrasted with capitalist profit, the term *ying-li*, a kind of hybrid of gain and profit, is sometimes used, apparently to designate profit under socialism.

In a socialist economy, social production does not involve the exploitation of wage-labor and the domination by, and the reproduction of, alien, antagonistic interests over labor power. Profit is neither the goal of production nor the yardstick by which resources are allocated and enterprise performance and viability judged. Politics commands production—at the national and enterprise level. Private gain ceases to be the organizing and motivating principle of society.

Under socialism, profit, or net income, refers to a social accumulation surplus. This social surplus is the product of a collective and nonexploitative socialist labor process and is utilized by the proletarian state to satisfy social need and to revolutionize society and the world. In monetary terms at the socialist enterprise level, this surplus derives from the difference between production cost and final price under conditions in which a) the enterprise's production activities are worked out as part of a central plan (prices and profits neither determine the composition and level of output nor the direction of technical innovation); b) prices of all inputs and outputs are given to the enterprise (it cannot charge what "the traffic will bear"); and c) profits of the individual production units are placed at the disposal of overall social and economic development.

However, and these are central themes of the text, exactly because profit plays a necessary, though secondary, role in a socialist economy, it can and does exert negative influence on allocation and efficiency criteria and on production activities—in the direction of maximizing income and return rather than serving social interest.

"higher-level profit", embodies the superiority of the socialist system. Of course, this is not to say that profits in individual enterprises and sectors are no longer important, or that excuses should be made for poor management on the part of individual enterprises. Profits of the whole national economy are ultimately based on profits from individual enterprises and sectors. Therefore, enterprises suffering temporary losses should try hard to improve operation, reduce production costs, reduce losses, and turn losses into profits in order to increase socialist accumulation.

From the above analysis, it can be seen that capital funds, costs, profits, and other value categories in socialist economic accounting reflect socialist relations of production. These categories are used by the proletariat to serve socialist construction. Hence, in handling the contradiction between use value accounting and value accounting, we cannot treat the question of fulfilling the value targets assigned by the state as unimportant but must rather take it seriously and actively strive to fulfill various value targets in an all-round way.

On the other hand, it must also be recognized that value categories are, after all, remnants of the economic system of private ownership. Value categories are bound up with the commodity system and embody bourgeois right. For example, since prices will deviate from values, enterprises expending an equal amount of labor to produce products of different varieties and specifications will obtain unequal amounts of output value and profit. If enterprises set out to produce more products yielding high value and high profit, they will have an easier time fulfilling the targets of output value and surrendered profits assigned them by the state. If enterprises find themselves producing more products yielding low value and low profit, they will have a much harder time fulfilling the targets of output value and surrendered profits assigned them by the state. Here we have another example of bourgeois right.

The class interest of the proletariat demands that, in handling the contradiction between use value accounting and value accounting, people consciously restrict this kind of bourgeois right, criticize the line of "output value first" and "profit in command," put the creation of use values that satisfy the needs of the state and the people in first place, and subordinate calculation in value to calculation in use value. The bourgeoisie and its representatives in the Party want to use and expand bourgeois right, carry out the line of "output value first" and "profit in command" in the departments and enterprises they control, produce more of what yields high profit, produce less of what yields low profit, and produce none of what yields no profit. The "total economic accounting system" implemented by the Soviet revisionist renegade clique is designed to carry out this thoroughly capitalist principle of profits in command. In the "total economic accounting system," "the most important summary indicators of the financial activities of enterprises are profits and the rate of profit." In actuality, the enterprise determines the variety and quantity of production according to the expected profits. To increase profits, the enterprises can dismiss workers and increase labor intensity to "reduce production costs." This "total economic accounting system," which puts profits in command, has already become a system of exploitation imposed on the working people of the Soviet Union by the Soviet revisionist bureaucrat-monopoly bourgeoisie, and is an important means through which capitalism has been restored in the Soviet Union.

Therefore we can see that, in the final analysis, the contradiction between calculation in use value and calculation in value in socialist economic accounting manifests itself as the struggle between the proletariat and the bourgeoisie, between the socialist road and the capitalist road. Only by grasping this key link in the struggle between the two classes and the two roads, and by restricting bourgeois right in the realm of value accounting, can we correctly understand and handle this contradiction, subordinate calculation in value to calculation in use value, and prevent economic accounting from following a deviant course.

Major Study References

Marx, Engels, Lenin, & Stalin on Communist Society (not available in English)

Mao, "Introductory Note to 'Running a Cooperative Diligently and Frugally' ", in *The Red Book*, p. 187

Mao, "Correct Handling of Contradictions," section 11

Notes

1. Marx, *Grundrisse*, p. 173.
2. Mao, "Correct Handling of Contradictions," *SR*, p. 474.
3. Mao, *The Red Book*, p. 187.
4. Mao, "Correct Handling of Contradictions," *SR*, p. 475.
5. Ibid., p. 459.
6. Marx, *Capital* 3, p. 396.
7. Ibid., 1, p. 83.
8. Ibid., p. 496.
9. Ibid., p. 337.
10. Ibid., p. 81.
11. Ibid., 2, p. 135.
12. Lenin, "To G.Y. Sokolnikov," *CW* 35 (1973), p. 546.

9

EXCHANGE IS AN ECONOMIC FORM THAT LINKS PRODUCTION TO CONSUMPTION

Exchange and Currency Circulation in Socialist Society

Most products of labor in socialist society can only enter into the realms of productive and personal consumption by being exchanged. What are the characteristics of exchange in socialist society? How is such exchange realized? What are the objective laws that govern it? These issues must be clearly understood if the socialist economy is to develop.

SOCIALIST EXCHANGE POSSESSES NEW QUALITIES, CHARACTERISTICS, AND FUNCTIONS

The characteristics of the three types of exchange in a socialist society

Exchange is determined by production. Production in socialist society has a dual character, and this determines the necessary complexity of socialist exchange. To understand the qualities and characteristics of socialist exchange, it is necessary, first and foremost, to identify the essential exchange relations that actually exist in a given socialist society.

After the socialist transformation of the ownership of the means of production had been basically completed in China, there existed three main categories of exchange relations:

(1) Exchange based on the system of private ownership (the vestiges of private ownership in industry and agriculture, private plots in the hands of collective farm members, and family sideline production.) This type of exchange materializes mainly in the form of trade at county fairs. But there is still another part that materializes in the form of selling to the socialist commercial sector.

(2) Exchange between socialist state enterprises and the collective economy, as well as exchange within the collective economy itself. Members of the rural collective economy buy commodities from the state-run shops with the money distributed by the collective economy. This is essentially exchange between the state-run economy and the collective economy.

(3) Exchange within the system of socialist ownership by the whole people, including exchange between socialist state-run enterprises, as well as exchange between the state and staff and workers.

The existence of these three types of exchange relations clearly reveals the transitional character of socialism, that is, as an historical period of transition from capitalism to communism.

The first type of exchange relation is commodity exchange with private ownership as the foundation. It is basically the same in nature as commodity exchange in the old society. This exchange relation does not constitute the main body of exchange relations in socialist society.

The second type of exchange relation is socialist commodity exchange based on two kinds of socialist public ownership. The qualities and characteristics of this type of exchange need to be examined from two different aspects. On the one hand, since this exchange relation is based on socialist public ownership, the commodities exchanged have the attributes of being direct products of a socialist system. Hence, based on the general principle that production determines exchange, the characteristics of socialist production will inevitably be reflected in exchange and thus reveal the following:

(1) The aim of this type of exchange is not profit, but rather satisfying the needs of the state and the people.

(2) This type of exchange is not carried out amidst competition and anarchy, but rather is conducted under the guidance of a state plan.

(3) Prices of products do not form spontaneously in the market, but rather are set by the socialist state.

These characteristics reveal that exchange based on two kinds of socialist public ownership is different from the exchange of commodities in the old society.

On the other hand, since this type of exchange remains exchange between different owners, it still has the general characteristics of commodity exchange, with these attributes:

(1) Since it is commodity exchange, it must, of necessity, be subject to regulation by the law of value, which objectively calls forth the practice of exchange at equal values.

(2) This type of exchange still requires the use of money as the medium of exchange. Between these two sectors of socialist public ownership, there still exists the relationship of buying and selling and exchange through money.

(3) The value of the exchanged commodity still must be expressed in terms of price. Thus, there will continue to be deviations between the price and value of commodities: the commodity whose price exceeds its value will still enable its owner to gain extra income through exchange; the commodity whose price falls below its value will reduce the income of the owner.

From these characteristics, we can see that bourgeois right continues to exist in the commodity exchange based on two kinds of socialist public ownership, and is not that much different from bourgeois right in the exchange relations of the old society.

The third type of exchange relation is commodity exchange within the state sector of socialist ownership by the whole people. There is a big difference between this type of exchange and any previously existing form of commodity exchange. Throughout history, all commodity exchange—from the exchange of commodities between primitive communes to commodity exchange under capitalism—involved exchanges among different owners. The type of exchange we are now examining is exchange within a unitary system of ownership, that is, exchanges among the same owners. Hence, the qualities and characteristics of exchange have already undergone change. Below, we will individually examine exchange between the state and staff and workers, and exchanges among state-run enterprises.

Exchange between the state and staff and workers assumes the concrete form of the staff and workers of state enterprises using money paid out as wages by the state to buy consumer goods from state shops. This type of exchange is different from previous forms of commodity exchange. Historically, all commodity exchange expressed the movement of "commodity to commodity" or "commodity to money to commodity." This was a relationship in which both parties were buying and selling. For example, in capitalist society the worker sells his labor power to the capitalist, and receives in return a monetary income. He then uses a part of the money to buy consumer goods from the capitalist. This type of exchange takes the form of "commodity [labor power] to money [wages] to commodity [consumer goods]." But in a socialist country, in the exchange relation between state and staff and workers, the staff and workers are the owners of the state and enterprise, so they are not in fact selling their labor power. Because of this, all commodity exchange manifests itself as a one-sided action: on the worker and staff side, there is only buying and no selling; and on the state side, there is only selling and no buying. This situation, where the state enterprise staff member or worker receives monetary wages and goes to a state-run shop to buy consumer goods, approximates the situation described by Marx in the *Critique of the Gotha Programme*: "[The worker] receives a certificate from society that he has furnished such and such an amount of labor (after deducting his labor for the common funds), and with this certificate he draws from the social stock of means of consumption as much as the same amount of labor costs. The same amount of labor which he has given to society in one form he receives back in another."[1] This is also a relation of exchange, and it follows the same principle that regulates commodity exchange: a definite amount of labor of one form can be exchanged in its entirety for the same amount of labor in another form. But the exchange between the state and the staff and workers constitutes a special kind of exchange relation. It is actually a form through which the socialist state uses commodities and money relations to distribute personal consumer goods among the staff and workers. Compared with traditional commodity exchange, this type of exchange already possesses new content and characteristics.

Exchanges among socialist state enterprises are manifested mainly as mutual buying of the means of production from each other. Since the system of socialist ownership by the whole people enters into relations of commodity exchange with the system of collective ownership and since each socialist state enterprise must maintain relative independence in operation and management, then it follows that if one state enterprise requires the product of another it still must calculate price, pay money, and practice the principle of compensation of equal value. Looking at it from this aspect, exchanges among state enterprises still have the character of commodity exchange as their nature. What distinguishes this type of exchange from other forms of commodity exchange in the past is this. Historically, commodity exchange was an exchange between different owners. On being exchanged, ownership of the product was being transferred. The seller lost ownership and the buyer obtained ownership of the product. Exchange between state-run enterprises, however, is exchange between the same owners. When a product is exchanged from one state enterprise to another, it is still the property of the state. This exchange does not result in any change of ownership. At the same time, since the object of exchange between state enterprises is mainly means of production, this type of exchange mediates production and productive consumption. It bears a direct relation to production, hence this commodity exchange relation requires stricter planning than the exchange of consumer goods would normally require. It should be brought even more directly into the orbit of the state plan so as to meet the needs of socialist direct social production. In the important exchanges of means of production among state enterprises, allocation and allotment should be state-planned and should not go through market transactions. This type of exchange, though still possessing the characteristics of commodity exchange, has already begun to acquire the elements of a future communist society, namely, the direct social distribution of products. This is one transitional form that socialist commodity exchange assumes as it progressively develops toward communist direct social distribution of products.

The three categories of exchange relations discussed above amply illustrate the complexity of exchange relations during the socialist period. Commodity exchange exists on the basis of private ownership of the means of production. Socialist commodity exchange exists on the basis of public ownership of the means of production. Importantly, commodity exchange continues to operate within the state sector of the socialist economy, that is, within the system of ownership by the whole people. Exchange within the state sector contains elements of commodity exchange as well as elements of the future communist direct social distribution of products. How to handle the three categories of exchange relations, according to their different qualities and characteristics, is a major problem that confronts the proletariat as it undertakes socialist construction and consolidates its dictatorship.

Bourgeois right in socialist exchange must be restricted

Since socialist exchange, to varying degrees, remains commodity exchange, bourgeois right will inevitably assert itself in exchange. We must recognize, and both utilize as well as restrict, such bourgeois right.

Bourgeois right in commodity exchange is the fertile soil engendering capitalism and bourgeois elements. Historically, capitalism and the bourgeoisie were incubated in commodity exchange and emerged out of the polarization of small commodity producers. Because commodity exchange continues to exist in socialist society, capitalism and new bourgeois elements will inevitably be generated. Under the conditions of practicing the commodity system, it is entirely necessary for socialist enterprises to calculate output value and profit. But this could possibly result in situations in particular departments and units in which the needs of the state and the people, and the requirements of the state plan, are disregarded, situations in which output value and profit are put in command, situations in which capitalist free operations are carried out. These practices will cause some socialist enterprises to degenerate into capitalist enterprises. Furthermore, under the conditions of commodity exchange, there will always be contradictions between supply and demand and there will always be deviations of prices from values. This will induce some people to unscrupulously take advantage of supply/demand and price/value contradictions in order to indulge in speculation, trafficking of goods, and the opening of underground factories—and thereby engendering batch after batch of new bourgeois elements.

Thus, if the state under the dictatorship of the proletariat does not restrict bourgeois right in commodity exchange, capitalism will develop even more rapidly. In the Soviet Union, new and old bourgeois elements have collaborated and used the old base of commodity exchange to corrode and disintegrate the socialist economic base through various legal and illegal means in order to bring about the all-around restoration of capitalism in the Soviet Union. This fact is of great significance. We must fully recognize the sharp and complex class struggle that exists in the process of socialist exchange.

The Soviet revisionist renegade clique has replaced the socialist planned economy with the market economy of capitalism in the sphere of circulation. Previously serving the development of socialist production and the betterment of people's livelihoods, socialist exchange has been completely transformed into a system of capitalist commercial activities serving the pursuit of profit. In view of the circulation of means of production, capitalist commercialization is already at work in the Soviet Union today. One-third of the means of production are exchanged through wholesale business channels, and the remaining two-thirds are exchanged via free trade between those enterprises supplying and those enterprises demanding means of production. The circulation of means of consumption also completely adheres to the principles of capitalist operation with the goal of seeking profit. State-run shops of Brezhnev and Company fleece consumers and bleed the staff and workers. Apart from the state-run shops, there are three kinds of free market for the buying and selling of consumer goods in the Soviet Union: collective farm markets, consumer cooperatives specializing in high-priced commercial goods, and free markets for consumer manufactures. Seventy percent of the Soviet revisionists' collective farm markets are set up in the cities, where "market prices fluctuate all day long" and all kinds of speculation and profiteering activities run rampant. The high-priced commercial cooperatives also carry agricultural subsidiary goods. They operate according to the principle of buying cheap and selling dear, and also do business on a commission basis. They are not much different from the collective farm markets. Many high-priced commercial cooperatives are set up in collective farm markets. Most goods sold in the free markets for manufactured consumer goods are obtained through fraudulent or corrupt means: through the back door, under the table, or by relying on special privileges and access to "internal shops" [within the factories producing a given good]. Otherwise, these goods are obtained from foreign tourists and seamen, and then resold in these free markets. The goods sold here are mainly items which are out of stock at the state-run shops for a long period of time or simply not available there. The prices are generally two to three times higher than what is charged at the state-run shops. Many of the sellers in these free markets are speculators and profiteers who travel back and forth logging thousands of miles trafficking goods for sale. Just like the collective farm markets, the free markets for manufactured consumer goods are also paradises for speculators.

In analyzing the relationship of commodity exchange in socialist society to the regeneration of capitalism, Lenin pointed out: "Commodity exchange and freedom of trade inevitably imply the appearance of capitalists and capitalist relationships."[2] The shocking manifestations of the all-round restoration of capitalism in the sphere of circulation in the Soviet Union, of the sort described above, have been justified under the rubric of "free trade." Such is the result of the expansion and strengthening without limit of bourgeois right in commodity exchange.

How does the proletariat restrict bourgeois right in the sphere of circulation? The most important thing is to bring the production and exchange of commodities into the orbit of the state plan. It is absolutely impermissible to carry out "free trade" in violation of state plans. The bourgeoisie and their representatives in the Party will use any means possible to oppose such restrictions. Whenever there is a chance, they will sabotage the state plan and carry on "free trade." Hence, sharp struggle between the proletariat and the bourgeoisie over the question of restriction and counterrestriction in the sphere of circulation is inevitable under the dictatorship of the proletariat. Such struggle in our country has been extremely acute. People like Liu Shao-chi and Lin Piao did their utmost to promote the revisionist line of "free trade," espousing the fallacies of "free market," "free pricing," and "free competition," etc. They strenuously opposed efforts by the proletariat to restrict bourgeois right in the sphere of circulation. They had tried to flood this realm with the capitalist forces of town and country. They trotted out contraband notions like "profit in command," "business first," etc., and tried to introduce the principles of capitalist management into socialist exchange. Liu Shao-chi also advocated that "people in a given field of economic activity can be permitted to buy more items of that field"; Lin Piao peddled the fallacies that "human dealings are above society's laws," "going through the back door" is legal, and so on. They tried to corrupt people's minds. Other old and new bourgeois elements in society are also trying to stir up trouble in the sphere of circulation and to attack the proletariat and socialism. They use bribery to corrupt cadres, and seek to turn state and collective assets into their own property. They carry on speculation and trafficking to disrupt and sabotage the socialist market.

Under the guidance of Chairman Mao's revolutionary line, and after repeated trials of strength, the people smashed the conspiracies of Liu Shao-chi and Lin Piao and company. Capitalist forces have been continually dealt heavy blows. But as long as commodity exchange exists, and with it bourgeois right, there will be fertile soil giving rise to capitalism and the bourgeoisie. Hence, class struggle between the proletariat and bourgeoisie in the sphere of exchange will have to continue. The proletariat must bring the exchange of basic means of production into the orbit of the socialist plan, provide leadership to unfold socialist cooperation, and prevent the old and new bourgeois elements from utilizing means of production to reinitiate capitalist operation. The proletariat must maintain the flow of exchange in materials and goods between town and country, strengthen management of the market and price, and prevent capitalist forces in town and country from disrupting and sabotaging the market. Only on this basis can we effectively restrict bourgeois right in exchange, continually dig out and eventually eliminate the soil breeding capitalism and the bourgeoisie, and can socialist exchange be made to better serve industrial and agricultural production, better serve the worker-peasant-soldier masses, and better serve proletarian politics.

Develop socialist exchange, promote the development of production, and improve the people's livelihood

In the process of social reproduction, production plays a determining role. However, exchange, both directly and indirectly, reacts back on production. Engels said: "Each of these two social functions [of production and exchange] is subject to the influence of what are for a large part special external factors, and consequently each has what are also for a large part its own special laws. But on the other hand, they constantly determine and influence each other to such an extent that they might be termed the abscissa and the ordinate of the economic curve."[3] This statement of Engels is applicable to socialist commodity exchange as well.

The development of socialist industrial and agricultural production is the material basis of socialist production and commodity exchange. As early as 1942, Chairman Mao pointed out, "The general policy guiding our economic and financial work is to develop the economy and ensure supplies."[4] This is to say, only when agricultural production is developed can there be enough means of production to satisfy the needs for further developing production and expanding economic construction and can there be enough consumer goods to maintain thriving markets and stable prices. Without the development of industrial and agricultural production, it is impossible to improve socialist commodity exchange.

On the other hand, socialist exchange also plays an immense, initiating role in the development of socialist industrial and agricultural production. Only through socialist exchange can the exchanges of material resources among various regions of the country and among various state enterprises in different sectors of the national economy be effected. Only through socialist commodity exchange can the relations between agriculture and industry, production and consumption, the economy under state ownership and that under collective ownership, and between the urban and rural areas be properly arranged. The state material supply departments and the commercial departments in charge of socialist exchange actively organize the exchanges of means of production among state enterprises. The socialist commercial departments responsible for socialist commodity exchange actively organize for the purchase of commodities at the appropriate time from the industrial and agricultural production sectors and sell them to consumers in a planned and systematic manner. This plays an enormous role in rapidly developing the national economy in a planned and proportionate manner and in improving the living conditions in the urban and rural areas. It is also an important aspect of consolidating the worker-peasant alliance.

In addition to recognizing and correctly dealing with bourgeois right in the sphere of socialist exchange, we must also correctly handle the contradictions specific to the various types of exchange relations, so as to give full scope to the role of socialist exchange in accelerating production and expanding consumption.

A very important link in the development of exchange within the sector of state-owned enterprises is the ability of the material supply departments to fully understand and correctly handle the contradictions between supply and demand for means of production. In the process of high-speed development of socialist construction, the supply of the means of production generally increases at a faster rate than does the supply of consumer goods. On the other hand, the quantity, quality, variety, and specifications of the means of production often do not fully meet the developmental requirements of socialist construction. Contradictions between supply and demand for means of production will objectively exist for a long time and will be reflected in the various departments of the national economy, in the various regions, and in the various state enterprises. Only through regular study and by properly balancing plans and matching supply with demand can a continuous relative balance between the production of and the requirements for means of production be maintained and can the rapid development of socialist production be promoted.

The process of exchange between the state economy and the collective economy, among the various levels and units of the collective economy, and between the state and staff and workers is even more complicated. The objects of commodity exchange are mainly consumer goods, but such exchange also includes a certain amount of means of production. The contradiction between supply and demand, as manifested in these complex exchange relationships, will exist for a long time. It will concretely express itself as the contradiction between the commercial sector and agriculture and between industry and the consumer.

The contradictions between socialist commerce and agriculture are mainly manifested in the proportions of sideline products that are purchased or retained, in purchase prices, in the forms through which products are purchased, and by the supply and prices of industrial products. A portion of agricultural and sideline production is commodity production to satisfy society's needs. The other portion is self-provided production to satisfy the peasant's own needs. Thus, in purchasing agricultural and sideline goods, it is necessary for the commercial departments to work out the proper ratios between what is purchased by the state and what is retained by the peasants—this so that the state can obtain the required amount of agricultural and sideline products and so that the peasants can also take care of their production and consumption needs. At the same time, when socialist state commerce purchases agricultural and sideline products, it must also be good at supplying industrial products to the rural areas. It must strive to ensure the inflow and outflow of goods and materials to fully meet the requirements of both socialist agricultural production and the peasant's livelihood. The purchase prices of agricultural and sideline products and the supply prices of industrial products directly influence the income of the peasant, the expansion of agricultural production, and state accumulation. It is necessary to determine reasonable purchase prices for agricultural and sideline products and set reasonable prices for industrial products. It is necessary to create conditions to progressively narrow the historically-long-standing "scissors" differential between industrial and agricultural prices. In this way, an exchange relationship based on exchange of equivalent values between industrial and agricultural products can be maintained. Handling the contradictions between commerce and agriculture in accordance with correct principles makes it possible to do a good job in commodity exchange between the urban and rural areas and is favorable to arousing the enthusiasm of the peasants in socialist production, promoting the development of industrial and agricultural production, and consolidating the worker-peasant alliance.

The contradictions between socialist commerce and industry are mainly contradictions internal to the state economy. State industry is engaged in production. State commerce is engaged in marketing. The contradictions between industry and commerce are mainly contradictions involving, on the one hand, the quantity, quality, variety, and price of industrial products and, on the other, market requirements. There is relative stability in industrial production. But market requirements change. The contradictions between relatively stable industrial production and variable market requirements often issue in contradictions between industry and commerce. Other contradictions flow from the lack of coordination between the production plan and the marketing plan, which results from inadequate investigation and research into developments and changes and into the laws of production and the market. The influence of capitalist ideas of operation, or

214

the interference of the revisionist line, further aggravates the contradictions between industry and commerce. To correctly handle the contradictions between industry and commerce, the commercial departments must obey the requirements of the fundamental economic law of socialism, strengthen investigation and research, duly report the requirements of consumers' to the industrial departments, foster closer cooperation between industry and commerce, and actively assist the industrial departments to develop production, expand variety, and raise quality in order to better satisfy both the needs of the state and the people.

The contradictions between production and demand in the commodity exchange process are ultimately manifested as contradictions between socialist commerce and the broad masses of consumers. With rapid industrial and agricultural development, the purchasing power of the people has been steadily raised. It is natural that they require of socialist commerce that it provide them with a greater and improved variety of consumer goods. However, the growth of social production always lags behind the growth of social demand. Therefore, correctly handling the contradictions between commerce and agriculture and between commerce and industry is a necessary condition for correctly handling the contradictions between commerce and the consumers. Furthermore, to correctly resolve the contradictions between commerce and the consumers, it is essential that those who work in commerce embrace the principle of wholeheartedly serving the people. China's commercial workers put it well: "The shelf is only three feet high, but service to the workers, peasants, and soldiers has no bounds." Only when this world outlook becomes deeply rooted can socialist commerce actively organize supplies of commodities, rationally distribute commodities, and properly arrange the socialist market according to the various requirements of the workers, peasants, and soldiers. At the same time, in organizing for the people's consumption needs, socialist commerce should not merely passively adapt to consumer demand; it should actively influence and guide consumption, and do a better job of organizing for people's living requirements according to the developmental conditions of socialist industrial and agricultural production and the conditions of national resources.

SOCIALIST EXCHANGE MUST HAVE
APPROPRIATE FORMS OF ORGANIZATION

Establish an appropriate supply system and appropriate exchange channels

The circulation of means of production between those state enterprises that produce them and those state enterprises that consume them is a very complex process. Appropriate forms of exchange, under the guidance of a central state plan, are required to facilitate the movement of means of production from the sphere of production to the sphere of productive consumption.* The means of production must circulate in a timely way, in the right amount, and must meet certain standards of quality if they are to promote the development of production.

Exchanges of means of production among state enterprises reflect the interrelations among enterprises owned by the whole people, the interrelations among regions, among departments, and between the central economic departments and the local economic departments. China's experience in socialist construction teaches us that it is very important to set up a rational system for supplying material resources as part of the process of handling these interrelations.

China's material resources supply system should adhere to the principles of "centralized leadership, level-to-level administration, and specialized operation" in keeping with Chairman Mao's great strategic policy that we must "be prepared against war, be prepared against natural disasters, and do everything for the people" and his teaching: "Let the local units do more things under a unified central plan." At present, based on the above principle, China's material resources supply system is selectively and gradually adopting in a step-by-step way the method of "regional balance, differential allocation, regulation of variety, and guaranteed delivery to the state under a unified state plan."** This requires, within the framework of a unified state plan and guaranteed

---

* That is, from the sphere where means of production are produced to the sphere where they are used as elements in the production process.

** What is being referred to here and throughout this paragraph are allocative and regulatory mechanisms and policies which aim to coordinate overall economic development on the basis of fostering regional self-reliance (and reducing interregional disparities). Planning authority and supply and purchase policies are key economic levers wielded by

delivery to the state, that locally produced raw materials and equipment should be kept in local balance and that complete sets of equipment should be manufactured locally. This method assists in carrying out the great strategic policy of preparing against wars, preparing against natural disasters, and doing everything for the people. It encourages the step-by-step establishment of industrial systems in the various coordinating regions, and even at the level of individual provinces, the mobilization of central and local initiative, the proper handling of the interrelations between the central and local units, as well as among regions and among enterprises, and it promotes the development of the productive forces.

After a proper material resources supply system is established, the appropriate forms of exchange, along with concrete channels for conducting such exchange, must be set up to expedite the flow of goods. With rational links in circulation, the means of production can be circulated from one state enterprise to another more quickly and economically. At present, the concrete forms of exchange of means of production in the state sector are of three basic types; there are three channels through which means of production circulate among China's state enterprises.

The first is direct supply. This is a form of exchange in which raw materials, equipment, etc., produced by a state enterprise are directly delivered to the user without going through any middle link. It is arranged under a unified state plan and according to supply contracts between enterprises. This form of exchange shortens circulation time, reduces circulation expenses, stabilizes supply-demand relations, and helps improve product quality. It is the direction of development of product exchange between state enterprises. But this form of exchange cannot be used under all circumstances. In general, it is a suitable channel of circulation for those enterprises where supply-demand volumes are large and supply-demand relations of products stable.

The second form of exchange is supply by material resources departments. This too is conducted under a unified state plan. Like the

the center. Specifically: in respect to the allocation of material supplies, central authorities must take account of differences in resource endowments and the general level of development of particular areas or regions, assisting poorer areas, and pay attention to the needs of agriculture and light industry; and in respect to regulation of product mix and product destination, the center, while also taking account of local characteristics, promotes food grain and agricultural self-sufficiency and industrial self-reliance in the local regions while also guaranteeing that locally-produced output flows to where it is needed overall in the economy.

previous form of exchange, it also falls within the scope of plan allocation. However, the product must go through the material resources departments. In other words, according to the product supply contract, raw materials, equipment, etc., produced by a state enterprise must first be collected and sent to state material resources branches. After necessary processing and arrangement by the material resources departments, they are supplied to enterprises for consumption. Raw materials and equipment subject to this form of exchange are generally in great demand, although the demand from some enterprises is small. Now if all goods were delivered directly by the producing enterprises to the consuming enterprises, the producing enterprise would have to develop a vast supply organization in order to deliver these goods on time. Consequently, although it seems slower and more expensive to use state material resources departments rather than the channels of direct supply, in fact, it means that storage charges and transportation fees can be reduced and means of production can be supplied faster to the consuming enterprises. In addition, because the state needs to maintain a reserve of some means of production and because state enterprises may also experience a sudden surge in demand for some means of production (due to changes in plan assignments), state material resource departments are needed as a middle link for managing and organizing supplies of the means of production.

The third channel of circulation is supply organized by commercial departments. This involves products which can be used either for productive consumption or personal consumption. Some are small spare parts and small metal tools of various specifications and of more limited use. It is more convenient to have these small and assorted means of production managed by commercial departments so that they can be bought by the user unit in the market at any time.

Bring the effects of socialist commerce fully into play

Exchange between socialist state enterprises is realized mainly by direct supply and through the material resources departments acting as intermediate links. The mediating role of the commercial departments is not essential in this kind of exchange. But in exchange between the state economy and the collective economy, within and between the levels and units of the collective economy, and between the state and staff and workers, it is essential for the commercial departments to fully function in their intermediary capacity. At the present stage, China's socialist commerce takes two forms: state-run commerce and collective-run commerce. Taken together, these constitute China's planned and unified socialist market.

State commerce constitutes the main body and leading force in the unified socialist market. It controls the overwhelming majority of retail shops and all commercial wholesale links. All consumer goods and a portion of producer goods manufactured by state industry are purchased by state commerce. Major agricultural sideline products and a portion of the industrial products turned out by the collective enterprises will also be purchased primarily by state commerce. Commodities are delivered to the consumer by the state commercial departments. These departments must take the whole population of the country into consideration in a planned manner and follow the principles of overall planning, making proper arrangements, and guaranteeing key points. In 1973, state commerce already accounted for 93.5 percent of the total volume of retail trade.

Collective commerce assists state commerce. Collective commerce refers mainly to rural supply and marketing cooperatives. Urban cooperative stores also belong to the category of commerce under the system of collective ownership.

In China, after the seizure of political power by the proletariat, there existed an exceedingly vast rural market in which the individual economy predominated. If socialism had failed to take over, this market would have fallen into the clutches of capitalism and become a hotbed for the growth of capitalism. While actively developing state commerce, it was also necessary to arouse the masses to energetically develop cooperative commerce through their own efforts. Cooperative commerce is an auxiliary to state commerce. It assists in regulating supply and demand, controlling the market, and stabilizing prices. Practice has shown that the establishment and development of supply and marketing cooperatives in China have played a very important role in augmenting the strength of socialist commerce, in cutting the connection between individual economy and capitalist economy, and contributing to the socialist transformation of the individual economy. After twenty years of development, there has been great change in the funding and management of the rural supply and marketing cooperatives. Whereas in their early period of formation, money was raised in the form of shares, today this accounts for only a small proportion of the cooperatives' funds. In fact, the supply and marketing cooperatives are now actually already a component of socialist commerce by the whole people.

The cooperative stores were originally formed by individual laborers in the urban areas. These cooperatives represented a transitional form from individual commerce to state commerce. Already in some areas of China, cooperative stores have largely been transformed into state-run stores. In other areas, various forms are being adopted to continue carrying out socialist transformation. Existing cooperative stores provide a convenience to the urban inhabitants, facilitating small purchases of daily commodities.

In 1973, collective commerce accounted for 7.3 percent of the total volume of retail trade. Apart from the two kinds of socialist commerce, state commerce and collective commerce, there still remains a certain amount of trade conducted at rural trade fairs. The rural trade fair is a form of trade that corresponds to commodity exchange on the basis of private ownership. Rural trade fairs are a supplement to the socialist planned market. There the peasants sell that part (relatively small quantities) of the farm produce grown on their private plots and household sideline products which they neither keep for their own personal needs nor sell to the state. The rural trade fairs are organized according to strict state regulations. Trade fairs are places where peasants exchange what they have for what they want and where peasants exchange directly with urban people. No middle merchants are allowed.

Rural trade fairs have a dual character. On the one hand, as adjuncts to the socialist planned market, they have the effect of increasing the social product, increasing the team members' income, and enlivening the rural economy. On the other hand, rural trade fairs are an unplanned market. If they are allowed to develop spontaneously and unchecked, they will interfere with the socialist planned market and nurture capitalist forces. If rural trade fairs are to be allowed to exist for a period of time under the socialist system, it is necessary to strengthen leadership and management over them in order to bring into play their positive effects and restrict their negative effects so that they serve the socialist economy better.

MONEY MUST BE THE SERVANT OF SOCIALIST EXCHANGE

Money under the socialist system begins to acquire new properties and functions

When commodity production and commodity exchange reached a certain level of development in human history, money appeared as the general equivalent (of all other commodities) and unit of account. Since commodity production and commodity exchange continue to exist in socialist society, money is still necessary.

Owing to the dual character of social production and the products of social labor in a socialist society, the nature and function of money begin to change.

Money, in its relation to commodity production and commodity exchange, is still a unit of account under the socialist system. But it no longer reflects capitalist relations of production. Capitalist commodity production and commodity exchange, which embody the exploitation of hired labor, are no longer associated with this money. Money is now associated with socialist commodity production and exchange, which embody the mutual exchange of labor within and between the two laboring classes: the proletariat and the peasantry. Let us examine the properties of money in socialist direct social production.

In its planned leadership over the national economy, the socialist state must use money as a unified standard to measure social labor—whether in the formulation of production targets, the allocation of material resources, or the distribution of the total social product. This means that money under the socialist system begins to acquire a new property, namely, as a means to measure labor in national economic planning work. And the further socialist direct social production progresses, the more important this new property of money becomes. In the course of development, with the gradual elimination of commodity production and commodity exchange, money as a unit of account will also gradually be eliminated. Even then, however, a means of measuring labor will still be necessary in national economic work.

In the distribution of personal consumer goods in socialist society, in addition to being a unit of account, money also serves as labor certificates. The distribution of personal consumer goods in the departments under socialist state ownership is conducted this way: the state pays money wages to the staff and workers following the principle of "from each according to one's ability, to each according to one's work," and the staff and workers use the money to buy the consumer goods they need. Here, the role of money is similar to that of labor certificates described by Marx: "The certificate of labor is merely evidence of the part taken by the individual in the common labor, and of his right to a certain portion of the common produce destined for consumption."[5]

The change in the nature of money under the socialist system reflects the characteristics of socialist relations of production. But this change is also embodied in the functions of money.

The first function of money is that of a measure of value. This is also the case in socialist society. In socialist society, apart from using money to measure the social labor embodied in commodities, money is also used as a tool for the planned management of the state economy. The socialist state uses money's function as a measure of value to set the prices of commodities and products and to fix targets of production, costs, and profits in value terms in order to exercise planned management of the national economy.

Money acts as a means of circulation in all three of the major exchange relations of the socialist system. In socialist society, this function of money is carried out by paper currencies. Paper currencies have no intrinsic value. They are merely symbols of value. In China, these symbols of value (or legal tender) are the Renminbi issued by the People's Bank of China. The socialist state uses money's function as a means of circulation to promote the economic relations between industry and agriculture, between the urban and rural areas, and among state enterprises. Although currency remains a means of circulation, the individual who possesses it has already been denied the right to buy substantial means of production or labor power, which is a condition basic to money under capitalism. Money can only be used to purchase some tools needed for handicrafts and personal items of consumption. Under such conditions, great limitations have already been placed on the effective range of action of money as a means of circulation.

In socialist society, money functions as a means of payment. Socialist state enterprises use this function of money to pay taxes and profits to the state and wages to the staff and workers and to repay loans from fraternal enterprises. The socialist state uses this function of money to centralize and distribute state budgetary and credit funds in order to ensure and promote socialist construction.

In socialist society, money also functions as a means of accumulation and savings. The net social income created by the laboring people becomes the socialist accumulation of the state in the form of money. The portion of the labor compensation of the laboring people that is not yet spent is also deposited in the state bank in the form of money also to be used to promote socialist construction.

In the foreign economic relations of the socialist state, gold functions as world money. In the socialist state's foreign aid and foreign trade, gold serves as a universal means of payment and an embodiment of social wealth. Because China's Renminbi is a rare and stable money in the world, it has earned an ever-higher reputation. In China's foreign trade, more and more countries are willing to use the Renminbi as a means of calculating prices and for international accounting.

In socialist society, by virtue of the establishment of public ownership of the means of production and the resulting changes in production and exchange, the production relations reflected by money and the functions it performs are vastly different from the situation in capitalist society. In capitalist society, money is converted into capital that the capitalist uses to buy labor power and means of production in order to extract surplus value from the worker. The bourgeois state uses its power to print money as a means of patching up its financial deficits. This leads to monetary inflation and increases the misery of the laboring people. The bourgeois state also uses money as a means to economically invade and expand outside its national borders and to grab superprofits. In socialist society, the issuance and management of money are mainly in the hands of the state under the dictatorship of the proletariat, and money is used to measure and calculate the expenditure of labor on the social product and to strengthen and expand the economic links between industry and agriculture and among various state enterprises. Money also facilitates the distribution of individual consumer goods, which follows the socialist principle of "from each according to one's ability, to each according to one's work." Money is a tool used by the state of the dictatorship of the proletariat to wage class struggle, to administer socialist production, and to distribute products.

But money is like commodities: it is a remnant of the private economy, "a survival of yesterday's exploitation."[6] In using money to serve the socialist economy, we must see this clearly. In socialist society, money as general equivalent and unit of account is still the direct incarnation of social wealth. Its functions as measure of value, means of circulation, means of payment, means of saving, and world money are still operative. This is not that much different from the old society. The existence of money remains the soil breeding capitalism and new bourgeois elements.

"The commodity of commodities [money] had been discovered, that which holds all other commodities hidden in itself, the magic instrument which can change at will into everything desirable and desired."[7] In the money form, bourgeois right has attained concentrated expression. Before money, people are formally equal. Anyone can own money. Everyone can use money to buy the commodities they need. It is the same for everyone. But this equality actually embodies inequality. Those who own more money not only can enjoy a higher standard of living but also can use it to exploit others under certain conditions. In capitalist society, operating a factory, speculation, usury, and corruption are essentially the same: they are all exploitative methods of owning another's labor and exploitative means of obtaining more money. In socialist society, not only does the system of distributing money income according to work embody inequality; there also exists the possibility of using exchange through money to secure ownership over another's labor. These exploitative activities are of course illegal under the dictatorship of the proletariat. But as long as money exists, the old and new capitalist forces of the city and countryside will risk disobeying the law to practice speculation, operate underground factories, engage in usury, etc., in order to secure ownership over another's labor and grab huge amounts of money. In his criticism of Duhring's discussion of economic communes, Engels made this point: "By accepting money in payment without any question, the commune leaves open the door to the possibility that this money may have been obtained otherwise than by the individual's own labor. *Non olet.* [It does not smell.] The commune does not know where it comes from."[8] Lenin also pointed out: "[Until] we can abolish money . . . we must put up with equality in words, in the constitution; we must put up with a situation in which everybody who possesses money practically has the right to exploit."[9]

The thesis of Engels and Lenin, that as long as money exists it will be transformed into capital under certain conditions and will engender new bourgeois elements, is extremely important. When we use money to serve socialist construction, we must do so with a clear head. The harmful effects of money must be restricted by the dictatorship of the proletariat. Illegal activities such as using money to employ and exploit workers and to engage in speculation and usury must be severely attacked and punished.

In a socialist society, the potentially harmful effects associated with the use of money are already held in check as a result of the establishment of public ownership of the means of production and the restriction of bourgeois right in commodity production and commodity exchange. The social and economic foundations of money fetishism will be greatly weakened. However, since money remains the independent form of exchange value, money is still "that absolutely social form of wealth ever ready for use."[10] Money can be exchanged for almost any commodity; consequently, money fetishism could not possibly disappear in a short period of time. Liu Shao-chi and Lin Piao and company advocated material incentives. "Make big profits with little capital." "Let us all get rich." We must repeatedly criticize and repudiate such ideas of the exploiting class as: "Money can bribe the gods," "With money even ghosts will grind wheat," and "Get promoted and make a fortune." Liu Shao-chi and Lin Piao and company did their utmost to poison the minds of the working people with money fetishes and undermine the socialist system. In taking further steps to weaken and progressively eliminate money fetishism, we must create the requisite conditions to weaken its social and economic base, and we must never cease struggling against old and new bourgeois elements who use money to conduct criminal activities such as corruption, theft, bribery, speculation, and opening underground factories. At the same time, we must pass severe judgment on the modern-day revisionists who advocate material incentives. We must propagate Marxism-Leninism-Mao Tsetung Thought among the masses of people, foster the advanced sentiment of working for the revolution and plowing for the revolution, and insist on continuing the revolution. The struggle against money fetishism is an essential means by which the proletariat exercises all-round dictatorship over the bourgeoisie. This is an important task of the proletariat and all laboring people throughout the historical period of socialism.

Master the law of money circulation to serve socialist construction

In the process of production, exchange, distribution, and consumption, there is a movement of money corresponding to the movement of commodities. In capitalist society, production and exchange are carried on blindly and spontaneously. The circulation of money in the market is also carried on blindly and spontaneously. In socialist society, production, exchange, and distribution are all carried on according to plans. The socialist state can expand and contract the money supply in a planned way, and can bring planning into money circulation and exchange through money. And it can restrict bourgeois right in exchange through money, guard against the dangers associated with the use of money and ensure that money serves socialist construction. To achieve planned money circulation, it is first necessary to understand the movement of money under the socialist system and to know the objective law of money circulation.

In socialist society, exchanges among state enterprises do not generally require actual money (cash) transactions. Price calculation in the exchange process is carried out by utilizing money as a measure of value. When money performs its function as a measure of value, no cash need be on hand. Only the concept of money is required. Payments in the exchanges among enterprises are generally settled through clearing accounts in the state bank, so no money transaction is required for this either.

In socialist society, there are four main channels for issuing and recovering money.

First, state enterprises, business units, and state organs obtain money from the state bank to pay wages to staff and workers. Staff and workers use their wages to buy personal consumer goods, or to meet other living expenses. In this way, money flows back to the bank through the commercial sector and the service industries. In addition, staff and workers can save by directly depositing money in the bank without any commodity exchange.

Second, the commercial branches obtain money from the state bank to purchase agricultural and sideline products from the rural collective economy. A part of the money income from the sale of agricultural and sideline products is used by the collective units to buy chemical fertilizers, insecticides, agricultural machines, and other means of production from the state. In this way, this part of the money again returns to the bank. Another part of the money income of the collective economy is distributed to the peasants of the collectives according to their labor contributions. The peasants use it to buy industrial products from commercial branches or save it. In this way, this part of the money also ultimately returns to the bank.

Third, through their purchases at trade fairs, a part of the money income of the urban people also circulates. However, it must also finally return to the bank through the peasants' purchases of industrial products and savings deposits.

Fourth, economic transactions among state enterprises, business units, and state organs are basically conducted by transfers of credit. But some assorted and small payments also require cash. State enterprises, business units, and state organs can only retain the amount of cash specified by the state. Any amount over and above this limit must be deposited in the state bank. Therefore, the amount of money needed for such circulation is limited.

These channels of money circulation are closely related to socialist commodity exchange. Money circulation is determined by commodity circulation. According to the law of money circulation explained by Marx, the formula for money circulation is:

$$\text{AMOUNT OF MONEY AS MEANS OF CIRCULATION} = \frac{\text{Total money value of commodities}}{\text{Velocity of money circulation}}$$

This formula is still valid under the socialist system. This formula says that the amount of money needed for circulation in a given period of time is directly proportional to the total money value of commodities which require money to be realized and inversely proportional to the velocity of money circulation. Since paper currencies are merely symbols of value, the issuance of paper currencies should correspond to the amount of money needed for circulation. Only in this way can the value of money be kept stable and its active role in a dynamic socialist economy be brought into full play. If too little money is issued, commodities may pile up in the circulation sphere (because the medium of exchange is lacking) and they will not reach the consumer in time. If too much money is issued, the result will be too much money chasing too few commodities. The prices of commodities will then rise in the trade fairs, and the value of the paper currency will fall. The socialist state consciously uses the law of money circulation to match money circulation with commodity circulation and promote the planned movements of socialist production, exchange, distribution, consumption, and other links through a planned regulation of the channels of money circulation.

As indicated, China's Renminbi is a rare and stable money in the world. Under the guidance of Chairman Mao's proletarian revolutionary line, China's industry and agriculture steadily develop, fiscal revenues are plentiful, and international payments are balanced. A strong socialist economy lays a stable material foundation for China's money and permits the state to steadily release a large amount of commodities into the market at stable prices to match the demand from the increasing purchasing power of the people. The stable value of the Renminbi is also a result of the state's conscious use of the law of money circulation and the planned management of money circulation to achieve a balance between income and cash payments. On the one hand, the state controls the release of money through planned regulation of the number of staff and workers, the rate of wage increases, and the purchasing power of state enterprises, business units, and state organs, and through regulation of purchase prices of agricultural products. On the other hand, the state organizes the withdrawal of money from circulation by duly and sufficiently supplying commodities required by the urban and rural populace, by regulating prices in a planned way, and by mobilizing the people to save. In this way, the amount of Renminbi in circulation is matched by the amount of circulation required, thus guaranteeing the stable value of the Renminbi.

The planned regulation of money circulation in the socialist state is carried on through the state bank. In China, the People's Bank is the state bank. The People's Bank of China, which issues and withdraws Renminbi and regulates money circulation in a planned way according to the development of production and the requirements of commodity circulation, becomes a nationwide cash income-outgo center. The People's Bank of China is a nationwide clearinghouse for all noncash transactions among all the state economic branches, enterprises, and units. It is also a nationwide credit center that seeks to achieve a fuller use of idle money through its holdings of receipts, payments, and deposits. In summary, all money accounting and payment activities develop from the central hub of the state bank. The socialist bank is not only an economic organization but also a state bank in charge of managing the national economy of the proletarian state. It plays a very important role in socialist revolution and socialist construction.

Major Study References

Marx, *Capital*, volume 1, chapter 3
Stalin, *Economic Problems of Socialism*

Notes

1. Marx, *Critique of the Gotha Programme*, p. 15.
2. Lenin, "Instructions of the Council of Labor and Defense to Local Soviet Bodies," *CW* 32, p. 385.
3. Engels, *Anti-Duhring*, p. 186.
4. Mao, "Economic and Financial Problems in the Anti-Japanese War," *SW* 3, p. 111.
5. Marx, *Capital* 1, pp. 97-98 n1.
6. Lenin, "First All-Russia Congress on Adult Education: Deception of the People with Slogans of Freedom and Equality," *CW* 29, p. 358.
7. Engels, *The Origin of the Family, Private Property and the State* (Peking: Foreign Languages Press, 1978), p. 201.
8. Engels, *Anti-Duhring*, p. 395.
9. Lenin, "First All-Russia Congress on Adult Education," *CW* 29, p. 358.
10. Marx, *Capital* 1, p. 132.

.

10

CORRECTLY HANDLE THE RELATIONS BETWEEN THE STATE, THE COLLECTIVE, AND THE INDIVIDUAL

The Distribution and Redistribution of Socialist National Income

Products produced in socialist society must generally be exchanged and distributed before they can be consumed. The process by which production, exchange, distribution, and consumption are repeated and continuously renewed is a process of reproduction. The correct handling of the relations between the state, the collective, and the individual with respect to distribution and the correct distribution of the social product and national income play an important role in the smooth management of socialist reproduction.

SOCIALIST NATIONAL INCOME COMES FROM THE PEOPLE AND IS EXPENDED ON THE PEOPLE

Socialist national income can increase steadily and rapidly

Socialist reproduction has its own characteristics. In essence, what is involved is simply the repeated occurrence of the characteristics of socialist production. The aim of reproduction is to satisfy the ever-increasing needs of the socialist state and the people. It is not for the purpose of exploitation as under capitalism. Socialist reproduction is carried on in a planned and proportionate way. It is not the blind competition of capitalism. Socialist reproduction is continuous expanded reproduction. It is not interrupted by cyclical economic crises as under capitalism. These characteristics of socialist reproduction are inevitably reflected in the creation and distribution of the socialist national income.

National income is the total social product produced by the laborers employed in the branches of material production in a given country over a given period of time (usually a year) minus the depreciation of the means of production. It is the wealth created by the laborers in the branches of material production.

Because of the dual character of socialist production, the national income created by socialist production is manifested in products as well as in value. National income in the form of products cannot be calculated by simple addition due to the wide variety of products. But since the total social product minus depreciation has value, its total and its rate of increase can be calculated at current or constant prices.

The main factors determining the creation and increase of national income are as follows: increases in social labor, increases in the productivity of labor, and savings in the social consumption of the means of production.

In general, other factors being equal, the greater the amount of labor engaged in social production, the greater the national income created, both in physical and in value terms. Under socialism, the aim of production and reproduction is to satisfy the ever-increasing needs of the state and the people. The scale of reproduction increases year after year, and the national income can sustain this growth. Under capitalism, the aim of production and reproduction is exploitation. The expansion of reproduction [extended reproduction] is often interrupted by economic crises. Relative overproduction is aggravated, leading to mass unemployment which is a unique social problem under capitalism. Thus the increase in the capitalist national income will certainly be adversely affected.

If the amount of labor is constant, then the faster that the productivity of labor in the production enterprise increases, the faster will the physical volume of national income grow, that is, national income, computed at constant prices, will increase. In socialist society, the initiative and enthusiasm of the laboring people can be fully mobilized. Advanced technology can be widely disseminated. Mass movements for technical innovation and technical revolution open a broad vista for increasing labor productivity and national income. In capitalist society, the laboring people are oppressed and exploited, and their initiative and labor activism are suppressed. Advanced technology is used only if it results in more surplus value. Thus, increasing the productivity of labor and increasing national income face tremendous obstacles.

Let us look at the third factor determining national income. If the total social product is fixed, then the greater the savings in the consumption of means of production in the production process, the smaller will be the deduction from the total social product and the faster will be the growth of national income. In socialist society, the laboring people are the masters. They can be actively concerned with saving, substitution, multipurpose use of raw materials, and with regular maintenance and full utilization of the means of production. The planned nature of socialist reproduction allows for the fuller and more rational utilization of the means of production on a society-wide basis. These conditions make it possible to economize on means of production, reduce their consumption, and increase national income. In capitalist society, although the capitalist tries to economize on means of production to reduce capital expenses, a large amount of waste results from competition and the anarchy of production. In addition, underutilization of capacity in the enterprises frequently idles a large amount of equipment. These conditions are unfavorable to increasing national income.

Because the factors determining the creation and growth of national income are different under different social conditions, the national income of the socialist country can increase faster in the long run than is possible in a capitalist country.

The distribution of national income corresponds to the basic interests of the laboring people

How is national income to be distributed after it has been created? The distribution of national income is ultimately determined by the form of ownership of the means of production. In socialist society, the means of production are publicly owned. The laboring people are the masters in production. Therefore, the distribution of national income must correspond to the interests of the laboring people and satisfy the ever-increasing needs of the state and the laboring people in a planned manner.

National income is created by the laborers of the branches of material production. It must first undergo an initial distribution within the branches of material production. In enterprises under socialist state ownership, national income is divided into two parts after this initial distribution: one part is wages to be used by the laborer in state enterprises for personal consumption; the other part is net income, which becomes the centralized net income of the state after it is turned over to the state in the form of taxes and profits.

In enterprises under collective ownership, after an initial distribution, one part of the national income is distributed as labor compensation to commune members for their personal consumption needs, while the other part becomes the net income of the collective. The net income of enterprises under collective ownership, unlike net income of enterprises under state ownership, is not remitted wholly to the state. Only a part of it is transferred to the state as taxes to become part of the centralized net income of the state. The other part is retained as a public accumulation fund and a public welfare fund to be used for expanded reproduction of collective enterprises and for collective welfare.

After the initial distribution in the branches of material production, the socialist national income becomes state income, income of collective enterprises, and income of individual laborers. It is an important matter of principle to correctly handle the relations between the state, the collective, and the individual with respect to distribution. Chairman Mao teaches us: "On the question of the distribution of income, we must take account of the interests of the state, the collective and the individual. We must properly handle the three-way relationship between the state agricultural tax, the cooperative's accumulation fund and the peasants' personal income, and take constant care to make readjustments so as to resolve contradictions between them."[1] This instruction of Chairman Mao was in reference to the collective economy. But this principle also applies to the distribution of the whole national income.

After the initial distribution, a part of the national income must be redistributed to form a second round of income.[2] Why must national income be redistributed? This is because in socialist society, in addition to the branches of material production, there are also cultural, educational, and health branches, some service industries, the armed forces, and state organs of administration. These branches of nonmaterial production do not create national income, but they are necessary for the development of socialist society, the enrichment of the material and cultural life of the laboring people, and the consolidation of the dictatorship of the proletariat. The personal income of the laborer in these branches of nonmaterial production is provided through a redistribution of the national income. In addition, a redistribution of the national income is required to satisfy the needs for social welfare and social assistance, and in this way, it becomes the personal income of those who benefit from such welfare and assistance.

The redistribution of the national income is carried out mainly through the socialist state budget. But the activities of the service industries can also bring about a redistribution of the national income. For example, barber shops and laundries charge certain fees to those who have received their services. From these charges, a part is used to pay wages to their employees. In this way, personal income from the initial distribution is transformed into personal income of laborers in service industries, constituting a redistribution of the national income.

The redistribution of national income is also, to a certain extent, brought about through price adjustments. For example, by lowering the prices of industrial commodities and agricultural capital goods and raising the purchase prices of agricultural products, the income of the peasant is in effect raised.

National income in socialist society is divided into two parts after distribution and redistribution. One part is under the control of the socialist state and enterprises under collective ownership to expand reproduction and satisfy other common social needs. The other part belongs to the individual laborer to satisfy his or her personal living requirements. These two parts of the national income are finally grouped into accumulation funds and consumption funds according to their different uses.

After distribution and redistribution of the social product and the national income, the final result can be categorized as appears in the accompanying table.

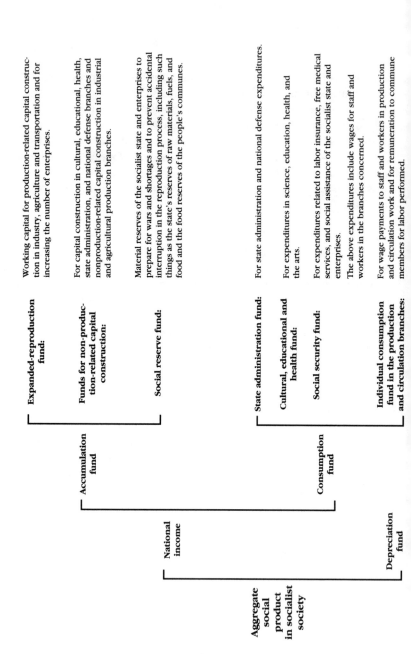

After distribution and redistribution, all the socialist national income is directly or indirectly used to serve the laboring people. The part that goes to society contributes to the laborers' collective welfare and their long-term interests. Just as Marx said: "The 'undiminished proceeds of labor' have already surreptitiously become converted into the 'diminished' proceeds, although what is withheld from the producer in his capacity as a private individual benefits him directly or indirectly in his capacity as a member of society."[3]

The socialist national income comes from the people and is expended on the people. It is fundamentally different from the distribution of the national income in the old society. In a society dominated by the exploiting class, the national income created by the laboring people is largely expropriated by the exploiting class to support a handful of parasites. People like Lin Piao sought to restore this order in which man exploits man. They followed in the footsteps of Mencius, a faithful disciple of Confucius, who declared: "Without the gentleman, no one will rule the uncultured, without the uncultured, no one will support the gentleman." In their eyes, domination and oppression of the laboring people were immutable laws. However, we live in the era of imperialism and proletarian revolution. The system of exploitation is doomed, and is in fact already extinct in socialist society. The laboring people will no longer support the "gentleman" of the exploiting class. People like Lin Piao who futilely attempted to turn the wheel of history back could not escape being crushed by that wheel.

THE IMPORTANT ROLE OF PUBLIC FINANCE IN THE DISTRIBUTION AND REDISTRIBUTION OF NATIONAL INCOME

The state budget is an important link in the financial system

In socialist society, the distribution and redistribution of national income is effected mainly through finance. The socialist financial system consists of the state budget, state bank credits and loans, and state enterprise finance. Of these, state enterprise finance is the basis of the socialist financial system. It systematically reflects the use and turnover of capital funds in the production activities of enterprises. It also brings about an initial distribution of national income to form the centralized net income of the state. State banks distribute temporarily idle funds in the national economy, in the form of loans, to meet the needs for short-term working capital in production. The state budget obtains its revenues from its participation in the distribution of national income to meet the needs of consolidating the dictatorship of the proletariat and economic and cultural construction. A fairly large part of the national income that is distributed, especially that which forms the major part of socialist accumulation, is brought about through state budget allocations. The state budget is an important link in the system of socialist finance.

How does the state budget participate in the distribution of national income? Because the state budget consists of revenues and expenditures, this question has to be answered from these two aspects of the budget. Budget revenues of the socialist state generally include income from enterprise and services, various taxes, and other income items. These income items of the budget derive largely from the net income of socialist enterprises. In China at present, the net income of socialist state enterprises is handed over entirely to the state budget in the form of taxes and profits. In the current budget revenues of China, more than 99 percent are payments from the state economy and collective economy. In China's budget, the items of public debt and foreign debt no longer exist. China has become a socialist country without any internal or external debt.

Socialist state budget expenditures generally include expenditures for economic construction, expenditures for social, cultural, and educational undertakings, and expenditures for national defense and foreign aid. Through these budget expenditures, various funds are established in a planned manner to meet the needs of consolidating the dictatorship of the proletariat, expanding production, and developing cultural, educational, and health services. Among budget expenditures, economic construction and social, cultural, and educational expenditures are of major importance. Expenditures for these two items increased from about 36 percent of China's state budget expenditures in 1950 to about 70 percent in 1973. By contrast, in the imperialist and social-imperialist countries, expenditures for armament expansion and government administration represent a very substantial proportion of state budget expenditures. Imperialism requires such expenditures in order to encroach upon and plunder the laboring people of foreign countries and to oppress and exploit the laboring people of the imperialist countries. Expenditures often exceed revenues, resulting in sizable budget deficits.

The conditions that have been described demonstrate that socialist finance is a distributive relationship centering on the socialist state's participation in the distribution and redistribution of national income. Socialist finance is a tool to consolidate the dictatorship of the proletariat, to develop the economy and cultural, educational, and health services, and to fulfill internationalist duties. The differences between socialist finance and capitalist finance lie in the fact that socialist finance ultimately serves the interests of the broad masses of laboring people, rather than encroaching on those interests, and that socialist finance participates in the distribution and redistribution of national income both within and outside of the sphere of production. Socialist finance links the state budget, state bank credit, and state enterprise finance closely together to serve the growth of production.

The economy determines finance, and finance influences the economy

Since socialist finance is a relationship of distribution and redistribution of national income centered on the state, it is bound up with the development of the national economy. Marxism tells us that production determines distribution and distribution in turn reacts back on production. Different forms of distribution in different societies are determined by different forms of social production. And the wealth made available by society for distribution is also determined by the national income created within the sphere of production. Chairman Mao instructed us on the dialectical relations between the economy and finance: "The general policy guiding our economic and financial work is to develop the economy and ensure supplies. . . . While a good or a bad financial policy affects the economy, it is the economy that determines finance."[4] Since liberation, the vast numbers of financial personnel have followed Chairman Mao's instruction. They first paid special attention to the economy to promote a sustained increase in industrial and agricultural production. As a result, a stable and reliable material base for China's finance has been secured, and the scale of revenues and expenditures has developed relatively rapidly. From

1950 to 1973, as measured in value terms, China's agricultural production has increased 1.8 times, light industrial production increased 12.8 times, and heavy industrial production increased 59 times. In this same period, China's financial revenues have increased approximately thirteenfold, while financial expenditures have increased elevenfold.

The economy determines finance. Thus, a one-sided emphasis on finance, the belittling of the importance of developing the economy, and the adoption of a purely financial viewpoint, which seeks to solve financial problems by purely financial means, are all erroneous. People holding a purely financial viewpoint do not understand the dialectical relations linking the economy, finance, production, and distribution and do not actively concern themselves with and promote the growth of production; they will not be able to solve the problem of financial revenues and expenditures.

The economy determines finance, but finance is not simply a passive or a negative factor. Finance in turn plays a very important role in economic development. When the state wants to carry out economic construction and the enterprise wants to increase production, the necessary funds must be arranged. Through its participation in the distribution of national income, socialist finance allocates budgetary funds from the centralized net income of the state to state enterprises, which then use these funds for economic construction. In the allocation of funds, a balance should be achieved in the distribution of material resources. In other words, if the movement of value can be coupled with the movement of material resources (use values), so that a certain amount of funds can be exchanged for a corresponding amount of resources, and if these resources are used economically and properly, then the high-speed development of the national economy in a planned and proportionate way can be guaranteed. Conversely, if socialist finance improperly funds, such that the movement of value is decoupled from the movement of material resources, or if material resources are not used rationally, then the development of the national economy will be hindered.

Socialist finance centralizes the national income that is created in the sphere of production in the hands of the state. This centralized net income of the state is then used to develop the national economy. But this by itself is not enough. The vast numbers of financial workers, having wide contact with and knowledge of the conditions of various enterprises, have an important role to play. They should assist enterprises in improving management and operation, in forging cooperative relationships, in perfecting mutual relations within the enterprise and among enterprises, and in doing a better job of tapping potentialities in order to steadily promote the development of social production and the increase in national income. In this way, and on the basis of developing the economy, the sources of socialist finance can be augmented and guaranteed.

THE PROPORTIONAL RELATIONS BETWEEN ACCUMULATION AND CONSUMPTION ARE OVERALL PROPORTIONAL RELATIONS

Socialist accumulation is the source of expanded reproduction

In the distribution and redistribution of national income, there are proportional relations between accumulation and consumption which directly affect the development of the national economy and the improvement of the people's livelihood.* Like the proportional relations between industry and agriculture and the proportional relations involving agriculture, light industry, and heavy industry, the proportional relations between accumulation and consumption are also overall proportional relations.

In the process of distributing and redistributing national income, socialist finance must ensure that a certain amount of accumulation be used for expanded reproduction. Accumulation is the source of expanded [extended] reproduction. However, in different societies, accumulation has different characteristics. In capitalist society, the means of production are in the hands of the capitalists, and the only form of accumulation is capitalist accumulation. This accumulation serves to further the exploitation and oppression of the laboring people by the exploiting class. In socialist society, the laboring people control political power and own the means of production. Consequently, they can accumulate funds through the state and the collective and use these funds to expand reproduction and to serve the interests of the laboring people. The more wealth accumulated by socialist society, the larger

---

* Livelihood in this context refers to the relationship between work/income and overall consumption and living standards.

241

the scale and capacity of social production and the higher the standard of material and cultural life. The result will be overall moral, intellectual, and physical development. The material and ideological conditions will also be gradually created for the transition to communist society. However, opportunists and revisionists of every hue have attempted to gloss over the essential difference between socialist and capitalist accumulation. Typically, they have advocated that the socialist national income be distributed in its entirety. More than a hundred years ago, a leader of the German workers' movement, Lassalle, proposed the so-called "undiminished proceeds of labor." Duhring proposed a similarly absurd "complete labor income." Like Lassalle, Duhring, and other swindlers of the same ilk, Liu Shao-chi also clamored that socialism meant "more distribution" and "more take-home pay." Lin Piao maliciously slandered China as "a rich state with poor people." He attacked socialist accumulation as "disguised exploitation" and conspired to liquidate socialist accumulation. Marx and Engels took such ridiculous propaganda head on in *Critique of the Gotha Programme* and *Anti-Duhring*. If the revisionist fallacies were implemented, there would be no social accumulation. As a result, the socialist economy would not be able to carry on expanded reproduction. It could only maintain simple reproduction, or the function of accumulation would be transferred to private parties. The end-result would be the restoration of capitalism. Thus we can see that the fallacies of distributing and spending everything, which were peddled by Liu Shao-chi and Lin Piao, represent a desperate attempt to undermine the socialist economy and restore capitalism.

There must be a proper ratio between accumulation and consumption

Aside from what is used as accumulation funds, what remains of the socialist national income is used as consumption funds. "To decide the proper ratio between accumulation and consumption within each of the two sectors of socialist economy . . . and also between the two sectors themselves is a complicated problem for which it is not easy to work out a perfectly rational solution all at once."[5*] For any given peri-

---

* The two sectors are that in which the means of production are owned by the whole people and that in which the means of production are collectively owned.

od of time, the national income is limited. If the proportion used to increase accumulation is raised, then the proportion used to increase consumption has to be somewhat lower. A higher level of accumulation will certainly accelerate the pace of socialist reproduction, but it will also mean that the improvement in the laboring people's livelihood will have to be temporarily slowed down. Conversely, if the proportion used to increase consumption is raised, the proportion used to increase accumulation must be somewhat lower. A higher level of consumption can, of course, better satisfy the current living requirements of the laboring people, but the pace of socialist expanded production must then be slower—which will adversely affect future improvement of the laboring people's livelihood. These conditions reveal that there are contradictions between socialist accumulation and consumption. But the contradictions are not antagonistic in nature. They are contradictions between state interests, collective interests, and individual interests. In other words, they are contradictions between overall interests and partial interests and contradictions between the people's long-term and short-term interests.

In arranging the proportional relations between accumulation and consumption, we must first base any increase in accumulation on appropriately improving the livelihood of the laboring people. At the same time, any increase in consumption must also be based on steadily expanding production and improving labor productivity. The interests of the state, the collective, and the individual must be considered simultaneously. If we pay no attention to improving the livelihood of the laboring people and one-sidedly emphasize accumulation, we will not have met the objective requirements of socialist economic development. This will dampen the laboring people's enthusiasm for labor. Conversely, if we pay no attention to accumulation and one-sidedly emphasize consumption, this will not be in the basic and long-term interests of the laboring people. In order to create favorable conditions for the correct handling of this contradiction, we must strive to develop social production. As long as production is developed and national income is increased, the livelihood of the laboring people can still be improved even if accumulation is appropriately increased. Therefore, for the overall and long-term interests of socialism, it is necessary to emphasize the revolutionary spirit of arduous struggle and building up the country through diligence and frugality.

Accumulation and consumption are a proportional relation in value terms. The proper handling of this proportional relation requires corresponding material resources as a guarantee. As for accumulation, it is used for capital construction and expanded reproduction. Once a certain amount of funds is available, there must also be a corresponding amount of the means of production.[6] Of the total social product in socialist production, only the added [newly-created] portion is to be used for expanded reproduction, while the other portion, equivalent to the previous year's consumption [depreciation of means of production], is to be used for simple reproduction. Therefore, to maintain a balance between supply and demand, accumulated funds must first accommodate the increase in the means of production. If this is not the case, then either the accumulation fund will not have sufficient means of production to purchase, making complete realization of expanded reproduction impossible, or the added means of production will not be sold, thereby creating an unplanned surplus. In either case, socialist expanded reproduction will be adversely affected.

As far as consumption is concerned, since consumption funds are used to meet the material and cultural needs of the socialist state and the broad masses of laboring people, an adequate supply of consumer goods must be available to guarantee that these needs will be satisfied. If the increase in consumption funds does not correspond to the increase in consumer goods, then either the supply of consumer goods will exceed the demand, resulting in unplanned inventory accumulation, or demand for consumer goods will exceed their supply, resulting in shortages. Either way, it will be difficult to properly attain the goal of satisfying the needs of the state and the laboring people.

It can thus be seen that in order to maintain the proper proportional relations between accumulation and consumption, it is necessary to vigorously develop production. Only when the production of the means of production and consumer goods is solved can both accumulation and consumption be increased and the contradiction between accumulation and consumption be better resolved. Here, it is of decisive importance to continually raise labor productivity, economize on the use of means of production, and create more material wealth while saving on manpower, material resources, and finance.

Major Study References

Marx, *Critique of the Gotha Programme*
Engels, *Anti-Duhring*, part 3, chapter 4
Mao, "Correct Handling of Contradictions," sections 1 and 3
Mao, "Economic and Financial Problems in the Anti-Japanese War"

Notes

1. Mao, "Correct Handling of Contradictions," *SR*, p. 453.
2. The centralized surplus [net] income which the state obtains through its participation in the first-round distribution of the national income is ploughed back into the economy for various purposes. However, not every item of national income-expenditure creates new income available for second-round distribution of income. Take the case of funds allotted by the state to state enterprises where no new income is generated and where there is no change in ownership; these funds fall outside the process of the redistribution of national income.
3. Marx, *Critique of the Gotha Programme*, p. 14.
4. Mao, "Economic and Financial Problems," *SW* 3, p. 111.
5. Mao, "Correct Handling of Contradictions," *SR*, p. 445.
6. A small part of accumulation funds is used to purchase consumer goods, but the major part is used to purchase means of production.

11

How Are Personal Consumer Goods Distributed in Socialist Society?

The Socialist Principle of "From Each According to One's Ability, to Each According to One's Work"

The distribution of personal consumer goods is an important aspect of the relations of production. Like the distribution of national income, the distribution of personal consumer goods is fundamentally determined by the form of the system of ownership of the means of production. But the form of distribution reacts back on the system of ownership, influencing its consolidation and development.

Personal Consumer Goods are Distributed in Accordance with the Socialist Principle of "From Each According to One's Ability, to Each According to One's Work"

Distribution is determined by the system of ownership of the means of production

In no society are the relations of distribution of articles of consumption determined by human will or choice. It is the relations of ownership that determine the relations of distribution. Who controls the means of production is a matter of decisive importance. Marx pointed out: "The prevailing distribution of the means of consumption is only a consequence of the distribution of the conditions of production themselves;

247

the latter distribution, however, is a feature of the mode of production itself."[1] In capitalist society, because the means of production are controlled by the capitalist, destitute workers can only sell their labor power and subject themselves to exploitation and oppression by the capitalist. In socialist society, because the means of production are controlled by the proletariat and the laboring people as a whole, a socialist system of public ownership is established. The power to distribute goods is in the hands of the proletariat and the laboring people, and the socialist principle of distribution favors the laboring people.

Therefore, distribution cannot be divorced from the system of ownership. To treat distribution without any reference to the system of ownership is "distribution determinism." More than a hundred years ago, Lasalle, a scab hidden in the German workers' movement, argued that poverty among the laboring people could be eliminated if there was "equitable distribution." Liu Shao-chi nonsensically asserted that "the contradictions between the relations and forces of production in socialist society are mainly manifested around the question of distribution"; a key member of the Lin Piao anti-Party clique wrote in his black notes: "distribution according to labor and the principle of material interests" are "the determining, motive force" in developing production. These are merely refurbished versions of distribution determinism. Under conditions in which the proletariat had yet to seize political power, those advocating distribution determinism were in effect praising the capitalist mode of production. According to them, the only fault with capitalism, and it was a minor one, was inequitable distribution. Therefore, the capitalist system did not need to be overthrown, all that was required was to improve distribution. However, since the means of production were controlled by the bourgeoisie, how could the relations of distribution be fundamentally altered? Distribution determinism is a poison that saps the fighting spirit of the revolutionary people. After the proletariat seized political power, those advocating distribution determinism were doing nothing less than attempting to divert the revolutionary people from the revolutionary goal, to lead them on to the path of bourgeois welfarism, and to make them forget the question of the consolidation and development of the system of ownership and the historical mission of continuing the revolution under the dictatorship of the proletariat—in order to facilitate the restoration of capitalism by such swindlers as Liu Shao-chi and Lin Piao.

In criticizing "distribution determinism," we must at the same time understand that distribution is not a completely passive element. Distribution is determined by the ownership system but also reacts back on the ownership system. To underestimate the role of distribution is also incorrect.

"From each according to one's ability, to each according to one's work" is a negation of exploitative systems

In socialist society, the social product belongs to the laboring people. Does this mean that the entire social product can be distributed directly to the laboring individuals in the various branches of production? Certainly not. Marx pointed out in his *Critique of the Gotha Programme* that in socialist society the following deductions should be made from the gross social product before distribution [to the laboring individuals]: first, funds for the replacement of means of production used up; second, additional funds for expanded reproduction; and third, reserve or insurance funds against natural disasters and for emergencies. And there are other deductions that must be made before distribution to individuals takes place: first, funds for general costs of administration not directly related to production; second, cultural and welfare funds intended to meet common social needs, such as educational and health facilities; and third, funds for disabled persons, and so forth.[2] Today, in addition to the above deductions, the socialist state must also set aside funds to support the revolutionary struggles of the world's people.

What remains of the gross social product after necessary social deductions becomes personal consumer goods that can be distributed to the laborers in the various branches of production. In socialist society, the basic principle governing the distribution of personal consumer goods is "from each according to one's ability, to each according to one's work." This is to say, all laborers must do their level best in productive labor, and then society will distribute to the individual laborers an amount of consumer goods which corresponds to the amount of labor each has provided.

The realization of the principle "from each according to one's ability, to each according to one's work" represents enormous progress in the system of distribution in human history. In the several thousand years during which class antagonism has existed in human society, there have been all kinds of systems by which man has exploited man, man has oppressed man, and man has destroyed man according to the principle of "those who labor do not reap, those who reap do not labor." In slave society, the slave owner treated his slaves as talking tools, and forced them to live like cattle and horses. In feudal society, the peasant had to deliver 50, 60, or even 80 percent of his harvest to the landlord while living in abject poverty. In capitalist society, the wages from the workers' labor are not enough to feed or clothe their families. Moreover, the worker is constantly threatened by unemployment. Inequality in the ownership of the means of production inevitably generates inequality between the exploiter and the exploited in the realm of distribution. In socialist society, public ownership of the means of production replaces private ownership. This makes it possible to realize the principle of "from each according to one's ability, to each according to one's work," which benefits the laboring people. This principle takes labor as a yardstick for the distribution of consumer goods. All able-bodied people must participate in labor. Those who do not work do not eat. This is a fundamental negation of the system of distribution in which man exploited man for several thousand years. It is a very big advance in the system of distribution.

In socialist society, why must the distribution of personal consumer goods follow the principle of "from each according to one's ability, to each according to one's work" rather than the principle of "from each according to one's ability, to each according to one's need"? This is because socialist society has barely emerged from capitalist society, and the differences between worker and peasant, between urban and rural areas, and between mental and manual labor have not yet been eliminated. For most people, labor has still not become their life's prime want.* The social product has not reached a level of abundance. And owing to the existence of classes and class struggle in socialist society, the exploiting class always spreads the evil thoughts of "loving

---

* "Under the conditions of public ownership of the means of production, everyone's labor is performed for the revolution and the collective, but, for most people, labor has not become their life's prime want" (*Peking Review*, 14 November 1975, p. 18).

leisure and hating labor" and "reaping without laboring" to poison the laboring people. Under these conditions, it is not possible or practical to institute distribution according to need. Only the principle of "from each according to one's ability, to each according to one's work" meets the developmental needs of the productive forces and can be understood and accepted by the broad masses of laboring people.

Distribution according to work differs very little from the old society

In the socialist stage, it is necessary to observe the principle of "from each according to one's ability, to each according to one's work" in the distribution of personal consumer goods. But distribution according to work definitely is not the highest ideal of the proletariat. What the proletariat strives to achieve in the future is the communist principle of "from each according to one's ability, to each according to one's need." This is because equal right embodied in distribution according to work "is still—in principle—[bourgeois right]."[3] "The inequality of 'bourgeois right' . . . *continues to prevail* as long as products are divided 'according to the amount of labor performed.' "[4] In his directive on the need to study Marxist theory, Chairman Mao pointed out that distribution according to work "differs very little from the old society."[5]

Why is it said that distribution according to work differs very little from the old society, and that the equal right that it embodies is still bourgeois right? The reason is that distribution according to work still follows the same principle that regulates commodity exchange, that is, the exchange between a given amount of labor in one form and an equal amount of labor in another form. This exchange principle is equal on its face, but unequal in fact. From the standpoint that society uses an equal yardstick—labor—as a measure to determine the distribution of consumer goods according to the amount of labor various individuals put in, everyone is equal. But conditions vary among laborers: some are stronger than others, and some have higher cultural and technical levels than others. Therefore, the amount of labor that they can contribute to society is unequal, and the equal right embodied in distribution according to work "tacitly recognizes unequal individual endowment and thus productive capacity of the worker as natural privileges."[6] At the same time, the family burdens of various laborers are not the same: some have to support more people, while others support only a few, and so forth. Under the conditions in which an equal amount of labor obtains an equal amount of compensation, the standard of living of those who are strong, skilled, and have few mouths to feed is higher. For those in the reverse situation, the standard of living is lower. De facto inequality results. This inequality is different from that in the old society. Here, the issue of man exploiting man does not arise. But it is still a "defect" compared with the ideal of common abundance shared by the proletariat and with the communist principle of "from each according to one's ability, to each according to one's need." "These defects are inevitable in the first phase of communist society as it is when it has just emerged after prolonged birth pangs from capitalist society. Right can never be higher than the economic structure of society and its cultural development conditioned thereby."[7]

On the one hand, the principle of distributing articles for personal consumption according to the labor provided is historically necessary and cannot be negated at will. On the other hand, the equal rights that it embodies are still bourgeois rights, and are the soil and condition out of which capitalism can be regenerated. Therefore, these rights must be restricted under the dictatorship of the proletariat. To view distribution according to work as something sacred that should be set in concrete, and to consolidate, expand, and strengthen bourgeois right, will inevitably lead to the polarization of society into rich and poor; capitalism and the bourgeoisie will develop faster. Therefore, with an ever-increasing abundance of the social product and an ever-higher communist consciousness among the people, it is necessary to make the transition from distribution according to work to distribution according to need. In socialist society, there are some elements of distribution according to need in the social welfare services run by the state or the collective, such as free medical care for staff and workers and the labor insurance provided by the state. Therefore, at present, we must adhere to the theory of development of the revolution by stages and implement the socialist principle of "from each according to one's ability, to each according to one's work." But we must also insist on the theory of uninterrupted revolution, actively create favorable conditions, gradually increase the elements of distribution according to need, and, when future conditions are ripe, replace "distribution according to work" with "distribution according to need."

Avoid two tendencies in the distribution of personal consumer goods

In socialist society, there is acute struggle over the issue of distribution according to work. The Liu Shao-chi clique advocated high wages, high bonuses, and high compensation for literary work. They attempted to create a large gap between the highest and lowest paid to undermine the solidarity among the people, to discourage the masses' initiative in production and enthusiasm for labor, to obstruct the development of the productive forces, and to nurture a privileged class as their social base for restoring capitalism. This conspiracy of the Liu Shao-chi clique was smashed during the Great Proletarian Cultural Revolution.

Opposing polarization and gradually narrowing differences in distribution are part of the revolutionary mission of the proletariat. In his summary of the experience of the first proletarian government in the world, the Paris Commune, Marx praised the commune heroes for adopting the principle which insisted, "From the members of the Commune downwards, the public service had to be done at [workmen's wages]."[8] He regarded that as a great innovation and fully upheld this revolutionary experience. In the early period following the establishment of the Soviet government, owing to the exigencies of the class struggle, Lenin temporarily had to resort to high salaries for the bourgeois-educated class. But he clearly pointed out: "The corrupting influence of high salaries—both upon the Soviet authorities . . . and upon the mass of the workers—is indisputable,"[9] and he deeply criticized and repudiated high salaries. Chairman Mao consistently teaches us: "All our cadres, whatever their rank, are servants of the people."[10] He opposes high salaries for the minority and demands of us that we rationally bring about a gradual narrowing of the differences in personal income between and among the working personnel of the Party, the state, the enterprises, the people's communes, and the people in general.

Why do the teachers of proletarian revolution repeatedly remind us to pay attention to this problem and repeatedly affirm the Paris Commune principle? First, because polarization in distribution is not consistent with socialist public ownership and socialist mutual relations between people. In socialist society, the laboring people are masters of the state and enterprises. Their labor skills are basically taught by society. Their labor contribution to society may vary as a result of the division of labor practiced in the old society and other conditions, but differences in the standard of living cannot be too large. A gradual narrowing of the three major differences is objectively required to advance on the road towards common abundance. Second, if polarization in distribution were allowed to develop, a privileged stratum in society would form. It would serve as a social base for a bourgeois restoration of capitalism. This is unfavorable to the consolidation of proletarian dictatorship. In today's Soviet Union, a bourgeois privileged stratum, which expropriates others' labor product, has formed into a bureaucrat-monopoly bourgeoisie. This is the new exploiting class represented by the Brezhnev renegade clique and which rules the laboring people of the Soviet Union. Third, polarization in distribution is unfavorable to strengthening solidarity among the laboring people. It also provides oxygen to bourgeois ideas like chasing after fame and gain. Therefore, we must guard against this tendency.

To oppose polarization in distribution does not mean absolute egalitarianism, whereby all labor compensation is equalized regardless of the difficulty of the work and the differences in labor intensity and individual contributions. The Paris Commune advocated that all state employees should only get salaries equivalent to those of the worker. However, it also accepted wage differentials among workers. But this differential could not be large. Absolute egalitarianism is totally inconsistent with the socialist principle of "from each according to one's ability, to each according to one's work." It must be opposed. More than forty years ago, Chairman Mao pointed out clearly that "absolute egalitarianism is a mere illusion of peasants and small proprietors, and that even under socialism there can be no absolute equality, for material things will then be distributed on the principle of 'from each according to one's ability, to each according to one's work' as well as on that of meeting the needs of the work."[11] As with polarization in distribution, absolute egalitarianism is harmful to labor activism, hinders the development of production, adversely affects the growth of the social product, and is unfavorable to socialist enterprise.

In socialist society, the distribution of personal consumer goods requires, on the one hand, that we implement the principle of distribution according to work and accept the existence of differences. On the other hand, socialist distribution also requires that we guard against polarization and consciously restrict the bourgeois right embodied in distribution according to work, in this way enabling the living standards among the laborers to gradually even out so as to achieve common abundance. This is a contradiction, and even if this contradiction is handled relatively correctly under given conditions, new contradictions will arise when conditions change. This requires that we seriously study Marxism, firmly grasp the Party's policies, investigate and do research in depth, firmly rely on the masses, and correctly handle these contradictions by putting proletarian politics in command.

THERE ARE TWO BASIC FORMS OF DISTRIBUTION OF PERSONAL CONSUMER GOODS

The wage system is the chief form of distribution in the state economy

Commodity production and commodity exchange still exist in the socialist stage. Under these conditions, the state pays out a given amount of money to the staff and workers as labor compensation for a given amount of labor provided to society. These money incomes of the staff and workers are known as wages, and they are paid out according to a fixed standard under the system of socialist state ownership.

Wages under the socialist system and wages under the capitalist system reflect different relations of production. Under the capitalist system, labor power is a commodity. Wages are incomes received in exchange for the sale of labor power. These wages embody the relations between employer and employee, the relations between exploiter and exploited that bind the worker to the capitalist. Under the socialist system, workers are masters of the state and the enterprises. Labor power is not a commodity. Wages are no longer a transformation of the value or price of labor power. They are a form of state distribution of personal consumer goods, through the use of money, according to the principle of "from each according to one's ability, to each according to one's work."

There are two major forms of wages, namely, time-rate wages and piece-rate wages. Time-rate wages are calculated on the basis of labor time. Within a given period, a fixed wage is paid by the day or month on the basis of the wage level set according to the socialist principle of distribution. Piece-rate wages are calculated on the basis of labor product. Wages are paid at a per-unit rate according to the number of pieces of product of a certain quality which the laborer completes. In China, these two forms of wages have undergone a process of development. Before 1958, the piece-rate wage system was used in a large number of occupations and jobs that were done by hand. This was consistent with the level of development of the productive forces in China and the degree of ideological consciousness among the broad staff and workers. It was instrumental in the rehabilitation and development of production. However, with the development of mechanization and automation, and with the enhancement of the ideological level of the staff and workers, especially after the Great Leap Forward in 1958, many defects and negative effects of the piece-rate wage system were revealed. First, with technical progress, it was increasingly difficult to implement individual piece-rates in many kinds of work. Also piece-rate wages adversely affect technical innovation. Second, the piece-rate system was unfavorable to solidarity among workers. It easily led to contradictions between time-rate workers and piece-rate workers, between new and old workers, between the upstream and downstream work processes, and between workers on different shifts. Third, the piece-rate system easily nurtured the idea of being primarily concerned with personal income and not with the collective enterprise. It was also unfavorable to raising political and ideological consciousness. Therefore, at the demand of the broad staff and workers, the piece-rate system was abolished in most enterprises and the time-rate system was adopted. The form of wages used in China today is mainly time-rate wages. Piece-rate wages are used only in some units and for some types of work.

The issue of wages is a complicated one. It involves not only the relations between the state, the collective, and the individual but also the relations among workers, between worker and peasant, and between worker and peasant on the one hand and other laboring people on the other. The issue of wages must be handled with extreme seriousness and caution. Despite several transformations in China's wage system, there still exist many problems that need to be resolved. Chairman Mao pointed out: "Our country at present practices a commodity system, the wage system is unequal, too, as in the eight-grade wage scale, and so forth. Under the dictatorship of the proletariat such things can only be restricted."[12] Inequality of the wage system is the expression of the inequality of distribution according to work. The eight-grade wage system is a wage system practiced among the production workers. It emphasizes the incentive role played by wage differences in stimulating enthusiasm for labor, and uses the complexity and skill of labor as the only standard to determine wage grades. The practice of the eight-grade wage system fosters significant differences in wage incomes—between complex and simple labor and between skilled and unskilled labor. Since it is more apparent that this wage system embodies bourgeois right, it is even more necessary that it be restricted under the dictatorship of the proletariat.

Besides wages, at certain times and under certain conditions in socialist society, the form of bonuses is also used to praise those staff and workers who have done better work and achieved certain results. The form of bonuses does not escape the bourgeois framework of "working to make money." Before the Great Proletarian Cultural Revolution, and under the influence of the revisionist line of Liu Shao-chi, many factories and enterprises in China did not promote proletarian politics and resorted to handing out bonuses. As Chairman Mao pointed out: "Not that there were no good people in the leadership of factories. But they followed that line of Liu Shao-chi's, just resorting to material incentive, putting profit in command, and instead of promoting proletarian politics, handing out bonuses, and so forth."[13] This experience revealed that when proletarian politics were not put in command, when the communist consciousness of the masses was not raised, and when, instead, bourgeois right was expanded and strengthened by resorting to material incentives and using bonuses as baits to unleash the activism of the masses in production, it was inevitable that the world outlook of the masses would be corroded—sowing discord among the workers and causing enterprises to veer off in the wrong direction and to slide into the mudhole of revisionism.

The experience in socialist revolution and construction shows that in handling the issue of wages, we must persist in putting politics in command and strengthen ideological education. We must also pay attention to the following principles. On the basis of developing production and increasing labor productivity, the wages of the staff and workers are gradually increased, but not excessively. The magnitude of wage increases cannot exceed the increase in labor productivity. To determine wage standards and increases, an overall arrangement must be made taking into account the relation between worker and peasant. In determining wage scales of staff and workers, we must oppose the tendency toward polarization and wider differences, while at the same time guarding against any development that may, by negating differentiation of wages, lead to absolute egalitarianism. Increments in wages and collective welfare must go hand in hand, so as to gradually raise the proportion of collective welfare to individual incomes and so as to bring forward and test out those factors that will result in distribution according to needs.

Under the socialist system, the conditions of distribution according to need have improved with the development of production. Therefore, any increase in the standard of living among the workers is reflected not only in wage increases but also in the improvement of the conditions of distribution according to need, such as social welfare. In the modern revolutionary Peking opera *On the Docks*, the retired wharf worker Ma Hung-liang sang: "In the new society, we wharf workers become proud masters. We are taken care of in birth, old age, illness and death. The benevolence of the Communist Party and Chairman Mao is higher than heaven!" These sentences represent the true feelings of the working class who are liberated in the new society. They reflect the immense superiority of socialist relations of production. It is very important to understand the fundamental difference between capitalist wages and socialist wages and the fundamental difference between the distributional relations of the new and the old societies. This understanding can strengthen our responsibility as masters of our destiny and raise the consciousness of socialist labor.

The work-point system is the chief form of distribution in the rural collective economy

The distribution of personal consumer goods in the collective economy of the rural people's commune also follows the principle of "from each according to one's ability, to each according to one's work." However, because the degree of public ownership in the system of collective ownership is different from that in the system of ownership by the whole people, its concrete forms of distribution have different characteristics. In units under ownership by the whole people, the means of production and products belong to the state and are allocated and distributed centrally by the state. Therefore, labor compensation in the whole society can be standardized and wages can be paid in money. In the collective economy of the rural people's commune, the system of "three-level ownership with the production team at the basic level" has been adopted at the present stage. The means of production and products belong to various collective units. Therefore, distribution cannot be carried out at the level of society as a whole. It cannot even break beyond the bounds of the communes or production teams to achieve egalitarian distribution. Distribution can only be carried out independently within a collective unit according to its own conditions of production.

With the exception of commune-run enterprises, in which the wage system is partially in force because their revenues are relatively stable, distribution according to work in the collective economy of the rural people's commune is carried out by means of work evaluation and points allotment. In some production teams, work points based on labor quotas for some farming activities also take into account the specific customs of the masses. Work points are a standard with which to measure the members' participation in collective labor. They are also a standard for the distribution of income for work. The amount of income obtained by a member from a production team is determined by the amount of work points as well as by the money value of each work point (the work-point value). The money value of work points is not specified in advance. It is determined by the annual income of the production team after a certain amount of funds have been deducted for accumulation. Owing to differences in management and operation, technique and equipment, and natural factors and conditions of transport, the income of various production teams will vary. And there may also be differences in the level of deductions for accumulation. Therefore, the incomes of members in different production teams are not uniform. These differences should be gradually reduced by actively helping the backward communes, brigades, and teams to catch up with the advanced units. But absolute egalitarianism must be avoided, or the development of agricultural production and the consolidation of the collective economy will be adversely affected.

"We should do everything possible to enable the peasants to raise their personal incomes year by year in normal years on the basis of

259

increased production."[14] It is important that this requirement be fulfilled. It is not only favorable to improving the livelihood of the peasant but is also favorable to consolidating and developing the collective economy and consolidating proletarian political power.

How then can the income of the peasant be increased? Ultimately, we must develop production before we can improve distribution. To develop production, we must persist in putting proletarian politics in command, educate the peasants with Marxism-Leninism-Mao Tsetung Thought, and promote the idea of farming for the revolution in order to fully mobilize the labor activism of the broad masses of peasants. We must insist on thorough implementation of the policy of taking grain as the key link to ensure all-round development and fully utilize manpower, material resources, and finance in the rural areas. We must strengthen management and operation and practice scientific farming to increase crop yields. We must budget carefully, practice strict economy, and find substitutes to reduce costs as much as possible and increase production and income, and so forth.

In calculating labor compensation for members of the production teams, we must not only oppose the method of putting "work points in command," paying no attention to ideological education, but must also carry out the principle of from each according to one's ability and to each according to one's work. Between male and female members, "the principle of equal pay for equal work for men and women must be carried out." Unequal pay for equal work in which "men get ten work points for each labor day but women should not get more than eight points" is contrary to the socialist principle of distribution.

CRITICIZE AND REPUDIATE THE IDEOLOGY OF BOURGEOIS RIGHT; NURTURE THE COMMUNIST ATTITUDE TOWARD LABOR

Building socialism and achieving communism require that we nurture the communist attitude toward labor

In socialist society, the principle of "from each according to one's ability, to each according to one's work" in the distribution of personal consumer goods must be carried out. This is for certain. But the principle of "distribution according to work" is not impervious to change. As conditions change, it will evolve, step by step, into "distribution according to need" and will be completely replaced by "distribution according to need" when we advance to the communist society in the future. This requires that we grasp the socialist principle of distribution in our work. But it also requires that we look further ahead, and that we repudiate the ideology of bourgeois right and warmly praise and fully support the communist attitude toward labor.

What is communist labor? Lenin said: "Communist labour in the narrower and stricter sense of the term is labor performed gratis for the benefit of society, labor performed not as a definite duty, not for the purpose of obtaining a right to certain products, not according to previously established and legally fixed quotas, but voluntary labor, irrespective of quotas; it is labor performed without expectation of reward, without reward as a condition."[15]

Only after the proletariat seizes political power and only when the laboring people become masters of the state and enterprises can communist labor arise and gradually develop. Under systems of exploitation, the laboring people all toil for the exploiting classes—thus, there cannot be any enthusiasm for labor or labor activism. In socialist society, things are completely different. The laboring people have been transformed from hired slaves into masters of the state and enterprises. Every job and every product of labor is related to the interests of the laboring people. The laboring people no longer labor for the exploiter but for their own class—thus, there is immense socialist enthusiasm and activism among the laboring people. This is a basic condition for the gradual development of the communist attitude toward labor.

The appearance and step-by-step development of the communist attitude toward labor are significant events in the history of human development. We should publicize and applaud the communist attitude toward labor. We should spread it and forge it into a powerful force for overthrowing the old world and establishing the communist new world.

The development of the communist attitude toward labor represents "the most radical rupture with traditional property relations, . . . the most radical rupture with traditional ideas,"[16] and a thorough rupture with the ideology of bourgeois right.

The ideology of bourgeois right is the reflection of bourgeois right in the realm of ideology. In the distribution of personal consumer goods, "'the narrow horizon of bourgeois right . . . compels one to calculate with the coldheartedness of a Shylock whether one has not worked half an hour more than somebody else, whether one is not getting less pay than somebody else."[17] If we did not make a thorough rupture with the ideology of bourgeois right and deeply criticize and repudiate the capitalist creed of working only for money, proletarian ideology would not triumph on this battleground, the communist attitude toward labor could not take hold, and socialist revolution and construction would be hindered. Therefore, we should "spread communist ideas more widely"[18] so that more comrades will become models who are willing to work hard without expectation of reward.

Nurturing the communist attitude toward labor can accelerate socialist construction and actively prepare favorable conditions for the achievement of communism. Communist society is the brightest and most beautiful form of human society; this is a goal for which the proletariat and the laboring people must strive. Although communist society is an irresistible trend of social development, it can only be achieved through the dauntless struggle and diligent and arduous labor of millions of revolutionary people. Before liberation, our revolutionary elders had only five cents per person per day for cooking oil, salt, and vegetables. They had no wages or welfare. Under extremely difficult conditions, they struggled against imperialism, feudalism, and bureaucrat capitalism and for the liberation of the proletariat. They worked hard and fought courageously. It was this communist spirit that helped our revolutionary elders defeat the reactionaries and establish a new China. Today, we still need to foster this communist spirit of arduous labor without concern for pay and carry on the revolutionary tradition of courageous struggle—if we are to build socialist society and achieve the communist society of the future.

In nurturing the communist attitude toward labor, we must criticize and repudiate material incentives

The appearance and step-by-step establishment of the communist attitude toward labor indicate the gradual growth of communist ideology and the gradual decline of capitalist ideology. Therefore, in the process of nurturing and fostering the communist attitude toward labor, it is inevitable that an acute struggle between the two classes, the two ideologies, and the two lines will unfold. It is of the nature of the bourgeoisie to be attracted by money and profit. But the bourgeoisie generalizes this as universal human nature. Proclaiming that the desire "to work for money" is "only human," they hope to poison the proletariat.

Modern revisionists try to replace the socialist principle of "from each according to one's ability, to each according to one's work" with "material incentives." They treat the laboring people as hired slaves and think that if money is not used as an incentive, there will not be any labor activism. The Soviet revisionists have consistently advocated "material incentives." They have nonsensically declared that material incentives are "a most important lever" for increasing labor productivity. In advocating material incentives, people like Liu Shao-chi and Lin Piao went so far as to base their arguments on such fallacies as Confucius's saying that "the gentleman pursues what is right, the small people seek what is profitable." They claimed that "the drive to work is stimulated by material incentives" and "labor activism will not be high if we don't use a little more money." They slandered the laboring people, declaring that the only thing on these people's minds is "financial windfalls" and thoughts of "wealth and treasure." They regarded material incentives as a panacea, praising "the strong role of wages." Why did they make so much noise? Their ultimate intention is to expand and strengthen bourgeois right in distribution, to nurture new bourgeois elements, and to restore capitalism. The worker comrades put it nicely: "material incentives are the opiate to paralyze the revolutionary fighting spirit, sugar-coated arsenic and a soft dagger that can kill without shedding a drop of blood."

In socialist society, the bourgeois preference for leisure over labor is inevitably reflected among the laboring people so that some of them do not work hard and their socialist labor activism is not high. What can we do about such cases? Should we insist on putting politics in command and on strengthening ideological education, or should we rely on putting material incentives and cash in command? This is an issue of fundamental orientation for the proletariat and the laboring people. It is an issue of which road to follow.

Politics is the commander and the soul. Only by persisting in putting proletarian politics in command, doing a good job in ideology and politics, continually imbuing the broad masses with the socialist and communist ideology, criticizing and repudiating capitalist tendencies, and at the same time seriously carrying out the principle of "from each according to one's ability, to each according to one's work" can the socialist enthusiasm and activism of the masses be fully mobilized. To educate the laboring masses with Marxist ideology is meticulous work. It has to be done with perseverance and a great deal of effort. But the activism thus unleashed is socialist, communist, solid, and long-lasting.

People who had been deeply affected by the poison of capitalist material incentives behaved differently. They had basic doubts about the effects of ideological work. Some began by doing some ideological work, but after a couple of unpleasant experiences, they would shake their heads, thinking that there were no lasting effects to ideological work. They would say: "It does not work. Only money can do the trick." They were afraid of conducting arduous and meticulous ideological work. Once difficulties were encountered, they would resort to bonuses. But the result was usually no better: "The more rewards are given, the worse it gets." Ideology would be declared bankrupt and evil practices would multiply. Such people were not good at discovering the essence of the masses' enthusiasm for socialism. They did not have faith that anything can be transformed under certain conditions. In fact, while it is true that the consciousness among the laboring people will not uniformly be at the same level and that the transformation of consciousness will proceed unevenly, favorable results can be achieved if we persevere in putting proletarian politics in command, conducting ideological education and being patient and meticulous in our work.

Chairman Mao consistently extols the communist attitude toward labor. He more than once has called upon us to learn from the selfless spirit of Comrade Norman Bethune and from the complete and thorough devotion to the interests of the people of Comrade Chang Szu-teh.* Their wholehearted devotion to revolution and to the people will forever illumine the communist path and encourage us to advance courageously along the road of revolution!

---

* Norman Bethune was a Canadian surgeon and member of the Canadian Communist Party. In 1936, he went to the front in Spain, working for the antifascist cause. He came to China in 1938 at the head of a medical team that served in the War of Resistance Against Japan. He contracted blood poisoning while operating on wounded soldiers and died in Hopei Province in 1939. Chang Szu-teh was a soldier in the Guards Regiment of the Central Committee of the Chinese Communist Party. He took part in the Long March and was wounded in service. In 1944, while making charcoal in the mountains of Shensi, he was killed by the sudden collapse of a kiln.

Major Study References

Marx, *Critique of the Gotha Programme*
Lenin, "A Great Beginning," *CW* 29
Mao, "On Correcting Mistaken Ideas in the Party," in *SW* 1
Mao, "Correct Handling of Contradictions"

Notes

1. Marx, *Critique of the Gotha Programme*, p. 18.
2. Ibid., p. 14.
3. Ibid., p. 16.
4. Lenin, *State and Revolution*, p. 112.
5. Quoted in Chang Chun-chiao, "On Exercising All-Round Dictatorship Over the Bourgeoisie," in Lotta, *And Mao Makes Five*, p. 211.
6. Marx, *Critique of the Gotha Programme*, p. 16.
7. Ibid., p. 17.
8. Marx, *The Civil War in France* (Peking: Foreign Languages Press, 1974), p. 64.
9. Lenin, "The Immediate Tasks of the Soviet Government," *CW* 27, p. 250.
10. *Liberation Daily,* Yenan, December 16, 1944.
11. Mao, "Correcting Mistaken Ideas," *SW* 1, p. 111.
12. Quoted in Chang Chun-chiao, "On Exercising All-Round Dictatorship Over the Bourgeoisie," in Lotta, *And Mao Makes Five*, p. 209.
13. Ibid., p. 215.
14. Mao, "Correct Handling of Contradictions," *SR*, p. 453.
15. Lenin, "From the Destruction of the Old Social System to the Creation of the New," *CW* 30, p. 517.
16. Marx and Engels, *Communist Manifesto*, p. 59.
17. Lenin, *State and Revolution*, p. 115.
18. Mao, "On New Democracy," p. 379.

12

ADVANCE TO COMMUNISM

From Socialist Society to Communist Society

The theory of socialist political economy advanced by Marxism-Leninism, Mao Tsetung Thought scientifically analyzes the laws of motion of the formation and development of socialist relations of production. It also reveals the historical necessity of socialist society developing into communist society. Communism is the highest ideal of the proletariat and the millions of laboring people. It is the most complete, most progressive, most revolutionary, and most rational social system. It is the ultimate goal of proletarian revolution. Chairman Mao pointed out: "The ultimate aim for which all communists strive is to bring about a socialist and communist society."[1] Every revolutionary warrior should struggle for communism for all of his or her life.

COMMUNISM IS AN IRRESISTIBLE TREND OF HISTORICAL DEVELOPMENT

Socialist society is a necessary stage on the way to communist society

Lenin pointed out: "From capitalism mankind can pass directly only to socialism, i.e., to the social ownership of the means of production and the distribution of products according to the amount of work performed by each individual."[2] In socialist society, public ownership of the means of production has been established, the laboring people have become masters of society and enterprises, and Marxism has become the guiding thought of society. In these respects, socialist society possesses elements of communism. However, socialist society is merely the first stage of communist society. It is still an immature communist society. In socialist society, as regards both the relations of production and the superstructure, there still exist capitalist traditions and birthmarks, and there still exist bourgeois rights and the ideology of bourgeois right. Viewed from the perspective of class relations, there exist classes, class contradictions, and class struggles from beginning to end. There is the struggle between the proletariat and the bourgeoisie, and there is the struggle between the socialist road and the capitalist road. In these respects, socialist society is different from communist society.

The historical task of the proletariat in the socialist period is to persevere in exercising all-round dictatorship over the bourgeoisie in all spheres and at all stages of development of the revolution, thoroughly defeat the bourgeoisie, abolish all classes and class distinctions generally, abolish all the relations of production on which they rest, abolish all the social relations that correspond to these relations of production, revolutionize all the ideas that result from these social relations, and propel socialist society toward a higher and more mature communist society. Therefore, socialist society constitutes the necessary preparation for communist society, and communist society is, in turn, an objective trend of development of socialist society.

Then what is a mature communist society?

Communist society is the most complete, most progressive, most revolutionary, and most rational society

There is precise content to scientific communism. According to Marxism-Leninism-Mao Tsetung Thought, communist society is a society that has completely eliminated classes and class distinctions. It is a society in which the entire people possess a high degree of communist consciousness and communist morality. It is a society in which the social product is abundant. It is a society in which the principle of "from each according to one's ability, to each according to one's need" is adopted. It is a society in which the state has withered away.

Marx pointed out: "In a higher phase of communist society, after the enslaving subordination of the individual to the division of labor, and with it also the antithesis between mental and physical labor, has vanished; after labor has become not only a means of life but itself life's prime want; after the productive forces have also increased with the all-round development of the individual, and all the springs of cooperative wealth flow more abundantly—only then can the narrow horizon of bourgeois right be crossed in its entirety and society inscribe on its banners: From each according to one's ability, to each according to one's needs!"[3]

According to the Marxist theory of scientific communism, the realization of communist society requires the creation of the following conditions.

First, the thorough elimination of all classes and class distinctions, including the differences between worker and peasant, town and country, and mental and manual labor, and the thorough elimination of bourgeois right. In communist society, the basis for capitalist restoration will have been thoroughly eliminated. Everyone will become fully-developed new communists. People will consciously grasp the objective laws of social development and propel communist society ceaselessly forward. Of course, the elimination of classes and class distinctions does not mean that there will be no contradictions and no struggles in communist society. There will still be contradictions between the superstructure and the economic base and between the relations and forces of production, and there will be struggles between the advanced and the backward and between correct and erroneous lines. Therefore, even in communist society, it will still be necessary to continue revolution.

Second, the achievement of a single communist system of ownership over the means of production by the whole people. In communist society, the communist system of ownership by the whole people will become the sole economic base. The most advanced communist relations of production, which are based on this system of ownership, will guarantee the fastest possible development of the productive forces so as to increase labor productivity at an ever-increasing pace. In order to achieve communist ownership by the whole people, it is necessary to create the conditions in the socialist stage of development, that is, ultimately eliminating bourgeois right in the system of ownership, gradually raising socialist collective ownership to the level of socialist ownership by the whole people, and then from socialist ownership by the whole people to communist ownership by the whole people. The people's commune created by the Chinese people is the best organizational form for facilitating this transition.

Third, the creation of a very abundant social product. When communist society is achieved, the social productive forces will have developed to a new level. People's ability to conquer nature will be incomparably greater than it is now. At that time, people will fully utilize all natural resources to serve human society and will create a very abundant social product to satisfy the needs of the whole society and all the laborers. At that time, commodity production will have ceased. Commodities and money, which are in the domain of the commodity economy, will finally be retired from the historical stage and relegated to the museum of history. In communist society, the level of development of the social productive forces cannot be compared with the present level of development of the productive forces. To realize communism, it is necessary to greatly develop the social productive forces.

Fourth, the cultivation of a high degree of communist ideological consciousness and moral standards among the whole people. Communist society will thoroughly sweep away bourgeois thought and all concepts of self-interest. Labor will no longer be merely a means of life [a way of earning a living] but will itself become life's prime want. The whole world will assume a completely new appearance, and the new thought, new culture, new customs, and new ideological standards of behavior of the proletariat will become common practice. Just as Chairman Mao pointed out, "The epoch of world communism will be reached when all mankind voluntarily and consciously changes itself and the world."[4] Of course, even at that time, there will still be contradictions between the advanced and the backward, between the correct and the incorrect, and between materialism and idealism, and there will still be struggle among people. But the nature and form of the struggle will be different than is the case in class society.

Fifth, the adoption of the principle of "from each according to one's ability and to each according to one's need." When communist society is achieved, because the means of production will all have been brought under a single communist system of ownership by the whole people, because the fundamental difference between mental and manual labor will be eliminated, because the social product will be very abundant and people's ideological consciousness will have been greatly heightened, and because labor will no longer be merely the means of life but itself life's prime want, the distribution of personal consumer goods will no longer be determined by people's contribution of labor to society but by their needs. By then, all the reasonable needs of people's material and cultural lives will be fully satisfied.

Sixth, the state will automatically wither away. With the thorough elimination of imperialism, capitalism, and all exploitative systems throughout the whole world, and with the elimination of classes and class distinctions, the state as an instrument of class struggle will of necessity disappear. Chairman Mao pointed out: "When classes disappear, all instruments of class struggle—parties and the state machinery—will lose their function, cease to be necessary, therefore gradually wither away and end their historical mission; and human society will move to a higher stage."[5]

Chairman Mao instructed us a long time ago: "Communism is at once a complete system of proletarian ideology and a new social system. It is different from any other ideology or social system, and is the most complete, progressive, revolutionary and rational system in human history."[6] Communist society is a society of boundless brilliance and boundless beauty. It is the most ideal society of mankind.

Phony communism is genuine capitalism

"The dialectics of history were such that the theoretical victory of Marxism compelled its enemies to *disguise themselves* as Marxists."[7] The Soviet revisionist renegade clique and swindlers like Liu Shao-chi and Lin Piao are contemporary pseudo-Marxists. They use the label "communism" to engage in capitalist restoration.

The phony communism of the Soviet revisionist renegade clique is a typical representative of all sorts of contemporary phony communism. The Soviet revisionists start from such reactionary positions as the "theory of the productive forces" and "human nature" and foolishly declare that "communism is the most humane and benevolent ideological system," is "all for the people and all for people's happiness," and is a good dish of "beef with beans." They have never mentioned the thorough elimination of all classes and class distinctions, nor the restriction and final abolition of bourgeois right, which is the soil that engenders the bourgeoisie and capitalism. They completely empty scientific com-

271

munism of its revolutionary content. This brand of communism is not only false but also very reactionary. This is "communism" centered on the decaying bourgeois outlook. This is "communism" modeled on the bourgeois lifestyle. This is phony communism and genuine capitalism.

In China, renegades like Lin Piao also strove to peddle phony communism. They proclaimed that communism was "public propertyism," that "'property' is the word to be stressed on the banner," and that communism was to make "everyone rich." The renegade clique never talked about eliminating the landlord and the bourgeoisie; all they cared about were the words "public" and "property." What class's "public" was it? What class's "property" was it? It is obvious. Their so-called "public" was what Confucius and his kind advocated: "When the great Tao prevails in the world, a public spirit will rule all under Heaven." Hence, it was the slave owner's "public," the landlord's "public," and the bourgeoisie's "public"! The so-called "property" was the slave owner's "property," the landlord's "property," and the bourgeoisie's "property." Getting rich could only mean that this handful from the exploiting classes would become millionaires. Had the renegades succeeded in carrying out their conspiracies, the proletariat and the broad masses of laborers would have once again lost all the means of production and would once again have been reduced to slaves in the abyss of hardship and suffering. This is what has happened in the Soviet Union. The Soviet revisionist renegade clique has already expropriated the wealth created jointly by the proletariat and the broad masses of laborers. This wealth has become the "public property" of a tiny bureaucrat-monopoly bourgeoisie. The broad masses of people of the Soviet Union are once again leading the miserable life of the tsarist period and are trapped in an abyss of agony. Chairman Mao pointed out incisively, "The Soviet Union today is under the dictatorship of the bourgeoisie, a dictatorship of the big bourgeoisie, a dictatorship of the German fascist type, a dictatorship of the Hitler type."[8] Therefore, it is evident that the "public propertyism" advocated by the Lin Piao clique contradicts the scientific communism of Marxism and is the same type of stuff as the phony communism of Soviet revisionism.

The history of the communist movement clearly shows: communism is irresistible. No matter how hard the reactionaries try to turn back the wheel of history, communism will ultimately win thorough victory throughout the whole world.

THE ACHIEVEMENT OF COMMUNISM IS
A PROFOUND SOCIAL REVOLUTION

**Persevering in continuing the revolution
under the dictatorship of the proletariat is the
only path for achieving communism**

In the transition from socialist society to communist society, the proletariat must thoroughly defeat the bourgeoisie and its ideology and eliminate all classes and class distinctions. Therefore, whether in the sphere of production relations or in the superstructure, this transformation represents a qualitative leap and comprises a series of profound social revolutions.

State power under the dictatorship of the proletariat, "like food and clothing, . . . is something a victorious people cannot do without even for a moment. It is an excellent thing, a protective talisman, an heirloom, which should under no circumstances be discarded before the thorough and total abolition of imperialism abroad and of classes within the country."[9] On the basis of the fundamental principles of Marxism, Chairman Mao summed up the historical experience of the dictatorship of the proletariat and put forward the theory of continuing the revolution under the dictatorship of the proletariat. Adhering to the theory of continuing the revolution under the dictatorship of the proletariat requires that we be good at applying the method, theory, and outlook of Marxism-Leninism-Mao Tsetung Thought in observing and analyzing socialist society, and that we persevere in the Party's General Line for the entire historical period of socialism. This is the key link in further strengthening the proletariat's all-round dictatorship over the bourgeoisie in the political, economic, ideological, cultural, and educational realms. This is the basic guarantee for building socialism and making the transition to communism.

Whether or not the exercise of all-round proletarian dictatorship over the bourgeoisie is firmly upheld and whether or not continuing the revolution under proletarian dictatorship is firmly upheld are issues of fundamental importance in determining whether we are advancing toward communism or retrogressing toward capitalism. The Soviet revisionist renegade clique tries hard to distort the Marxist theory of scientific communism, claiming that neither revolution nor class strug-

273

gle nor the dictatorship of the proletariat is necessary in the transition from socialism to communism. They absurdly declare that "there are no antagonistic classes in socialist society" and that, therefore, "the passage from socialism to communism does not involve social revolution or class antagonism." Although this renegade clique also calls for the realization of communism, this is merely a smokescreen to deceive the people, sabotage the dictatorship of the proletariat, and restore capitalism. It is by means of negating the basic Marxist theory in respect to the existence of classes, class contradictions, and class struggle that the Soviet revisionist renegade clique abolishes proletarian dictatorship, ceases continuing revolution under proletarian dictatorship, mobilizes the bourgeoisie to attack the proletariat, converts proletarian dictatorship into bourgeois dictatorship, and converts the socialist system into the capitalist system.

Only by persisting in continuing the revolution under the dictatorship of the proletariat can the dictatorship of the proletariat be consolidated, the restoration of capitalism be prevented, socialism be built, and all the conditions necessary for the realization of communism be created.

Uphold proletarian internationalism and support world revolution

The era we live in is the era of imperialism and proletarian revolution. Chairman Mao pointed out, "Ever since the monster of imperialism came into being, the affairs of the world have become so closely interwoven that it is impossible to separate them."[10] To achieve communism, we must thoroughly eliminate imperialism, capitalism, and all systems in which man exploits man, so that all of humanity can be thoroughly emancipated. Therefore, the seizure of political power in one country or several countries and the establishment of a socialist society by the proletariat do not mean the end of revolution. Only by emancipating all mankind can the proletariat finally emancipate itself. This is because capital is an international force. As long as imperialism, capitalism, and exploitative systems still exist, imperialism and social-imperialism will certainly use the two reactionary methods of armed intervention and peaceful penetration and fragmentation to oppose the socialist countries. Under these conditions, the socialist state will always face the threats of aggression and sabotage from imperialism and social-imperialism. Since capital is an international force, the proletarian cause cannot but be an international cause. When the Russian proletariat seized political power in the October Revolution and began unfolding socialist revolution and socialist construction, Lenin clearly and precisely pointed out, "Final victory is only possible on a world scale, and only by the joint efforts of the workers of all countries."[11] In his struggle with Trotsky, Stalin firmly adhered to, and defended, Leninism. But the Khrushchev-Brezhnev renegade clique repeatedly claimed that in the Soviet Union, "socialism has achieved not only a complete victory, but a thorough victory." This is a downright betrayal of Leninism. Domestically, the purpose of the ridiculous claims of this renegade clique was to obscure the acute struggles between the proletariat and the bourgeoisie and conceal its conspiracy to restore capitalism internally. Internationally, this betrayal of Marxism was designed to spread the illusion that the aggressive nature of imperialism has changed and to conceal the ugly features of this clique in its struggle for hegemony with the other "superpower."

Against the distortion and betrayal of Leninism by modern revisionism, Chairman Mao has defended and enriched Leninism. Chairman Mao pointed out: "We have won a great victory. But the defeated class will still struggle. These people are still around, and this class still exists. Therefore, we cannot speak of a final victory. Not even for decades. We must not lose our vigilance. According to the Leninist viewpoint, the final victory of a socialist country not only requires the efforts of the proletariat and the broad masses of the people at home, but also involves the victory of the world revolution, and the abolition of the system of exploitation of man by man over the whole globe, upon which all mankind will be emancipated. Therefore, it is wrong to speak lightly of the final victory of the revolution in our country; it runs counter to Leninism and does not conform to the facts."[12] To attain final victory in the socialist revolution and to achieve communism throughout the whole world, the proletariat of various countries is holding high the banner of proletarian internationalism, supporting each other, struggling together, and advancing courageously, keeping firmly to the Marxist general line of international communism.

In the era of imperialism and proletarian revolution, part of the capitalist system has already entered the museum of history; the remaining, moribund part, like a setting sun dangling precariously on a western hill, is struggling for its last breath, and it too will soon enter the museum. It is the communist doctrine and its social system that are sweeping across the world like ten thousand thunderbolts striking at the same time, powerful as towering mountains and mighty as billowing oceans. Communism shall ever retain its youth and vitality. Basing itself on the objective laws of development of human society, Marxist political economy analyzes the motion and development of the production relations of various forms of society and arrives at the scientific conclusion that the capitalist system is bound to perish and that the socialist and communist systems are bound to prevail. Marxist political economy reveals the general trend of historical development and is a powerful ideological weapon for the proletariat in making revolution

History develops through struggle. The world advances amidst instability. The dawn of a new world in which there will be no imperialism, no capitalism, and no exploitative systems is within sight. The great Chairman Mao teaches us, "The future is bright; the road is tortuous."[13] Let us raise high the victorious banner of Marxism-Leninism-Mao Tsetung Thought, unite with the international proletariat and the oppressed people and nations of the world, be resolute, fear no sacrifice, and surmount every difficulty to win victory!

Major Study References

Marx and Engels, *Communist Manifesto*
Marx, *Critique of the Gotha Programme*
Lenin, *State and Revolution*, chapter 5
Mao, "On New Democracy," *SW* 2

Notes

1. Mao, "The Chinese Revolution and the Chinese Communist Party," *SW* 2, p. 331.
2. Lenin, "The Tasks of the Proletariat in Our Revolution," *CW* 24 (1974), pp. 84-85.
3. Marx, *Critique of the Gotha Programme*, p. 17.
4. Mao, "On Practice," *SW* 1, p. 308.
5. Mao, "On the People's Democratic Dictatorship," *SW* 4, p. 411.

6. Mao, "On New Democracy," *SW* 2, p. 260.

7. Lenin, "The Historical Destiny of the Doctrine of Karl Marx, *CW* 18 (1973), p. 584.

8. Cited in "Leninism or Social-Imperialism," *Peking Review* 17 (24 April) 1970, p. 7.

9. Mao, "Why It Is Necessary to Discuss the White Paper," *SW* 4, p. 444.

10. Mao, "On Tactics Against Japanese Imperialism," *SW* 1, p. 170.

11. Lenin, "Report on Foreign Policy Delivered at a Joint Meeting of the All-Russia Central Executive Committee and the Moscow Soviet, May 14, 1918," *CW* 27, pp. 372-73.

12. Quoted in Lin Piao, "Report to the Ninth National Congress of the CPC," in *Important Documents on the Great Proletarian Cultural Revolution in China* (Peking: Foreign Languages Press, 1970), pp. 62-63.

13. Mao, quoted in CPC, *Tenth Party Congress Documents*, p. 37.

AFTERWORD

THE THEORY AND PRACTICE OF MAOIST PLANNING: IN DEFENSE OF A VIABLE AND VISIONARY SOCIALISM*

by Raymond Lotta

Introduction

Can a socialist planned economy really work, and can it work to lead forward and away from the inequality and dehumanization of class society?

The ideologues of capitalism claim that a socialist economy not only has *not* worked, where and when it has been tried, but could *never* work. Usually two reasons are given for this. First, it is said that a modern economy is just too complex to be centrally planned and run effectively. Planners would have to obtain and process an unmanageably large amount of information. Since, it is argued, that's not possible, socialist state planning inescapably leads to misjudgment, waste, and bureaucracy. So only through the free market and the interplay of competing firms can economic information be reliably generated and acted upon.

Second, socialism is said to crash against insurmountable motivational obstacles. A planned economy does not operate with the rewards and penalties that promote rational (read: capitalist) economic behavior. If self-interest is suppressed, enterprises will have no spur to economize, innovate, and satisfy consumer demand; and individuals will have no incentive to work hard and well.

* A version of this essay appeared in the Spring 1992 issue of *Revolution* magazine.

And so the bourgeois experts chant their mantra: there is no workable alternative to the market. That, the argument goes, is the lesson of the demise of the Soviet Union.

Yet 20 years ago, one quarter of humanity was engaged in a remarkable effort to create a society and economy profoundly different from the private-monopoly capitalism of the West and, after 1956, the state-monopoly capitalism (that masqueraded as socialism) of the former Soviet Union. This was socialist China. Millions of the formerly poor and powerless were consciously uprooting feudalism and capitalism. Workers and peasants were consciously building a different kind of society—one based on cooperation, community, and the common struggle to do away with the class divisions and dog-eat-dog social relations of capitalism and its imprisoning "cash nexus." This was the highest development yet of human society.

China's socialist revolution—which lasted from 1949 until 1976, when it was overthrown by capitalist forces—was living testimony to the fact that a socialist planned economy can release creative energies on a scale unseen in human history; can enable the masses to consciously utilize the productive forces to overcome economic and social inequalities and foster the transformation and socialization of work, living, and learning; and can promote the conscious involvement and increasingly all-sided capability of the majority of society.

This more profound dimension of economic performance and progress is not captured by the conventional data of bourgeois economics; more to the point, it doesn't compute with bourgeois economics! But even as measured by standard growth indicators, revolutionary China stacked up quite well during the Maoist years. Still, the experts and ideologues have their way of evading any substantive discussion of the Maoist achievement. They simply dismiss it as utopian totalitarianism. Communist revolutions, we are told, must resort to unspeakable evil because they seek to impose social change on an unwilling population. After firing this ideological mortar, presumably nothing more need be said.

One would expect as much from the defenders of privilege and exploitation. But even among many professing socialist convictions, one encounters what can only be described as a willful refusal to deal seriously with the Maoist achievement. Western Marxism's treatment of Mao has been conditioned by a deeply ingrained Eurochauvinist prejudice. It is all too common among socialist scholars to write off revolutionary China as too backward to be of any possible relevance to Western society and its "rational" and "democratic" traditions; to dismiss Mao as too crude a thinker (he wrote for the masses!); and to view the Cultural Revolution as nothing more than an exercise in "mob terror" (regrettably, many who should know better have bought into the lies and distortions churned out by the anti-Maoists who rule China today and by the Western bourgeois "experts").

There have been two great revolutions in this century, the Bolshevik and Chinese, and many intellectuals familiar with matters of socialist economics have a certain fluency with the Soviet experience. They can tell you about Bukharin's line on agriculture, or Preobrazhensky's views on the financing of industrialization. But the discussion rarely takes the theory and practice of Maoist economics into account. Outside the universe of China specialists, very few socialist intellectuals know about Mao's insights into agricultural–industrial interrelations contained in his essays "On the Question of Agricultural Cooperation" and "On the Ten Great Relationships," or the farsighted ideas of appropriate technology that informed the Great Leap Forward, or the bold principles of socialist enterprise management summed up in the Constitution of the Anshan Steel Works, or the lofty mass debates on material and moral incentives that raged during the Cultural Revolution.

More often than not, Western socialists conceptualize Maoist China as a variety of "Stalinist command economics" (defined by highly centralized party–ministerial control over investment and production and tight control over enterprise management) punctuated by wild utopian episodes. So no need to bother with Mao . . . even though Mao's critiques of Soviet economic theory and practice rank among the most important writings on socialist political economy,[1] even though Mao had broken with Stalin's approach of "micromanagement from above" and had led in forging a multileveled planning system over the whole of China that took in even the smallest cooperatives. Revolutionary China traveled a rather different path of economic construction than had the Soviet Union (although Mao had learned greatly from the Soviet experience under Stalin). The Maoist revolutionaries developed a coherent and innovative approach to planning that combined nonbureaucratic methods of central coordination with forms of administrative decentralization and enterprise flexibility (without giving free play to the market and its polarizing forces). They linked planning with mass participation and mass supervision. They integrated economic priorities with issues of urban–rural relations, health and population, and ecology. They grasped that socialist construction was inextricably bound up with waves of mass struggle and experimentation. But much of this would come as news to many socialist scholars.

The prejudices of Western Marxism have mixed with the contaminants of the ideological assault mounted against communism by the Western ruling classes. Seizing upon the collapse of the oppressive societies in the former Soviet Union and in Eastern Europe, the ruling classes have tried to pound into people's heads the idea that communism has failed and can only fail. This message has left its mark and taken its toll in contemporary discussion about the future of socialism. On the one hand, it has produced a deep pessimism in many progressive quarters about socialism. This is truly ironic, since the Soviet Union had not been socialist for decades. It was a society which in its essential aspects was not fundamentally different than what exists in the West. The collapse of the former Soviet bloc proves nothing about the vitality and viability of socialism, but much about the moribund nature of capitalism. Let the dead bury their dead!

On the other hand, the pageantry of failure has inspired all manner of attempts to "reinvent" socialism. One hears the refrain that socialism must be "freed" of its supposedly unhappy historical legacy. Socialism, on this account, must redefine its politics, which usually means adopting electoral, multiparty democracy (and which has suited Western imperialism just fine), and must redefine its economics, which often goes no further than glorified versions of the welfare state. A veritable cottage industry of socialist economic model-building has sprung up. The models are stitched together and spun out: conceptually fanciful, mathematically formal, and characteristically nonrevolutionary. This is not liberating. It is not a project to overthrow bourgeois dictatorship; it is not a project to remake society on the basis of proletarian rule. It is warmed-over capitalism.

Here is the rub. The Chinese revolution pioneered solutions to some of the most critical and difficult problems of planning and managing an economy to meet social needs and to revolutionize society. It stands as the most advanced, practical model of an emancipatory socialism. But this rich and inspiring body of socialist economic theory and practical experience has been largely hidden and greatly distorted. One of the challenges of this period is precisely to bring that suppressed history and achievement into the light of day.

Socialism is a historical movement and historical process that has engaged the energies, sacrifice, and daring of much of oppressed humanity. It has passed through one historical wave. The initial breakthrough was the short-lived Paris Commune of 1871. The next, and more thoroughgoing, assault on capitalism was the 1917 Bolshevik Revolution, which represented the first attempt to construct a socialist economy and to defend, deepen, and spread socialist revolution. In 1949, the Chinese Revolution gained victory. The high-water mark of this "first wave" of proletarian revolutions was the Great Proletarian Cultural Revolution in China. We are now at the end of a historical period that began with the founding of the First International (the international federation of working class organizations that Karl Marx helped to establish and guide) in 1864.[2]

There are no socialist countries in the world today. Is this because socialism is inherently flawed and thus doomed to fail? No, socialism met defeat (in the Soviet Union in the 1950s and in China in 1976) by the still more powerful material and ideological forces of world capitalism. It is a bitter truth, but one that must be put in historical context. The socialist revolution seeks to rip up every strand in the web of oppression that ensnares humanity and to cast off the dead hand of the past. Is it any wonder that such a revolution has encountered difficulty?

The world proletarian revolution does not go forward in a straight line of unbroken triumphs. It is not an arithmetic sum of separate national revolutions where socialism is simply and decisively secured in one country after another. Rather, it moves in spirals: with upsurges and advances, consolidation and retreat, setbacks and reversals. It proceeds through struggles between revolution and counter-revolution, restoration and counter-restoration. The communist revolution is a complex, protracted, and tortuous world-historic process. But it is not back to square one. In the great accomplishments of the working class where and when it has held power and in the understanding (including of its mistakes and short-comings) that has been gained through the struggle to create a new world lie a foundation and inspiration to carry forward.

That is the spirit in which this essay is offered. Capitalism has turned the world into a nightmare for the majority of humanity. It is a world that must be radically transformed if the fundamental needs of the masses are to be met. Revolution must be made. This is happening in the jungles and shantytowns of Peru, where Maoism is illumining a path to liberation. As Mao said, where there is oppression, there is resistance. Society must and can be run differently.

This essay examines the principles, methodology, and practice of Maoist planning, focusing on three elements: the role of politics in the planning process, the relationship between centralization and decentralization, and the nature of economic balance under socialism. It aims to uncover the Maoist achievement in the realm of socialist planning, and in so doing not only to stimulate consideration of a socialism that is both visionary and viable, but also what is even more important, to assist the struggle to make it a practical reality.

I. Politics in Command

Without a correct political approach to the matter the given class will be unable to stay on top, and consequently will be incapable of solving its production problem either.

—*Lenin*[3]

Grasp revolution, promote production.

—*slogan of the Cultural Revolution*

What is the fundamental objective of socialist planning—economic growth per se, or moving beyond the framework of commodity production and money and forging a new society? What should be its main criteria of success—efficiency, productivity, and profitability, or the degree to which collective mastery over society is promoted? The issue boils down to this: what kind of growth, and for what purpose?

A socialist society must mobilize productive resources and accumulate and deploy a social surplus (the portion of social product above and beyond what is necessary to reproduce society at the same level of development). But as Bob Avakian, Chairman of the Revolutionary Communist Party, has pointed out, "the decisive question is not whether a surplus will be produced, nor its exact size, nor the most 'efficient' means for producing the greatest surplus but whether the surplus will be produced through means, guided by principles, and utilized in such a way as to make the greatest possible strides at every point toward the revolutionary transformation of society and the world, above all."[4] In socialist society, the invisible hand of the market must be replaced by the visible hand of politics. This is not to deny that socialist planning must pay attention to cost and strive to economize on labor power, materials, and funds. But that must be subordinate to revolutionary politics. (For instance, when the Chinese revolutionaries decided to locate industry in the less developed interior regions, this was not undertaken because it was the most efficient way of expanding total industrial production. It served the goal of reducing regional differences and inequalities. But once these factories were established, efforts were made to run them efficiently.)

There is no aspect of economic development, no form of economic organization, no organization of the labor process that exists outside of specific production and class relations. The most basic issues of economic development—what to produce, how, for whom, and for what—cannot be answered, indeed cannot be understood, except in class terms. Capitalist "efficiency" is class-bound; it is based on maximizing worker output and minimizing worker resistance, on shackling the producers and their collective creative capacities. Economic "rationality" has no meaning apart from the class relations it embodies and reproduces and the ends it serves. This is an incredibly important component of Maoist thought.

For the Maoist revolutionaries, socialist development had to be linked with overcoming disparities between industry and agriculture, between town and country, nationalities, men and women, and between mental and manual labor. And putting politics in command fundamentally meant making sure that economic strategy promoted the revolutionary transformation of society, relied on social mobilization and the spread of socialist values, and served the cause of world revolution.

In a socialist society, the masses must be politically armed. They must know what is needed and what the problems are, learn from advanced experience, have initiative in their hands, and be engaged in struggle over the goals and nature of planning. The lesson Mao summed up was that by putting politics in command—not experts, not computers, not regulations and production quotas, and certainly not profits—problems of economic development could be solved and the economy could be pushed forward in the interests of the masses.

Guiding and Measuring Economic Development

It has been observed that Western economists often encountered great difficulty in making sense of the Chinese planning system because so many noneconomic objectives were fed into it. Revolutionary China's standards of economic performance were far broader than the achievement (and overachievement) of production targets. The revolutionaries weighed the social and long-run economic effects of economic development. In assessing the efficiency of particular production methods, techniques, and factory organization, the revolutionaries widened the very concept of efficiency to include the social benefits and educational side-effects, as well as the contribution to local developmental needs, of such processes and forms of organization.[5]

And the Maoists did not accept, indeed they deliberately struggled against, the supposed "logic" of modern industrialization—the idea that economic development necessarily implies big and concentrated industry, massive urbanization, and regional specialization. In terms of plan fulfillment, quantitative goals were important and had operational significance at the national and enterprise level. But these were secondary to and served qualitative goals (for instance, the important thing for a factory producing agricultural equipment was not simply that it meet its financial targets but that it really understand the needs of agriculture and strive to do a better job in meeting those needs).

In working out and evaluating plans, the insistence on putting politics in command entailed subordinating individual and sectoral (this or that branch of industry's or particular region's) interests to the collective interest and to advancing revolution; relying on the masses; acting in accordance with what was called the "general line" on economic development of "going all out, aiming high and achieving greater, faster, better and more economical results in building socialism"; and implementing a series of principles which included "be prepared against war, be prepared against natural disasters, and do everything for the people" and "taking agriculture as the foundation and industry as the leading factor."

All this had very real practical consequences. Here we can delineate four significant elements of socialist planning, both with respect to its goals and its methods that reflected and served the "politics in command" orientation.

First, the Western pattern of industrial investment and urban growth was rejected. China sought to disperse industry and prevent the uncontrolled growth of cities and the clustering of industry around large cities. In fact, for the first time in history a process of industrialization was not simultaneously a process of unrestrained urbanization. Efforts were made to stabilize (or reduce) the size of large cities and to promote the growth of small and medium-sized cities, to shift industry to such cities, and to site new industrial zones on the outskirts of cities to better cope with residential needs and control of pollution.[6] Industrial policy was also aimed, as mentioned earlier, at narrowing regional growth and income differentials.

The planning system facilitated the development of relatively independent and comprehensive industrial systems in each of China's provinces and encouraged self-sufficiency in grain production. New kinds of production complexes in which industry would be more directly integrated with agriculture, and residence with work, were created. China's industry was oriented toward serving agriculture, at the same time that rural industrial and technical networks were promoted as a means of harnessing productive potential in the countryside and reducing the social gaps between town and countryside. By 1973–75, rural small-scale industry accounted for close to 60 percent of China's cement and fertilizer output, 35 percent of its hydroelectric power generating capacity, and 15 percent of its steel output.[7] Most farm machinery and equipment, except for the heaviest, was produced in local small and medium-scale plants.

But not only did these policies begin to profoundly break down age-old patterns of economic and social development in which cities ruled over the countryside, and not only did such policies contribute towards narrowing the difference between mental and manual labor. These measures also contributed to a profound break with the imperialist world economy and the dependency that imperialism foists on oppressed nations. There was an important strategic dimension here. The self-reliant, self-generating, and decentralized development that China embarked on would enable it to better stand up to imperialism's economic pressure, to resist possible attack and invasion, and to do more to serve the needs of the world revolution.

Second, plan was primary, price was secondary. At the society level, profits, prices, and various financial measures of capital effectiveness could not determine where investments would be made, what would be produced, the rate and direction of technological change, or the purpose of enterprise activities. If price and profit were made principal, the state could not redistribute investment resources from the richer regions to the less developed regions. Neither could it encourage the development of industries supporting agriculture which themselves were not highly profitable, nor increase the output and subsidize the selling price of basic consumption goods, nor extend comradely aid to revolutionary movements.

The structure of prices was still connected to underlying cost conditions; prices were not totally arbitrary. But prices were set consciously and uniformly (throughout the country) to achieve certain goals. They reflected political line. One striking example was how the price system favored agriculture (and the peasantry) in the terms of trade between industry and agriculture: prices were kept low for agricultural equipment and fertilizer, while the prices paid by the state for agricultural produce were raised (which is totally opposite to what typically happens in Third World countries). Prices and monetary return could not be allowed to play an autonomous guiding function in the economy.

At the enterprise level, making plan primary over price meant that the costs and benefits of economic activities could not be calculated in narrow financial terms or judged from the narrow point of view of maximizing the income of the individual production unit. As the revolutionaries explained:

> In some cases, judging from appearances, the loss might be bigger than the profit to an individual factory. However, judged from the overall situation, the profit [the overall benefit to society] might be bigger than the loss. . . . If we are concerned only with petty profits and ignore the major issues, if we pay attention only to the present and not the future, if we only take care of our own unit instead of considering the overall situation, and if we exert efforts only in proportion to the amount of [individual] gains expected, we must have been poisoned by the . . . theory of putting profits in command.[8]

Was it enough simply to fulfill the production plan regardless of the larger social costs, such as worker alienation, harm to worker health, and harm to the environment? These were issues which the Maoists insisted could not be treated as separate problems of secondary importance. Enterprise efficiency (or profitability) could not be placed above everything else: individual units had to take into account the needs of the whole of society, and workers and staff had to be guided by the spirit of doing anything of benefit to the people. The revolutionaries insisted that costs and benefits could not be determined on the basis of immediate monetary return.

What if worker initiative created temporary problems in production—should strict fulfillment of plan targets be an excuse to suppress workers? A common experience in factories in the years prior to the

Cultural Revolution was that when workers pioneered new designs and methods of production, they would often be disciplined and punished by managers. These managers worried that such innovations would disrupt established practices and thereby threaten the fulfillment of quantitative plan targets (and their bonuses). This attitude towards plan fulfillment and this contempt for workers came under sharp attack during the Cultural Revolution. As a result, an atmosphere was created that encouraged workers to break with all kinds of convention, whether in building ships in ways that had never been attempted before in China or in rethinking machine design. This had the long-run effect of promoting production.

Pro-market ideologues attack socialism as a system where quantities mean everything, where factories just churn out shoddy goods to meet production quotas. This is the so-called "plan-fulfillment-indicator problem"—in other words, managers simply do whatever is easiest to meet production (and value) targets, even if it means disregard for quality.[9] Actually, one of the issues of struggle between the Maoists and the capitalist roaders (who now run China) concerned precisely whether revisionist forms of management, which one-sidedly emphasized quantity or financial return, and which in general took a narrow approach to plan fulfillment to the detriment of party and state goals, would dominate economic management.

In revolutionary China, success indicators cut against the "tonnage mentality" of Soviet-type planning. Indeed, one of the slogans raised by dock workers and popularized during the Cultural Revolution was "Be masters of the wharves, not slaves to tonnage." In judging output performance, the primary concern was whether resources and output were serving larger policy goals; getting the right mix and quality of products and promoting socialist enterprise cooperation were more important than output value or rate of return. The key yardstick was neither price nor quantity but social use values (that which serves the needs of society) and the overall content and direction of economic activity.

This is not to say that cost-accounting and efficiency were abandoned. On the contrary, great efforts were made to minimize expenditure, to reduce cost, and ensure output quality. But this became the responsibility of the workers, both through forms of group accounting, analysis of economic activities, and financial management, and through mass movements to innovate and cut costs.

Managing, Administering, and Motivating Through Politics

Third, industrial organization and management were socialized and revolutionized. Plan objectives included limiting the alienation and social fragmentation that accompanies job specialization. Craft distinctions were broken down, personnel were periodically rotated between jobs (and factories would dispatch workers into the countryside as well), oppressive work rules were discarded, and bonus systems that pitted workers against one another were eliminated. Technicians were trained from among workers, and technicians and workers joined together in technical innovation teams. Collective forms of management were developed, and management was simplified. Enterprise leaders would spend regular periods working on the shop floor. The industrial enterprise was more than a self-contained economic unit: it would cooperate with others, even at the expense of short-term gains, it would take account of local community needs and social services, and, above all, it would be redefined as a site of political and class struggle.

Fourth, the economy was administered mainly through political and ideological means. For a plan to be effective, there must be a society-wide commitment to carry it through. Otherwise, there can be no real coordination, no real planning. This objectively poses the question of "compliance"—with the goals and norms of a plan as it is transmitted and translated at different levels, especially at the industrial enterprise level. Capitalist theorists contend that socialist planning authority is faced with the insuperable task of coaxing and pressuring enterprise managers to implement a plan's mandates. The problem is said to derive from plans that are unrealistically conceived and from the necessarily clashing perspectives of planners and managers. The result, according to the bourgeois account, is a tug-of-war between planning and managerial authority that grows wearying and which eventually resolves itself institutionally into a planning system characterized by the repressive and unresponsive transmission of directives from above and by passive and pragmatic adaptation from below.

Plan execution is an imperative task of a socialist economy. But how is this to be conceptualized? During the period that the Soviet Union was socialist, plan coordination and implementation were generally viewed as regulatory issues, and enterprise compliance was exacted through a control and inspection network that tended to bureaucratically expand.

The Maoist revolutionaries summed up that an administrative system that tries to rule by regulation and that mainly tries to police people into sticking by regulation would not only become excessively bureaucratic but also wouldn't work. It is relatively easy for any level of authority to get around external controls and regulations issued from above. As Mao pointed out in 1957, "regulations alone will not work . . . men's minds must change."[10] Thus the importance of the ideological dimension, the need to shape the ideological environment in which decisions are taken at all levels, and the importance of collective responsibility, of people internalizing goals and engaging in vigorous political struggle.

The point is that planning is not only subject to technical and administrative constraints but to political factors and to the limitations imposed by ideology. It takes place in the context of class struggle in society. Towards what kinds of transformations is planning oriented? For whom and for what? These are not givens but issues of struggle. For Mao the issue to solve was not principally one of the enforcement mechanisms of planning authority versus the prerogatives of managers, but rather the role of the masses. The masses must grasp what is politically necessary and have wide knowledge of the whole system—its economic laws, its goals, its contradictions—so that they themselves become the actors rather than the inert material acted on by market or bureaucratic planning processes, so that they can analyze and act on contradictions . . . so that they can regulate the regulators.

Rather than administering by technical and economic standards, the Chinese revolutionaries fostered non- and anti-bureaucratic methods for communicating policy and raising a different kind of standard, that of advanced experience and moral example. They popularized and encouraged people to learn from model institutions—rural brigades, communes, or factories—that implemented the general line. These were studied (and, in many cases, first-hand, with peasants and workers from various parts of the country visiting actual sites). But these models were not studied to be strictly copied, as if they were blueprints. The idea was for people to learn how problems were analyzed and overcome, how breakthroughs were made in the face of resistance from capitalist roaders, what advances were made in reorganizing property and social relations as well as the continuing political and technical problems, and how to apply these lessons to local conditions. The experience of building the Red Flag Canal (a monumental collective effort by peasants that vastly increased the amount of irrigated land), or fighting cruel natural conditions in the rural Tachai Brigade when it was a revolutionary stronghold, were examples of the masses conquering all kinds of difficulties and defying convention in economic construction. The Anshan (Steel Works) Constitution set a standard of revolutionary industrial management. In short, these models enabled people to grasp more deeply both the goals and methods of the communist revolution.

At the same time, national political campaigns were vehicles to focus mass attention on and sharpen awareness about key issues confronting society. Several such campaigns, like those to criticize and restrict bourgeois right and to criticize Confucian ideas of subservience and blind submission to authority, were launched by the revolutionary forces in the early and mid-1970s in the context of the struggle between the capitalist and socialist roads and the two-line struggle in the party. The aim was to arm people to make decisions and evaluate activities with broader interests in mind and to figure out what class interests were in fact being served by particular institutions and policies, and to strengthen the capacity of the masses to wage the struggle to maintain and extend political power.

The proletariat's political power is concentrated in its state. The proletariat needs a state to represent its interests. It is not enough to leave things at the local level or at the level of the individual factory. The proletariat needs to take up questions of society and the world—politics, culture, and ideology. One of the guiding insights of the Cultural Revolution was that the laboring people, through their experience in struggle and study of Marxism, had to grasp the link between two-line struggle over questions of economics and two-line struggle over issues in other realms. The revisionists' economic policies were part of an overall program to turn the masses back into beasts of burden. And if the masses were to wage, much less win, the battle on any front, including economics, and prevent capitalist restoration, they had

293

to be concerned with and influence what was happening in society overall. And so it was extremely significant that enterprises were transformed from mere production units into what Mao called "universities of class struggle" where theoretical study groups were set up, where proletarian cultural activity took place among other things. At the same time, worker and peasant teams came in to the universities in connection with the larger political struggle. The fact is that it would not have been possible to initiate and carry through the radical transformations in economic organization, management, and the labor process that have been discussed if ordinary laboring people were not politically mobilized around these broader issues.

The proletariat needs to transform society in its entirety—the condition of women, the oppression of minority nationalities, the values promoted by the education system, and so on. It needs a state to see to it that political, social, and economic transformations are carried out in a way that serves the world revolution. And it needs a state to defend its rule against the forces that would bring back and impose the old order. But all this means nothing unless the workers are actually becoming masters of the state, waging struggle over the nature and actions of this state. Because who controls the state will ultimately determine who controls the means of production.[11] This is why politics must command economics.

Fundamentally, a plan must concentrate the advanced experiences and aspirations of the masses; it must be constructed for their use, and it must unleash their initiative. This requires political leadership of a specific type—not a dominating clique but a real vanguard party with links to and serving the people, a vanguard capable of leading people forward through the complex struggle to bring a new society into being and to revolutionize the vanguard itself. This too is what it means to put politics in command.

II. Centralization, Decentralization, and the Problem of Information

Only this state [dictatorship of the proletariat] can represent the fundamental interests of the working class and the masses of laboring people and determine the principles and policies to be followed by enterprises, the orientation for their development, the production and distribution of their products, and the disposal of their assets. In dealing with enterprises, the state practices democratic centralism, that is, centralized power on major issues and decentralized power on minor issues, centralized leadership and level-to-level administration.

—Writing Group, Kirin Provincial
Revolutionary Committee[12]

Under no circumstances can history be regarded as something the planners rather than the masses create.

—Mao Tsetung[13]

Perhaps the central criticism of socialist planned economy is that it is built on a totally unrealistic assumption: that planners can somehow obtain and process all the necessary, and ever-changing, information about production and consumption that truly effective planning at the society level would require. Here is how the argument goes. Modern industrial society is so complex, and its aggregate knowledge and skills so widely dispersed, that it is plainly impossible for a central planning authority to process and communicate all the relevant information that is necessary for the many different economic actors to coordinate their actions. Only the price mechanism—detecting changes in the relations between the supply and demand for goods—and the bargaining that goes on between contracting parties can functionally convey this kind of information. To attempt to run an economy according to central guidance will only lead to bureaucratic nightmare (a request for a minor repair will have to pass through countless levels). And once a central plan becomes the sole or primary source for providing relevant information to producers, then what follows is extreme centralization of decision-making. Since the central planners are trying to hold together what fundamentally can't be held together—a vast centrally-run economy—they have no choice but to run things with an iron, dictatorial hand.

This critique sets up a straw man, the "all-knowing planner" who is supposed to operate with perfect information and perfect foresight. And it sets out the task or challenge facing a socialist economy to be essentially computational and administrative: to crunch the right numbers in order to *micro*manage the economy from the central bank down to the smallest factory. Planning, a profoundly political task for which the masses must take collective responsibility and over which they must assert collective control, becomes a computational and accountancy exercise by which state planners attempt (successfully or unsuccessfully) to achieve detailed control over the economy.[14]

Capitalism and the Problem of Information

Before turning to some of the political and operational issues bound up with the transmission of economic and social information in a genuine socialist planned economy, a few points need to be made about the supposed superiority of capitalism in this regard.

First off, in the Western market economies, private capitalists and consumers are nowhere close to possessing all or most price information (cheapest suppliers, lowest price for a consumer good, etc.) when it comes to making economic decisions and choices. So there is no full or "perfect" information in a modern market economy. It should also be noted that the inability of capitalism to solve major social problems, such as homelessness in the United States, has very little to do with insufficiency of information—the problem is well-known, as are many potential solutions. Nor can it be said there is insufficiency of social demand; the poor certainly demand decent housing. But whether capitalism recognizes and meets a particular "demand" is principally determined by profits to be made and money income to be spent.

Secondly, the claim is made that while a socialist economy lumbers under a sprawling command apparatus to find things out and to direct economic activities, a capitalist economy has an automatic and efficient means of transmitting essential information to producers. It is to be found in the operations of markets and prices—if a price is rising, there is demand to be filled and capitalists proceed to produce more of that product. But this must be seen for what it is: an indirect and anarchic mechanism of communication and coordination. Under capitalism, economic development is not guided and shaped by any prior plan or social purpose. Society's overall production needs and requirements are not, and cannot be, confirmed and planned in advance, because the productive activity of society is fragmented into privately organized units of capital. These individual capitals attain a high degree of organization (and even plan) at the firm and enterprise level. But there is no coordination at the society-wide level and these individual capitals do not know ahead of time for whom and in what necessary quantity they are producing, or even if what they produce is really needed. They are engaged in a battle for profits and market share, and they expand production and introduce new technologies to wage the battle. But whether the labor processes under their command are actually needed or up to competitive standard . . . that news and information only comes later—when the market clears or doesn't clear what is thrown on to it for sale, and by movements of prices and profits. In response to these market signals, investments are steered here or there, the labor force increased or contracted, etc. Thus the discipline of the market expresses itself through a hit-and-miss, too-much-and-too-little, trial-and-error process of *after the fact* adjustment.

Further, if the market and price mechanism work so efficiently, one has to ask why capitalism requires a bloated army of stockbrokers, market researchers, and advertising personnel to make its markets function profitably. The answer is that competing firms and corporations must gather ever more information ever more rapidly in the anarchically moving market in order to gain competitive advantage. The ensuing waste and squandering—whether it is the proliferation of all manner of technologies and activities to "read" the market and capitalize on market information, or the $130 billion that is spent each year in the U.S. on advertising to stimulate and steer demand—is a major indictment of capitalism.

Finally, while it is true that market prices convey information upon which capitalists base their production decisions, there is some absolutely crucial social information, like the environmental and health damage caused by a polluting steel mill, that the market-price mechanism fails to register and in fact systematically ignores. Individual firms and enterprises do not take into account the effects of things they do that do not fall within their particular (private) universe of cost and price calculation; and they do not take into account things they do that do not have prices—pollution is not generally bought and sold. Actually, the market tends to reward firms for ignoring the larger social costs and longer-term effects of their activities, because this raises profits.[15]

Still, the opponents of planning argue, look at the economy of the former Soviet Union in the 1970s and 1980s, where central administrative expenditures were enormous, where individual enterprises were routinely sending false information to the planning agencies, and where central planners really did not know what was going on. How can this be regarded as an advance over capitalism? Clearly, there was no efficient and informed coordination of production. This is certainly a correct description of the situation that had existed. Enterprises would deliberately overstate their resource needs and understate their production capabilities in reporting to and bargaining with planning authorities. At the same time, layers of the bureaucracy multiplied as planners hopelessly tried to monitor and control the economy.

But these were not the workings of socialism. Misreporting and concealment of production capabilities by enterprises were a reflection of the competition among state capitalist enterprises for centrally supplied credit and resources in a system of profit maximization. In a perverse way, this was a strategy to "outplan" a plan that wasn't really functioning—so enterprises tried to accumulate and hide supplies—and in the long run it only made things worse, as planning became even more unreliable and chaotic.

Let's talk about a genuine socialist economy. To be sure, complete and perfect economic information would not be obtainable even under its conditions. But this is not a terribly profound or useful observation . . . and it is hardly an argument against planning. Socialist planning is a process of continuous discovery arising from the interplay of knowledge and action, with information flowing in many different directions to coordinate production, increase understanding, and serve social need. Moreover, planning must make allowance for unforeseen circumstances and upheavals, for adjustment to new conditions and the correcting of mistakes. In short, a plan cannot be a precise (and never to be altered) numerical forecast or frozen blueprint; rather, it involves fundamental approximations, estimations, and projections in the pursuit of basic goals (in technical language, it must be cast in probabilistic terms), and the key thing is to learn from experience.

Nevertheless, it is quite realistic for a socialist society to identify and rank economic and social priorities, to determine what social needs have to be met and which are the most pressing (like building new hospitals versus new sports stadiums). It is possible to formulate broad targets and to evaluate appropriate and alternative means and methods of meeting them. It is possible to carry out the necessary material–supply balancing, that is, to figure out how a desirable output of goods can be produced, or industrial construction and expansion undertaken, given the resources, available technology, and production and labor capabilities of society—and Maoist economics emphasized the role of the human factor in opening new possibilities in solving production problems—and to arrange the necessary links between different sectors of production. In the case of socialist China, agriculture was consciously made the starting point in planning. This meant first making a realistic estimate of potential agricultural output and the resources (fertilizer, iron and steel, and machinery, etc.) required to meet agricultural targets and on that basis working out a detailed plan for industry. In this way it was possible to formulate reliable plans that promoted mutually supportive relations and arrangements between agriculture and industry, as part of a larger project of overcoming the division between town and country. In sum, it is possible to conduct conscious economic calculation. It is a form of calculation that proceeds from social needs and politically defined goals and that takes measure of long-term impacts (such as the ways in which patterns of production and consumption react on the resource base and the ecosystem).

Maoist Decentralization and Area Planning

A major issue posed by opponents of planning concerns the nature of centralized control. Does a planned economy necessarily lead to massive and oppressive bureaucracy? In fact, it is capitalism that requires hierarchical and bureaucratic control over people—one need only consider the internal organization of the modern corporation with its many echelons of managers, technocrats, and supervisors, not to mention the vast governing and political apparatus of modern capitalism. Mao emphasized that *socialist planning must combine centralized leadership and direction with decentralized initiative and administration.* This is what enables a socialist society to bring economic processes under conscious control and to maximize mass participation in running the economy—something that is impossible under capitalism. The proletariat needs to exercise its centralized state power to defend the revolution against internal and external enemies and to carry the revolution forward. It needs strong political leadership to concentrate advanced experience and understanding. It needs central

299

planning to coordinate social production. But on this basis, there must be extensive decentralization in order to unleash people and solve problems at the most appropriate levels.

Mao had summed up that too much top-down (vertical) control over the economy stifled popular initiative. Such a system of planning could not give full play to local capabilities and allow for creative utilization of local resources. It also undermined unified leadership over the economy as a whole, since there was no way that a complex and diverse economy could be managed on the basis of detailed commands from the top, no matter how thorough the statistical information and price calculations may be. This kind of detailed management and control of the economy by industrial ministries and central planning authorities, which was practiced when the Soviet Union was socialist, also distorted economic calculation and produced certain irrational practices. For instance, if a plant needed extra supplies it would have to make a request to the appropriate industrial ministry and sometimes wait for months to receive them from a geographically distant supplier that was under the control of the same ministry . . . instead of obtaining the supplies from a nearby producer that happened to be tied to another ministry.

In Maoist China, the national plan projected the principal requirements of the provinces. But, and this was a sharp break with the approach developed under Stalin, substantial powers of economic planning and administration were delegated to the provinces and localities. Mao understood that central planning could not encompass all the decisions that have to be made to run an economy. The principle was to pass decision-making power down to the level at which decisions would be carried out. This was decentralization to local *political* authority, and its purpose was to allow tasks to be defined and carried out, and problems to be solved, at the local level and to allow for greater mass initiative. In Eastern Europe in the 1960s, decentralization had taken place, but this was entirely different, it was capitalist decentralization—some authority was transferred from central planners to *managers* of industrial enterprises and this was combined with greater reliance on market forces, not people.

Before the Great Leap Forward of 1958–60, which saw the rise of the people's communes and tremendous revolutionary upheaval and innovation, the Chinese planning system shared many of the features of the Soviet planning system developed under Stalin. The central ministerial authorities drew up plans for their own industries and large manufacturing enterprises were placed under fairly tight control of the ministry of the branch of production concerned. But this was changed "from a system of planning and management in which each item [industrial product] is the main focus, to one in which the *localities* are the focus."[16]

What was developed was a system of "dual track" planning. Plans were drawn up by the industrial ministries to meet the needs and requirements of particular branches of production (one track) and plans were also drawn up to promote the development and meet the needs and requirements of geographic areas (the other track); they were then coordinated with one another by the planning commission. But the main track was that of "area" planning. As indicated earlier, a goal of Maoist planning was to develop comprehensive and self-reliant regional and local industrial systems with links to agriculture and to encourage more initiative from below. For these reasons, production plans were formulated principally in terms of *areas*. By having local areas take responsibility for basic production decisions and allocating resources, the whole process of coordinating social production was simplified and efficiency was raised. And this freed up central planning authority from a lot of "superficial calculations" and daily management, enabling it to focus instead on major questions of overall national economic planning.

Provinces assumed responsibility for supplying key goods to enterprises within their borders. Area planning broke down the rigid separation of enterprises by the products they manufactured. Neighboring producing units were encouraged to establish extensive linkages so that they could coordinate with, aid and learn from each other, and serve the surrounding population. Where possible, components and supplies were to be produced within localities. The flexibility built in to this kind of planning made it easier to cope with shortages or interruptions in supply. When an enterprise required additional supplies that weren't covered by the plan, it could go to the provincial authority, it could organize for supplies locally, or it could seek out and develop substitutes or find ways to economize on materials. The revolutionary line also encouraged enterprises to diversify their production activities and to develop the capability of meeting more of their parts, supplies, and repair requirements from *within* the enterprise, and this too made for simpler administration of planning.[17]

This kind of area planning and integration fostered all-round industrial-agricultural development, instead of leaving ministries to develop and locate industry based on the existing level of development of the regions (which would keep the backward backward). And it was an approach that could more effectively link economic growth to broader societal concerns. It had been summed up that vertical ministerial-based control and organization reinforced tendencies to put production above all else, and this cut against noneconomic goals. Clearly, these were problems in the Soviet Union when it was socialist in the pre-1956 period. In pursuit of efficiency and rapid economic growth, planners went in for gigantic industrial enterprises and put intense pressure on enterprises to maximize output. At the same time, the industrial ministries tended toward "departmentalism"—primary concern for enterprises in the same industry. All this had negative economic and social, as well as environmental, consequences. Area planning, on the other hand, could concern itself in a more all-round way with issues of population density, pollution, health, the ways in which residential areas could be developed into new kinds of units of collective economic and social life (which has tremendous implications for the emancipation of women), and urban-rural differences and interrelations. Here it might be added that decentralization was also reflected in scale of production: the Maoists were not spellbound by large factory size but sought flexibility in the spread of small and medium-sized and popularly-managed enterprises.

Once Again on Centralized Direction, Local Coordination, and Social Information

While the Maoist revolutionaries put great stress on local initiative and local responsibility, the central government remained intimately involved in the planning process. The levers of central control in the planning system included: the material supply system and transfers of resources and finances between provinces; national financial policy, including centrally determined and uniform prices; and the system of joint management of enterprises by the appropriate central government ministry (this was the centralized aspect) and the relevant local political authority at the province or municipality level (this was the decentralized aspect). Thus there was centralized direction over output levels of major products, over the distribution of industries between provinces, over retail prices of key commodities, and over the distribution of funds between ministries. In order to mobilize resources for priority needs and sectors, to effect rapid structural transformation, and to prevent political and economic fragmentation, centralization of this sort was essential.

However, the number of central ministries and other central planning bodies was reduced through the Cultural Revolution. Except for a few "key" enterprises decisive to defense and nationwide economic construction, most state industrial and commercial enterprises were, by 1970, placed under local control. Of 5,000 large and medium-sized enterprises some 2,000, or fewer than 40 percent, were under direct central control in the early 1970s.[18] At the same time, the planned activities of centrally-controlled industrial units were integrated into provincial and municipal plans. The provinces had prearranged financial obligations to the center. But provincial and local governments had control over a worked-out proportion of revenues above their assigned targets.

As far as major investment projects were concerned—for example, the construction of large, technologically-advanced steel mills—decisions about national industrial capacity of a given type were taken at the center and materials and finance were centrally allocated. Here the industrial ministries had an important role to play. But the specific plans to increase industrial capacity were integrated into provincial plans. And the number of materials placed under centralized allocation was reduced through the Cultural Revolution. It was in the range of 200–300 in the early 1970s, as compared with a much higher number during the time the Soviet Union was socialist (and as compared with as many as 65,000[!] materials controlled by the Soviet central authorities in the 1970s and 1980s).[19] All told, and this is rather extraordinary in modern economic history, administrative and planning channels were simplified in China, despite increasing diversity and complexity of the economy.

Socialist planning requires material balancing. This means estimating the quantity of inputs required for each unit of output, for instance how much steel is needed to produce a desired amount of machine tools. In other words, it means making sure the necessary production

303

resources are made available to meet production requirements and that different branches are in synch with each other's needs and linked to each other, in order to carry out the plan. And it also means that "norms" be set, that is, standards of how much labor or raw materials should be necessary to produce a given unit of this or that commodity. In China, the national plan would set broad production targets for particular commodities, but it did not set down exact quotas. The regional and local governments managed detailed material balancing. The broad commodity targets would be broken down into specific products (with specific quality standards, etc.) and delivery contracts through face-to-face meetings between producers, planners, and consumers at supply and sales conferences.

This conference system was something new in socialist planning, an innovative attempt to bring together representatives of economic units and organizations to work out arrangements between enterprises and supply and delivery contracts, and meet the requirements of balancing. This was a way to distribute materials for production that neither relied on the market nor on far-removed planners. This conference system, with its institutionalization of direct personnel linkages, improved the flow of information between enterprises (not just between units connected to each other in a given branch of production but between units producing and units consuming the items in question), and this made planning more efficient and flexible.

As for consumer needs, the planning system sought to sensitize itself to consumer likes (and dislikes). The commercial departments of the state economy made considerable efforts to conduct consumer research and surveys. At the same time, factories producing consumer goods would routinely dispatch worker-representatives to stores selling their particular items in order to size up consumer satisfaction and preference (it was not unusual for such representatives to visit communes for the same purpose). The Chinese showed that a socialist economy could assess and respond to consumer need and taste (although the concern was with the needs of the broad masses, not an elite consuming luxuries).[20]

The discussion has focused on society's *collective* understanding of production and consumption needs. But there is another crucial dimension of the "information problem." This is society's ability to share and spread knowledge of what has been learned in the struggle for production. In a capitalist economy, there is "a fundamental tension between the privatization of innovative ideas and the diffusion of those ideas into the economy."[21] A capitalist economy rewards innovators for keeping their ideas from others. A capitalist firm can get a leg up in the competitive battle by developing a new product or technology and using secrecy, patents, etc., to prevent others from utilizing or benefiting from it (on the other hand, if a firm feels it cannot profit from an innovation, or that others may benefit from its efforts, it may hold back). Socialism eliminates the barrier of private ownership. Innovations and knowledge become social property. One task of the planning system in China was exactly to socialize such knowledge. This process included the establishment of cooperative links between producing units so that new ideas could be spread and new production technologies learned; worked out donor–recipient relationships for equipment and on-the-spot assistance; the practice of sending technicians out from more developed to less developed areas and production units; the establishment of special worker institutes in factories and schools in the countryside in which technical and political study were combined; the sending down of educated youth into the countryside; and the widespread use of popular manuals.[22] By broadening the capabilities and experiences of ordinary workers, and by breaking down narrow specialization in tasks and skills, a socialist economy can generate far more useful information (to the well-being and advance of society) than is possible under conditions of capitalist specialization and hierarchy.[23]

Planning Through Line

The Maoists insisted on "two-way" initiative in planning, from the center and from the local areas, and on giving the local areas as much responsibility as possible. But how within this system were immediate and long-term interests balanced, competing interests reconciled? What safeguards were there to prevent provinces and areas from just looking out for their own interests? How would coordination be achieved across these many different units of planning?

Here the centralizing aspects of the planning system come back into play. There were certain basic guidelines which had to be observed: the structure of management was generally uniform throughout the country; individual units could only exercise decision-making powers and the authority to act on their own in various matters on the basis of sticking to the general political line and directives; profits of state-owned enterprises were transferred to the state, and the specific performance of an enterprise did not determine its wages and salaries (these were centrally set); and key plan targets, once set, could not be altered by autonomous decision of the production unit.

The Chinese relied on a kind of "indirect" centralization in which politics not heavy-handed control was principal to coordinate planning and make sure that it had mass support. This was accomplished by means of what the revolutionaries called the "Five Unifiers." In an important study of the Chinese planning system, Roland Berger spells them out:

(i) **unified understanding,** that is, people were acting on the basis of a revolutionary political and ideological understanding of where society needs to go and were raising that understanding through study and political struggle;

(ii) **unified policy,** which meant that this general political line would be applied at each level of the economy and in each phase of development to solve specific problems;

(iii) **unified plan,** that is, there would be coordination of different sectors and interests in applying this policy;

(iv) **unified direction,** which was a principle by which leadership for each economic and social unit would come from the next unit above;

(v) **unified action,** which meant that the masses had to be relied on and unleashed at each level.[24]

Thus the policy of giving greater scope to local authority was carried out in dialectical unity with unified central leadership and unified planning. Local initiative would have the effect of strengthening, not weakening, centralized leadership and unified planning. But *the real glue of this system ensuring that the interests of the whole and the overall needs of the revolution were being met was political and ideological.* And decisive to this was the practice of the "mass line," from the masses to the masses, to ensure that planning was carried out in accordance with the interests of the masses and on the basis of mobilizing the masses.

The Maoists had a phrase to describe planning that was divorced from the masses, that put planning in the hands of "experts." They called it "planning by the typewriter, the computer, and the telephone." Maoist planning was based less on detailed gathering of statistics than it was on in-the-field, in-person investigation and consultation by planning authorities, in fact-finding away from work benches, and exchanging of experiences among enterprises. "We must leave our offices, and go amongst the masses, have confidence in and rely on their strength, and not merely close the doors while doing estimates and calculations," [25] said one article written during the Great Leap Forward. The key directional flow of information was from the bottom up: "in the overall coordination of production . . . , it is the Center that has to be bombarded with reports, data, and returning 'planners,' who have been to the localities and conducted investigations." [26]

In drawing up and reviewing plans, the revolutionaries emphasized the importance of continuous consultation at each stage of the planning process and of "planning through line" (through mass political discussion and debate). The application of the "mass line" meant that discussions of proposed plans would take place at the grassroots level and that suggested modifications would work their way upward, as back-and-forth exchanges continued between upper and lower levels, and with the most valuable suggestions getting incorporated along the way.

This overall process was described by the Chinese as "the two ups and the two downs." An initial plan, based on mass experience flowing upward and the overall needs of advancing the revolution, would be formulated and sent down through all administrative and production levels. It was then put to mass review, with suggestions getting transmitted upward. Then a final modified plan would be sent back down. The main thrust of these procedures and mechanisms was that plan goals and norms (standards of production) were the object of mass discussion and evaluation, according to the general political line. But planning through line not only required this back-and-forth process through which a more correct plan could be drawn up. It required that people be won politically to the plan, so that they could define and carry out their specific responsibilities with the interests of the whole revolution in mind. If this approach were not taken, then the spontaneous tendency would be for people either to take a passive attitude and just figure out the easiest way to fulfill their particular assignments, or to twist the plan and go in for whatever would bring the greatest immediate or local gain.

Planning methods are not neutral. They exert effects on class structure—on who and what is being controlled. And the very means by which information is gathered and evaluated reflects the class struggle. China's planning system was cohesive yet flexible, and it was based on mass participation. This was the result of a unique combination of centralized and decentralized planning mechanisms and the practice of a mass revolutionary politics. It was a new kind of socialist planning.

III. Economic Laws, Balance, and Plan Flexibility

The revisionist approach to planning denies the dialectical movement of things and attempts to impose order and balance from the top, through bureaucratic methods and decrees divorced from and opposed to the masses and mass initiative as well as the actual laws of development of the economy.

—Bob Avakian[27]

Balance is relative to imbalance. Without imbalance there is no balance. The development of all things is characterized by imbalance. That is why there is a demand for balance. . . . Plans constantly have to be revised precisely because new imbalances recur.

—Mao Tsetung[28]

Socialism cannot be built in an atmosphere of calm seas and gentle breezes.

—Mao Tsetung[29]

The nature of economic laws under socialism was the object of continuing investigation and theorization by the revolutionary forces in China. This is clear in studying *The Shanghai Textbook*. Mao defined objective laws as things that appear over and over, not accidentally, in the movements of phenomena.[30] Economic laws refer to basic, yet dynamic, connections and relationships that regulate social production and economic development and that compel economic units to organize and behave in certain ways within certain ranges. These laws are rooted in the objective economic structures and processes of society as it has historically developed. It must be frankly admitted that much more needs to be understood about the operation of economic laws under socialism. But the experience of socialist construction has shown that the force of economic laws will invariably be asserted, even if negatively by failure to understand and act in accordance with them. Socialist construction must be consciously guided.

Here it might be said that one law-like characteristic of socialism is that there is no "invisible hand" that directs socialist economic development. But this is not the same as voluntarism (Mao is often charged by Western and Soviet ideologues with having the view that you can just do anything at any time regardless of material and ideological conditions). The formulation and execution of plan involves the conscious study and utilization of objective laws, and, through application, investigation, and summation, the gaining of a more comprehensive grasp of the nature of these laws. On this basis, the scope for intentional and purposeful human activity, including restricting the range of operation and negative effects of certain laws, vastly increases, as does what the Maoists called the "initiating role" of the superstructure (broadly understood to mean the dynamic play of politics, culture, and ideology).

With respect to planning, the Maoists focused attention on three laws. The law of value reflects the quality of exchangeability of commodities (commodities exchange in proportion to the labor time socially necessary for their production). In a socialist economy, this law continues to play a role in economic planning in calculating cost, in influencing price determination and the ratios in which different products exchange for one another, and in spotting inefficiencies in production. But it did not play a controlling and regulating role. As a holdover from capitalism, this law had to be restricted. The law of planned (and proportionate) development requires that social labor and means of production be distributed in correct proportions between different branches and spheres of the economy so that the economy can harmoniously develop as a whole. This law reflected the requirements of social production under conditions of public ownership. But it did not set the direction of social development; this, *The Shanghai Textbook* points out, was determined by a more fundamental economic law under socialism: the satisfaction of the ever-increasing needs of the proletarian state and the people.

309

Economic laws operate as tendencies. They are influenced by other laws and factors, as well as by historical circumstances, and these laws are themselves contradictory. So the actual movements and effects of economic laws are complex, not simple and straight line. This remains the case in socialist society.

Socialism is a transition between capitalism and communism, and economic development cannot but be a struggle between the road of socialism and the road of capitalism, a transition marked by upheaval and transformation. One of the common misconceptions of socialist economics, or, perhaps better said, one of the tenets of the "law and order" phony socialism of Soviet-style revisionism is that socialism is a stable social formation whose economic laws will enable production to develop smoothly and society to evolve gradually and ever so surely towards communism. Hence a preoccupation with equilibrium . . . and with order.

The Soviet revisionists would appeal to economic laws that supposedly put society on a kind of "automatic pilot" to communism. Ideologically, this served the function of politically demobilizing the masses. The state bourgeoisie would tell the masses not to worry about politics; everything that exists is what is supposed to exist, and socialism will take care of itself—provided, of course, that leadership (i.e., the new bourgeoisie) manages the economy "scientifically" in accordance with economic "laws." The reality of the Soviet Union was of course quite different. Hyper-rigid mechanisms of state-capitalist planning only intensified economic disorder in the long run, because capitalism and its laws cannot be controlled.

Stability is not the Highest Goal

In a genuine socialist economy, conscious regulation of the whole economy (macroeconomic regulation) becomes possible. By this is meant that *society can control all branches of the economy on a regular and system-wide basis.* But this raises some important questions. Does this ability to control social production mean that a planned socialist economy can achieve macroeconomic stability? And to what degree should that be an overriding objective of socialist economy? Clearly, part of the argument for, and objective superiority of, the socialist system is that socialized management of the productive forces enables society to coordinate production according to a conscious plan based on social need. This eliminates the economic dislocations and social misery inflicted by the capitalist drive for profit and the violent fluctuations and market adjustments to which it gives rise. Socialism overcomes the underlying anarchy (planlessness) of capitalist social production and the condition whereby blind economic forces rule people's lives. Again, conscious macroeconomic regulation becomes possible. But socialist society is in motion; there is struggle and change, and stability and control are relative. In the Maoist conception, the task of planned socialist construction was not to achieve equilibrium in each sector of the economy or at each phase of development—this was an impossible quest anyway—but rather to unleash and harness dynamic forces, the most important of which is people, in the pursuit of specified political and social objectives. Here is how Mao explained the motion of socialist economic development:

> Economic construction is not devoid of forward and backward motion; it is not steady, straight-line advance . . . Economic construction is wave-like; there are peaks and troughs with one wave following each other. This is to say, there is balance, disruption, and after disruption, balance is restored. Of course these fluctuations in wave-like advance should not be too great, otherwise it would be adventurism followed by conservatism. But wave-like advance is an inevitable and recurring feature of economic construction.[31]

Mao rejected the linear (undynamic) approach of the traditional planning model which took production capacities, supplies of reserves, and technological capabilities as fixed givens, and which viewed balanced growth in terms of static input-output planning (*x* amount of machines require *y* amount of steel . . . just put the right pieces in the right places to get the right results). The Maoists certainly paid attention to the technical requirements of coordinated production, as discussed in the previous section. But their emphasis was much more on the stimulus that came by unleashing people to solve problems, on grassroots innovation, on creatively mobilizing human and material resources as part of "digging out potential" and this would hardly be neat and orderly.

In the unfolding of plans and mass mobilizations, imbalances were bound to crop up. Some imbalance was economically and socially undesirable and had to be promptly and resolutely corrected; bottle-necks and weak points would have to be overcome. Some imbalance was the result of obstruction and interference by capitalist roaders. But some imbalance and disruption opened up whole new avenues for development, as did the bursts of social, economic, and technical change that occurred during the Great Leap Forward. Some imbalance was the unavoidable side-effect of the pursuit of larger policy objectives. For instance, bringing industry to the countryside enabled peasants to master industrial production processes and to transform rural society, but it also created short-term labor and supply demands in some situations that adversely (though temporarily) affected agricultural production. Finally, much imbalance actually represented advanced experience to be learned from—thus the Maoist call to "take a positive attitude towards imbalance."

Balanced–imbalanced development was the very process through which growth unfolded. The task of planning was not to avoid or "out-plan" imbalance as such but to "ride" those waves Mao speaks of in order to push development forward, and to utilize and more deeply grasp the spiral-like adjustment cycle of balance-imbalance-balance to achieve the ever-more conscious social regulation of production.

One-sided insistence on balance would have three negative impacts. One, it would restrain some of the "irregular" but dynamic elements of the economy, like China's small-scale industries in the countryside and cities which Mao's revisionist opponents regarded as a threat to economic order. Two, it would actually make it more difficult to cope with difficulties and unforeseen circumstances by reining in sectors and units in the name of short-run balance. And, three, it would stifle mass initiative and experimentation. The revisionist approach to planning made an absolute out of balance, order, and control, whereas for Mao the key thing was not economic or political stability but change, revolutionary change.

Plan Flexibility

Mao's dialectical approach to balance found concrete expression in planning methodology. Long-, medium-, and short-term plans all reflected overriding political principles. As far as time horizons were concerned, broad economic and social goals were embodied in long-term plans, but these plans served more to indicate the future shape of society than to function as quantitative "master" plans. More operational five- and especially one-year production plans were formulated in more detailed numerical form.

But targets and assumptions could not be etched in granite. As Mao wrote, a five- and one-year plan could not meet all the requirements of economic law; this could only be obtained through practice. In China's specific conditions, overall economic balance was very much conditioned by fluctuations in agricultural production. And there were the unpredictable "variables" of political struggle, war, and revolution.

Advance coordination is essential to effective planning. But socialist society is not a clockwork mechanism set in motion by planners nor, as mentioned earlier, mechanically governed by economic laws. A planned economy must have feedback mechanisms: the feedback of political debate and discussion on the shape and priorities of development, and the feedback that comes from experience in the struggle for production. A plan must be proven in practice and subject to modification. Observance of goals and norms is essential to effective planning, as is the commitment to fulfill specific plan targets. A plan must be implemented. But the Maoists rejected the idea—as enshrined in revisionist Soviet planning methodology—that "the plan is the law."

The planning system in revolutionary China did not insist on rigid quotas. Now, this did not mean that targets had no purpose, authority, or motivating role. But it did mean that targets should be sufficiently broad so as to allow for continual review and adjustments, within the framework of keeping the plan consistent and on the basis of level-to-level consultation, in the course of their execution. (And, again, these targets were mainly based on conscious political inquiry, not price data.) In short, it was more important that the economy be able to accommodate itself to making readjustments than that it be tied to rigid targets.[32] It also meant that problems should be solved at the lowest levels concerned, through self-reliant and cooperative means.

Importantly, the revolutionaries moved away from what has been called "taut," or tight, planning—high output targets with low input allocations, in other words, asking for more than could be reasonably delivered. Such excessively rigid planning causes frequent supply problems. It also reacts on the morale of the masses:

Plan targets should be advanced. But this does not mean that the higher the targets, the better. Plan targets that are too high to be practicable not only fail to unleash the enthusiasm of the masses but will dampen it. Leave some leeway.[33]

The "leeway" in the plan was a margin (or surplus amount) of material and financial resources, as well as labor, that would enable regions, provinces, or county levels to meet emergency situations and enterprises to cope with problems or new conditions. State-owned enterprises were granted a ten percent (and sometimes higher) allowance in the use of production factors for unexpected circumstances and for local initiative. Quantitative targets were centrally set for enterprises. But as Table 1 shows, of the twelve major targets, eight could be changed without permission by the enterprise. This added another measure of flexibility. The revolutionaries had summed up that a complicated and compulsory set of targets, as was the practice of the Soviet Union when it was socialist (and which the Chinese had emulated in the early years of their planning system), actually worked against coherent planning. It often led enterprises to concentrate on some targets at the expense of others, or even to falsify statistical performance. Technical conditions varied considerably among enterprises; and economic and political circumstances were bound to change, and this had to be taken account of by the plans. The net effect of these kinds of planning innovations was that changes and adjustments could be made in the course of carrying out a plan without throwing the whole plan out of whack or forcing it to be abandoned altogether.[34]

Plan flexibility was not merely a question of cutting enterprises and units some slack. Fundamentally, the way to adjust for imbalances caused by uneven development and to overcome various bottlenecks and shortfalls was to encourage all levels of the economy to tap the potential of resources previously unknown, unnoticed, or wasted, and to mobilize positive factors through mass movements. This was the principle of "active" balance, which meant searching out solutions to reach goals that had been set, and using the experience of the advanced to inspire the less advanced to catch up. It stood in contrast to "passive" balance, which proceeded from the need to attain a formal balance, even if it meant putting a halter on the dynamic sectors

TABLE 1. FLEXIBILITY GRANTED INDUSTRIAL ENTERPRISES IN MEETING QUANTITATIVE TARGETS

	Targets That Could Not Be Changed By Enterprises Without Permission	*Targets That Could Be Changed By Enterprises On Their Own Initiative*
Physical	1. Output of main commodities produced	1. Trial production of new commodities 2. Main technical and economic norms (e.g., units of electricity produced per unit of coal)
Financial	2. Total profit	3. Total value of output 4. Total value of cost reduction 5. Rate of cost reduction
Labor	3. Average size of workforce 4. Total wage bill	6. Year-end size of workforce 7. Average wage 8. Productivity of labor

Source: Adapted from Christopher Howe, *China's Economy* (New York: Basic Books, 1978), Table 17, p. 42.

In a planned socialist economy, industrial enterprises are guided by a central plan. They strive to meet targets and goals set by central, regional, and local political authorities so that social production can function as an integrated whole and satisfy society's needs. But too often central planning systems have tied enterprises to rigid targets, which makes it hard to adapt to changing conditions and which can also stifle worker initiative. This table shows that enterprises in revolutionary China had the flexibility to adjust a great many targets within the framework of a unified plan.

(pulling down the high to suit the low), and which tended to promote passivity at the lower levels.

A Deeper Sense of Balance

If imbalance was viewed as the necessary condition for society to advance and for future balance to be established, this did not mean that the Chinese planning system under Mao was unconcerned about balance or did not view balance as a desirable goal of a planned economy. One can go back to Mao's 1956 speech, "On the Ten Major Relationships." This was a critique of major features of the Soviet growth model under Stalin, in particular the one-sided emphasis on heavy industry which took too much of the product from the peasants and left them too few funds for further accumulation through their own efforts. In this work, Mao conceptualizes socialist construction as a whole series of contradictions, and he sets forth a dialectical approach to arranging priorities and proportionalities (it was in this speech that Mao also criticized over-emphasis on central control).

Proportionate development required that certain key proportional relations be handled correctly: between agriculture and industry; within agriculture, between food grain production and other lines; within industry, between key links and secondary links; between agriculture and industry, on the one hand, and communications and transport on the other; between economic construction and cultural and educational activity; and between accumulation and consumption. Approaching these relationships correctly called for attention to investment priorities, growth rates in key spheres of the economy, and their effects on proportionalities between different sectors and industries. But it also called for attention to how these proportionalities affected class relations within Chinese society. Industry required certain agricultural materials to produce goods in social demand. But getting the proportionalities right between these two branches of production (industry and agriculture), getting the right ratios of inputs (from agriculture) and outputs (what industry produced with them) was not simply a technical matter. It was also political: if the peasants were squeezed to achieve the "correct" input-output balance, or taxed too heavily to achieve financial balance, this could undermine the confidence of the peasants in the system and erode the worker-peasant alliance.

Maoist planning showed a profound concern with balance. But, as with every other aspect of Maoist political economy and strategy, this was seen through the filter of the advance to communist society. Balanced development hinged on three key elements: broad *sectoral balance,* fundamentally between agriculture, light industry, and heavy industry; *regional developmental balance,* that is, reducing the economic and social inequalities between regions; and *technological balance,* meaning there should be a balanced spectrum of techniques of production in society, not just the big, the modern, and the foreign.[35] The central planning system was more concerned with these kinds of balances than with detailed material balancing and target setting. And in the 1949–76 period, the Chinese economy made notable gains in achieving this kind of balanced development.

Agriculture received major attention (as mentioned, it was the starting point in the planning process). Considerable resources in the industrial sector were devoted to supplying agriculture with modern industrial products; substantial direct state investment was made in agricultural infrastructure, like water conservancy projects; and mass-run rural industries were developed. Earlier in this essay, the question of prices was discussed. During the Maoist years, the terms of trade between agricultural and industrial goods improved dramatically. Chart 1 provides dramatic evidence: between 1952 and 1974, the prices of farm products paid by the state increased by 64 percent while prices of industrial goods sold in rural areas increased by less than 1 percent. Concern with technological balance brought forward the policy of "walking on two legs," or utilizing both advanced and simple (or traditional) technologies, and spreading technology and scientific know-how that people could master and apply (for example, peasants learned and practiced seed-selection and seed-crossing).

Regional balance was aimed at avoiding what is sometimes called "air-bubble" development, wherein modern and fast-growing industry is concentrated in a few coastal areas cut off from the rest of the country, which is condemned to stagnation. (This kind of lopsided development is reasserting itself with chaotic vengeance in China today under the banner of reform and modernization.) A policy of rational dispersion of industrial capacity was pursued. New industrial centers appeared in the interior regions, and there was a steady increase in the share of industrial output by inland provinces. This can be seen in

Afterword

CHART 1. IMPROVING THE TERMS OF TRADE BETWEEN AGRICULTURE AND INDUSTRY, 1950–1974

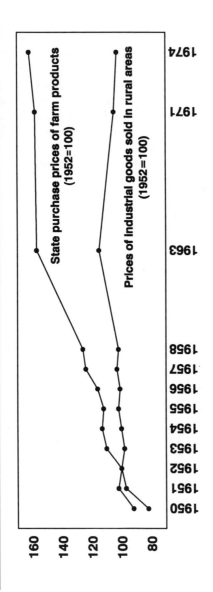

Source: Nicholas Lardy, "Economic Planning and Income Distribution in China," *Current Scene*, November 1976, p. 6.

This chart shows that in Maoist China prices of industrial goods (like equipment and fertilizer) held relatively constant from 1950 to 1974, whereas the state steadily increased the prices at which it purchased agricultural goods. This is totally opposite to the general situation of Third World countries both internally and in their relation to the world market—whereby the terms of trade for agricultural producers tend to be unfavorable and to deteriorate over considerable stretches of time. The Maoist price policy is an illustration of taking agriculture as the key link and the determination to overcome differences between industry and agriculture and between town and country.

TABLE 2. SHARE OF TOTAL OUTPUT PRODUCED BY COASTAL PROVINCES, 1952–1970 (in percentages)

	1952	1957	1965	1970
Electric power	66	60	54	57
Coal	34	36	36	40
Crude oil	75	40	16	13
Steel	85	83	64	56
Chemical fertilizer	100	88	49	50
Cement	72	62	41	36
Paper	50	44	40	39
Machine tools	90	*	*	80
Cotton cloth	82	70	61	61
Sugar	40	33	47	47

Source: Charles R. Roll, Jr., and Kung-Chia Yeh, "Balance in Coastal and Inland Industrial Development," *China: A Reassessment of the Economy,* Joint Economic Committee of the U.S. Congress, 1975, Table 4, p. 89.

One of the goals of socialist economic development in China was to effect a more balanced distribution of productive capacity between the coastal regions and the poorer interior of the country. Before 1949, most of China's industry was concentrated in Shanghai and Tientsin (coastal areas) and Manchuria. The revolution rejected the capitalist logic of focusing investment resources on these already developed areas ("building on the best") as well as the Soviet model of constructing highly centralized production complexes. Instead, the revolution set out to create a wide net of industry that could both supply basic necessities for the local population and meet local industrial needs. The table reveals that the relative share of output of key industrial items accounted for by noncoastal areas increased substantially over the 1952–1970 period.

TABLE 3. GOVERNMENT REDISTRIBUTION OF FINANCIAL RESOURCES TO POORER REGIONS: REVENUE SHARING BETWEEN THE CENTRAL GOVERNMENT AND PROVINCES

Province (listed in descending order of industrial development)	Percentage of Total Provincial Revenue Kept by Province*	
	1959	Post-1960
Shanghai	19.8	10 (1972)
Liaoning	36.1	18 (1972)
Kiangsu	54.4	30 (1972)
Yunnan	11.8	115 (1974)
Inner Mongolia	88.5 (1957)	**
Kwangsi	108.6 (1957)	**
Sinkiang	125.9	135 (1955–72)
Ninghsia	**	152 (1958–74)
Tibet	183.5	150+ (1960–73)

* *Percentages above 100 indicate a net subsidy from the central government to the province. Those provinces receiving such subsidies could spend more to cover their expenditures than would have been possible given the revenues they could generate on their own.*

** *Expenditures in these provinces were greater than anticipated revenues, resulting in a subsidy from the central government. However, the size of this subsidy in relation to expenditures is not known.*

Source: Adapted from Nicholas Lardy, *Economic Growth and Distribution in China* (Cambridge: Cambridge University Press, 1978), Table 4.3, p. 162.

This table illustrates one way in which the planning system in China sought to overcome differences between the more industrially developed and urbanized regions and provinces and the more rural, agricultural, and backward areas of the country. The areas of highest industrial development, like Shanghai, sent the vast majority of their revenues to the center. The poorest areas, like Tibet, received subsidies from the center that amounted to over half of their spending requirements. These poorer areas received other kinds of support as well. This policy of redistributing financial resources from the richer to the poorer areas was strengthened by the Cultural Revolution. After a socialist revolution in a country like the United States, the application of such a policy would involve a vast redistribution of resources towards the inner cities and poorer rural areas.

Table 2, which shows the declining share of output (with the slight exceptions of two categories) by China's coastal provinces, which were the traditional centers of industrial development. The central government also made determined efforts to redistribute investment and financial resources from the rich to the poor areas. As illustrated by Table 3, highly industrialized areas sent well over half their revenues to the center while less developed areas received considerable subsidies. Skilled labor and technical labor power were systematically transferred from more developed to less developed regions. By the early 1970s Shanghai had supplied over half a million skilled workers to industry in the interior of the country.[36] As a result of these and other policies, the least industrialized regions had experienced the highest rates of growth (although their absolute level of development still remained considerably behind that of the advanced regions).[37]

For Maoist planning, the proper handling of key economic and social relationships was more important than growth or balance per se. In the long run this approach to balanced development promoted sustainable growth that both increased collective mastery over the economy and narrowed social, economic, and regional inequalities.

IV. It Worked and Opened New Possibilities

Revolutionary China scored great economic successes. It can be seen from Table 4 that in the 1952–1966 and 1966–76 subperiods agricultural and industrial output grew steadily. In the countryside, the food problem was solved, mass hunger and disease wiped out. A basic consumption level was established below which people were not permitted to fall and living standards for the masses rose. During the years of the Cultural Revolution (1966–1976), when Maoist China was supposedly on the brink of economic disaster according to its detractors, industrial production achieved an impressive average annual rate of growth of over 11 percent. There were major industrial breakthroughs, like the development of a large machine-building industry and advances in ship construction capabilities, and major scientific breakthroughs, like the development of synthetic insulin. Consumption for both urban and rural inhabitants grew at a moderately good rate of over two percent a year. Revolutionary China's quantitative growth

TABLE 4. REVOLUTIONARY CHINA'S ECONOMIC GROWTH, 1952-1976

	Phase I (1952-1966)			Phase II (1966-1976)	
	1952	1966	Annual rate of growth	1976	Annual rate of growth
1. National income (net domestic material product)—billion yuan in 1970 prices	65.4	151.0	4.0%	245.6%	7.0%
2. Total value of industrial output—billion yuan in 1970 prices	27.5	144.8	10.6	326.1	11.3
3. Of which, heavy industry production—billion yuan in 1970 prices	8.7	72.3	14.4	183.1	13.6
4. Of which, light industry production—billion yuan in 1970 prices	18.7	72.3	7.4	143.0	8.5
5. Total value of agricultural production—billion yuan in 1970 prices	63.6	94.7	1.4	131.7	3.8
6. Amount of food grain production—unprocessed, in millions of tons	163.9	213.9	0.6	286.30	3.4
7. Population—yearly average in millions of persons	568.2	735.6	1.7	926.19	2.4
8. Per capita national income—yuan in 1970 prices	115.0	205.3	2.3	265.2	4.4
9. Per capita food grain output—unprocessed, in kilograms	288	291	-1.0	309.0	1.0

Source: S. Ishikawa, "China's Economic Growth Since 1949," *China Quarterly*, June 1983, Table 1.

This table illustrates China's growth during two periods. The first was the early phase of socialist construction, when China was laying the foundations of a planned socialist economy. The second covers the years of the Cultural Revolution, when there was enormous political upheaval and social experimentation. This table shows that the trends of growth for most of the agricultural and industrial indicators were quite high—especially as compared with other developing countries. It also shows that the economy performed quite well during the Cultural Revolution, which has often been attacked by critics as a total disaster. That success was not an accident but the result of the Maoist policy of Grasp Revolution, Promote Production.

record as measured against that of other countries stood up well. Compared with the growth rate of contemporary advanced industrial countries during the periods between 1870–1900 and 1900–1971, only Japan's performance in growth of per capita income may have been better. Compared with other low-income Third World countries during the 1965–75 period, China's growth rate was quite high.[38]

But more important was the quality of this planned growth, its emphasis on reducing social inequality, its refusal to allow the market to determine the allocation of resources and the distribution of income, its insistence on growth on the basis of collective control by those on the bottom of society. And this was its reality. Urban income and consumption differentials were, by any standard, extremely low (no other low-income country came close). Within industry, the highest-paid managers and technical personnel were typically paid only about five times the wage of unskilled workers (a 5:1 pay ratio), whereas in many Third World countries of Africa and Asia it was not unusual for the ratios to range from 30:1 up to 50:1.[39]

Urban–rural inequality was addressed through a series of measures that included the previously mentioned efforts to improve the terms of trade in favor of agriculture, as well as the development of rural industrial and technical networks, expansion of secondary schooling, recruitment of peasants into the universities, sending down of university youth to the countryside, and vast expansion in rural health and welfare services (prior to the Cultural Revolution, two-thirds of budgetary funds for medical and health care were spent in urban areas; as a result of the Cultural Revolution, this proportion was reduced to 40 percent). A large, underdeveloped, and overwhelmingly rural society had an average life expectancy that ranked far above that of other low-income countries.[40] As for China's largest city, Shanghai, by 1975 its infant mortality rate was lower than New York City's.

This was a radically different kind of economy and society. Take the workplace. Social control was asserted over technology. The labor process and the social division of labor became the object of transformation. Administrative bureaucracy and technical hierarchy with their oppressive pecking orders, rules and regulations, and their institutionalized antagonisms between manual workers and "mental" experts were criticized, overhauled, and simplified. Management was made accountable to workers. And bold worker and peasant innovation was made the order of the day. Throughout society, base-level institutions of popular control developed. No authority was exempt from criticism by ordinary workers and peasants. Above all, the masses were drawn into debate and struggle around the cardinal political issues of the revolution. Imagine a society organized around the principle of serving the people. That was Maoist China.

The fact that Maoist China was a very poor country with a large peasantry has led some observers to conclude that while there is perhaps much to admire about revolutionary China's strategy for economic development, this is essentially only relevant to overcoming underdevelopment. These observers suggest that there is little else about the Maoist experience that is relevant to advanced industrial society. But this is quite mistaken and, it must be frankly stated, quite Eurocentric. To begin with, the proletarian revolution is a complex and world-embracing struggle that must, as one of its key objectives, overcome the existing (unequal) distribution and concentration of productive forces. The majority of the world's population live in a Third World dominated and penetrated by imperialism. In these neocolonial areas, revolution must completely recast the lines of dependent and distorted development that result from this domination. The Maoist road to socialism in the Third World, what it actually means to *delink* from the imperialist world economy and to achieve self-reliant and sustainable *socialist* growth, is of enormous relevance in the world today. (It might also be added that high on the agenda of any victorious revolution in an advanced capitalist country must be the dismantling of exploitative relations with the oppressed nations in the context of promoting world revolution.)

Secondly, the Maoist strategy of economic development has even wider applicability. Many of the particular issues of industrial development with which revolutionary China was grappling—such as location and scale of industry; forms of integration of residence with work, and industrial production with nonindustrial activities; pollution and waste management; and breaking with lopsided urban population–industrial transportation growth and consumption patterns—are certainly issues and experiences that matter very much, indeed urgently so, in Western industrial society.

There is a larger issue. To seriously confront and solve the kinds of problems that exist in advanced capitalist society—whether we are talking about health needs, education, pollution, or the condition of the inner cities—requires a revolution that will not only focus resources according to priorities based on human need, but a revolution that will catalyze total participation and emancipate people's minds. The experience of revolution in the 20th century has shown that a socialist society must develop and release human energy and creativity by promoting socialist values, raising consciousness, and encouraging mass initiative at all levels. The Maoist project in China was exemplary in this regard.

The experience of socialist revolution in the 20th century has also shown that a socialist economy must combine socialized productive forces, which require a significant degree of centralized coordination, with extensive decentralization and local initiative. The Soviet model of planned economy, as it evolved under Stalin, went way overboard with centralization. On the other hand, capitalist market mechanisms—erroneously construed by some as a counterweight to entrenched bureaucracy—lead inescapably to concentration of wealth and power, the subordination of living labor to the accumulation of capital, and anarchy of production. Maoist planning represents the most advanced synthesis of centralization and decentralization, of structural coordination and mass participation.

Lastly, there is the question of planning itself. A plan is not an end as such but must serve and be evaluated from the standpoint of abolishing commodity production and classes. It must attack the material and social basis of exploitation and oppression, transform and ultimately eradicate the conditions and relations which give rise to class, national, and male-female divisions. It must, in association with deepgoing political and ideological struggle, aim at breaking down the distinctions between mental and manual labor, between intellectual and worker, between state functionary and ordinary member of society. This was the path of planned socialist economy in revolutionary China.

Is this to say there were no difficulties or problems in Maoist China? Of course not—society was, after all, being sprung in the air. Workers, peasants, women, and other former "nobodies" were entering and conquering the "forbidden" arenas of intellectual knowledge, technical expertise, and culture. There was not a lot of experience, there were not many models, to draw on. Much of what was being undertaken had a certain experimental quality to it; so lessons and mistakes had to be summed up and modifications made. And it cannot be forgotten that the changes brought about by the Cultural Revolution challenged the privileges and positions of those who had lorded over the masses . . . and they fought tooth and nail to prevent or undermine these changes.

As for the economy per se, despite the overall and quite positive thrust of economic development, there were problems and new challenges. The revolutionaries were keenly aware of them: structural weaknesses in certain sectors, like power, coal, iron ore, and transport; a static growth rate in agriculture; still significant differences in living standards between communes; difficulties in making most productive use of capital inputs; and new tasks in resource management and environmental control posed themselves with the further development of the economy. The Maoists were prepared to tackle these and other problems and challenges, and had the only approach for doing so.

But Maoist policies, including the planning principles discussed in this essay, were not implemented in a vacuum. They were being fought for and carried out in the context of two-line struggle within the Communist Party and a continuing contest for power. The mid-1970s saw a new round of class struggle shape up which, as it intensified, affected economic performance, spilling over to planning, enterprise management, struggle over discipline and forms of payment, and eventually the quantity and quality of output. The revisionist forces grouped around Zhou En-lai and Deng Xiaoping had a vast network of functionaries under their organized control and they resorted to bureaucratic intrigue and all kinds of disruptive tactics. The Maoist forces on the other hand sought support from below. This was the reality of the situation and owing to a variety of internal and external factors, the alignment of forces was not favorable to the revolutionaries. Socialism in China did not collapse in failure or wither away in utopian irrelevance but rather met defeat in a battle with the domestic and international forces of capitalism.

V. More Relevant than Ever

At a time when capitalism's triumph is trumpeted, the basest motives of human behavior glorified, and revolutionary hopes and dreams declared unrealistic, the ideological defense of socialist revolution assumes heightened importance. This is a world in which the organization of social production divides people from each other and from their creativity, a world that has never been more polarized into haves and have-nots, a world in which blind economic development threatens ecocide. And the reason is not hard to pinpoint: the world is dominated by a system that uses profit as measure and motor of social development. But the material basis exists to organize society on a planetary scale on a nonexploitative foundation, while the oppressiveness of this world system breeds resistance. At such a time in such a world, the struggle for socialism must not only be upheld in principle, but taken up and fought for in practice with renewed urgency.

The collapse of the Soviet Union proves not the failure of socialism but that nothing less than a liberatory socialism, a revolutionary communism, will challenge the structural and ideological foundations of exploitation and class rule. And that is why the experience of revolutionary China is so crucial. It demonstrates that socialism can and must be both visionary and viable, and charts a direction for defending and advancing revolution against would-be exploiters. The legacy of Maoist China is a storehouse of experience and insight, method and principle, and theory and practice for uprooting the old and forging the new. Can we learn from and build on it? Can we afford not to?

Notes

1. Mao's critical assessment of Soviet economics is discussed in the Introduction to this volume.
2. *See* the discussion in Bob Avakian, "The End of A Stage—The Beginning of a New Stage," *Revolution*, Fall 1990.
3. Lenin, "Once Again on the Trade Unions," *CW*, 32, p. 84.
4. Bob Avakian, unpublished correspondence.
5. *See* Stephen Andors, *China's Industrial Revolution* (New York: Pantheon, 1977), pp. 217-18.
6. *See* "Planning and Urbanism in China," special issue of *Progress in Planning*, Vol. 8, Part 2 (1977); Charles Bettelheim, *Cultural Revolution and Industrial Organization in China* (New York: Monthly Review Press, 1974), pp. 87-89; Dwight Perkins (ed.), *Rural Small-Scale Industry in the People's Republic of China* (Berkeley: University of California Press, 1977), pp. 218-22; Leo

Orleans, "China's Environomics," in Joint Economic Committee, Congress of the United States, *China: A Reassessment of the Economy* (Washington, D.C.: U.S. Government Printing Office, 1975), pp. 116-44; and the earlier but quite valuable book by Keith Buchanan, *The Transformation of the Chinese Earth* (New York: Praeger, 1970).

7. Christopher Howe, *China's Economy* (New York: Harper, 1978), p. 128, Table 47. The proportional figure for hydroelectric generating capacity tends to be lower in other studies owing to definitional differences.

The data cited here is derived from official Chinese sources and Western studies that generally made use of figures provided by Chinese statistical bureaus. Is this data trustworthy? Thomas Wiens's "Agricultural Statistics in the People's Republic of China," in Alexander Eckstein (ed.), *Quantitative Measures of China's Economic Output* (Ann Arbor: University of Michigan Press, 1980), argues that aggregate figures in agriculture are, for the most part, dependable. As for official reporting of economic performance during the Cultural Revolution, even the current anti-Mao, anti-Cultural Revolution leadership of China has had to acknowledge that the data generated in that period is basically reliable. *See* Li Chengrui, "Are the 1967–76 Statistics on China's Economy Reliable," *Beijing Review* (12), 19 March 1984. These references are cited in a useful discussion in Stephen Endicott, *Red Earth* (New York: New Amsterdam, 1991), pp. 222, 258.

8. Hua Ching-yuan, "In Multipurpose Utilization of Materials, It is Necessary to Promote What is Beneficial and Eliminate What is Harmful," *People's Daily* (7 September 1971), quoted in K. William Kapp, " 'Recycling' in Contemporary China," *Kyklos*, Vol. XXVII (1974).

9. One of the weaknesses in the planning system under Stalin was that the overwhelming pressure to meet quantity targets sometimes resulted in a decline in the quality of products; the lower quality of goods forced factories to consume them in greater quantity; and this prompted planners to intensify the pressure to increase quantity. Mao emphasized that this vicious circle could only be broken by grasping the interconnection between quantity and quality (neither one nor the other could be negated) and

by grasping that the key to handling these contradictions was to arouse and rely on the activism of the masses to correctly combine quantity, speed, quality and cost in order to push the economy forward.

10. Quoted in Han Suyin, *Wind in the Tower* (Boston: Little, Brown and Company, 1976), p. 55. Mao was dealing more broadly with solving problems of right and wrong among the people in socialist society. But this orientation clearly applies to matters of economic administration as well.

11. *See* Bob Avakian, *There's Nothing More Revolutionary Than Marxism-Leninism, Mao Tsetung Thought* (Chicago: RCP Publications, 1982), p. 111.

12. Writing Group of the Kirin Provincial Revolutionary Committee, "Socialist Construction and Class Struggle in the Field of Economics," *Peking Review* (16), 17 April 1970, p. 9.

13. Mao Tsetung, *Critique of Soviet Economics* (New York: Monthly Review Press, 1977), p. 79.

14. Some socialist theorists have attempted to answer the bourgeois critique on its own terms, arguing that developments in computer and telecommunications technology will effectively enable central planning authority to have all the information necessary to carry out this kind of micromanagement. In effect, the illusory guiding hand of "perfect competition" is replaced by the illusory guiding hand of "perfect computation." The pivotal question of the role of the masses, and of the class struggle, in the planning process is passed over.

15. *See* Nicholas Costello, et al., *Beyond the Casino Economy* (London: Verso, 1989), pp. 68-70.

16. Liao Jili, "Discussing the 'Double Track System,' " *Jihua Jingji* (1958), No. 8, reprinted in Christopher Howe and Kenneth R. Walker, (eds.), *The Foundations of the Chinese Planned Economy* (London: Macmillan, 1989), p. 74. The critique developed during the Cultural Revolution of what came to be known as the "trust system" of industrial organization and planning is summarized in Andors, *China's Industrial Revolution*, pp. 187-95. Vertical planning was resurrected by the forces grouped around Deng Xiaoping and Zhou En-lai as they made their bid for power against Mao and revolutionary forces. What may be the

329

last critique by Maoism in power of an emergent state-capitalist "trust system" can be found in Kao Lu and Chang Ko, "Comments on Teng Hsiao-ping's Economic Ideas of the Comprador Bourgeoisie," in Lotta, *And Mao Makes Five*, pp. 301-08.

17. The discussion of planning principles in this section draws on Joan Robinson, *Economic Management* in *China, 1972* (London: Anglo-Chinese Educational Institute, 1973).

18. Thomas P. Lyons, *Economic Integration in China* (New York: Columbia University Press, 1987), p. 213.

19. Christine P.W. Wong, "Ownership and Control in Chinese Industry: The Maoist Legacy and Prospects for the 1980s," in Joint Economic Committee, U.S. Congress, *China's Economy Looks Toward the Year 2000* (Washington, D.C.: U.S. Government Printing Office, 1986), p. 577 and Table 7, p. 603.

20. *See* "Socialist Commerce, Not for Profits," *Peking Review*, 30 July 1976, pp. 13-15. For a more detailed explanation of the conference system of materials allocation in revolutionary China, *see* Michael Ellman, *Socialist Planning* (Cambridge: Cambridge University Press, 1979), pp. 36-37, and Robinson, *Economic Management*, pp. 20-21.

21. Fred Block, *Post-Industrial Possibilities* (Berkeley: University of California Press, 1989), p. 208.

22. *See* Perkins, *Rural Small-Scale Industry*, and Jon Sigurdson, "Rural Industrialization in China: Approaches and Prospects," *World Development*, Vol. 3, Nos. 7 & 8, July–August 1975. One of socialist China's great technical accomplishments was the pioneering, and wide diffusion, of high-yielding varieties of grain.

23. This point is made in John Gurley, *China's Economy and the Maoist Strategy* (New York: Monthly Review Press, 1976), p. 18.

24. Roland Berger, "Economic Planning in China," *World Development*, Vol. 3, Nos. 7 & 8, July–August 1975.

25. "Break the Old Balance: Establish New Balance," *Renmin Ribao*, 28 February 1958, reprinted in Howe, *Foundations of Planned Economy*, p. 66.

26. Philip Corrigan, et al., *For Mao* (Atlantic Highlands, New Jersey: Humanities Press, 1979), p. 132.

27. Bob Avakian, *Mao Tsetung's Immortal Contributions* (Chicago: RCP Publications, 1978), p. 119.

28. Mao, *Critique of Soviet Economics*, pp. 80-81.
29. Mao Tsetung (ed.), *Socialist Upsurge in China's Countryside* (Peking: Foreign Languages Press, 1957), p. 253.
30. Mao, *Critique of Soviet Economics*, p. 113. In this text (*see* p. 54), Mao emphasizes that economic categories and laws, such as distribution according to labor and the law of value, are not eternal and unchanging. They are historically relative and will cease to exist at some point as a result of societal development and transformation.
31. Mao Tsetung, "Examples of Dialectics," in *Miscellany of Mao Tsetung Thought (1949-68)*, Part I (Arlington: Joint Publications Research Service, 1974), p. 224. The translation here is different.
32. Howe, *China's Economy*, p. 53. An important statement of Mao's approach to planning methods can be found in Mao Tsetung, "Talk on the Third Five Year Plan," in Howe and Walker, *Foundations of Planned Economy*, pp. 131-34.
33. *The Shanghai Textbook*, pp. 154-55.
34. See Jan Prybyla, *The Chinese Economy* (Columbia, S.C.: University of South Carolina Press, 1978), p. 92; James Stepanek, "Plan Flexibility in the PRC," *Contemporary China*, Vol. 1, No. 3; and Howe, *China's Economy*, p. 42.
35. See Suzanne Paine, "Balanced Development: Maoist Conception and Chinese Practice," *World Development*, Vol. 4, No. 4, 1976.
36. Alexander Eckstein, *China's Economic Revolution* (Cambridge: Cambridge University Press, 1977), p. 364.
37. See Nicholas Lardy, *Economic Growth and Distribution in China* (Cambridge: Cambridge University Press, 1978), pp. 153-64.
38. See Carl Riskin, "Judging Economic Development: The Case of China," *Economic and Political Weekly* (India), 8 October 1977.
39. Alexander Eckstein, *China's Economic Development* (Ann Arbor: University of Michigan Press, 1975), pp. 348-49. In 1974, the basic salary of the highest paid administrative official in Canton (chairman of the Provincial Revolutionary Committee) was eight times the basic wage of the least skilled worker in the province's

modern industrial sector. (Prybyla, *The Chinese Economy*, p. 120.)

40. Some of the relevant data is summarized in Carl Riskin, *China's Political Economy* (Oxford: Oxford University Press, 1987), chapter 10. Per capita consumption in China doubled between 1952 and 1975 (Eckstein, *China's Economic Revolution*, p. 305). But the rate of growth of consumption (of foodstuffs, clothing, and other material goods) per person, or of per capita income, is only one—and not always the most meaningful—measure of improved living standards. Trends in infant mortality, literacy, average life expectancy, and so forth are highly important indicators of social progress. As indicated, these improved astoundingly in China between 1949 and 1976—the result of the expansion and increasingly need-based allocation of health, education, and other social welfare "goods," as well as of the mass mobilization approach to dealing with social problems that had characterized socialism in China. On living standards, narrowing of social differentials, and "quality of life" issues in Maoist China, the literature is vast, but see, for example, Maria Antonietta Macciocchi, *Daily Life in Revolutionary China* (New York: Monthly Review Press, 1972); Wilfred Burchett and Rewi Alley, *China: The Quality of Life* (Middlesex: Penguin, 1976); and Jan Myrdal and Gun Kessle, *China: The Revolution Continued* (New York: Vintage Press, 1972).

SUGGESTED READINGS
ON SOCIALISM AND THE POLITICAL
ECONOMY OF SOCIALISM

Karl Marx, *Critique of the Gotha Programme* (Peking: Foreign Languages Press, 1972).

Marx did not set down a systematic account of how a socialist economy would function. But in this brief work, written towards the end of his life, he does offer more extensive comments on the conditions of emergence and the economic and social organization of socialist and communist society.

V.I. Lenin, *The State and Revolution* (Peking: Foreign Languages Press, 1973).

Taking Marx's ideas further, and defending them against revisionist assault, Lenin discusses the nature of the proletarian state and the economic and political factors involved in the transition from socialism to communism.

Joseph Stalin, *Economic Problems of Socialism in the U.S.S.R.* (Peking: Foreign Languages Press, 1972).

In this essay, written in 1952, Stalin attempts to identify and address key problems arising from the remnants of capitalism still surviving under socialism. The discussion ranges over such issues as the law of value, commodity production, and their effects on the regulation of socialist production, and the continuing contradiction between the forces and relations of production. A serious work of socialist political economy, although also seriously flawed. See next reference.

Mao Tsetung, *A Critique of Soviet Economics* (New York: Monthly Review Press, 1977).

Pathbreaking writings dating from the late 1950s and early 1960s. Mao critically examines the Soviet model of socialist construction and its associated principles of socialist political economy. Set against the canvas of the Great Leap Forward, Mao probes the process of continuing revolution and the nature of the transition from socialism to communism—and in so doing stakes out new conceptual territory for Marxism.

Chang Chun-chiao, "On Exercising All-Round Dictatorship Over the Bourgeoisie," in Raymond Lotta, ed., *And Mao Makes Five* (Chicago: Banner Press, 1978); also in *Peking Review* (14), 4 April 1975.

Chang was a key leader of the Cultural Revolution and part of the radical leadership core on whom Mao relied during his last great battle. This essay was written in 1975, as the struggle within the Chinese Communist Party over whether China would remain on the socialist road was coming to a fateful head. It is a highly important analysis of the relations of production under socialism, the contradictions within its ownership system, and the material and ideological conditions giving rise to new privileged and exploiting forces.

Bob Avakian, *Mao Tsetung's Immortal Contributions* (Chicago: RCP Publications, 1979).

A lucid synthesis of Mao's contributions to various fields of Marxism, including the political economy of socialism, that is also a stimulating survey of the development of Marxist theory. The work provides grounding as well for understanding key historical and developmental issues of the Chinese revolution.

Index

Accounting
  and collective economy,
    194-96
  and economic development,
    188-90
  and law of value, 146-48
  and management, 191-94
  and masses (role in), 190-91
  "profit in command" of,
    199-201
  in Soviet Union, 201
  and state economy, 191-94
  and value accounting, 197-201
Accumulation and consumption
  (of national income), 241-44
Agriculture
  as foundation for national
    economy, 157-61
  and industry, 167-69, 177-79
  proportional relations with
    industry, 137-38, 316-21
  proportional relations within,
    138-39
  (*See also* Socialization of
    agriculture; Collective
    economy)
Anshan Charter, 83-89, 293
Avakian, Bob, xxii, xviin
  on socialist planning, 285, 308

Balance
  "active" and "passive," 151,
    156 n.8, 315-16
  and imbalance, 311, 316-18
  Mao's view towards, 312-13
  of materials, 303-04
  in planning, 136-37, 150-53,
    308-12
  and proportional relations,
    150-53
  regional, 141-42, 318-21
  sectoral and technological,
    316-21
Bourgeoisie
  comprador, 42-43
  and confiscation of capital,
    41-43
  inside the party, Mao on,
    xxxiii, xli, 95-103
  national, 43-44, 72-73, 96
  new, xxxi-xxxiii, 29-30,
    95-103
  under socialism, xxxi-xxxii,
    62-67, 96-103
  (*See also* Capitalist roaders)
Bourgeois economics, iv-v
Bourgeois right
  and accounting, 200-201
  and collective ownership, 58

and mutual relations between
agriculture and industry,
167-69
proportional relations within,
137-42
stability in, 310-12
(*See also* Economic
development)
National economic plan, 148-53
National income
accumulation and consumption
of, 241-44
development of, 231-33
distribution of, 233-39

"One man management," 65
(*See also* Management)
Ownership system, socialist
and agriculture, 49-58
class nature of, 48-49
and class struggle, 45-46
consolidation of, 62-67
and distribution of consumer
goods, 247-49
establishment of, 41-46
importance of, 39-41
national bourgeoisie in, 43-44
scope of, 46
in Soviet Union, 58-61
and state capitalism, 44-45
and state economy, 47
and state farm, 48
Oil, 174-76

Paris Commune, xvin, 98, 283
and establishment of social
public ownership, 42
and proletarian dictatorship, 15

and salaries, 253-54
People's communes
and accounting, 194-96
establishment of, 54-56
and management, 194-96
Peru, 284
Planning
and allocation of labor, 134-35
area (horizontal), 300-02
balance in, 136-37, 150-53,
and balanced economic
development, 316-21
centralism and local initiative
in, 153-55, 216-19, 299-305
and commodity exchange,
210-11
in contrast to capitalism,
133-36
and Cultural Revolution, 303
and economic laws, 308-10
and economic stability, 310-12
and environmental issues, 287,
302, 326
and free trade, 209-11
and industrial development,
287-88
and information problem,
295-99
and law of value, 143-48
and management, 191-94
Maoist model of, xi, xxix-xxx,
300, 313
and material supply, 216-19
and national economic plan,
148-53
objective of, 285-87